Diaspora and Multiculturalism

Common Traditions and New Developments

C|**ross**
C|**ultures**

Readings in the Post / Colonial
Literatures in English

66

Series
Editors

Gordon Collier
(Giessen)

Hena Maes–Jelinek
(Liège)

Geoffrey Davis
(Aachen)

Diaspora and Multiculturalism

Common Traditions and New Developments

Monika Fludernik, Editor

Rodopi

Amsterdam - New York, NY 2003

The paper on which this book is printed meets the requirements of "ISO 9706:1994, Information and documentation - Paper for documents - Requirements for permanence".

Transferred to digital printing 2007
ISBN-10: 90-420-0906-3
ISBN-13: 978-90-420-0906-6
©Editions Rodopi B.V., Amsterdam - New York, NY 2003
Printed in the Netherlands

Table of Contents

AMERICAN, BRITISH AND OTHER DIASPORAS: MULTICULTURALISMS AT PLAY

Acknowledgements

THIS VOLUME developed from research conducted within the framework of the Freiburg Sonderforschungsbereich (SFB 541: "Identities and Alterities") and, specifically, from project A5 ("Identity and Alterity in the New Literatures in English; Postcolonialism and Multiculturalism"), which was funded by the German Research Council (DFG) beween 1997 and 2002. My very first vote of thanks thus goes to the Deutsche Forschungs-gemeinschaft for having made possible this interdisciplinary research and for having supported a number of dissertation projects on Indian literature in English and South African English writing. The interdisciplinary setup of the SFB and of our project A5, which combined scholars from two chairs in English literature and participants from the Department of Philosophy, proved extremely fertile and resulted in a climate of stimulating intellectual exchange. In this place I would like to thank Professor Hans–Joachim Gehrke for his initiative in founding the SFB and my colleagues Professor Paul K. Goetsch and Hans–Helmuth Gander for their participation in A5 and their continued support on and dedication to the project. Our regular seminars, at which we discussed recent publications in post-colonial literary theory and the theoretical literature on multi-culturalism, were the highlight of my SFB-related activities. I greatly appreciated the intellectual honesty and passionate intensity of our debates and hold in fond recollection the atmosphere of mutual respect and familiarity that developed during our meetings. The generosity of the intellectual and personal give-and-take symbolizes for me the ideal of what a university should be: a forum for the ongoing exchange of ideas between students and faculty in their common goal of scholarly enquiry.

My second paragraph is dedicated to acknowledging the time-consuming efforts and dedication expended on this volume by Kerstin Fest and Miriam Nandi, who read and re-read, formatted and reformatted, edited and checked the text of the following essays before they could go into print. If it had not been for them, this volume could not have appeared in all its present splendour. Thanks are also due to my secretary, Luise Lohmann, and to Thomas Lederer, for typing, proofreading and correspondence in connection with the project.

My thanks go, additionally, to all the contributors to this collection, who kept faith with me and thereby helped the project to its successful completion. I would also like to express my warmest gratitude to Gordon Collier who – as Co-Editor of the Cross/Cultures series – encouraged and supported this project and, moreover, did an expert job in solving all our layout, final-editing and indexing problems.

Monika Fludernik
Freiburg im Breisgau

INTRODUCTION

MONIKA FLUDERNIK

The Diasporic Imaginary
Postcolonial Reconfigurations in the Context of Multiculturalism

V IJAY MISHRA, in his essay "The Diasporic Imaginary," has coined a term that is extremely evocative.[1] It links the current concern for diasporic self-styling with Benedict Anderson's "imagined communities,"[2] and it suggests that people who identify themselves as part of a diaspora are creating an 'imaginary' – a landscape of dream and fantasy that answers to their desires. The term 'imaginary', moreover, implies that this landscape is stocked with a variety of perhaps contradictory landmarks and that, when dreams of a diasporic identity congeal, they sometimes do so around some of these landmarks rather than others. Nobody has the same dream entirely; and nobody's diaspora therefore looks wholly like their neighbour's. Mishra's useful term makes apparent what has been troubling recent explicators of the concept of 'diaspora', from Khachig Tölölyan to William Safran, James Clifford and Robin Cohen: the referent seems to resist precise definition. The term is used by different (ethnic) groups whose commonality consists in their earlier migration to foreign parts where they have established a separate community.

---

[1] Vijay Mishra, "The Diasporic Imaginary: Theorizing the Indian Diaspora," *Textual Practice* 10.3 (1996): 421–47.

[2] See Benedict Anderson, *Imagined Communities: Reflections on the Origin and Spread of Nationalism* (1983; London: Verso, 1991).

Among the critics presenting a definition of 'diaspora', Clifford, Tölölyan and Cohen are the most incisive. Of the nine criteria that Robin Cohen mentions in his 1997 book *Global Diasporas*, taken as a point of critical reference by several contributors to the present volume, not all can be said to be definitive, but at least some out of these nine must apply for a diaspora to come into existence. Thus, Cohen's first and second categories are mutually exclusive – a diaspora is formed *either* by "dispersal from an original homeland, often traumatically, to two or more foreign regions" (this corresponds to the classic case of the Jewish diaspora and to all victim diasporas); *or* "alternatively," says Cohen, from "the expansion from a homeland in search of work, in pursuit of trade or to further colonial ambitions."[3] The second type therefore characterizes the most prominent present-day diasporas of South Asians in the USA or Canada, Mexicans and Cubans in the USA, but it also refers to the ethnic groups that have dispersed into foreign regions as part of a colonial venture (the German colonization of the Slavic territories from the ninth century onwards, the Islamic conquest of North Africa, the Iberian peninsula, the Near East and all the way to India). These latter groups differ from more traditionally conceived diasporas in that they belong to the conquering nation and, though perhaps small in number, wield great political, military and economic power as well as dominating the cultural realm.

Cohen's second category of migration in search of work can perhaps be usefully divided into three very different groups: the colonial diaspora; and the old and new diasporas in Mishra's terminology.[4] Mishra's distinction refers to the Indian diaspora, but can be generalized to include all types of slavery and de-facto permanent displacement through emigration under the label of the "old diaspora." The

---

[3] Robin Cohen, *Global Diasporas: An Introduction* (Seattle: U of Washington P, 1997): 26.

[4] Vijay Mishra, "The Diasporic Imaginary," 421–22.

new diaspora, according to Mishra, is characterized by greater mobility and a tendency to see one's exile as negotiable, semi-permanent or
even merely temporary. Mishra cites the Chicano and Korean immigration to the USA. Mexican immigration (see the essay by Jussawalla
in this volume) should be mentioned as well. In contrast to Mishra, I
see this type of new diaspora as a more recent version of (admittedly
free) labour movements across the globe. The really different, new
diaspora, and my third category, would therefore be motivated by
professional considerations – the movement of individual professionals and their families to mostly anglophone industrial nations. This is
the type of diaspora represented in most recent South Asian fiction and
which mirrors the personal background of many expatriate Indian
writers who have migrated from India to the UK and on to Canada
(Suniti Namjoshi), or from Canada on to the USA (Bharati Mukherjee), and who are in 'permanent transit' mentally and professionally.
They belong to a cultural elite in their country of origin.

This insight takes us to the further point that diasporas, though
prototypically associated with *victim* diasporas, can also include cultural and political *elites*. John A. Armstrong, in an early and highly
interesting essay, distinguishes between two types of diaspora, the
elite (or "mobilized diasporas," as he calls them) and the exploited (so-
called "proletarian diasporas" in his model).[5] The distinction is important for two reasons. On the one hand, it highlights the inflationary
use of the term 'diaspora' to cover just about any type of existence
away from the homeland. (For instance, according to Cohen's
definition, the early American settlers were a British diaspora in North
America, though soon outnumbering the native tribes and immigrants
from outside England.) The definition, therefore, does not pronounce
on numeric proportions. The traditional type of diaspora illustrated by

---

[5] John A. Armstrong, "Mobilized and Proletarian Diasporas," *American
Political Science Review* 70.2 (1976): 394–408, repr. in *Migration, Diasporas
and Transnationalism*, ed. Steven Vertovec & Robin Cohen (Cheltenham:
Elgar Reference, 1999): 199–214.

the Jewish or Armenian victim diasporas used to correlate with
minority status in the host community, since these peoples were not
merely driven away from their homelands but found themselves
unwelcome minorities at their destination. Armstrong's and Cohen's
analyses, however, correctly demonstrate that some exile communities
acquired great social power and advanced to the status of cultural
elites; and they additionally observe that many groups that settle
abroad for economic reasons soon begin to establish a diaspora
identity even though they lack a traumatic history of eviction from
their home country.

The second important consequence of including non-victim diasporas lies in the implicit countering of current diaspora politics,
which has been determined largely by notions of victimhood and the
right to be included in affirmative-action programmes. These moves
can be observed quite clearly in the case of the Indian (South Asian)
diaspora, where the hitherto readily forgotten history of indentured-
labour settlements moved into the foreground as a means of highlighting the community's victim-status. This was all the more absurd
as most South Asians in the USA did not have a personal family
history of indenture but merely absorbed this background via writers
like V.S. Naipaul or David Dabydeen. A related and much politicized
issue has been that of South Asian 'racial identity'. Whereas most
discussions of South Asian immigration tended to argue that South
Asians were accepted as 'white' immigrants before the 1970s, Susan
Koshy has recently presented convincing evidence of South Asians'
'non-white' status on the basis of discrimination: ie, their subjection to
American racism.[6]

Cohen's criteria three ("a collective memory and myth about the
homeland, including its location, history and achievements") and
four ("an idealization of the putative ancestral home and a collective

---

[6] See Susan Koshy, "Category Crisis: South Asian Americans and the
Questions of Race and Ethnicity," *Diaspora: A Journal of Transnational
Studies* 7.3 (1998): 285–320.

approbation") seem to apply to all immigrants. These features become functional in a diasporic context when immigrants group together and establish cultural and religious centres that re-activate native mythology. Cohen's fifth category (wish for return to the home country) is the one least relevant to most diasporas that are currently being apostrophized. For obvious reasons, return played a crucial role in the Jewish diaspora, but except for Armenia and more recently the Kurds and Palestinians, in most diasporic communities there is no political movement trying to (re)establish a home state, because the home state has always continued to exist. What is a live issue with all migrants, however, is the hope to return home – a hope that in many cases persists well beyond the point where one has settled down permanently abroad. Nevertheless, sending money back home and participating in the home country's politics do signal more interest in a return than merely a general feeling of community. This type of involvement is particularly common among Armstrong's proletarian diasporas. Cohen's next four points –

> 5.   the development of a return movement that gains collective approbation;
> 6.   a strong ethnic group consciousness sustained over a long time and based on a sense of distinctiveness, a common history and the belief in a common fate;
> 7.   a troubled relationship with host societies, suggesting a lack of acceptance at the least or the possibility that another calamity might befall the group;
> 8.   a sense of empathy and solidarity with co-ethnic members in other countries of settlement

– do not feature in equal measure in the current diasporas. Group consciousness is, of course, a prerequisite for identifying oneself as part of a diaspora in the first place. The troubled relationship to the host society is really an offshoot of the victim-diaspora model and concerns proletarian diasporas more than others. However, I find Cohen's eighth criterion extremely important, since this significantly enhances the communal myth of belonging and establishes a properly diasporic identity.

Cohen's ninth multicultural category ("the possibility of a distinctive creative, enriching life in host countries with a tolerance for pluralism") is different from the other criteria and deserves comment. In fact, what Cohen is presenting here is an alternative to the myth of return. In present-day diasporas, one encounters utopian visions (we are again with Mishra's diasporic 'imaginary') that promise peaceful existence in a tolerant society, a society in which one's collective identity can be cherished and preserved despite physical distance from the homeland. These multicultural societies figure as places where one can be 'at home' even when not at home. We are here broaching the subject of multiculturalism, to which I will return shortly.

One of the unanswered questions about the proliferation of self-styled diasporas has been why this should have become an issue in the 1990s. Or, to put it differently, why do the terms exile, immigrant, expelled, refugee, expatriate or minority[7] no longer fit the experience? One possible answer to the question lies, I believe, in the communitarianism that has been sparked off by the multiculturalist movement. Traditional prototypes of exile or emigration have focused on the individual, on the personal trauma of leaving family and *Heimat* behind and having to face a strange and hostile new environment abroad. The scenario typically has its setting in the USA and integrates elements of the rags-to-riches plot. Thus, the tale frequently continues as a success story, with the immigrant doing well, marrying an American girl, and ending up rich and happy as an assimilated American citizen. That success-story was never the rule, and has recently been discredited by the sheer mass of the American underclass and by the issue of ethnic rights.

---

[7] Dominique Schnapper, "From the Nation-State to the Transnational World: On the Meaning and Usefulness of Diaspora as a Concept," *Diaspora: A Journal of Transnational Studies* 8.3 (1999): 225.

Whereas the civil-rights movement had managed to establish indivi-dual rights for minorities, these rights did not include – in fact, were meant to supersede – 'separate but equal' formulas that had been so detrimental during the period of segregational politics. When it be-came clear that individual rights did not tend to improve the situation of blacks as a group, that – unlike Jews or Irishmen – African Ameri-cans could not profit equally from the legal provisions that basically guaranteed non-discrimination but did not provide for positive dis-crimination, movements for political representation by ethnic classi-fication began to emerge. Individuals hence no longer have merely personal rights as individuals but, additionally, rights as members of an underprivileged group whose culture and political interests must not be subordinated to those of mainstream (WASP) Americans.

℘

Which finally brings me to the topic of multiculturalism.[8] The present volume sets out to clarify the precise interrelationship between the recent rise in diasporic consciousness and the American concept of multiculturalism. The main thesis of this study could be summarized as follows: Only in the wake of American pluralism and the sub-sequent move into multiculturalism as a key issue of educational policy did it become possible for ethnic minorities to style themselves as discrete diasporas. What is particularly noteworthy in this link between multicultural politics and diasporic consciousness is the way in which it relates to the development of American societal self-

---

[8] See esp. *Identity: Community, Culture, Difference*, ed. Jonathan Ruther-ford (London: Lawrence & Wishart, 1990), Charles Taylor et al., *Multicul-turalism: Examining the Politics of Recognition*, ed. Amy Gutman (Princeton NJ: Princeton UP, 1994), *Multikulturelle Gesellschaft: Modell Amerika*, ed. Berndt Ostendorf (Munich: Wilhelm Fink, 1994), and Kwame Anthony Appiah, "The Multiculturalist Misunderstanding," *New York Review of Books* 44.15 (9 October 1997): 30–36.

understanding from a politics of assimilation (the melting-pot ideology) to the 'salad-bowl' vision of American pluralism and on to the
craze for 'hybridity'. Diaspora consciousness belongs to a stage
beyond hybridity, to what is now frequently called 'identity politics'.
This development is also one from individualism to communitarianism, from American citizens' understanding of themselves as unique
individuals possessing rights and obligations to a newer conception of
self as situated within an ethnic and cultural community to which one
belongs. This new type of (collective) identity therefore relies on a
politics of difference, since the identity in question can arise only from
a differentiation between groups, each vying for attention on the stage
of American politics.

The odd man out in this setting is the default American, W A S P to
the core, whose identity goes under the very vague label "Caucasian."
So far, 'white' Americans have not reacted to the onslaught of non-
white groups by creating a 'white' identity.[9] Conservative critics and
theorists such as Alan Bloom have, rather, shielded themselves behind
the European tradition, usually condensed to the Judaeo-Christian
world-view as it is now called and to the 'classics' (Homer, Aristotle,
Plato, Virgil, Augustine, Dante). These, it is opined, are key texts in
the Western tradition and superior to a great deal of what is taught in
multiculturalism courses.

The canon wars trace the main problem posed by multiculturalism
for the educational curriculum: how to be fair to the many different
cultures that students belong to. As has been demonstrated,[10] the
British Empire initiated English studies as a means of integrating 'the
natives' into British civilization (or, from the native perspective,
indoctrinating them), with the result that students in India and South
Africa would, via Shakespeare, Wordsworth or Keats, be familiar with

---

⁹ There are, however, some studies of 'white trash' and the history of how
the Irish and the Jews managed to be accepted as quasi-W A S P s.

¹⁰ Gauri Viswanathan, *Masks of Conquest: Literary Study and British Rule
in India* (London: Faber & Faber, 1990).

daffodils and snow and robins but would have read no poetry about their own landscapes or cultural background. It therefore makes good sense to say that the American canon was serving a similarly integrative and assimilative function in American schools and universities by introducing immigrant subjects to the mainstream culture and endorsing the melting-pot ideology. Indeed, the teaching of US history in high schools still performs this very function. Criticism of white supremacy has now led to the paradoxical situation of proportional representation: each group has the right to get its own texts into the curriculum. From a blind neglect of anything that was not white, the canon has thus moved to (utopian) mimesis of the multiculturalist status quo. Since the individual ethnicities represented in this multicultural canon are defined by maximum diversity, such teaching necessarily works against establishing cultural unity and communality and prepares the ground for a diasporic conception of group consciousness.

The current situation presupposes the equal validity of all manifestations of cultural distinctiveness – critics call this cultural relativism. These tenets are enshrined in the ideology of political correctness. A comparative glance at the European situation points the way towards a more comprehensive view of the problem. Many areas of Europe have resident minorities, usually defined as *linguistic* minorities. This is the prime factor distinguishing European from American multiculturalism. Although the Latin American constituent of the American population is a linguistic minority in the European sense of the term (but in some states a majority), most other ethnic minorities use English as their first language. Cultural identity is – except for visible minorities – predicated less on language than on customs and habits, myths, religion, moral attitudes, etc. For this reason, cultural 'identity' becomes a tricky business. Although all cultural identities are constructed, American ethnic identities – in the absence of a linguistic factor – are perhaps more constructed than others. The current politics of difference, in fact, forces ethnic groups to foreground their specificity and to create distinct identities that frequently have little bearing on actual origins. In the case of the South Asian diaspora, for instance, people who belong to quite different groups at home fuse into a new identity of geographical ascription that, if at all, had a reality only under British colonial rule. The supposed 'identity' of South Asians is merely mythic. The Indian subcontinent is divided denominationally (Sikhs, Parsis, Hindus, Muslims, Christians); the Indian caste system separates people; and political dissidence is rife. Bangladeshis, Indians and Sri Lankans would certainly assert their difference on Indian territory, but they are happy to join together as South Asians in the USA because they see themselves as different from East Asians and Chicanos. It is precisely on account of the great variety of native customs, religion and beliefs that South Asian identity in the USA cannot be anything but *ethnic* in orientation: ie, ultimately undefinable.

What has gone wrong with American integrationalism? In order to measure the extent to which the tide has turned, one could focus on the example of Jewish immigration to the USA. The American Jewish population, following closely on that of the Irish and the Italians, is able to tell one of the most resounding success-stories. Jewish Americans these days belong to mainstream culture, increasingly referred to as the Judaeo-Christian world-view, and they have been able to preserve their religious and ethnic identity. That identity only rarely conflicts with mainstream values and attitudes. Orthodox Hassidim are a minority among Jewish Americans, as are the Amish among Protestants. Like the Irish, Italians, Poles or other Europeans, Jewish Americans are regarded as Caucasians and as nominal WASPs, an achievement so far denied to immigrants of Arab background, particularly practising Muslims. The crucial question for the workability of integration is whether the identity espoused by a particular group is at odds with American culture at large. Given the de-facto segregation of most ethnic minorities in the USA, conflicts are bound to arise most prominently in the realms of the law, of medicine, and of education.

So far, the law has been able to adjudicate a number of conflicts, but the potential for further conflict is high, since in some areas emotions have soared. Thus, although Quakers are allowed to avoid the draft and Amish children may be taught at home rather than at 'corrupting' public schools, hate crimes, the exercise of 'free speech' in the form of hate speech, the canon wars, and the Rushdie affair have been causes of major unrest. The problems are equally unresolved when it comes to genital mutilation or the refusal to allow one's children blood transfusions. Indeed, the case here appears almost as hopeless as the conflict between pro-life versus pro-choice constituencies. Women as a distinct group are empowered to make their own choice, but that choice appears to be criminal to a broad sector of the population.

These are problematic cases within the framework of multiculturalism,[11] and they remain unresolved in theory except by ad-hoc solutions. Diasporic consciousness can be demonstrated to be closely linked to these conundra of multiculturalism. If one calls oneself a diasporic, then one would like to imitate the Jewish success-story – to be the same but different. It is thus no coincidence that economically advantaged groups were the first to take up the label 'diaspora'; they, too, were on the way to becoming rich and respected despite holding on to their cultural difference. As soon as this self-congratulatory label was first applied to immigrants from Asia, it also started to be used for African Americans and Hispanics, and immediately veered towards a reading of the diaspora as exile, exploitation and discrimination. For underprivileged groups, the term 'diaspora' implied a claim to cultural rights when really involving a claim to economic, educational and employment rights. In this manner, the politics of empowerment has shifted from civil to educational rights and on to cultural and econo-

---

[11] See Stanley Fish, "Boutique Multiculturalism, or Why Liberals Are Incapable of Thinking about Hate Speech," *Critical Inquiry* 32 (1997): 378–95. Another recent publication that clearly focuses on the as yet unresolved tension within the multiculturalist framework is Susan Moller Okin's *Is Multiculturalism Bad for Women?* (Princeton NJ: Princeton UP, 1999).

mic rights. It stands to reason that, the more underprivileged the immigrant, the more profitable the reliance on one's own ethnic community. In a sense, the political force of identity politics lies precisely in the "Black is Beautiful" strategy of foregrounding and valorizing discriminatory difference. It is also a way to have one's cake and eat it – to move to where there are jobs but to assert one's difference and love of home in the face of the grim necessity of living abroad.

Such a shift from individualism to communitarianism is to some extent paradoxical and regressive. People who have been motivated by the American success-story to leave their frequently repressive home countries in order to test their individual talents and chances abroad are now forced back into the fold of their native communities. If women emigrated in order to be rid of the constraints of paternalistic culture, they now not only encounter discrimination as representatives of the home culture but find themselves additionally caught in the net of an identity politics that frustrates their chances for American assimilation. Diaspora is not only a consequence of globalization; it is itself determined by the effects of globalization. Emigrating to another country no longer allows one to make a clean break with the past; on the contrary, one's ethnic affiliation with all its attendant responsibilities re-emerges – a ghost that has followed the emigrant and catches up with him after arrival. The contemporary scenario of diasporic communities privileges communal collective rights over individual rights, collective identity over private self. Hate crimes are the reverse of a medal whose obverse portrays individuals who define themselves as representatives of their respective (diasporic) communities.

The diasporic consciousness displayed so prominently at this historical moment, one could argue, constitutes a second and more successful attempt to engage positively with the experience of exile. It supplants the earlier key concept of 'hybridity' as a cultural catch-all of alien positivity. What, then, is the difference between the buzzword 'hybridity' and that of 'diaspora'? And how do they relate to multiculturalism?

The first thing to note about both multiculturalism and hybridity is that these concepts have been employed in a fairly utopian manner. Different groups living in propinquity to each other or hybrid identities empowering subjects or groups to manipulate their patterns of behaviour between conflicting sets of expectations have been presented as positive scenarios of self-fulfilment, freedom and opportunity. The praise given to the concept of hybridity could, in fact, be interpreted as an answer to the constraints inherent in the practice of multiculturalist identity politics, which, as we have seen, tends to confine subjects within ethnic boundaries. To the extent that assimilation is allowed to remain on the horizon as a frame within which multiculturalism operates (as in Richard Rorty's views on the marketplace), hybridity opens a way out of ethnic reification by proposing a 'both–and' solution: subjects can be both Indians at heart *and* good American citizens establishing themselves as hyphenated Asian-Americans, as South Asians in the USA or as expatriate Hindus in North American academia. At least, this is still the salad-bowl idea – immigrants remain ethnically distinct but acquire some American veneer.

Homi Bhabha's celebratory redefinition of hybridity as more than a merely 'both/and' phenomenon, as a deconstruction and an instrumentalization of competing frames of identity, takes the salad bowl a step further to the stage where chemical reactions occur between the salad dressing and its individual ingredients. Bhabha's hybridity sketches the subversive character of alterity within identity, the way in which hybrid subjects are enabled to manipulate features of one identity frame for the purpose of refunctionalization in another, but he also clearly demonstrates that such manipulation can only reach so far and that ultimately no destruction of the frame conditions is possible. Like Stephen Greenblatt's ruminations on the containment of dissent within existing power structures, hybridity is never a free-floating order of

existence beyond identity politics but the result of a dual affiliation
and of an opening-up of unilateral reifications.

The invention of diaspora politics, one could argue, takes a step in
the direction of preserving the celebratory tenets of hybridity and of
couching hybridity in the language of identity politics rather than that
of individualist self-fulfilment. The concept has the additional advantage of allowing reflection on not-so-happy types of migratory experience by linking the diasporic imaginary with its Jewish prototype
and thereby creating a diasporic category of victimization.

I would therefore like to suggest that the function of the diaspora
concept consists in resolving problems inherent in the individualistic
design of the hybridity concept, and that both scenarios are answers to
the tensions and contradictions present in the politics of multiculturalism which are exacerbated in the current climate of aggressive identity
politics, hate crimes and increasing threats to affirmative-action programmes. The topicality of these issues is underlined by the two
personal statements included in this volume – Uma Parameswaran's
introductory reflections on the politics of memory, and Feroza Jussawalla's plea for the cultural rights of Muslims.

✀

This brings me to a few remarks on the purposes of this collection and
to a brief explanation of my choice of issues and themes. The volume
is in three main parts: an introductory section, to which the present
essay and Uma Parameswaran's belong; a section on the Jewish diasporas in the UK and the USA; and a third section on diasporic
scenarios in the USA, the UK, the Caribbean, and Germany. This
arrangement is designed to permit comparative analysis between the
prototypical Jewish diaspora in the contemporary situation and the
more recent contenders for diasporic existence. In addition, the multiculturalist situation in the UK and the USA is contrasted with a brief
glance at the Caribbean and Germany. These two additional settings

have been chosen because, in the one case, the Caribbean is so frequently apostrophized as the home of creolization and successful hybridity, and, in the other, because Germany has a particularly problematic record of failed multiculturalism. For obvious reasons, the range of essays cannot be exhaustive, but they are, it is hoped, fairly representative of the major theoretical issues and the currently contested political terrains.

As is generally the case, the selection of essays also reflects the vagaries of the volume's history. This collection developed from research on expatriate Indian writing conducted in Freiburg, Germany, and for this reason several essays deal with the South Asian diaspora. I subsequently contacted a number of scholars to persuade them to contribute to the volume, as a way of providing complementary versions of diaspora. Since the Jewish diaspora is usually taken to be the prototype, one main section of three essays is devoted to this important topic. A second, longer section contains four essays on the South Asian diaspora and an essay each on the Mexican, Caribbean and Turkish diasporas. The essays additionally treat, from a multiculturalist perspective, diasporic situations in Canada, the USA, the UK, Germany and Australia.

The comparison between the Jewish diaspora and more recent diasporas has been extremely fruitful and surprisingly rich in both parallels and major differences. Two key results of this comparison should be noted right here. It is usually argued that the Jewish diaspora, on account of the original dispersal and elimination of the homeland, is decidedly different from, say, the Caribbean or South Asian diasporas on account of the presence of a homeland to which one – at least in principle – could return. The entire discussion has, therefore, first and foremost concentrated on the relation of Jews to their home in Palestine, with the result that the establishment of the state of Israel caused severe reorientation in the diasporic self-image of American Jewry. However, what this primary focus on Israel has concealed is the *similarity* between the situation of American Jews and that of South Asians in terms of their relationship to the country from which they migrated to America. Thus, the situation of Polish or German Jewish emigrants to the USA was closely resembled that of non-Jewish Polish or Italian immigrants, in the sense that their immediate nostalgia was focused on the country in which they had been born and raised, rather than on a mythic homeland in Palestine. The parallel becomes even more arresting when one sets East (Caribbean) Indians or East African Indians who have emigrated to the UK or North America side by side with Jewish immigrants to the USA. South Asians, like European Jewry, had made themselves a home in a primary diaspora and were then displaced a second time when they went to England or the USA.

Such a double or even triple diasporization has not yet been analysed as much as it deserves to be. In particular, the recognition that the Jewish diaspora in the USA stands in a twofold relationship to both Israel and European nation-states constitutes a crucial insight into the appropriateness of the term 'diaspora' to Jews and non-Jews alike. The double and triple diasporization of South Asians has been noted also in relation to the Parsi community, which – at least officially – is as constitutively diasporic as the Jewish diaspora (the Parsis having lost their original Iranian homeland).[12] In the case of the Parsis, double diasporization comes about through emigration to the West, and intermarriage may be treated as yet another, third entry into a kind of diaspora. It is worth noting in this context that a large number of the most recent novels about the South Asian diaspora (by Hanif Kureishi, Sunetra Gupta, Meena Alexander) treat intermarriage and ethnic mixture within the context of multiculturalist or cosmopolitan settings.

The second point to note about the significance of the Jewish situation in current debates about diasporas concerns the relationship

---

[12] See Nilufer E. Bharucha, "Imagining the Parsi Diaspora," in *Shifting Continents/Colliding Cultures: Diasporic Writing of the Indian Subcontinent,* ed. Ralph J. Crane & Radhika Mohanram (Cross/Cultures 42; Amsterdam & Atlanta GA: Rodopi, 2000): 73–74.

of expatriates to their home country. Whereas sociological studies of diaspora all emphasize the family contacts with the home country and the financial investment of, say, South Asians in businesses in India, this involvement of the diaspora with affairs in India, Pakistan or Sri Lanka – even if given its full due – pales beside the commitment of American Jews to the state of Israel.[13] The Zionist focus on Israel belongs to a category of its own and cannot be equated with Chicano or South Asian support for their countries of origin. In fact, it is only thanks to globalization and the post-multiculturalist lobbying for ethnic diversity that South Asians, among others, have been moving towards closer involvement with home, a commitment additionally strengthened by the media (CNN, email). Meena Alexander, whose novel *Manhattan Music* (1997) explicitly treats the South Indian diaspora, contrasts old and new types of staying in touch with home:

> Mrs. Mathai, whose husband owned the shop, was making chitchat with Sandhya, their hometowns in India were quite close, just a river and a bridge separated them, and a few acres of palm groves.[14]

> "Now you must admit that were it not for the new internationalism, the whole Rushdie business would not have blown out of proportion. Faxes, e-mail, CNN, the whole lot. Why, some of the death threats, I was told on good authority, came via fax. If TV in Lahore hadn't carried what began in Iran, and then if Bradford hadn't carried the news, things might have been very different. Islam is getting a bad name in the West, not of course that I'm a believer. Just a cultural Muslim if you wish."[15]

---

[13] See Yossi Shain, "American Jews and the Construction of Israel's Jewish Identity," *Diaspora: A Journal of Transnational Studies* 9.2 (Fall 2000): 163–201.

[14] Meena Alexander, *Manhattan Music* (San Francisco CA: Mercury House, 1997): 56–57.

[15] Alexander, *Manhattan Music*, 67–68.

Rashid, who expresses these views, is a typical example of postcolonial cosmopolitanism. His Egyptian-Arabic origins have been hybridized with French, Greek, Hindi, German and British English grafts.[16]

In what follows, we will be dealing with literary representations of the diaspora and with theoretical negotiations of the topic by literary scholars. This perhaps requires a brief justification. Why should one deal with the topic from a literary perspective? After all, the diaspora would appear to be a sociological, economic and historical fact.

True, migration has risen tremendously in recent times and become one of the trademarks of the process of globalization that has us all in its grip. What we are discussing in this volume, however, is less a sociological analysis of facts than the diasporic imaginary – that web of images and dreams which creates a consciousness of ethnic belonging and collective identity in the hearts and minds of expatriates. Wanting to retain one's origins is, to some extent, a paradoxical wish:

> Letting go of the old culture, allowing the roots to wither is natural, change is natural. But the unnatural thing is to hang on, to retain the old world. What is the point of hanging on to a culture that's thousands of miles away, and that probably not you, not your children, not your grandchildren will ever see? Why not adjust and accommodate to the world around you?[17]

The paradox expressed here by Bharati Mukherjee is not really such – how, except by clinging to what one knows, can one manage to face the new and survive the challenge? Given this dilemma, the memory of the past and its re-invention as an imaginary homeland are of the

---

[16] Alexander, *Manhattan Music*, 67. For explicit passages about the diaspora, see pp 158 and 163.

[17] Bharati Mukherjee, "Interview with Bill Moyers, 'Imagining Ourselves'," in *Bill Moyers: A World of Ideas II*, ed. Andie Tucher (Garden City NY: Doubleday, 1990): 8, quoted from Lothar Bredella, "Interpreting Cultures: Yasmine Gooneratne's Novel *A Change of Skies*," in *Critical Interfaces: Contributions on Philosophy, Literature and Culture in Honour of Herbert Grabes*, ed. Gordon Collier, Klaus Schwank & Franz Wieselhuber (Trier: Wissenschaftlicher Verlag Trier, 2001): 372–73.

utmost psychological significance. Identity operates through narrative, and narrative needs to start in the past and pace its way to a future that embraces and resolves the discrepancies between past and present. What better story than that of a return to one's origins, a negation of the present in the light of messianic redemption?

From these insights it becomes more obvious that the mythicizing of the homeland can best be performed through literature, which is thus both the creator and the critical analyst of diasporic consciousness. The texts with which the following essays will be dealing reflect diasporic settings in their fictional worlds and comment on them. By focusing on one aspect of the diaspora rather than another, by foregrounding the positive or negative consequences of cultural displacement, these works discuss the dilemmas of exile and at times suggest solutions to the problems facing expatriate communities and individual emigrants. The critical essays about these texts in turn document the status of such representations within the current debate on multiculturalism and the diaspora.

℘

This collection starts with a personal intervention by Uma Parameswaran on the status of the South Asian diaspora in Canada. It is a plea for tolerance and for mutual recognition through memorialization of past discrimination. The essay points out, in particular, one of the traditional drawbacks of a diasporic stance – the threat of being relegated to the status of the 'Other', as were all those who died in the Air India disaster of 23 June 1985. Parameswaran's piece reminds us that only when immigrants and long-time residents have been acknowledged as citizens with equal rights within a multicultural setting can an explicit politics of diaspora avoid reinforcing negative heterostereotypes directed against all foreigners and ethnic Others. The essay, quite apart from its warm and personal tone, its humanity of sympathy and grief, therefore also serves to point up the realities behind, and sometimes the inadequacies of, recent discussions of models of diaspora.

The section on the Jewish diaspora is headed by Ursula Zeller's essay on the American Jewish diaspora. It provides some necessary background information for the section and in turn discusses three prominent American stances in reference to American Jewry's relation to Israel and Zionism. Zeller contrasts Cynthia Ozick's Rabbinical approach to the diaspora with Daniel and Jonathan Boyarin's critique of a Zionist nationalism and concludes with an appreciation of Philip Roth's literary impersonations in *Operation Shylock*. Zeller's main topic is the legitimization of the American Jewish diaspora after the creation of the state of Israel.

The American framework dominates in discussions of the Jewish diaspora. The essays of Bryan Cheyette and Beate Neumeier shift this emphasis, focusing instead on the situation in England and the UK generally. Cheyette's essay is broadly concerned with the peculiarities of the British situation but also analyses closely the treatment of diasporic Jewish consciousness by three writers – Muriel Spark, George Steiner and Clive Sinclair. Unlike American Jewry, British representatives of the Jewish diaspora are less concerned with their relationship to Israel than with their status within a context of British notions of Englishness, with the issues of conversion, the trauma of the Shoah and the limits placed on the creation of imaginary home-lands. On the theoretical side, Cheyette's essay usefully contrasts traditional readings of the Jewish diaspora as both *galut*, the traumatic displacement from home, and *golah*, a liberating expansion into foreign parts, arguing that these two notions anticipate and prefigure present-day schemata that contrast victim diasporas with Bhabhian celebrations of diasporic hybridity.

Beate Neumeier's contribution highlights another key event in the British landscape of the Jewish experience – the scheme to save Jewish children by shipping them to England and thus rescue them from the Shoah. In her rendering of the plight of these children,

Neumeier significantly adds to recent accounts such as Tony Kushner's[18] of British postwar insensitivity to the Jewish trauma. In an analysis of both literary and biographical texts, Neumeier sketches with sympathy and some sarcasm what the diasporic experience of these children was like. Significantly, for many of them exile in England was primarily exile from their German or Polish homes, and a proper consciousness of their specifically Jewish diaspora, their relationship with Israel, arose only as a reaction to their alienation within British society. These case studies therefore come closest to the typical scenario of more recent diasporas treated in the closing section of this volume.

This final section opens with another document of personal concern. Feroza Jussawalla's case for cultural rights takes the situation of Mexican immigrants rather than her own South Asian origins as a starting-point and engages pluckily with the current anti-Muslim atmosphere in the Judaeo-Christian American mainstream. Jussawalla's proposals need to be seen in two contexts: American multiculturalism (a radical reading); and international migrancy under the dictates of economic globalization. The first aspect foregrounds agency and self-determination, while the second correlates with the realities of enslavement through the labour market and political and economic disfranchisement under global capitalism.

The first of these issues, multiculturalism, is taken up in Roy Sommer's analysis of the British multicultural novel. This essay provides an in-depth analysis and criticism of Stanley Fish's concept of "boutique multiculturalism," linking this scenario to discourses on hybridity and diasporic identity. Sommer's illustrative texts are by two recent novelists, Courttia Newland and Zadie Smith.

Minoli Salgado's essay on Ondaatje and Rushdie significantly addresses the second issue noted above, that of migrancy, and treats the

---

[18] Tony Kushner, "Remembering to Forget: Racism and Anti-Racism in Postwar Britain," in *Modernity, Culture, and "the Jew"*, ed. Bryan Cheyette & Laura Marcus (Stanford CA: Stanford UP, 1998): 226–41.

diaspora in metaphoric correlation with chaos theory. This original approach highlights some of the vagaries and uncertainties of diasporic existence and the migrant condition. The theoretical insights gained from the chaos concept are then applied to a comparative discussion of Ondaatje's *Running in the Family* and Rushdie's work.

Salgado's contribution also serves to open a series of essays that focus on the South Asian diaspora. It is M.G. Vassanji who figures next, in an essay by Vera Alexander which provides a close analysis of Vassanji's *No New Land* in the context of immigration to Canada. The diaspora figures here less as an abstract concept, a diasporic consciousness or imaginary, than as the expatriate South Asian community into which Vassanji's protagonist is thrown on arrival from Dar es Salaam. It can be observed that the South Asian diaspora is here practically synonymous with a ghetto situation reminiscent of early immigrant days among American Jews.

Makarand Paranjape's essay also considers the problems of assimilation among diasporic South Asians, this time in Australia rather than Canada. The essay starts with a survey of the historical migrant streams on which South Asians have been borne, then takes two stages of Australian Indian literature as paradigmatic for South Asian literary reflection on the diaspora.

My own essay, which follows Paranjape's, concludes the analysis of South Asian fiction. My main concern is to contrast the features of diasporic communities as outlined in the critical literature with the depiction of diasporic settings in novels and short stories of the South Asian diaspora in North America and the UK. The essay focuses on work by Shauna Singh Baldwin, M.G. Vassanji, Harold Sonny Ladoo, Meera Syal and Meena Alexander.

The final two contributions to this collection turn to the Caribbean and the Turkish diasporas. Ulfried Reichardt's essay concentrates on

the extension of the diasporic concept to the black diaspora,[19] analysing Caribbean poetry by Walcott, Brathwaite and Linton Kwesi
Johnson. Besides adding an important focus on poetry rather than
fiction, this essay provides an important theoretical corrective to the
South Asian diaspora. Despite the central place of colonialism in
Indian affairs, the diaspora literature discussed in this volume is concerned more with expatriate existence than with properly postcolonial
traumas. This lack is significantly offset in Reichardt's essay by the
creative Caribbean negotiation with the Afro-Caribbean colonial
trauma, and it thereby also forges an associative link with the Jewish
diaspora and its victimization.

In the final essay, the leading issues of this volume are applied to
the Turkish population of Germany and to recent German-Turkish
authors' literary negotiations of their displacement, hyphenated identities and diasporic consciousness. Sandra Hestermann starts with an
historical section providing background information on the size and
development of the Turkish German diaspora since the 1970s. In the
subsequent discussion of two major representatives of the German
Turkish community, she highlights the two authors' literary evolution
of a 'kanakster' identity and the creation of a linguistic 'kanaksteriza-
tion' of German literary prose. It is stressed that many aspects of the
diaspora observable in the American, Canadian and British contexts
presented elsewhere in the volume do not figure in the German setting,
since Germany has not yet adopted a policy of multiculturalism on the
lines of Canada, the USA, the UK or Australia.

The essay therefore also underlines the fact that the existence of
more recent diasporas is wholly independent of multiculturalist settings, arising instead from a globalized capitalist economy. Nevertheless, this comparison with the Turkish diaspora helps to focus on
those aspects of anglophone or anglo-resident diasporas which do

---

[19] Ronald Segal, *The Black Diaspora* (London: Faber & Faber, 1995); Paul
Gilroy, "'It Ain't Where You're From, It's Where You're At...': The Dialectics of Diasporic Identification," *Third Text* 13 (1991): 3–16.

indeed rely on multicultural reinforcement. These relate less to the diasporic imaginary in the imaginary-homeland formulation than in the combative campaign for cultural rights, collective recognition as autochthonous others and an associated willingness on the part of the host country to welcome hybrid conceptions of the native subject as doubly or even triply diasporized. Such tendencies must contend with the drift towards assimilation that is strongly articulated in German public policy but which equally emerges from multicultural and cosmopolitan settings in the British and American texts discussed in this collection.

What all these essays demonstrate, then, is not a solution to the problems of identity but the increasing complexity of the issues involved in the globalization process. Diasporas create chaos and dilemmas for the traditional nation-state and for those caught between the battle-lines. These dilemmas have to be negotiated on both a personal level and a theoretical plane.

WORKS CITED

Alexander, Meena. *Manhattan Music* (San Francisco CA: Mercury House, 1997).

Anderson, Benedict. *Imagined Communities: Reflections on the Origin and Spread of Nationalism* (1983; London: Verso, 1991).

Appiah, K. Anthony. "The Multiculturalist Misunderstanding," *New York Review of Books* 44.15 (9 October 1997): 30–36.

Armstrong, John A. "Mobilized and Proletarian Diasporas," *American Political Science Review* 70.2 (1976): 394–408, repr. in Vertovec & Cohen, ed. *Migration, Diasporas and Transnationalism*, 199–214.

Barkan, Elazar, & Marie–Denise Shelton, ed. *Borders, Exiles, Diasporas: Cultural Sitings* (Stanford CA: Stanford UP, 1998).

Bharucha, Nilufer E. "Imagining the Parsi Diaspora," in *Shifting Continents / Colliding Cultures: Diasporic Writing of the Indian Subcontinent*, ed. Ralph J. Crane & Radhika Mohanram (Cross/Cultures 42; Amsterdam & Atlanta GA: Rodopi, 2000): 55–82.

Biale, David et al., ed. *Insider/Outsider: American Jews and Multiculturalism* (Berkeley CA: U of California P, 1998).

Blatter, Silvio. "Salad Bowl," *World Literature Today* 69.3 (1995): 463–68.

Boyarin, Jonathan, & Daniel Boyarin. *Powers of Diaspora: Two Essays on the Relevance of Jewish Culture* (Minneapolis: U of Minnesota P, 2002).

Brah, Avtar. *Cartographies of Diaspora: Contesting Identities* (1996; London & New York: Routledge, 1998).

Bredella, Lothar, "Interpreting Cultures: Yasmine Gooneratne's Novel *A Change of Skies*," in *Critical Interfaces: Contributions on Philosophy, Literature and Culture in Honour of Herbert Grabes*, ed. Gordon Collier, Klaus Schwank & Franz Wieselhuber (Trier: Wissenschaftlicher Verlag Trier, 2001): 371–82.

Cheyette, Bryan, & Laura Marcus, ed. *Modernity, Culture, and "the Jew"* (Stanford CA: Stanford UP, 1998).

Chow, Rey. *Writing Diaspora: Tactics of Intervention in Contemporary Cultural Studies* (Bloomington: Indiana UP, 1993).

Clarke, Colin, Ceri Peach, & Steven Vertovec, ed. *South Asians Overseas: Migration and Ethnicity* (Cambridge: Cambridge UP, 1990).

Clifford, James. "Diasporas," *Cultural Anthropology* 9.3 (1994): 302–38.

Cohen, Robin. *Global Diasporas: An Introduction* (Seattle: U of Washington P, 1997).

Dayal, Samir. "Postcolonialism's Possibilities: Subcontinental Diasporic Intervention," *Cultural Critique* 33 (1996): 113–49.

Fish, Stanley. "Boutique Multiculturalism, or Why Liberals Are Incapable of Thinking about Hate Speech," *Critical Inquiry* 23 (1997): 378–95.

Fludernik, Monika, ed. *Hybridity and Postcolonialism: Twentieth-Century Indian Literature* (Tübingen: Stauffenburg, 1998).

Ghosh, Amitav. "Diaspora in Indian Culture," *Public Culture: Bulletin of the Project for Transnational Cultural Studies* 2.1 (1989): 73–78.

Gilroy, Paul. "'It Ain't Where You're From, It's Where You're At...': The Dialectics of Diasporic Identification," *Third Text* 13 (1991): 3–16.

Goldschmidt, Henry. "'Crown Heights is the Center of the World': Reterritorializing a Jewish Diaspora," *Diaspora* 9.1 (2000): 83–106.

Hall, Stuart. "Cultural Identity and Diaspora," in Rutherford, ed. *Identity: Community, Culture, Difference*, 222–37.

JanMohammed, Abdul R., & David Lloyd, ed. *The Nature and Context of Minority Discourse* (Oxford: Oxford UP, 1990).

Kim, Elaine H. "Defining Asian American Realities through Literature," in JanMohammed & Lloyd, ed. *The Nature and Context of Minority Discourse*, 146–70.

Koshy, Susan. "Category Crisis: South Asian Americans and the Questions of Race and Ethnicity," *Diaspora: A Journal of Transnational Studies* 7.3 (1998): 285–320.

Kushner, Tony. "Remembering to Forget: Racism and Anti-Racism in Postwar Britain," in Cheyette & Marcus, ed. *Modernity, Culture, and "the Jew"*, 226–41.

Mishra, Vijay. "The Diasporic Imaginary: Theorizing the Indian Diaspora," *Textual Practice* 10.3 (1996): 421–47.

Miyoshi, Masao. "A Borderless World? From Colonialism to Transnationalism and the Decline of the Nation State," *Critical Inquiry* 19.4 (1993): 726–51.

Mohanty, Satya P. "Colonial Legacies, Multicultural Futures: Relativism, Objectivity, and the Challenge of Otherness," *PMLA* 110.1 (1995): 108–18.

Okin, Susan Moller. *Is Multiculturalism Bad for Women?* (Princeton NJ: Princeton UP, 1999).

Ostendorf, Berndt. "Der Preis des Multikulturalismus," *Merkur* 46.9–10 (1992): 846–62.

——, ed. *Multikulturelle Gesellschaft: Modell Amerika* (Munich: Wilhelm Fink, 1994).

Panossian, Razmik. "Between Ambivalence and Intrusion: Politics and Identity in Armenia-Diaspora Relations," *Diaspora: A Journal of Transnational Studies* 7.2 (1998): 149–96.

Parekh, Bhikhu. *Rethinking Multiculturalism: Cultural Diversity and Political Theory* (London: Macmillan, 2000).

Radhakrishnan, R. "Ethnic Identity and Post-Structuralist Differance," in JanMohamed & Lloyd, ed. *The Nature and Context of Minority Discourse*, 50–71.

Ramraj, Victor J. "Diasporas and Multiculturalism," in *New National and Post-Colonial Literatures: An Introduction*, ed. Bruce King (Oxford: Clarendon, 1996): 214–29.

Rushdie, Salman. *Imaginary Homelands: Essays and Criticism 1981–1991* (London: Granta, 1991).

Rutherford, Jonathan, ed. *Identity: Community, Culture, Difference* (London: Lawrence & Wishart, 1990).

——."A Place Called Home: Identity and the Cultural Politics of Difference," in Rutherford, ed. *Identity: Community, Culture, Difference*, 9–27.

Safran, William. "Diasporas in Modern Societies: Myths of Homeland and Return," *Diaspora: A Journal of Transnational Studies* 1 (1991): 83–99.

——. "Comparing Diasporas: A Review Essay," *Diaspora: A Journal of Transnational Studies* 8.3 (1999): 255–92.

Saldívar, José David. *The Dialectics of Our America: Genealogy, Cultural Critique, and Literary History* (Durham NC: Duke UP, 1991).

Schnapper, Dominique. "From the Nation-State to the Transnational World: On the Meaning and Usefulness of Diaspora as a Concept," *Diaspora: A Journal of Transnational Studies* 8.3 (1999): 225–54.

Segal, Ronald. *The Black Diaspora* (London: Faber & Faber, 1995).

Shain, Yossi. "American Jews and the Construction of Israel's Jewish Identity," *Diaspora: A Journal of Transnational Studies* 9.2 (2000): 163–201.

——. "Multicultural Foreign Policy," *Foreign Policy* 100 (1995): 69–87.

Shreiber, Maeera Y. "The End of Exile: Jewish Identity and its Diasporic Poetics," *PMLA* 113.2 (1998): 273–87.

Sheffer, Gabriel. "A New Field of Study: Modern Diasporas in International Politics," in *Modern Diasporas in International Politics,* ed. Gabriel Sheffer (New York: St. Martin's, 1986): 1–15.

Shohat, Ella. "Taboo Memories and Diasporic Visions: Columbus, Palestine, and Arab-Jews," in *Performing Hybridity,* ed. May Joseph & Jennifer Natalya Fink (Minneapolis: U of Minnesota P, 1999): 131–56.

Singh, Gurharpal. "A Victim Diaspora? The Case of the Sikhs," *Diaspora: A Journal of Transnational Studies* 8.3 (1999): 293–308.

Sternberg, Claudia. "' We're not Jews': Blending Postcolonial and Jewish Discourses in Contemporary British Literature," in *Colonies – Missions – Cultures – in the English-Speaking World: General and Comparative Studies,* ed. Gerhard Stilz (Tübingen: Stauffenburg, 2001): 191–203.

Stratton, Jon. "(Dis)placing the Jews: Historicizing the Idea of Diaspora," *Diaspora: A Journal of Transnational Studies* 6.3 (1997): 301–29.

Taylor, Charles et al. *Multiculturalism: Examining the Politics of Recognition,* ed. Amy Gutman (Princeton NJ: Princeton UP, 1994).

Teraoka, Arlene A. "*Gastarbeiterliteratur*: The Other Speaks Back," in JanMohamed & Lloyd, ed. *The Nature and Context of Minority Discourse,* 294–318.

Tölölyan, Khachig. "Introduction" to *Diaspora: A Journal of Transnational Studies* 1.1 (1991): 3–7.

——. "Rethinking Diaspora(s): Stateless Power in the Transnational Moment," *Diaspora: A Journal of Transnational Studies* 5.1 (1996): 3–36.

van der Veer, Peter. *Nation and Migration: The Politics of Space in the South Asian Diaspora* (Philadelphia: U of Pennsylvania P, 1995).

Vertovec, Steven. "Three Meanings of 'Diaspora', Exemplified among South Asian Religions." *Diaspora: A Journal of Transnational Studies* 6.3 (1997): 277–99.

——, ed. *Aspects of the South Asian Diaspora* (Oxford University Papers on India 2.2; Delhi: Oxford UP, 1991).

——, & Robin Cohen, ed. *Migration, Diasporas and Transnationalism* (International Library of Studies on Migration 9; Cheltenham: Elgar Reference, 1999).

Viswanathan, Gauri. *Masks of Conquest: Literary Study and British Rule in India* (London: Faber & Faber, 1990).

Voestermans, Paul. "Alterity/Identity: A Deficient Image of Culture," in *Alterity, Identity, Image: Selves and Others in Society and Scholarship*, ed. R. Corbey & J.T. Leerssen (Amsterdam Studies on Cultural Identity; Amsterdam: Rodopi, 1991): 219–50.

✑

Uma Parameswaran

Dispelling the Spells of Memory
Another Approach to
Reading Our Yesterdays

O NE OF THE NEW REALITIES of the contemporary era is
the increasing prominence of diasporic communities. Given
the distinctive notions of history and identity arising among
diasporic populations, I would like to explore new ways of reading our
yesterdays.

Since I am both a writer and a critic, bear with me if I wear both
hats, alternately and sometimes concurrently. I am interested in what
we need to do as writers and critics. I see neocolonialism on the one
hand, and the increasing prominence of diasporic communities on the
other, as the new realities of the contemporary era. One would think
they are antipodal forces, but there is a danger that they may conflate
unless there is constant dialogic friction between them. While neocolonialism is of ongoing and global concern, in this essay I focus on
diasporic realities and think aloud on possible ways of reading our
yesterdays, hoping to lead you through a series of tenuously connected
thoughts on my present area of research, which is in the literature of
the Indian diaspora. More specifically, I am interested in what I see as
a reticence among Canadian writers of the Indian diaspora to deal
directly in their works with the Canadian locations in which they live.
Because of the intersections of Caribbean Canadian literature with
SACLIT (my acronym for the more cumbersome "South Asian

Canadian Literature"), for the sake of comparison I use some literary
and cultural examples from the Caribbean diaspora in Canada.

✇

Exile, Memory, and Desire are concepts which have been dealt with in
different ways in each of the three eras – the colonial, the postcolonial,
and the present (what I call the diasporic) age. In the decades before
1950, for instance, for colonial writers in English, exile referred to
having left Britain, and their desire was directed towards such goals as
bearing the white man's burden and making sure the sun never set on
the British Empire. But with the end of Empire came a series of shifts.

Shifts of awareness in each of the last four decades have helped
shape a distinctive approach to what we now call postcolonial literatures; each decade has re-named this body of literature in line with its
own new reading strategies. The 1960s and 1970s formed the beginnings of this development, with recognition being granted to writers
such as Chinua Achebe, Wole Soyinka, Wilson Harris, Witi Ihimaera,
Patrick White, Raja Rao and R.K. Narayan, to name a few. Here were
people from the "British Commonwealth" whose writings blew us
away because as readers we were granted access to unfamiliar cultures
and traditions. Though Salman Rushdie in *Imaginary Homelands*
satirizes the emergence of "Commonwealth Literature" as an academic
ploy, I think the term served the cause at least as well as such later
names as "New Literatures in English" and "World Literature in
English," and now "Postcolonial Literatures."

As readers in the 1980s, in the wake of new modes of critical
theorizing, we became more aware of the nature of Orientalist discourse. We re-read earlier classics in the light of the presence in them
of what Mary Louise Pratt calls the "imperial eye" or "imperial gaze,"[1]

---

[1] See Mary Louise Pratt, *Imperial Eyes: Travel Writing and Transculturation* (London: Routledge, 1992).

a strategy for exercising power that reified the colonized by 'othering' them. We became aware of what Edward Said and Frantz Fanon had to say about the way Orientalism and colonialism brainwashed whole generations of European-educated members of colonized countries into denigrating their own cultural heritage. The re-reading process started in the 1980s and saw the imprint of colonialism not only on colonial and Commonwealth literature but also on works of the traditional canon, such as Shakespeare's *The Tempest*, Defoe's *Robinson Crusoe*, Melville's *Moby-Dick* and Charlotte Brontë's *Jane Eyre*. For example, Nancy Armstrong and Leonard Tennenhouse, in *The Violence of Representation*, see Jane Eyre as donning the garb of helplessness in order to be powerful; they identify the character of Jane Eyre as a prototype of the missionaries who wielded great power through appearing to be impotent. By the end of the 1980s, the term 'postcolonial studies' had come to stay.

In the 1990s, we became acquainted with the concept of hybridity in such texts as Gauri Viswanathan's *Masks of Conquest* (1989), Aijaz Ahmad's *In Theory* (1992) and Partha Chatterjee's *The Nation and Its Fragments* (1993), and finally Homi K. Bhabha's *Location of Culture* (1994). Viswanathan makes an intriguing point: using the Gramscian notion of hegemony, she demonstrates that cultural domination "works by consent, and can, and often does, precede conquest by force."[2] Bhabha, by contrast, takes a Lacanian position in seeing both colonizer and colonized as undergoing a splitting of their identity positions.

I was never happy about the term 'postcolonial literature', because it can often give more weight to colonial power than is warranted. Moreover, postcolonialism soon became a scholarly hold-all into which a great many concepts got thrown, the assumption being that world literature could be seen through a common lens because the whole world in one form or another had been influenced by the com-

---

[2] Gauri Viswanathan, *Masks of Conquest: Literary Study and British Rule in India* (London: Faber & Faber, 1990): 1.

mercial and territorial take-overs of European colonialism. While this outlook has a core of truth, it certainly is not the whole truth. It perpetuates the privileging of the West by taking the latter's paradigms as the yardstick and normative base by which to measure the rest: in short, all it does is continue the oppressions of the Western hegemonic order. As I say in an earlier essay,

> All this endless talk about colonial and patriarchal oppressions [...] abuse of power and consequent loss of self-esteem in the victim, the scars etched forever and a day in the psyches of the colonized and of women bothers me because they often make the erstwhile colonized and the female of the species as weak and helpless as macho sexist masculinity do [sic]. Listening to some academic papers on Indian-English literature, one would think three thousand years of India, Indians and Indian culture were totally crushed by the British...[3]

Also, as Anne McClintock points out in her essay "The Angel of Progress," the use of the prefix 'post' has "shifted the binary axis of power (colonizer/colonized) to the binary axis of time, an axis even less productive of political nuance since it does not distinguish between the beneficiaries of colonialism and the casualties of colonialism."[4]

So it was good to hear the counter-discursive arguments put forward in the mid-1990s by such critics as Abdul JanMohamed and Harish Trivedi. We need to formulate new paradigms for where we are at: a post-postcolonial age where the two new realities, I repeat, are neo-colonialism and the diasporic movement of people across the world.

∅

---

[3] Uma Parameswaran, "I see the glass half full," in *Between the Lines: South Asians and Postcoloniality*, ed. Deepika Bahri & Mary Vasudeva (Philadelphia PA: Temple UP, 1996): 360.

[4] Anne McClintock, "The Angel of Progress: Pitfalls of the Term 'Postcolonialism'" (1992), in *Colonial Discourse, Postcolonial Theory*, ed. Francis Barker, Peter Hulme & Margaret Iversen (Manchester: Manchester UP, 1994): 254.

A common anguish and outrage expressed in the works of diasporic writers is against the loss of their mother tongue that colonists impose on the colonized. Ngugi wa Thiong'o of Kenya and Rajagopal Parthasarathy of India turned away from English and started writing in their mother tongue. For others, it was not so easy. Derek Walcott, of the Caribbean, in his poem "A Far Cry from Africa," has his mulatto self cry out:

> I who am poisoned by the blood of both,
> Where shall I turn, divided to the vein?
> I who have cursed
> The drunken officer of British rule, how choose
> Between this Africa and the English tongue I love?[5]

and Kamala Das, of India, responding to those who say she should write in her mother tongue, says:

> Leave me alone...
> The language I speak becomes mine...
> Half English, half Indian, funny perhaps,
> but it is honest...[6]

Before I take up the Indian diaspora, I would like to start with a text that exemplifies for me the interconnections between Exile, Memory and Desire in the context of many diasporas. It is a four-page poem, "Discourse on the Logic of Language," by Marlene Nourbese Philip.[7] I consider Nourbese Philip an exemplar of a diasporic writer who says what can and should be said about exile, memory and linguistic desire; as a writer. As a fellow writer I give priority to linguistic desire and so

---

[5] Derek Walcott, "A Far Cry from Africa," in Walcott, *Collected Poems 1948–1984* (New York: Farrar, Straus & Giroux, 1986): 18.

[6] Kamala Das, "An Introduction," *The Old Playhouse and Other Poems* (Hyderabad: Orient Longman, 1973): 26.

[7] Marlene Nourbese Philip, "Discourse on the Logic of Language," in Nourbese Philip, *She Tries Her Tongue, Her Silence Softly Breaks* (Charlottetown, P.E.I.: Ragweed: 1989): 56–57. See the Appendix to the present essay, below, which reprints the poem, with the kind permission of the author.

have chosen this poem. Nourbese Philip was born Afro-Caribbean and is now one of the most forceful of Canadian poets. Her *A Genealogy of Resistance* (1997) and *Looking for Livingstone: An Odyssey of Silence* (1991) are volumes of essays interwoven with poems.

Nourbese Philip uses her father tongue, the language of oppression, to put the oppressors in their place and then to break free of them. Her counter-discursive strategy uses both words and the page. The first and third pages are formatted to have three columns. In the middle column is a poem; to its right is an "Edict," a direct quotation from an historical tract on how to manage slaves. On the left edge of the page is a paragraph of poetic prose, to read which one has to turn the page ninety degrees anti-clockwise. The way I read this poem is that Exile is flanked by Memory and Desire. The legacy of the colonists is that they very effectively imposed on the colonized an exile from their mother tongue. Exile is thus centre-stage. But to the left, and subverting the standard layout of the page, is Memory in the image of the mother cat licking her newborn: note that she licks her kitten "clean of the creamy white substance covering the body." In Kristevan terms, when the child moves from the Symbolic to the Imaginary, the white cream of identity will accrete again, but the fact remains that the original stamp of the father was at one point cleaned out.

In exile, the movement of the tongue is varied to denote loss: "I have no mother/tongue/no mother to tongue/no tongue to mother/tongue/me." The open-ended "tongue/me" is an imperative to action, an imperative that is continued on the next page, where the vertical lines of Memory in summary say that the mother then put her fingers into her child's mouth and blew "her words, her mother's words, those of her mother's mother, and all their mothers before – into her daughter's mouth."[8]

My reading of the third column argues that the blank white space under the heading "Edict I" is where Nourbese Philip has written a

---

[8] Nourbese Philip, "Discourse on the Logic of Language," 56.

subversive call to action which she herself carries out – a clarion call
to others to come together and foment rebellion and revolution. The
irony lies in the fact that this revolution will be engineered through the
very language of the masters. Philip thus gives a twist to Audre
Lorde's assertion that "the master's tools will never dismantle the
master's house."[9]

℘

Not much has been written on the characteristics of the Indian diaspora. Unlike those who have arrived in North America from central
Europe and South America, Indians have not come as refugees fleeing
from an oppressive regime; unlike those who have come from Africa
or the Caribbean, Indians do not come with the widely shared cultural
memory of slavery and enforced exile from their original mother
tongue that we see in the poetry of Nourbese Philip. The sense of
exile, so strong a component of the Jewish diaspora, means something
entirely different from the way I see my diasporic experience, in which
I have felt a sense of both exile *and* of home within Canada.

Any literary or sociological theory of the diaspora must consider the
significance of borders. My own positioning as a member of a diaspora is fraught with a variety of tensions, and I know I am not alone
in this. People who move away from their native countries occupy (not
only inherit but also bequeath to subsequent generations, actually) a
liminality, an uneasy pull between two cultures. In my poetry, I call
this Trishanku's curse, after the mortal king in Hindu lore.[10]

Trishanku wanted to reach heaven in his mortal state. He enlisted
the aid of the sage Viswamitra, who propelled him skyward with his
yogic powers. But Heaven refused him entry, saying that only those

---

[9] Audre Lorde, "The Master's Tools Will Never Dismantle the Master's
House," in Lorde, *Sister Outsider: Essays and Speeches* (Crossing Press Feminist Series; Trumansburg NY: Crossing Press, 1984): 110–14.

[10] Uma Parameswaran, *Trishanku* (Toronto: TSAR, 1988).

who have left their body can enter heaven. He was sent back, but Earth refused to accept him, saying she would grant entry to no-one once they left Earth. Viswamitra, meanwhile, seeing this as a challenge to his own yogic powers, kept Trishanku in motion. Trishanku, disowned by both heaven and earth, was, as a face-saving device, given his own constellation by the supreme deity.

Added to the tension of liminality between cultures is a problem peculiar to diasporas in Canada: as a Canadian, I believe in borders but as a member of a diaspora I can see that strength lies in the erasure of borders.

As a Canadian I know I am part of the oppressor group. I get distraught at the presence and pace of global neocolonialism, by the fact that the rest of the world is being consumerized by the Coca Cola–McDonald's empire, and enslaved by multinational conglomerates seeking to acquire patents on and monopolies over the natural fauna and flora of the world. This is imperial history all over again: cotton taken from India, made into cloth in the mills of England and sold back to India.

At the same time, as a Canadian, I also feel a victim. I believe in borders because I feel strongly about the threat to Canadian sovereignty from US acquisition of Canada's industries, cultural property and natural resources. People usually think only of non-Western countries as victims of neocolonialism. I know it is much closer to home, with Canadian lumber and wheat moving south of the border, and Canada's cultural heritage being taken over by American superbookstores and television stations. I get angry at the way the history of my native land is repeating itself in my new homeland, with a foreign power taking over our resources and browbeating us at every turn, be it about fishing waters off the west coast, or grain control in the prairies, or the diversion from North Dakota to Manitoba of water potentially harmful to our waterways.

However, as a literary member of the Indian diaspora, I actually feel closer to my fellow Indians south of the border than to fellow Canadians. The internet has opened up a whole new world of links to men and women born in India, people who have occupied the same geographical, historical, literary, linguistic, social and political spaces that I did growing up in India. I have been saying for years that Salman Rushdie's most appreciative readers are the ones he seems to scorn: the English-educated people of India, many of whom are now spread all over the world but connected by computers.

Publishers and editors, too, have joined in this realization of the strong bonds between members of diasporas. The anthologies that erase borders speak not only to a larger market but are also useful in the formulation of critical parameters. For example, the second edition of Cyril Dabydeen's *Another Way to Dance* contains poems by writers on both sides of the border, the connecting element being that all the poets are non-white. Nurjehan Aziz's two anthologies of short stories titled *Her Mother's Ashes* likewise span the continent, the binding elements being that all the writers are women and of South Asian descent. Sunaina Maira's *Contours of the Heart* is another such anthology. Even more pertinent to the critical charting of diasporic writing are volumes such as *Between the Lines*, edited by Deepika Bahri and Mary Vasudeva, and *Living in America*, edited by Roshni Rustomji–Kerns.[11]

William Safran contends that "diaspora consciousness is an intellectualization of an existential condition," a sad condition that is

---

[11] Cyril Dabydeen, ed. *Another Way to Dance: Contemporary Asian Poetry from Canada and the USA* (Toronto: TSAR, 1997), Nurjehan Aziz, ed. *Her Mother's Ashes and Other Stories by South Asian Women in Canada and the USA* (Toronto: TSAR, 1994) and *Her Mother's Ashes 2: More Stories by South Asian Women in Canada and the USA* (Toronto: TSAR, 1998), Sunaina Maira, ed. *Contours of the Heart: South Asians Map North America* (New York: Asian American Writers' Workshop, 1996), Deepika Bahri & Mary Vasudeva, ed. *Between the Lines: South Asians and Postcoloniality* (Philadelphia PA: Temple UP, 1996), and Roshni Rustomji–Kerns, ed. *Living in America: Poetry and Fiction by South Asian American Writers* (Boulder CO: Westview, 1995).

ameliorated by an imaginary homeland to which one hopes one will some day return.[12] Though this statement might apply accurately to the earlier Indian diaspora in the Caribbean so eloquently delineated in V.S. Naipaul's *A House for Mr. Biswas*, I do not see it as applicable to the modern Indian diaspora. Instead, I make a slight distinction between diaspora consciousness and diaspora experience. The former is a positive and celebratory linking across political borders of people who are of the same family. A.K. Ramanujan has a half-jocular, half-profound poem, "Love Poem for a Wife," which begins:

> Really what keeps us apart
> at the end of years is unshared
> childhood.[13]

This is true indeed; a metaphor for the divided self of an immigrant who is a member of a distinct diaspora. Wedded though we are to the new homeland, our deepest bonds are often with our diasporic family.

The dangers of this literary bonding are as deep as social bonding is in everyday life: namely, that a diaspora could end up ghettoizing itself, as is happening in larger centres of North America where one can have all the social and emotional networking one needs without going outside one's own ethnocentric community. Vijay Mishra says that diasporic cultural identity is "by its very nature predicated upon the inevitable mixing of castes and peoples."[14] While I would welcome that mixing, I do not see it happening. I have myself seen an increasing trend towards ghettoization over my last thirty years in Canada: from the initial access to spice stores and restaurants to sate culinary hunger, to live music and dance concerts that make Western ballet and

---

[12] William Safran, "Diasporas in Modern Societies: Myths of Homelands and Return," *Diaspora: A Journal of Transnational Studies* 1.1 (1991): 87.

[13] A.K. Ramanujan, "Love Poem for a Wife," in *Ten Twentieth Century Indian Poets*, ed. Rajagopal Parthasarathy (Delhi: Oxford UP, 1976): 100.

[14] Vijay Mishra, "New Lamps for Old: Diasporas Migrancy Border," in *Interrogating Post-Colonialism: Theory, Text, Context*, ed. Harish Trivedi & Meenakshi Mukherjee (Manchester: Manchester UP, 1986): 67.

orchestra needless, and now the easy access to videos from one's original homeland which has accelerated the insularization of Indo-Canadians in our larger cities.

Such self-ghettoization is unhealthy, in life and in literary studies. I see ghettoization as a pothole that just might throw the much vaunted Canadian policy of multiculturalism off the road. Ghettoization comes from two sources – from within and from beyond the diasporic community. Once the numbers of any particular ethnic group increase, there seems to be a stronger move towards self-ghettoization. This phenomenon has to be considered in any formulation of diaspora theory. Both exile and home are here, within the new homeland.

℗

When I first started working on this essay about counter-discursive strategies of understanding the diasporic experience, I chanted to myself those three theme words like a mantra – Exile, Memory, Desire. I tried to visualize something that would get me started on what I wanted to say. What I first saw was the inside of a composite cathedral and temple: a large hall with carved pillars where deities hold up Gothic arches, stretching symmetrically in a pattern of visionary splendour, with the altar in the far end of the distant regress of pillars. and on either side of me and above were stained-glass windows brilliantly lit against the sky.

And I knew I was in the corridor of time, standing between the past and the future. I made a full turn, thinking I would get a further clue to the topography of the space and about the direction in which desire lay. But, as Eliot says in "Burnt Norton," a cloud passed and the lotos that had risen quietly disappeared. I then walked out of the pillared hall with its ribbed vaults and flying buttresses and frescoes of dancing deities. Once outside, I knew where I was. I was in exile.

Stained-glass windows – that image has always had a spell on me. Brilliant and magical when seen against the light, they are dark, jagged lines of dull opaque glass when seen from outside. Inside looking out; outside looking in, because only from the inside can one enjoy the stained glass; inside looking at the altar; inside looking at the brilliant stained-glass windows; outside wanting to get in; outside not wanting to get in. All the permutations and combinations of memory, exile and desire, past and future. But, most importantly, even from the outside, going away altogether was out of the question, because that would be perpetual exile.

Later, I thought about the vision to see how it could be developed. What was the icon at the altar? Maybe it was Memory for some and Desire for acceptance for others; or, as many contemporary scholars would argue, Memory itself could be the Desire. In this context, the diasporic longing for the homeland becomes both the altar and the trajectory of being. Stuart Hall says that the bitter racial memories of a culture's colonial past begin to be deployed productively only when the ruptures and discontinuities of the experience of slavery and migration are once more set in place.[15] Nourbese Philip sets this in place in her works, especially in *A Genealogy of Resistance* and in *Livingstone*. Hall's reference to bitter racial memories needs to be amended somewhat for the more recent wave of the Indian diaspora.

∅

Indian diasporic literature, then, differs from other North American diasporas in its retrieval and recording of Exile. Wilson Harris says that if one lives in a country without history, one has to discover it or invent it, for Memory is the cornerstone of identity. Harris, in fact, has carried out his self-imposed mandate in his *Palace of the Peacock* (1973). Authors of other diasporas have done this work of retrieval and invention with power and poignancy: Toni Morrison's *Beloved*,

---

[15] Stuart Hall, "Cultural Identity and Diaspora," in *Identity: Community, Culture, Difference*, ed. Jonathan Rutherford (London: Lawrence & Wishart, 1990): 39.

for instance, is a sustained lyric of excruciating pain that discovers and records through stream of consciousness the memory of exile and slavery. But there is no such epic in miniature in the Indian diaspora. The writings of such authors as M.G. Vassanji, Rohinton Mistry and Rienzi Crusz do not display the sharp pangs of separation one sees in the writings of Canadians of African origin. Mistry in *Tales of Firozsha Baag* (1992) and Vassanji in *Uhuru Street* (1994) sensitively record their past, but there is no anguish of exile. On the other hand, in *Creation Fire* (1990), an anthology of Caribbean women's poetry edited by Ramabai Espinet, there are sixteen poems by twelve writers in the section titled "Exile." In the life-writings included in Hazelle Palmer's *...but where are you really from* (1997), one feels the throbbing pulse of pain.

For the literature of exile among the larger Indian diaspora, one needs to go to South Africa, East Africa, the Caribbean and Fiji. The sense of exile in the Indian diaspora of Fiji is well documented in Subramani's *Indo-Fijian Experience* (1979) and Vijay Mishra's *Rama's Banishment* (1979). Elsewhere, Mishra has written extensively on the Indian diaspora, especially the double displacement of those who went as indentured labourers to the Caribbean and Fiji. Ramabai Espinet and Frank Birbalsingh have edited anthologies that record Indo-Caribbean exile in the nineteenth and early twentieth centuries.[16]

Indo-Canadians, especially of the second wave, romanticize the past, tending to see no evil and brooking no negative views about their native country. Given this sociologically proven observation, one is led to wonder why better-known writers of the diaspora such as

---

[16] *The Indo-Fijian Experience*, ed. Subramani (St. Lucia: U of Queensland P, 1979), *Rama's Banishment: A Centenary Tribute to the Fiji-Islands*, ed. Vijay Mishra (Auckland: Heinemann, 1979), *Creation Fire: A Cafra Anthology of Caribbean Women's Poetry*, ed. Ramabai Espinet (Toronto: Sister Vision, 1990), and *Frontiers of Caribbean Literature in English*, ed. Frank Birbalsingh (New York: St. Martin's, 1996).

Rohinton Mistry, Bharati Mukherjee and Anita Desai tend to fore-ground some of the most negative images of India. These authors are like Canadian writers of Caribbean-Indian origin such as Neil Bissoon-dath, the short-lived Harold Sonny Ladoo, and the new writer Rabin-dranath Maharaj, all of whom tend to have bitter memories, not of the colonial masters but of their native cultures. I find this dissonance between diasporic feelings as held in real life and as delineated in diasporic fiction very curious. Is it that writers are usually loners and so position themselves outside their ethnic communities? Or is it that they write what readers outside of diasporic communities wish to hear? Or is it that the establishment imposes its slants on what comes onto the market? Nourbese Philip, for her part, argues that the Cana-dian media collude with establishmentarian moghuls in "acting as handmaiden to the elites of the dominant culture, and airing an apparent range of opinion."[17]

Rather than having only Memory *or* Desire as icon, I next thought of the cathedral having two altars, with Memory on one side and Desire on the other. The cathedral, then, is like the pleasure-dome in Coleridge's "Kubla Khan," and we must stand "where was heard the mingled measure of the fountain and cave." I spoke about that meta-phor of stained-glass windows to two colleagues. Neither agreed with what I had in mind, but what they said is worth sharing. One, citing Julia Kristeva, said that Memory and Desire cannot be differentiated; they both occupy the same space and devolve to the centre; but the centre is located in a sense of exile, in a place that never was; hence the perpetual interplay, the endless torment. The second colleague said that the cathedral had lost its privilege of centrality in pluralistic Canada, and that each ethnic community had built its own figurative churches and temples and mosques, thus preempting the need to enter the cathedral.

---

[17] Nourbese Philip, *Showing Grit: Showboating North of the 44th Parallel* (Toronto: Poui, 1993): 61.

I disagree with both. The cathedral is Canada, and I think we, racial minorities, just have to make room for ourselves within that space and not on the peripheries, no matter how spacious and independent the alternative cultural space. The centre is not a space of exile, nor is it the original homeland that never was. The centre is here and now, the place, as Earle Birney says, on which we stand. What is needed, though, is for us to stand facing the windows of Desire, with Memory energizing us from behind. There will always be an interplay of tensions, but it will be empowering, and not crippling as it would be were we to face in any other direction. And I think we are on our way to claiming that space within the cathedral. In February 2000, India-born Ujjal Dosanjh, the new Premier of the Canadian Province of British Columbia, took the oath of office to the sounds of Punjabi drums and the distribution of Indian sweetmeats. I think the metaphors that I have used in my poem-cycle *Trishanku* – of a mythic persona, suspended between two worlds, who will one day see and make everyone else see Ganga in the Assiniboine – will become reality. One day, soon, the dancing deities of the pillars in Hindu temples will be part of the cathedral.

In an unpublished essay titled "Towards an East–West Aesthetics," Shehla Burney comes close to what I am searching for:

> An East–West aesthetics is a Brechtian cultural practice, a deliberate discursive strategy, that uses the East and the West as equal, simultaneous, and important referents of "our" culture, thereby undercutting the hegemony of Eurocentric, ethnocentric, and dominantly Western literary discourse that creates marginalization and exclusion of the "other." It is a practice where both East and West work deconstructively as what Derrida calls the "supplement of knowledge" as "brisure" or "joining," cut and paste.

I look forward to the time when our writers engage in this Brechtian cultural practice. Though I celebrate the browning of Canadian politics, in literature the writers of the Indian diaspora in Canada have not yet fully found their diasporic voice. Writers, of course, have the freedom to choose their subjects, but as a diaspora reader, I have my opinions on what I would like writers and critics to do.

We often think of minority literatures as writings in opposition to mainstream writings; however, in being less 'oppositional' and more devoted to claiming space within larger national discourses, diasporic literatures can perform cultural work that is actually more subversive of hegemonic ideologies. As Nalini Natarajan says in the introduction to her *Writers of the Indian Diaspora*, "the transnational potential of diasporic populations can go a long way toward interrupting the mono-logic discourses of contemporary nation states."[18] It is thus more pro-ductive to see diasporic writings as works that enlarge national con-sciousness by introducing new elements, both in style and in content. Immigrant writings need not advocate assimilation; they can assert differences and move out of the insecurities that encourage protec-tionism.

How can writers dispel the spells of memory and how do we read our diasporic writers? The first question is, of course: *should* we dispel them? Not entirely; but I believe that both writers and critics of the Indian diaspora need to shift their focus from the original homeland to the present homeland. In our creative-writing classes we tell students to write about what they know best because, one, that will evoke the authentic voice in themselves and, two, it is a safe space.

As critics, we have to recognize that while writers are entitled to write on what they will, we should read between the lines of their content and intent, and see where the text fits in with the larger context of diasporic realities. If we note that most of our diasporic writers are still occupying that safe space of their original homelands, we need to figure out why this pattern persists. Are they afraid of writing about the place they are standing on? Or is it that they are not really standing here but back there? Or is it because they have realized it is more

---

[18] Nalini Natarajan, "Introduction: Reading Diaspora," in *Writers of the Indian Diaspora: A Bio-Bibliographical Critical Sourcebook*, ed. Emmanuel S. Nelson (Westport CT: Greenwood, 1993): xix.

marketable to stand there and not here? Is it because the world around us dictates the marketability of our writings in the eyes of publishers, establishment and readers? Do we write what readers want to hear? Or, rather, is it that the only ones who get published are those who write what the establishment wants readers to see? Is it that writers, too, are conscious of these pressures and so choose to write in a safe space where they can narrate, satirize and occasionally celebrate the obsessions of their original homeland?

Let me take two specific groups of writers who wrote about their adopted homeland. The theatre of protest, as I call it, is strong in SACLIT. Playwrights such as Rana Bose, Rahul Varma and Sadhu Binning write about life in Canada. They are totally unrecognized. The second example concerns the novelists Kamala Markandaya and M.G. Vassanji.

Last year while I was working on a study of Kamala Markandaya's novels, I had a profound insight about diasporic realities in the publishing world. Markandaya is an accomplished writer, with ten fine novels to her credit. She left India in 1948 and has lived in England ever since. Her first novel, *Nectar in a Sieve*, was published in 1954. Her first three were set wholly in India, while her fourth and sixth were set in both England and India. The next book, *The Nowhere Man* (1972), was set in England, and dealt with the life of an immigrant who, after thirty years in London, suddenly awakens to the racism around him. This novel met with a conspiracy of silence. I believe that this deafening silence made her go back to the safe space of setting her subsequent novels in India. Things have changed in England since her last novel, published in 1982. Racial-minority writers like Hanif Kureishi, who satirizes social and political conditions, are given space. One notes, though, that Salman Rushdie still feels most at home using the setting of the Indian subcontinent. In Canada, we have not yet reached that phase where we have fiction that is anchored here, not there. M.G. Vassanji's *No New Land* (1992), set in Toronto, like Markandaya's *The Nowhere Man* quickly sank into oblivion. After that, Vassanji went back and set his next works, *The Book of Secrets* (1994) and *Uhuru Street* (1994), in his native East Africa.

∅

I have three main points to make about reading our yesterdays: that is, about how diaspora writers and critics need to retrieve and record our diasporic history with a focus not on exile from the original country but on archival memories in the new country:

> 1. These writers need to introduce and establish archetypes and cultural allusions out of their own historical experiences, and make them part of the national literary culture.
> 2. Those who study a diaspora need to see where its members are located in other North American texts, and why they have been located there.
> 3. Critics need to educate themselves and others on how to read Canada in the writings of the diaspora so that the memory and culture of each diaspora become part of the cathedral.

Let me briefly develop these three points with reference to the Indian diaspora. As I have suggested, Indian diasporic writers have not done much to develop archetypes or establish cultural allusions, and not for want of historical data. Two historical events that need to become the cornerstones of the Indo-Canadian ethos are the Komagatamaru incident of 1914, and the Air India tragedy of June 1985. We have to write about these events, talk about them, cross-reference them at every turn until they become literary and cultural archetypes of the history in Canada.

The Komagatamaru was a ship carrying 376 passengers of whom most were potential immigrants from India, with a handful who were returning to Canada after a visit to India. It reached Vancouver harbour on 23 May 1914. Following a series of racist uprisings against the Brown Peril and Yellow Plague, as the inflows of Indians and Chinese were called, Wilfrid Laurier's federal government and local

British Columbia officials saw to it that the ship was sent back to India with its unwanted brown immigrants so that Canada could be kept white. The second event is the crash of *Emperor Kanishka*, as the aircraft was called. On 23 June 1985, Air India flight 182 crashed off the coast of Ireland with 329 people on board (307 passengers and 22 crew), most of whom were Canadian citizens or landed immigrants. The then Canadian Prime Minister Brian Mulroney's first reaction summed up how he and his government perceived Indo-Canadians' place in Canadian society: he sent a message of condolence to Indian Prime Minister Rajiv Gandhi on India's great loss.

These two incidents should, I feel, become part of the blood-consciousness of Indo-Canadians and, indeed, of every Canadian, just as should other events such as the wartime internment of Japanese Canadians or the long-term discrimination suffered by Jewish Canadians.

For balance, we do not have any single episodes to celebrate, and so must discover and rediscover the achievements and experiences of such collectives as *Vancouver Sath*, led by Sadhu Binning, and such journals as the *Toronto South Asian Review*, *Kala* and *Montreal Serai* that have published on the diaspora. The *Toronto South Asian Review* brings out the *Toronto Review of Contemporary Writing Abroad*, as well as a series of books. *Kala* is a small magazine oriented towards diasporic Indian fine arts, and *Montreal Serai* leans towards issues of social justice. The latter two are examples of the extreme difficulties encountered by any idealistic collective when it seeks to serve a community that is not willing to support it through as simple an action as annual subscriptions that would help keep them afloat. *Montreal Serai*, for instance, has moved to an online format to save on publication and postage costs. Online magazines may be the trend of the future, but as of now, it is merely a stress on the eyes and so cannot attract subscribers. As a member of the Indo-Canadian diaspora, I am curious about whether this unsupportive attitude is common to other diasporas.

In my effort to record the retrieval of Indo-Canadian memory, I would like to mention several artists who have incorporated into their

art the two potential archetypes mentioned above. One is Srinivas
Krishna of Toronto, who wrote, directed and acted in a movie called
Masala (1991), not to be confused with the American movie *Missis-
sippi Masala*. The film's protagonist, Krishna, is a young man whose
family died in this air crash; the image of the crashing plane serves as
a leitmotif in what is otherwise a hilarious and rather risqué satire on
Indo-Canadian society. But it also shows life as lived by average Indo-
Canadian citizens. Krishna's uncle runs a fabric store; his well-wisher,
Tiku, works at the Post Office; Tiku's mother is a devout Hindu with
her own little niche for incense and offerings to her deity; Tiku's
daughter works at a tourist bureau; Krishna himself has been into
drugs and promiscuous relationships. The movie is a fine mix of the
banal and the sensitive, humour and tragedy: everyday life.[19]

The second example is a video by Leila Sujir of Calgary called
Dreams of the Night Cleaners (1995), an ambitious piece of work with
several themes, including the American takeover of Canadian airlines,
the contractual takeovers of janitorial services, and the history of
Indian immigration to Canada's west coast through the personal
history of a Punjabi pilot as pieced together by his Caucasian wife and
their daughter. This last theme is powerfully presented through clips
from real newspaper headlines of the times. I have used this video in
my classes, and the impact of the irrefutable evidence of those newspaper clips on the screen has always been an eye-opener to each group
of students. Another film producer of significance is Charan Singh
Gill, who made a documentary on the lives of farm-workers and other
Indo-Canadians in British Columbia in the early 1980s. A more recent
producer is Jayasri Majumdar Hart. His documentary *Roots in the
Sand* (1991) is about Punjabi immigrants to the west coast of the USA

---

[19] See esp. Thomas Waugh, "Home is not the place one has left: Or,
Masala as 'a multi-cultural culinary treat'?" in *Canada's Best Features:
Critical Essays on 15 Canadian Films*, ed. Eugene P. Walz (Cross/Cultures
56; Amsterdam & New York: Rodopi, 2002): 255–72.

at the turn of the century who could not bring women from India – but were allowed to marry Mexican women.

In literature, there are two books that retrieve and record Indo-Canadian history in an involved manner. Both are from and about the Canadian province of British Columbia. The novel *Maluka* by S.S. Dhami, though published only in 1978, is set at the turn of the twentieth century, and describes Indo-Canadian life on lumber-factory sites. The second is a recent book of poems by Kuldip Gill, *Dharma Rasa* (1999). This sequence of poems reconstructs a collage of memories that foreground poignant feelings of desire, both for the past from which the persona is exiled and for the present that offers no respite, thus retrieving life as lived by Punjabis in British Columbia in the early decades of the twentieth century. One of her characters, Inderpal Singh, feels exiled in Canada, and draws nurture from memories of his honeymoon in distant Punjab, but memories only stir up desires that must subside, for he must "walk alone from the mill with hemlock, cedar sawdust, pitch, slivers in my skin."[20] Other poems show the lighter side of life:

> I asked you to keep saying
> on the bus
> on the way to Woodward's store
> so you could tell the clerk,
> > I want a mousetrap.
> > I want a mousetrap.
> > I want a mousetrap.
> > I want a mousetrap.
> Why did you say to the clerk, I want a rat peetie?[21]

Then there is the question of where the Indian diaspora is located in the writings of other Canadians. In Britain, racial minorities seem to be visible not only as writers but also as characters in fiction, plays and TV serials. Here in North America, except for Apu on the TV pro-

---

[20] Kuldip Gill, *Dharma Rasa* (Roberts Creek, B.C.: Nightwood, 1999): 15.

[21] Gill, *Dharma Rasa*, 85.

gram *The Simpsons* or Asok in the cartoon strip *Dilbert*, we are absent from the works of non-South Asian writers. The few times we do appear we are stereotyped by the Imperial Eye. We are an erased group, and we need to figure out why we are either erased or caricatured.

Theorizing on this, I can see several reasons. As I said earlier, in the Canadian context, at least part of this erasure is due to the controversial ongoing debate over voice-appropriation. It has made people walk as though on eggshells, wary of treading on other people's territory and becoming more jealous of their own territorial rights, be these ethnic roots, religion or sexual orientation. But the fact remains that fiction *is* voice-appropriation. The moment we create a character, even an autobiographical one, we are moving into another space and appropriating a voice, often different from our own even in such basics as gender, race, class or sexual orientation. This voice-appropriation can be called cross-cultural communication. All of us who interact with a text as writers or as readers inhabit a liminal world, between cultures. So, in one way or another, all of us are outside looking in. I make this point not as a futile semantic dissection but to show that diasporic writing is doubly liminal. Often diaspora writers are outsiders looking in at the new culture, but they are also outsiders to the homeland, looking in at a past of a space that has changed in their absence. This is an aspect of diasporic experience that we would do well to consider when studying diasporic writings.

Furthermore, diasporas sometimes make an impact in an ironic way, in that they get erased and exploited at the same time. Langston Hughes says it most eloquently when he writes:

> You've taken my blues and gone –
> You sing 'em on Broadway...
> and you fixed 'em
> so they don't sound like me
> ... You also took my spirituals and gone.[22]

---

[22] Langston Hughes, "A Note on Commercial Theatre," in Hughes, *Collected Poems* (New York: Alfred A. Knopf, 1995): 216.

Salman Rushdie's second-latest novel, *The Ground Beneath Her Feet*, treats this idea of borrowing in his usual extravagant way.

Finally, critics need to read Canada into the setting of diaspora writings. I have said that most South Asian-Canadian writers who have achieved any semblance of recognition have set their stories outside of Canada. I believe that, perhaps despite themselves, writers draw connections between the two homelands in a serendipitous way. Editors and readers resist these interconnections because they don't like anything that strikes too close to home. It is easier to read texts against the non-threatening backdrop of a faraway space.

Here are two examples of reading a text in the light of present space. In her review of Rohinton Mistry's *Such a Long Journey*, Arun Mukherjee reads Prime Minister Mulroney's government in the novel's Indira Gandhi sections. Mukherjee is brilliant, as always, but the review is seldom cited. Another example: when I reviewed Shyam Selvadurai's *Funny Boy* for a Winnipeg newspaper, I pointed out the similarities between the Quebec question in Canada and the Tamil question in Sri Lanka, and carefully packed in old and contemporary history of Canada and Sri Lanka in two paragraphs. Sure enough, the editor excised those two paragraphs, ostensibly because of space constraints, and highlighted only the homosexual elements.

Such readings are not currently welcomed, yet represent perhaps the most potentially productive steps towards making space in the cathedral for all citizens, to the end that all of our various interconnections of history and memory may become part of the total Canadian repertoire. That project is a long-term challenge, but we are beginning to make progress in the right direction.

WORKS CITED

Ahmad, Aijaz. *In Theory: Classes, Nations, Literatures* (London: Verso, 1992).

Armstrong, Nancy, & Leonard Tennenhouse. "Introduction: Representing Violence, or 'How the West was Won'," in *The Violence of Represen-*

tation: Literature & the History of Violence, ed. Armstrong & Tennenhouse (London: Routledge, 1989): i–vii.

Aziz, Nurjehan, ed. *Her Mother's Ashes and Other Stories by South Asian Women in Canada and the USA* (Toronto: TSAR 1994).

——, ed. *Her Mother's Ashes 2: More Stories by South Asian Women in Canada and the USA* (Toronto: TSAR, 1998).

Bahri, Deepika, & Mary Vasudeva, ed. *Between the Lines: South Asians and Postcoloniality* (Philadelphia PA: Temple UP, 1996).

Bannerji, Himani, ed. *Returning the Gaze: Essays on Racism, Feminism and Politics* (Toronto: Sister Vision, 1993).

Barker, Francis, Peter Hulme & Margaret Iversen, ed. *Colonial Discourse, Postcolonial Theory* (Manchester: Manchester UP, 1994).

Bhabha, Homi K. *The Location of Culture* (London: Routledge, 1994).

——, ed. *Nation and Narration* (London: Routledge, 1990).

Birbalsingh, Frank, ed. *Frontiers of Caribbean Literature in English* (New York: St. Martin's, 1996).

Burney, Shehla. "Towards an East–West Aesthetics" (unpublished).

Chatterjee, Partha. *The Nation and Its Fragments: Colonial and Postcolonial Histories* (Princeton NJ: Princeton UP, 1993).

Chow, Rey. *Writing Diaspora: Tactics of Intervention in Contemporary Cultural Studies* (Bloomington: Indiana UP, 1993).

Dabydeen, Cyril, ed. *Another Way to Dance: Contemporary Asian Poetry from Canada and the USA* (Toronto: TSAR, 1997).

Das, Kamala. *The Old Playhouse and Other Poems* (Hyderabad: Orient Longman, 1973).

Dhami, Sadhu S. *Maluka* (New Delhi: Arnold Heinemann, 1978).

Espinet, Ramabai, ed. *Creation Fire: A Cafra Anthology of Caribbean Women's Poetry* (Toronto: Sister Vision, 1990).

Fludernik, Monika, ed. *Hybridity and Postcolonialism: Twentieth-Century Indian Literature* (Tübingen: Stauffenburg, 1998).

Gill, Kuldip. *Dharma Rasa* (Roberts Creek, B.C.: Nightwood, 1999).

Hall, Stuart. "Cultural Identity and Diaspora," in *Identity: Community, Culture, Difference*, ed. Jonathan Rutherford (London: Lawrence & Wishart, 1990): 222–37.

——, "The Local and the Global: Globalization and Ethnicity," in *Culture, Globalization and the World-System*, ed. Anthony D. King (Binghamton NY: SUNY Press, 1991): 19–39.

Harris, Wilson. *Palace of the Peacock* (1960; London: Faber & Faber, 1973).

Hart, Jayasri Majumdar, dir. & prod. *Roots in the Sand*, written by William Hart (Hart Films, 1991).

Hughes, Langston. "A Note on Commercial Theatre," in Hughes, *Collected Poems* (New York: Alfred A. Knopf, 1995): 215–16.

Krishna, Srinivas, dir. *Masala* (Toronto: Divani Films, 1991).

Kristeva, Julia. *Desire in Language: A Semiotic Approach to Literature and Art*, ed. Leon S. Roudiez, tr. Thomas Gora, Alice Jardine & Leon S. Roudiez (New York: Columbia UP, 1982).

Lorde, Audre. "The Master's Tools Will Never Dismantle the Master's House," in Lorde, *Sister Outsider: Essays and Speeches* (Crossing Press Feminist Series; Trumansburg NY: Crossing Press, 1984): 110–14.

Maira, Sunaina, ed. *Contours of the Heart: South Asians Map North America* (New York: Asian American Writer's Workshop, 1996).

Markandaya, Kamala. *Nectar in a Sieve* (New York: John Day, 1954).

——. *The Nowhere Man* (New York: John Day, 1972).

McClintock, Anne. "The Angel of Progress: Pitfalls of the Term 'Post-colonialism'," in Barker et al., ed. *Colonial Discourse, Postcolonial Theory*, 253–66.

McGaw, William, ed. *Inventing Countries: Essays in Post-Colonial Literatures* (Murdoch, WA: SPAN: Journal of the South Pacific Association for Commonwealth Literature and Language Studies, 1987).

Mishra, Vijay. "New Lamps for Old: Diasporas Migrancy Border," in *Interrogating Post-Colonialism: Theory, Text, and Context*, ed. Harish Trivedi & Meenakshi Mukherjee (India: Indian Institute of Advanced Study, 1986): 67–85.

——, ed. *Rama's Banishment: A Centenary Tribute to the Fiji-Indians* (Auckland: Heinemann, 1979).

——, ed. *SPAN: Journal of the South Pacific Association for Commonwealth Literature and Language Studies* 34–35 (special double issue on "Diaspora"; November 1992–May 1993).

Mistry, Rohinton. *Such A Long Journey* (Toronto: McClelland & Stewart, 1991).

——. *Tales from Firozsha Baag* (Markham, Ontario: Penguin, 1992).

Morrison, Toni. *Beloved: A Novel* (New York: Knopf, 1987).

Mufti, Aamir R. "Auerbach in Istanbul: Edward Said, Secular Criticism, and the Question of Minority Culture," *Critical Inquiry* 25 (Autumn 1998): 95–125.

Mukherjee, Arun. "Narrating India," *The Toronto South Asian Review* 10.2 (1992): 82–91.

Naipaul, V.S. *A House for Mr. Biswas* (1961; New York: Alfred A. Knopf, 1984).

Nandan, Satendra, ed. *Language and Literature in Multicultural Contexts: ACLALS Proceedings* (Suva: U of the South Pacific P, 1983).

Nasrallah, Emily. *Flight Against Time*, tr. Issa J. Boullata (Charlottetown, P.E.I.: Ragweed, 1987).

Natarajan, Nalini. "Introduction: Reading Diaspora," in *Writers of the Indian Diaspora: A Bio-Bibliographical Critical Sourcebook,* ed. Emmanuel S. Nelson (Westport CT: Greenwood, 1993): xii–xix.

Nourbese Philip, Marlene. *A Genealogy of Resistance and Other Essays* (Toronto: Mercury, 1997).

——. *Looking for Livingstone: An Odyssey of Silence* (Stratford, Ontario: Mercury, 1991).

——. *She Tries Her Tongue, Her Silence Softly Breaks* (Charlottetown, P.E.I.: Ragweed, 1989).

——. *Showing Grit: Showboating North of the 44th Parallel* (Toronto: Poui, 1993).

Olinder, Britta, ed. *A Sense of Place: Essays in Post-Colonial Literatures* (Gothenburg University Commonwealth Studies; Gothenburg: English Department, Gothenburg University, 1984).

Palmer, Hazelle, ed. *...but where are you really from? Stories of Identity and Assimilation in Canada* (Toronto: Sister Vision, 1997).

Parameswaran, Uma. "I See the Glass Half Full," in *Between the Lines: South Asians and Postcoloniality*, ed. Deepika Bahri & Mary Vasudeva (Philadelphia PA: Temple UP, 1996): 351–67.

——. *Trishanku* (Toronto: TSAR, 1988).

Pratt, Mary Louise. *Imperial Eyes: Travel Writing and Transculturation* (London: Routledge, 1992).

Ramanujan, A.K. "Love Poem for a Wife: 1," in *Ten Twentieth Century Indian Poets,* ed. Rajagopal Parthasarathy (Delhi: Oxford UP, 1976): 100.

Roy, Anindyo. "Postcoloniality and the Politics of Identity in the Diaspora: Figuring 'Home,' Locating Histories," *Postcolonial Discourse and Changing Cultural Contexts: Theory and Criticism*, ed. Gita Rajan & Rahhika Mohanram (Westport CT: Greenwood, 1995): 101–15.

Rushdie, Salman. *The Ground Beneath Her Feet* (London: Jonathan Cape, 1999).

——. *Imaginary Homelands: Essays and Criticism 1981–1991* (London: Granta, 1991).

Rustomji–Kerns, Roshni, ed. *Living in America: Poetry and Fiction by South Asian American Writers* (Boulder CO: Westview, 1995).

Safran, William. "Diasporas in Modern Societies: Myths of Homeland and Return," *Diaspora: A Journal of Transnational Studies* 1.1 (1991): 83–104.

Selvadurai, Shyam. *Funny Boy* (Toronto: McClelland & Stewart, 1994).

Spivak, Gayatri Chakravorty. *Outside in the Teaching Machine* (New York: Routledge, 1993).

Subramani, ed. *The Indo-Fijian Experience* (St. Lucia: U of Queensland Ps, 1979).

Sujir, Leila, dir. *Dreams of the Night Cleaners* (Calgary: LRS, 1995).

Vassanji, M.G. *The Book of Secrets: A Novel* (Toronto: McClelland & Stewart, 1994).

——. *No New Land: A Novel* (Toronto: McClelland & Stewart, 1992).

——. *Uhuru Street: Short Stories* (Toronto: McClelland & Stewart, 1994).

Viswanathan, Gauri. *Masks of Conquest: Literary Study and British Rule in India* (London: Faber & Faber, 1990).

Vlassie, Katherine. *Children of Byzantium* (Winnipeg, Manitoba: Cormorant, 1987).

Walcott, Derek. *Collected Poems 1948–1984* (New York: Farrar, Straus & Giroux, 1986).

Waugh, Thomas. "Home is not the place one has left: Or, *Masala* as 'a multicultural culinary treat'?" in *Canada's Best Features: Critical Essays on 15 Canadian Films*, ed. Eugene P. Walz (Cross/Cultures 56; Amsterdam & New York: Rodopi, 2002): 255–72.

Yegenoglu, Meyda. *Colonial Fantasies: Towards a Feminist Reading of Orientalism* (Cambridge: Cambridge UP, 1998).

℘

APPENDIX: **Discourse on the Logic of Language**

English
is my mother tongue.
A mother tongue is not
not a foreign lan lan lang
language
l/anguish
 anguish
– a foreign anguish.

English is
my father tongue.
A father tongue is
a foreign language,
therefore English is
a foreign language
not a mother tongue.

What is my mother
tongue
my mammy tongue
my mummy tongue
my momsy tongue
my modder tongue
my ma tongue?

I have no mother
tongue
no mother no tongue
no tongue to mother
to mother
tongue
me

I must therefore be tongue
dumb
dumb-tongued
dub-tongued
damn dumb
tongue

WHEN IT WAS BORN, THE MOTHER HELD HER NEWBORN CHILD CLOSE: SHE BEGAN THEN TO LICK IT ALL OVER. THE CHILD WHIMPERED A LITTLE, BUT AS THE MOTHER'S TONGUE MOVED FASTER AND STRONGER OVER ITS BODY, IT GREW SILENT – THE MOTHER TURNING IT THIS WAY AND THAT UNDER HER TONGUE UNTIL SHE HAD TONGUED IT CLEAN OF THE CREAMY WHITE SUBSTANCE COVERING ITS BODY.

EDICT I

Every owner of slaves
shall, wherever possible,
ensure that his slaves
belong to as many ethno-
linguistic groups as
possible. If they can-
not speak to each other,
they cannot then foment
rebellion and revolution.

Those parts of the brain chiefly responsible for speech are named after two learned nineteenth century doctors, the eponymous Doctors Wernicke and Broca respectively.

Dr. Broca believed the size of the brain determined intelligence; he devoted much of his time to 'proving' that white males of the Caucasian race had larger brains than, and were therefore superior to, women, Blacks and other peoples of colour.

Understanding and recognition of the spoken word takes place in Wernicke's area — the left temporal lobe, situated next to the auditory cortex; from there relevant information passes to Broca's area — situated in the left frontal cortex — which then forms the response and passes it on to the motor cortex. The motor cortex controls the muscles of speech.

THE JEWISH DIASPORA

Ursula Zeller

Between *goldene medine* and Promised Land
Legitimizing the American Jewish Diaspora

I believe in the Diaspora, not only as a fact but a tenet. I'm against
Israel on technical grounds. I'm very disappointed that they decided
to become a nation in my life time. I believe in the Diaspora. After all,
they *are* the chosen people. Don't laugh. They really are. But once
they're huddled in one little corner of a desert, they're like anyone
else: Frenchies, Italians, temporal nationalities. Jews have one hope
only – to remain a remnant in the basement of world affairs – no, I
mean something else – a splinter in the toe of civilizations, a victim to
aggravate the conscience.
    […] I sighed. My needle was now deep in the clouds which were
pearl gray and late afternoon. I am only trying to say that they aren't
meant for geographies but for history. They are not supposed to take
up space but to continue in time.
— Grace Paley, "The Used-Boy Raisers"

WITHIN THE SOCIAL LANDSCAPE of US minorities,
American-Jewish diaspora takes a special position. It
makes a double claim to exceptionalism, one concerning
each side of its hyphenated identity. As a *Jewish* diaspora, constituting
the paradigm for a generalized use of the term in recent multicultural
discussions, it claims to be exceptional also in relation to other transnational communities. As an *American* diaspora, its claim to uniqueness concerns the inner-Jewish debates about exile and return to the

Land: America is different from all other Jewish diasporas and cannot
be called exile in the traditional negative sense of the term.

What distinguishes the Jewish diaspora from other (later) diasporas
is the fact that exile, or *galut*, and homecoming are central Jewish
religious concepts and as such have always been essential to Jewish
self-definition and identity. No other diasporic group attaches an equivalent eschatological meaning[1] to its return, and this premodern origin
of the Jewish diaspora affects even the politicized version of exile and
homeland as envisioned in Zionism. The theology of the Land established a hierarchical relationship between centre and margin, between
sacred space and spiritual deprivation, which has a secular analogue in
the polarity between authenticity and (self-) alienation. It is for these
reasons, I believe, that the need to justify and revaluate their diasporic
condition has proved particularly pressing for American Jews. In fact,
the rightful claim that their situation in America is unique in the entire
history of the Jewish diaspora constitutes an important element in their
strategy of legitimization. At the same time, as a result of Americans'
far-reaching acceptance of Jews into the American mainstream, diaspora has been of diminishing importance to American Jewry –
ironically, at a time when it has become increasingly important to
other groups as a central concept of their identity-politics.[2] However,
recently Jewish discussions of diaspora have received crucial impulses
from the postcolonial definition of diaspora, as one of my examples
will show.

This essay examines the diasporic situation of American Jews
between exceptionalism and prototype, between a separatist particular-

---

[1] For the term, see William Safran, "Diaspora in Modern Society: Myths
of Homeland and Return," *Diaspora: A Journal of Transnational Studies*
1.1 (1991): 94.

[2] Cheryl Greenberg, "Pluralism and Its Discontents: The Case of Blacks
and Jews," in *Insider/Outsider: American Jews and Multiculturalism*, ed.
David Biale, Michael Galchinsky & Susannah Heschel (Berkeley: U of California P, 1998): 76.

ism and a multicultural position. After a survey of the term 'diaspora' in Jewish tradition and the Jews' role in social theories of immigrant America, I will discuss texts by the writer Cynthia Ozick and the cultural critics Daniel and Jonathan Boyarin (one of whom is a Talmudic scholar, the other an anthropologist), and will conclude with a brief look at Philip Roth's novel *Operation Shylock*. While the Boyarins' rethinking of the Jewish diaspora is clearly positioned in a multicultural context, even the work of the inward-looking and exclusivist Ozick necessarily displays traits of cultural hybridity and occasionally comes close to a multicultural definition of diaspora. All three authors are practising Jews, and they argue from within that tradition to reach different, conflicting conclusions. From a basically Zionist position, Ozick arrives at a near-legitimization of an (exclusively?) American diaspora, which remains vitally connected to the centre. The Boyarins, in their turn, even go so far as to argue against the state of Israel and in favour of a diasporic identity – a plea that is (half-)ironically taken up in Roth's novel.

Jewish Interpretations of Exile

According to some scholars, exile is the most genuine and original religious conception attached to Judaism, whereas other Jewish essentials like monotheism can be found in neighbouring cultures as well.[3] It has been variously argued that the process by which Jews became Jews began with the diaspora two millennia ago. "In the beginning there was exile," writes Arnold Eisen in his foundational study of *galut*;[4] the history of mankind according to the Hebrew Bible began

---

[3] Paul Mendes–Flohr, "Zion und die Diaspora: Vom babylonischen Exil bis zur Gründung des Staates Israel," in *Jüdische Lebenswelten: Essays*, ed. Andreas Nachama, Julius Schoeps & Edward van Voolen (Frankfurt am Main: Jüdischer Verlag/Suhrkamp, 1991): 261.

[4] Arnold Eisen, *Galut: Modern Jewish Reflections on Homelessness and Homecoming* (Bloomington & Indianapolis: Indiana UP, 1986): xi.

with the expulsion and alienation from the soil of paradise. Later, in the Torah, this universal view of *galut* as the *condition humaine* evolves into a full pattern underlying the particular history of the people of Israel, beginning with prosperity in the Land, followed by eviction from the Land and the resultant diaspora, and moving towards closure in an eventual Return. As Adam and Eve's original sin helps explain Christians' existential homelessness on earth, a similar interpretative key transforms the recurrent pattern of exile and return in early Jewish history into a meaningful narrative of divine and human interaction: transgression – punishment – repentance – redemption.

From the very beginning of this tradition, the political and spiritual dimensions of exile are joined. Whereas the righteous shall be blessed by a life of abundance in their Land, dispersion and desolation are to be the severest form of punishment for transgressing against God and his Law (Deuteronomy 28:64).[5] The Land and the Law are seen as mutually dependent, in that the Land needs the Law for the right government of the Land, for the establishment of an ideal society, while the Law needs a space in order to develop its full force. From this interrelation derives the Israelites' legitimation for their territorial claims; if they do not keep to the Law, they lose their rights to the Land and will be cursed by expulsion.[6] A similar interrelation marks the contrasting twin concepts of exile and idolatry; the ultimate transgression is both the cause and effect of *galut*. In essence, diaspora entails idolatry: ie, assimilation to pagan rule, a view which will provide the ideological frame and rhetoric for Ozick.

---

[5] In the Hebrew Bible, Hebrew *galut* (*galah*) and Greek *diaspora* (*putz/ hefitz*) are initially used indiscriminately to describe the process of dispersal, not only of the people of Israel. It is only in the context of the divine promise, and the connection Land – Law, that the terms become charged with deeper meaning. Later, in the prophetic writings, *galut* increasingly dominates and acquires its darker meaning.

[6] Eisen, *Galut*, 24.

The reading of history as a recurring pattern of punishment and atonement, of exile and return, also offered consolation, in that it made exile temporary. After the destruction of the second Temple in 70 CE and the loss of national sovereignity to the Roman colonizers, however, exile seemed a permanent condition disrupting the pattern as well as its explanation. Rabbinic Judaism, which emerged in the wake of that national and religious catastrophe, had to give exile a new and extended meaning. According to the Rabbis, God went into exile with his people and, like them, would return to the Land only with the coming of the Messiah at the end of time: "Exile had indeed become co-extensive with the world itself."[7] And so, in a sense, had God. Instead of a localized presence in the holy Temple, God was now said to reside in the Torah and the Law, whose force had been expanded from the demarcated space of the Land. But it was the Talmud in particular, compiled by generations of Rabbis in this new and permanent exile, that helped to ensure Jewish identity under pagan rule. Its elaborate legal code, which drew strict boundaries between pure and impure, sacred and profane, allowed the Rabbis to create a sacred space amidst and beyond a pagan idolatrous environment. This vicarious "reconquest"[8] of the Land from the Roman invaders came to replace the aspirations of a physical return; as a consequence, the longing for Zion became ritualized. The homeland was turned into "a place of metaphysical desire for wholeness"[9] and was thus removed from geography into a spiritual category. It is this deterritorializing trend and the increased acceptance of exile in the classical framework of Judaism that provides American Jews with a structure within which they can situate and defend their diasporic position.

The decisive turn in Jewish conceptions of *galut* from a theological to a politicized view of exile occurred in the wake of the general

---

[7] Eisen, *Galut*, 36.

[8] Eisen, *Galut*, 37.

[9] Michael Galchinsky, "Scattered Seeds: A Dialogue of Diasporas," in Biale et al., ed. *Insider/Outsider*, 197.

secularization within modernity. Spinoza's redefinition of salvation as a political category thoroughly demystified the Land, whereas Moses Mendelssohn's universalizing of "Jerusalem" further severed Jewish faith from the Land and combined separate religious practice with full participation in the host country's culture and society – a position which makes him sound like an early advocate of pluralism.[10] After Jewish Emancipation, the experience of exile consisted, if anything, in the denial of full civic rights. The centre of Jewish concerns, religious as well as political, shifted to exile, while the term itself was replaced by the theologically less charged and less negative notion of diaspora, which recalls the voluntary exile of hellenized Jews in Antiquity.

When Zionism brought a reorientation towards geography, it was originally in terms of a mere territorialism, a secular nationalist movement born of the disappointment with Emancipation and the continued experience of antisemitism.[11] First and foremost, Zionism is to be understood in the context of European nationalist emancipation movements and the emergence of nation-states in the second half of the nineteenth century. At the same time, it shared the traditional view that *galut* was incompatible with a secure and wholesome Jewish existence, but offered a rational, sociological explanation as well as solution for it. Therefore any land which could take in masses of people

---

[10] Spinoza (1632–77) developed his ideas in his *Tractatus Theologico-Politicus* (1670); the key text by Moses Mendelssohn (1729–86) is his essay "Jerusalem" (1783). See Eisen, *Galut*, 61–65.

[11] Theodor Herzl, who convened the first Zionist Congress in Basel (1897), is usually considered the founder of political Zionism. But Herzl with his *Der Judenstaat* (1896) is unthinkable without ideological precursors like Moses Hess's *Rom und Jerusalem* (1862) and especially Leo Pinsker. In his pamphlet *Autoemanzipation* (1882), Pinsker argued that the anti-Semitism endemic to European societies was a natural result of the Jews' ghostly existence as an uprooted and stateless people. He was thus the first to articulate the idea that the solution to the Jewish question could lie only in a Jewish national territory. The term 'Zionism' was first used by Nathan Birnbaum, one of Pinsker's followers.

could become the site of the Jewish state. Soon, however, Zionism was overlayed by religious elements of exile: a paradoxical move, insofar as the traditional conception of *galut* lacks any political claims. But, as Eisen puts it, Herzl needed "an idea," a more emotional driving force to mobilize Jews for his rationally conceived project.[12] Yet Zionism was more than just a political instrumentalization of messianic religious rhetoric in order to create what Jacob Neusner called a "myth of mission."[13] The collective memory of two thousand years of diaspora was bound to make a powerful impact on any modern rethinking of homecoming, even if that rethinking amounted to a subversion of the diasporic tradition. The advocates of the Land would thus soon get the better of the territorialists in the movement. Zionism's inherent contradiction, the incongruous mix of political and religious elements, constitutes a major point of criticism of the state of Israel in the Boyarins' argument.

With the establishment of the state of Israel, by contrast, the controversies around exile and return took on a new quality and urgency. The very achievement of its aim brought a crisis to Zionism, since the majority of Jews nevertheless continued to live in the diaspora. The diaspora, in turn, faced a new challenge in view of the real possibility of a return to the Land. How can Jews choose exile; how could they prefer a life of assimilation and compromise to an 'authentic' Jewish existence in a Jewish state and society? It was one of Herzl's contemporaries and opponents, the Hebrew essayist and philosopher Ahad Ha'am, who provided a major source for all modern Jewish diasporist positions. While not strictly antiterritorialist, Ahad Ha'am claimed that spiritual regeneration was a more vital issue for the Jewish nation, and that the spiritual and the political dimensions of exile were not necessarily interdependent. His spiritual, or culturalist, version of

---

[12] Eisen, *Galut*, 59.

[13] Quoted in Jon Stratton, "(Dis)placing the Jews: Historicizing the Idea of Diaspora," *Diaspora: A Journal of Transnational Studies* 6.3 (1997): 327.

Zionism designated the Land as the spiritual centre of the Jewish
nation and in this way tried to ensure the continuity of Jewish cultural
life in the diaspora. Ha'am's replacement of faith by culture – be faithful to your people, rather than to your God – is a considerable shift
away from a traditional understanding of Jewish identity.[14] Moreover,
in his reinterpretation of the function of diaspora, the centre has
actually come to serve the periphery. Nevertheless, the centre was still
needed, and the hierarchy between centre and margin continued to
exist.[15] After the founding of the State of Israel, the philosopher Simon
Rawidowicz restructured Ha'am's image of the circle with a centre
and a periphery, proposing instead an ellipsis with two equal centres.
This metaphor derived from the dual role of Babylon and Jerusalem,
the two great post-national Jewish centres in Antiquity. It was eagerly
adopted by American Jews and applied to their own situation.

In the ideological debates between diaspora and centre, American
Jews have had a particularly strong point in their favour: the material
argument of sociological facts. Early immigrants from Europe envisioned America in messianic terms as the promised land, and the
enormous social, cultural and economic success of the later generations seemed to turn the promise into a fulfilment. America was
viewed and experienced as the *goldene medine*, the golden land, not

---

[14] The Boyarins will create their own postmodern synthesis of it; being
faithful to one's God is ultimately understood as a practice of being faithful to
one's people. Conversely, Ozick redefines Jewish cultural creativity as a religious act. Common to both positions is their focus on the cultural domain, the
traditional link between homecoming's political and metaphysical dimensions.

[15] A more radical anti-territorialism can be witnessed in the "Diaspora
nationalism" of the Bundists. The "Allgemeiner jüdischer Arbeiterbund" defined Jewish identity in cultural and linguistic terms and demanded autonomy
along these lines, together with political participation in the host society. The
emerging socialist movement was the other inter- or transnational element in
the Jewish Bund's identity. On both the universalist and the particularist level,
it was a movement truly antagonistic to Zionism, multicultural and transnational *avant la lettre* (see Mendes–Flohr, "Zion und die Diaspora," 274–75,
and Stratton, "(Dis)placing the Jews," 312).

only in the material sense. As Biale emphasizes, Jewish immigration
to the USA, like Zionist immigration to Palestine, was nurtured also
by idealistic motives, by the belief in the Jewish – *and* liberal American – values of freedom and equality.[16] On all levels, then, the Jewish
American story reads like the quintessential realization of the American dream; a reality which can hardly be described as exile in the political sense. Its metaphysical dimension had come to be seen by many
religious thinkers as equally applicable to the new nation-state established on the Land, arguing for the promise of a golden land in
Palestine. Conversely, the American condition of exile (if at all) could
be overcome by a 'spiritual *alyjah*' (return to Zion) even within
America, as the leader of Conservative Judaism, Abraham Heschel,
echoing Ha'am, put it. On the other hand, exile was also experienced
in secular terms as the modern *condition humaine* of alienation and
homelessness, a universalized understanding of the diaspora which
reveals the high degree of assimilation of second- and third-generation
Jews. This process of universalization can be described as a self-
allegorization. As Bernard Malamud famously put it: "all men are
Jews." By this argument, Jews are refined out of their particular
existence.[17]

This universalism had, significantly, begun with the immigrant
generation, and is what distinguished their ideological motives from
those of their Zionist counterparts. In her autobiography *The Promised
Land*, Mary Antin adopted the biblical rhetoric of the Exodus story to
narrate her own passage from the Russian pale, a diaspora vividly
described as little short of *galut*, to a secondary diaspora which she
mythologized as the place of ultimate redemption: "Next year – in
America!"[18] Already, back in Polotzk, the New World had replaced

---

[16] David Biale, "The Melting Pot and Beyond: Jews and the Politics of
American Identity," in Biale et al., ed. *Insider/Outsider*, 18.

[17] Allen Guttmann, *The Jewish Writer in America: Assimilation and the
Crisis of Identity* (New York: Oxford UP, 1971): 118.

[18] Mary Antin, *The Promised Land* (Harmondsworth: Penguin, 1997): 113.

Jerusalem in the Passover ritual as the site of longing. Ironically, Antin employed the Israelites' particular narrative to describe the process of her reinvention of herself as an American and her submersion in the American mainstream. "I have been made over," she writes, and claims to be "absolutely other" than the young immigrant Jew whose story she is about to tell.[19] Antin fully embraced the prevalent melting-pot ideology as also envisioned by Israel Zangwill in his play by that name. The melting-pot ideology amalgamated and homogenized ethnic identities into the figure of the new American, to whom each immigrant group would make their contribution at the same time that the group itself would re-emerge entirely reformed, "made over."[20] The melting pot replaced assimilation to the WASP majority by an ideally more democratic form of mutual transformation, or coalescence. At the same time, its underlying universalist ideal of equality left no room for cultivating any sense of difference.

Thus, the possibility of Jewish life in an all-too-inviting and assimilating environment largely free of antisemitism became the central issue of the Zionist–diasporist debate. Related to this was the question of how to reconcile allegiance to two promised lands, a question which had to be answered also both in relation to Israel and to the American host-country, which increasingly felt like home. Their experience as the quintessential alien in Europe had made early immigrant Jews highly sensitive to the issue of loyalties, and they were reluctant to compromise their hard-won Americanness by a reorientation to a Jewish homeland. A defence of the legitimacy of dual loyalties was initiated in the first decades of the last century by Horace

---

[19] Antin, *The Promised Land*, 1.

[20] For all the differences between a universalist and a particularist movement, this attempt to transcend the Old-World Jew offers an interesting ideological parallel between the two contrasting positions. In the Zionist nation-building process Jews would also be completely "made over," casting off the image of the weak, effeminate diaspora Jew, and define themselves as Israelis rather than Jews.

Kallen and Louis Brandeis, the leading figures of secular American
Zionism, and constituted perhaps the greatest possible achievement in
a pre-multicultural age. Kallen, a social activist and philosopher, had
almost completely turned away from Judaism when, during his studies
at Harvard, he became aware of the influence of the Hebraic tradition
on the Puritan mind and on the development of the American character.[21] If the Hebrew Bible was the source of "the American idea," if it
was the inspiration for establishing a free society of justice and
equality, then Zionism, the movement to create another such state, was
as much American as it was Jewish: the classical Jewish, or prophetic
ideals had informed the making of American society, which now in
turn became the model for the Zionist state.

Brandeis was an influential figure within mainstream America who
was to become the first Jewish Justice to the Supreme Court, and it
was through him, by virtue of his double position within American
Jewry and society at large, that Kallen's ideas made an impact on
American Zionism. Brandeis proclaimed that the Jewish spirit was
"essentially modern and essentially American" and that "loyalty to
America demands [...] that each American Jew become a Zionist."
Such a position by no means negated the American diaspora; in fact,
very few American Zionists believed that their commitment entailed
an obligation to live in Zion. Jewish statehood was necessary only for
the victims of antisemitism, and helping to secure a home for them
would only make every American Zionist "a better man and a better
American."[22] Exile was limited to Europe, and there was little difference between the golden and the promised land as a refuge and home.

Kallen's attempt to justify dual allegiance and a particularist position within the American mainstream consisted in cultural pluralism.
America, he argued, had been founded with the guarantee to preserve

---

[21] Sarah Schmidt, "Messianic Pragmatism: The Zionism of Horace M.
Kallen," *Judaism* 25.2 (Spring 1976): 219.

[22] Quoted in Eisen, *Galut*, 157.

differences. Its democracy aimed "through union, not at uniformity but
at variety, at a one out of many."[23] Against the image of the "melting
pot" with its assimilative or totalizing ideology, Kallen created the
metaphor of the "American symphony," in which the voices of diverse
but consonant groups were still to be distinguished.[24] Kallen's critics
might have argued that his version of Zionism did not need cultural
pluralism to make it acceptable to American loyalists, since all its
Jewish values had been thoroughly americanized in the process, so
much so that his recasting of Zionism undermined the very tenets of
cultural pluralism.[25] On the other hand, one could argue that to some
extent Kallen and Brandeis also judaized American ideals – syn-
thesized the values of Judaism and Americanism in a way that helped
assimilated Jews like themselves to renew a sense of their ethnic identity. What in particular this identity consisted of, beyond those abstract
'prophetic' ideals, remained unclear. When Brandeis compared
American Zionist activity with the Irish-American advancement of
Home Rule in Ireland – which also made them better Americans[26] –
then he seemed to imply that being Irish American was the same as
being Jewish American. Irish and Jewish ethnicity manifested itself in
the degree of their Americanness, their commitment to American
democratic ideals which determined their loyalty and attachment to

---

[23] Quoted in Schmidt, "Messianic Pragmatism," 221.

[24] Kallen, one could argue, anticipated the 'salad-bowl' metaphor of
American multiculturalism (Ed.).

[25] Jerold Auerbach provides some examples of the ways in which Zionist
history was recast as part of American history, in terms of the American fron-
tier experience, or of progressive Liberalism. American Zionist youth movements discussed topics like "The kibbutz and the American stockade," "The
ideals of the Pilgrims and the Chalutzim [the Zionist settlers in Palestine]," or
"Abraham Lincoln and the Jewish Spirit"; Auerbach, *Are We One? Jewish
Identity in the USA and Israel* (New Brunswick NJ & London: Rutgers UP,
2001): 67–69.

[26] Quoted in Chaim I. Waxman, "The Centrality of Israel in American Jewish Life: A Sociological Analysis," *Judaism* 25.2 (Spring 1976): 181.

their homelands. Lacking any specific cultural or religious content, ethnic consciousness and solidarity was constituted mainly by the "myth of homeland and return."[27] In the case of the Jews, moreoever, the very religion that had lost its validity was now reclaimed by isolating its universalist trends, and employed to allegorize Jews as the quintessential Americans.

The incongruence between Kallen's writings on pluralism, criticizing as they did the enforced americanization of the melting pot, and those on his very American brand of Zionism reveals not only his estrangement from his own tradition, but also the limits of pluralism itself. Through its compartmentalization – "ethnic at home and American in public" – pluralism, like its European precursor, Jewish Emancipation, still exerted some assimilative pressure. While recognizing and even encouraging cultural difference in private, "American in public" still meant an identity as close to the WASP label as possible. In that sense, pluralism, like the melting pot, was still a monocultural idea and very much a 'white' concept. Therefore pluralism proved largely successful for those European ethnicities which could pass for white and thus had access to power, so that eventually they became 'white'. When peoples of colour realized that the pluralist promise of an all-inclusive society did not extend to them, precisely because they could not pass for white, they challenged the traditional pluralist model with its emphasis on ethnicity and posited racial identification as the new paradigm for addressing societal problems. The black civil rights movement demanded political recognition of their group rights and interests, since in view of continuing structural racism, theoretical equality of all, as individuals, was not enough. Equal opportunity was a mirage, based on the illusion of individual meritocracy, which did not take into account the racist bias of society. Thus, multiculturalism

---

[27] Safran, "Diaspora in Modern Societies," 91.

was born of the limitations of pluralism; it was pluralism without public conformity.[28]

As Biale argues in his essay "The Melting-Pot and Beyond," in both
the melting-pot model and the pluralist model of American immigrant
society Jews became protagonists. Since the Anglo-conformism prevalent in the nineteenth century left no room for Jews, they became the
main proponents of the new theories. Moreover, they were considered
the paradigmatic minority, which was alternatively but also often
simultaneously described as the most easily adaptable to ever-new
circumstances, yet the most resistant to complete absorption, being
"the most group-conscious of groups" with a strong cultural heritage
of their own (Kallen). This group consciousness came from the Jews'
centuries of diasporic experience as a minority, as well as their status
as double aliens, by both religion and ethnicity, which made them the
test-case in the building of a new society. If successfully integrated,
they were "believed to hold the key to how the American polity would
define itself."[29] Thus, at one and the same time, Jews were considered,
and considered themselves, to be the quintessential outsiders and the
quintessential Americans. Until today, their self-image is marked by
the interplay of two obverse aspects, European allegorization of the
Jew as the prototypical Other, and Jewish self-allegorization as the
prototypical American.

With the advent of multiculturalism, Jews lost their centrality in
discussions of American self-definition, and other minorities moved
into the foreground of attention. Whereas in Europe Jews had been
constructed as the opposite of white, they were now considered as
insiders by non-white groups and especially by blacks, who had taken
the place of the paradigmatic outsider. On the one hand, this reflected
the social reality of the outstanding success of American Jews, particularly since World War II, when formal discrimination like educa-

---

[28] Greenberg, "Pluralism and Its Discontents," 57.

[29] Biale, "The Melting Pot and Beyond," 26.

tional quotas was abolished and antisemitism decreased. On the other hand, the Jewish self-image was, in part, still that of a minority, though their victimization had taken on relatively subtle forms. In any case, Jews no longer saw themselves in relation to African Americans. Blacks as the Jews of America or Jews as the blacks of Europe – this trope, which had been an important force behind the Jewish–black alliance in pre-Second World War America, still lingered, albeit no longer with much validity. Rather, there emerged two entirely different and simultaneous narratives of America as "Jewish Eden and black inferno."[30] The traditional Jewish identification with African-American causes was based on their collective memory of victimization which was still essential to their self-perception, but in the light of contemporary Jewish success that kind of brotherhood increasingly came to be felt by African Americans as presumptuous, if not traitorous.[31] Thus, for the first time Jews found themselves "doubly marginalized": marginal to the majority culture and marginal among the vociferous minorities and in the ongoing multicultural debate.[32] As a result, Jews now occupy a unique intermediate position as both insiders and outsiders in American society.

Jews, in turn, were (or still are) sceptical of multiculturalism with its emphasis on group rights rather than individual merits. Affirmative action in particular reminded them of the discrimination they had suffered merely by virtue of being a member of a certain group; hence their "love of America is based in large measure on its [...] insistence that rights and privileges accrue to individuals rather than groups."[33]

---

[30] Cynthia Ozick, "Literary Blacks and Jews," in Ozick, *Art and Ardor: Essays* (New York: Alfred A. Knopf, 1983): 94. Although Ozick acknowledges this fundamental incongruence, she then typically attempts to reclaim the Jews' status as the chosen minority by invoking the memory of their European experience.

[31] Ozick, "Literary Blacks and Jews," 94.

[32] Biale, "The Melting Pot and Beyond," 27.

[33] Greenberg, "Pluralism and Its Discontents," 78.

Thus, despite – or, rather, thanks to – their own past experiences, Jews remained as race-blind as the liberal, pluralist ideology which they embraced, since for them the system of meritocracy had proved so successful in America. They sometimes failed to see that meritocracy was often nothing but a white privilege by means of which peoples of colour were excluded from power.

Moreover, given its assimilationist dynamic, pluralism might in another sense have proved fatal for Jews. The pace of integration and the rate of intermarriage, along with the waning of group consciousness, made the danger of disappearing entirely into the mainstream a very real one. Multiculturalism thus has something to offer to Jews, too; it can raise awareness that they have become too closely linked to the WASP establishment. In a post-assimilation era, where Jews are reasserting their cultural and ethnic roots, multiculturalism's celebration of hybridity can teach them that no facet of identity need be suppressed in favour of another.

Similarly, when the concept of diaspora acquired a larger meaning in multiculturalist identity politics, diaspora and homeland again became topics for Jewish writers. The postcolonial theories of diaspora agree with the traditional American Jewish attitude in stressing the non-hierarchical relation between diaspora and centre, if not in fact privileging the former over the latter. American Jews, both religious and secular, had always been very ambivalent about Israel. While Israel was often proclaimed to matter in ultimate terms, it was of little consequence to their actual life and to their sense of Jewishness. Waxman even goes so far as to qualify American Zionism as a merely "pro-Israel sentiment."[34] If anything, it is the Old World – the primary diaspora ambivalently experienced as *galut* and as home – which for many American Jews constitutes Jewish "homeland," if an imaginary, sentimentalized one. This was true for the immigrant generation and is again true of contemporary Jews, who often consider themselves the

---

[34] Waxman, "The Centrality of Israel," 180.

inheritors of old *Yiddishkeit*[35] rather than as diasporic participants in
Israel's new Hebrew culture.[36] If the European origins of American
Jewry replace Israel as the real diasporic homeland, this conception
brings the American Jewish diaspora very close to the situation of,
say, Ugandan, Kenyan or Tanzanian South Asian Americans who have
passed from their exile in Africa to a new exile in the New World and
consider Africa their real homeland.

Nevertheless, the Six-Day War of 1967 and its existential threat to
the young state of Israel has marked a turning-point in Americans'
relation to Israel, bringing with it a wave of solidarity and proud identification with the image of a strong, successful Israel. Since these
events coincided with the general trends of identity politics and new
ethnicity, they became instrumental in the rediscovery of Jewishness.
As a result, for American Jews Israel has turned into what has repeat-

---

[35] The term *Yiddishkeit* encompasses a variety of cultural phenomena, both
religious and secular, as they developed and flourished in the nineteenth and
early twentieth centuries in Eastern Europe and to some extent also in immigrant America. Common to them all is the use of Yiddish as the main linguistic
medium. Movements opposed to traditional Jewish ways, such as Zionism or
Haskalah (the Jewish Enlightenment) looked down on Yiddish either as a
ghetto jargon and the language of the diaspora, or as a parochial and adulterated form of German. Hence, Zionists and (diasporist) Bundists were also
divided in their support of Hebrew or Yiddish respectively as the Jewish
national language. See Irving Howe, *World of Our Fathers* (1976; London:
Phoenix, 2000).

[36] In fact, Israel may even be an alienating experience, as in Joanna Spiro's
short story "Three Thousand Years of Your History ... Take One Year for
Yourself." In this story, the Californian visitor to her "ancestral home" is confronted with the heterogeneity and unfamiliarity of Israel's Jews, specifically
the presence of Israel's Moroccan immigrants. This makes her aware of the
fundamental difference arising from the non-Jewish side of their hyphenated
identity, and ironically reveals their common 'roots' as both portentous and
meagre. The irony is increased by the fact that it is a member of multicultural
American society who is confused by Israel's multiculturalism. To her, as an
American, Jews are homogeneously white and Ashkenazic: ie, of European
origin.

edly been called the new secular religion of American Jews. If most
recently American-Jewish identification with Israel has once more
been intensified, it is now with the hierarchy reversed: the vulnerable
centre is again in need of a powerful 'periphery'. And this is precisely
Cynthia Ozick's Zionist argument for the *raison d'être* of the American diaspora.

Toward a Poetics of Homecoming

Among the three authors I wish to discuss, Cynthia Ozick is certainly
the one who feels most keenly the paradoxical situation of being both
an insider and an outsider in American society, being at once "perfectly at home and perfectly insecure, perfectly acculturated and yet
perfectly marginal."[37] The conflicts of diasporic existence dominate
her writing, even where she does not address the issue of exile; in fact,
her entire work may be best described as the site of contesting
demands made on her identity as a Jew and an American, as a religious person and as a writer.

For Ozick, the Jewish position at the intersection of mainstream and
margin arises not merely from living in several worlds at once, but
specifically from two radically different and, as she constructs them,
opposing modes of life. While this opposition is initially one between
the religious and the secular, it is ultimately the opposition between
two cultures, the Jewish and the Christian, or Western. Inevitably, the
way in which she tries to come to terms with the conflict is not without
contradictions: The idea of a "Jewish writer" is for her nothing less
than an oxymoron.

Ozick remembers one of her formative experiences as a child in the
1930s, which illustrates what marked her as the outsider in the midst
of ethnic diversity:

---

[37] Cynthia Ozick, "Toward a New Yiddish," in Ozick, *Art and Ardor*, 172.

> "Cynthia, what are you?" (This always meant what is your religion.)
> Me: "I'm Jewish." "Yes, but are you Protestant or Catholic?" Me:
> "I'm Jewish." Jane Jones, getting exasperated...: "Well, I *know* that,
> you said it already. But are you Protestant or Catholic?" Me: "I'm
> *Jewish*." Jane Jones (now really exasperated): "O.K. O.K., you're
> Jewish. BUT ARE YOU PROTESTANT OR CATHOLIC? YOU HAVE
> TO BE ONE OR THE OTHER!"[38]

Even though it is only a child who reveals such annihilating ignorance,
the scene is nevertheless telling of the way in which the majority culture imposed public conformity on the members of its pluralist society.
American society has come a long way since the days of Ozick's
childhood, and Judaism has become one of the three "American"
religions. Today you have to be "one or the other" *or* Jewish. And yet,
there are echoes of that earlier situation when Ozick describes her
dilemma as a Jewish writer in America: "When I write English, I live
in Christendom."[39] Just as, in her naivety, the WASP Jane was, in a
way, trying to silence Cynthia's distinct voice, so Ozick's linguistic
medium has been shaped by the Western hegemonic ideology, and as
such it does not and cannot give room to other voices. While she con-
cedes that American Jews today are granted full cultural and religious
freedom, there is an assimilative and alienating force more subtle than
outright denial and repression which tends to subvert that freedom. Put
in contemporary terms, Jews may even share in the "regime of power,"
but to the extent to which they try to assert their separate identity in
the public cultural arena (ie, beyond the strictly religious practice),
they will, in her view, still feel subject to what Stuart Hall calls its
"regime of representation," which inevitably leads to an "inner expro-

---

[38] Quoted in Victor Strandberg, *Greek Mind/Jewish Soul: The Conflicted Art of Cynthia Ozick* (Madison: U of Wisconsin P, 1994): 6.

[39] Cynthia Ozick, *Bloodshed, and Three Novellas* (New York: Alfred A. Knopf, 1976): 9.

priation of cultural identity" in the colonized person.[40] For Jews, unlike other (postcolonial) minorities, the English language and its canon is the one domain left in which the exilic condition still acutely manifests itself. And consequently, the one who is mostly confronted with exile is the writer.

Against this near-impossibility of living an authentic Jewish life in the diaspora Ozick develops her vision of a new Jewish language in her essay "Toward a New Yiddish." First, from one perspective, she locates the problem, as well as the key to a meaningful diasporic existence, in culture rather than religion – as far as these dimensions can be that neatly separated. As such, the problem presents itself in the same way for other minorities; they all need to create a medium of self-expression against the regime of representation. As for religion, Jews can practise theirs and worship God anywhere – except for the fact that the very notion of religion, hence of religious freedom, is affected by a Protestant, post-Enlightenment understanding of religion as a private, compartmentalized creed: "synagogues [...] nowadays are only cathedrals, and we have always done without cathedrals."[41] In that sense, the religious issue is one instance within the larger cultural conflict, and, from this perspective, Ozick would subscribe to a multi-cultural definition of diaspora as the meeting-ground or, rather, "battleground," of cultures.

From a second perspective, however, the conflict for Ozick is very much a religious one, precisely because in the traditional view, which is basically also hers, religion permeates all aspects of life: "when a Jew becomes a secular person he is no longer a Jew."[42] Here she moves from the generalized, postmodern understanding of diaspora to the Jewish concept of diaspora as spiritual *galut*. She opens her essay

---

[40] Stuart Hall, "Cultural Identity and Diaspora," in *Identity: Community, Culture, Difference*, ed. Jonathan Rutherford (London: Lawrence & Wishart, 1990): 225–26.

[41] Ozick, "Toward a New Yiddish," 172.

[42] Ozick, "Toward a New Yiddish," 169.

with a classical *shlilat ha-golah*, a 'negation' (ie, rejection) of diaspora, repeating its dualistic world-view with the irreconcilable dichotomy of Jewish and non-Jewish, Zion and exile. This is not only in tune with political Zionist ideology, it is already a major characteristic of Rabbinic thinking with its rigid distinctions between pure and impure, sacred and profane. Ozick's emphasis is clearly on the latter and, within it, on its isolationist tendency (whereas the Boyarins will legitimize their position with a dialogic countercurrent in Rabbinic tradition). Her criticism of the diaspora is

> centered on a revulsion against the values [...] of the surrounding culture itself; a revulsion against Greek and pagan modes, whether in their Christian or post-Christian vessels, whether in their purely literary vessels or whether in their vessels of *Kulturgeschichte*. It is a revulsion [...] against what is called, strangely, Western Civilisation.[43]

Much of her argument for a Jewish particularism and a New Yiddish is directed not inward, to a recovery of Jewish values, but at a radical critique of mainstream culture, which does not understand Judaism as one of the roots of Western civilization but positions it as an entirely separate counterculture. Western culture, Ozick maintains, has become – if it has not always been – a "religion of Art."[44] Her main target of criticism is postmodern literature, which, however, in her view, only highlights the inherent tendency of all art towards pure form. With the so-called death of the novel, narrative, history and psychology were played out and superseded by a narcissistic preoccupation with language in and for itself. This dehumanized and aestheticized literature has turned the text into an idol, to be contemplated and venerated for its own sake, indulging in a "ceremony of language"[45] as its pagan rite. Defined in this way – as gentile *ersatz* religion – art becomes a violation of the Second Commandment, the prohibition against idolatry:

---

[43] Ozick, "Toward a New Yiddish," 156.
[44] Ozick, "Toward a New Yiddish," 157, 165.
[45] Ozick, "Toward a New Yiddish," 164.

"The problem of Diaspora in its most crucial essence," she writes, "is the problem of aesthetics," while Jews have always defined themselves through ethics and remained indifferent to aesthetics: "covenant and conduct are above decoration."[46] The oppositions that she constructs – religion of Art (or idolatry) vs faith, imagination vs history, dead matter vs life, form vs Idea – all come together in the fundamental dichotomy between a (pagan) aesthetic and (Jewish) ethics.[47] These dichotomies question the very possibility of a Jewish art in any medium, not only "Christian English" art.

Concurring with the Rabbis, Ozick locates the preservation of diasporic Jewish identity in the Second Commandment (and, by implication, in the First, complementary, Commandment, concerning monotheism): estrangement from God is the ultimate form of self-alienation.[48] However, she then extends her arguments to a terrain completely foreign to premodern Judaism: ie, to culture in the secular form of art and literature. As a result, the challenge Ozick has to face is even greater than that of the Rabbis: to assert her Jewish religious identity while taking part in a mainstream culture which by her own definition is antagonistic to that religion, both in its function as mainstream and as culture. This is the paradox which marks her essay on New Yiddish, in which she claims and strives for that which she

---

[46] Ozick, "Toward a New Yiddish," 165.

[47] Ozick, "Toward a New Yiddish," 165. Ozick here denies the Christian religion a fundamentally ethical orientation. Rather, she emphasizes its idolizing tendency in the eucharist; the word made flesh, spirit become matter, shares more with the pagan religion of Art than with Jewish faith.

[48] Referring, in his context, to Christianity, Hall also links the notion of a homogeneous, unadulterated and separatist identity to the tradition of monotheism, which makes monotheists resistant to absorbing foreign elements of the surrounding culture. By contrast, polytheistic systems like African religions, which were formative in Caribbean culture, have a pluralist disposition, so that a hybridized religious universe could emerge, with its mixture of "Haitian voodoo, pocomania, [...] Black baptism, Rastafarianism ..." (Hall, "Cultural Identity and Diaspora," 227).

rejects as non-Jewish. Her revulsion at pagan values is balanced by the equally great allure of the aesthetic and its seduction through language: "Why do I, who dread the cannibal-touch of story making, lust after stories more and more and more?"[49]

Ozick's moral diasporic dilemma could not be resolved in a synthesis of those antithetically constructed, irreconcilable values without a qualification of her earlier verdict on Western art as idolatry. Thus, she posits that the nineteenth-century novel, if not altogether a reconciliation of the conflict, already contains the seeds of a new Jewish language, since, dealing with human (hi)stories, it inevitably involves ethical questions. She therefore calls realist literature a "Judaized form" of writing and in that sense deems George Eliot and Tolstoy to be more Jewish – "touched by the Jewish covenant"[50] – than Norman Mailer or Allen Ginsberg. By dissociating "Jewishness" from Jewish authors and from biography, she moves one step away from pure essentialism to a more complex and "hybrid" form of identity, which, connecting Jewishness and textuality, suggests an interplay between the mainstream and its counterculture. In her description, nineteenth-century realism becomes an example of majority culture absorbing values from the minority.[51] As a manifestly Jewish form, New Yiddish will, however, surpass realist literature as a "Jewish force." Like Old

---

[49] Ozick, *Bloodshed*, 12. The "touch of story making" echoes that of lovemaking: there is an interesting parallel to the Rabbinic subdivision of the Decalogue into two sets of five corresponding commandments. The Seventh Commandment, which complements the second, concerns adultery, specifically sexual relations with gentile women. Idolatry and adultery are thus, in a sense, synonymous.

[50] Ozick, "Toward a New Yiddish," 164.

[51] This may be her vision rather than historical accuracy, since the Jewish covenant was mediated to the Victorians or Tolstoy through the Christian religion, Ozick refuses to acknowledge the white Jewish, ethical element in Christianity. Rather, when she speaks of post-realist literature as a "rejection" of the old novel as a "Jewish force," the implication is that contemporary mainstream culture suppresses values from a Jewish counter-culture previously absorbed.

Yiddish, it will contain numerous Hebrew words essential to its intention. With English as its basic linguistic vessel, it will, unlike Old
Yiddish, have the advantage of speaking also to the surrounding
gentile world. "We can do what we have never before dared to do in a
Diaspora language: make it our own, [...] understanding ourselves in
it while being understood by everyone who cares to listen or read."[52]
Beyond the question of its linguistic viability, Ozick's vision of a
hybridized idiom reveals a different understanding of the diaspora
from the earlier separatist model of her bipolar world-view: as a way
of "making English our own," her New Yiddish bears some resemblance to the way in which colonial subjects adopt, transform and
subvert the standard imperial code to forge their own variety of
"english."[53] She thus keeps oscillating between a particularist position
turned inward defensively and one that engages in a dialogue with the
world and tries to make "assimilation a two-way street."[54]

Literature written in New Yiddish, then, shall again reverse the
modernist postulate that, according to Susan Sontag, hermeneutics be
replaced by the eroticism of a text to reintroduce moral judgement and
interpretation. This is what Ozick means by "a liturgical language";
less a literature of explicit religious concerns than the expression of a
communal voice committed to Jewish values. In another essay, she
reveals what lies at the heart of the New Yiddish literature, there
calling it "redemptive," a term which more clearly expresses its quasi-
messianic potential.

> In that steady interpretive light we can make distinctions; we can see
> that one thing is not interchangeable with another thing; that not
> everything is the same; that the Holocaust is different, God knows,

---

[52] Ozick, "Toward a New Yiddish," 177.

[53] Bill Ashcroft, Gareth Griffiths & Helen Tiffin, *The Empire Writes Back.
Theory and Practice in Post-Colonial Literatures* (London: Routledge, 1989):
41-42.

[54] Quoted in Strandberg, *Greek Mind/Jewish Soul*, 32.

from a corncob.[55] So we arrive at last, at the pulse and purpose of literature: to reject the blur of the 'universal'; to distinguish one life from another; to illuminate diversity [...] *Literature is the recognition of the particular.*[56]

Hermeneutics and ethical judgement ultimately serve to recognize the possible danger of another Holocaust, of which a pagan '*galut* literature', preoccupied as it is with itself, remains unaware, so that in a sense it becomes complicit in the crime itself. The primary argument of political Zionism against the diaspora is thus re-employed in Ozick's poetic as an argument against cultural assimilation in general and the artistic norm of aestheticizing indifference in particular – both expressed in "the blur of the 'universal'." Her poetics instead proposes a homecoming in a Jewish liturgical language. With the implication that both assimilation and the Holocaust have their source in the totalizing universalism and ethical indifference of mainstream culture, the reassertion of particularity becomes a moral imperative. At the same time, the significance of redemptive literature is expanded beyond Judaism, which becomes – once more – the paradigm of particularity: within New Yiddish, it is the recognition of the particular per se (with no specifying adjective attached) that constitutes redemptive literature, and in recognizing *any* particular, it is inherently "Jewish."

Ozick's plea for a (re-)judaization of art and discourse, her endeavour to transform a cultural activity into a religious practice, place her somewhere between Ahad Ha'am's cultural Zionism and Heschel's spiritual *alyjah*. But unlike them she is also a devout Zionist who considers Israel the centre, both culturally and politically, and ultimately the locus of aspirations for all Jews. Her reasoning lacks the cele-

---

[55] Ozick is here referring to a celebrated (but unnamed) American writer quoted earlier as saying that, from a purely aesthetic and craftsmanship point of view, there is no difference as artistic subjects between the Holocaust and a corncob.

[56] Ozick, "Innovation and Redemption: What Literature Means," in Ozick, *Portrait of the Artist as a Bad Character and Other Essays on Writing* (London: Pimlico, 1996): 136.

bratory note of multicultural diasporism. She is, rather, trying to reconcile herself to her diasporic state, torn as she is between her ideological conviction and the recognition of her personal history and
identity: "Diaspora, *c'est moi.*"[57] Thus the primary legitimation of diasporic existence does not consist in her poetics of homecoming, but (at
least superficially) in the straightforward political argument of Israel's
insecurity and vulnerability, which makes the American diaspora and a
New Yiddish necessary – though only "for a while."[58]

Given her profound ambivalence as a religious Orthodox and
Zionist deeply immersed in the Western literary canon, who is unable
to synthesize but is equally unwilling to compartmentalize, the only
way for Ozick to square the circle is to make this conflict the topic of
her art: to write stories against storytelling. Her story "The Pagan
Rabbi," a variation on the oxymoron of Jewish art, is an instance of
this artistic credo. A promising young Rabbi is lured away from his
Talmudic studies by the figments of his poetic imagination as they
become incarnated in a beautiful, sensuous water nymph. The conflict
is one of life and death and can only be resolved in tragedy. The tale
reads like a midrash on her essay on New Yiddish, as well as on the
story's motto, which is taken from the Rabbinic *Pirkei Avot* or *Ethics
of the Fathers.*[59] Midrash is a Rabbinic form of Biblical exegesis comparable to allegory or parable, bringing out its moral and theological
implications. The tradition of narrative-as-exegesis, exegesis-as-narra-
tive thus provides Ozick with the perfect redemptive mode by means
of which to transcend her existential conflict.

✍

---

[57] Ozick, "Toward a New Yiddish," 158.
[58] Ozick, "Toward a New Yiddish," 173.
[59] Rabbi Jacob said: "He who is walking along and studying, but then
breaks off to remark: 'How lovely is that tree!' or 'How beautiful is that fallow
field' – Scripture regard such a one as having hurt his own being."

Contra Autochthony:
Towards a Genealogical Multiculturalism

Like Ozick, Daniel and Jonathan Boyarin variously criticize the (cultural) annihilation of Judaism through Western, Christian universalism. Even in its liberal form, Christianity is unable to accommodate difference, assimilating it instead. Unlike Ozick, however, Boyarin and Boyarin acknowledge Western universalism's inherently positive qualities, while equally recognizing the potential dangers of a Judaic particularism.

> Judaism and Christianity, as two different hermeneutic systems for reading the Bible, generate two diametrically opposed and mirror-image forms of racism – and also two dialectically opposed forms of antiracism. The genius of Christianity is its concern for all the peoples of the world, and the genius of Judaism is to leave other people alone. The evils of the two systems are the precise obverse of these genii."[60]

From these two antithetical discourses about identity they manufacture a synthesis combining their relative virtues, out of which they develop their ideal of a diasporic identity.

The problematic of the particularist position is explained in their critique of Zionism and of the nation-state, which they consider antithetical to Judaism. They define Zionism, like all nationalist ideologies, as a particularism extending over a special piece of land, and ultimately as a particularism combined with state power. Thus, ethnic exclusivism, which may have been a necessary strategy for a minority's cultural survival in the diaspora, becomes an oppressive force in that group's nation-state, now in turn negating the right of its Other to be different, if not to be (there) at all. It "will inevitably produce a discourse not unlike the Inquisition in many of its effects" (712); in an earlier passage, the comparison is to fascism (706).

---

[60] Daniel Boyarin & Jonathan Boyarin, "Diaspora: Generation and the Ground of Jewish Identity," *Critical Inquiry* 19 (Summer 1993): 707. Where the context is clear, further page references to this essay are in the main text.

In short, Jewish particularism became problematic with modernity and its shift from the religious to the political as the major paradigm of Jewish experience. As Stratton writes, "the modern rhetoric of diaspora is fundamentally political and [...] its politics are bound up with the nation-state."[61] Zionism, the Boyarins argue, reconnects the nation and the land in a way fundamentally different from the traditional Jewish theology of the Land. It is its territorial orientation in particular, the imperialist sway over others, that makes Zionism an objectionable, westernized form of Jewish nationalism. It replaced the divine promise of the Land by the myth of autochthony, which is characteristic of nationalisms trying to legitimate their political claims (as in the Israeli Declaration of Independence). Autochthony is not to be confused with indigeneity, as the authors stress, although the two notions are often significantly conflated in nationalist ideologies. Indigenes are "the people who belong here, whose land this rightfully is – a political claim, founded on present and recently past political realities" (715). The myth of autochthony, by contrast, imagines a "people who [was] never anywhere else but here and ha[s] a natural right to the land" (715). While such political realities never yield more than relative claims – other resident people can make similar claims to that space – the myth of autochthony satisfies the desire for uniqueness and thus legitimates ethnic exclusivism and the dispossession of others. Autochthony is what I would call the spatial analogue to the myth of national authenticity. Crucial to both are essentialist notions of the original and genuine, the natural and pure, and both function "as a quasi-religious locus of transcendence,"[62] which therefore cannot and need not be further negotiated. The seemingly political argument of geographical origin is in fact a pseudo-religious one.

---

[61] Stratton, "(Dis)placing the Jews," 312.

[62] Vincent Cheng, "Authenticity and Identity: Catching the Irish Spirit," in *Semicolonial Joyce*, ed. Derek Attridge & Marjorie Howes (Cambridge: Cambridge UP, 2000): 244.

The Boyarins and Stratton agree in their criticism of autochthony, which they regard as a highly problematic mystification within an otherwise secular and 'rational' discourse. They disagree, however, about the historical preconditions of this modern myth. Stratton sees a continuity between the Biblical divine promise of the Land and the unique tie between nation and Land created through "autochthony," and it is certainly true that both share the premodern "distinction between land and Land."[63] The Boyarins – although they do not further discuss the concept's genesis – do not consider it an originally religious idea but, significantly, a *quasi*-religious one which operates within a political, nationalist context. Its ideological source seems to lie in Romanticism rather than the Jewish Bible. As Cheng points out concerning the concepts of authenticity and national uniqueness, these notions – as well as autochthony – embody the Romantic legacies of the sublime and the transcendent.[64] By contrast, the Boyarins claim that the idea of autochthony is foreign to the traditional Jewish narrative. While conceding that the Jewish attachment to the Land ("natural connectedness") is similar to that of most other "indigenous" peoples, they stress that "the Biblical story is [...] one of always already coming from somewhere else," hence is "perpetually an unsettlement of the very notion of autochthony" (715).

To the territorial or spatial definition of national identity which they reject on ethical grounds, the Boyarins oppose an alternative model based on its temporal dimension: it is one that recovers the idea of a genealogical, rather than geographical, origin in the Jews' common descent from Abraham. Such a genealogically defined identity finds its

---

[63] Stratton, "(Dis)placing the Jews," 313.

[64] Cheng, "Authenticity and Identity," 243. Of course, the Biblical narrative of Exodus, the story of Moses leading his people out of bondage and into the Promised Land, has been appropriated by the nationalist rhetoric of a number of colonized peoples as various as the Irish or African Americans. In that sense, the myth of autochthony does get overlayed with the theology of divine promise, though only as a theological trope.

expression in the rituals of collective memory (Jewish history) and the
practice of Jewish traditions. This is basically the Rabbinical position
that formed *galut* consciousness until the advent of modernity. After
the loss of national sovereignty, the Rabbis redefined the notion of a
return to the Land in strictly messianic terms. They transcended the
loss of the Land by "displac[ing] loyalty from place to memory of
place" (719). Projected into the future, that memory calls up the idea
of messianic redemption and return to the Land. In this way, the
Rabbis did not merely substitute genealogy for geography; they additionally succeeded in transforming the spatial quality of Jewish
identity into a temporal one, thereby maintaining it while at the same
time overcoming it. By conceiving of identity as a purely temporal
existence, the Rabbis ended up inventing the Diaspora.

As the Boyarins see it, the redeeming potential of premodern Rabbinical discourse of the Land lies in its retention of a connection to the
Land without deducing any territorial claims from that affilation. The
so-called natural right to the land exists only as a transcendental claim
beyond human agency, and therefore the return has to be infinitely
deferred. It is through this messianic argument, by relocating all claims
to the utopian domain, that the Boyarins articulate their radically
diasporist stance, an attitude that is informed as much by (cultural)
politics as it is by religion. At the same time, in grounding their vision
in a historical Jewish model they also place themselves firmly within
their ancestors' tradition. Their theoretical position is thus also a first
instance of their genealogical credo. What Stratton calls an anachro-
nistic and problematic insistence on the traditional Jewish narrative in
a modern context here becomes a radical subversion of nationalist
politics.

It is certainly true, as Safran writes, that many if not most other
diasporas today do not seek a physical return to their homeland either,
while the memory and myth of the homeland and eventual return to it
still play an important emotional role in "solidify[ing] ethnic consciousness and solidarity." But if Safran sees the "return" of these

communities as a largely "eschatological concept," he confounds the
Jewish and the multicultural concepts of diaspora. That is, he meta-
phorizes the religious notion when he characterizes the infinitely
deferred "return" as "holding out a utopia – or *eutopia* – that stands in
contrast to the perceived *dystopia* in which actual life is lived."[65]
Where Safran psychologizes, the Boyarins politicize the concept, without, however, abandoning Jewish religious tradition, which lends
moral weight to their anti-Zionist argument. Also, Safran remains
within the politics of the nation-state; in his analysis, the homeland has
two faces, the mythic, nostalgic one, but also the very real one of a
state which nationalist diasporans support politically and financially
from afar. While the same dynamic is to a large extent at work in the
American-Jewish diaspora, the Boyarins concentrate on the situation
in Israel and want to stress the post-national lesson for the Jewish
diaspora that "a people does not need a land in order to be a people"
(723). As they see it, with its eschatological component, the unique
relationship of Jews to their homeland can be conducive to a multicultural approach not only in reference to the host-country but also to
the homeland, which in multicultural theories of the diaspora has often
been viewed in terms of the nation-state.

℘

The two different constructions of Jewish identity, the territorial and
the genealogical, in some sense also reflect the dichotomy between
Western and indigenously Jewish discourses about it. Western, or
Christian, ideology privileges space[66] over genealogy and spirit over
body – a valuation which the Boyarins trace back to Paul, the Jewish

---

[65] Safran, "Diaspora in Modern Societies," 94, 91.

[66] 'Space' not in the strictly territorialist sense, but in the sense that Christianity's aspirations are global and hence an imperialist imposition on the rest
of the world.

founder of Christianity. Rabbinic Judaism, in turn, reversed this valuation in favour of physical connectedness through family relations.

In the Boyarins' reading, Rabbinic politics and Pauline Christianity
offer a historical parallel to today's situation. Both are seen as movements which emerged from, and responded to, the 'multicultural'
dilemma of hellenized Palestine, as two antithetical approaches to
'identity politics'. This antithesis has constituted the matrix of all
debates around identity between a majority and its minorities. Paul's
radical and revolutionary challenge to overcome and erase all difference lies at the heart of the universalist "discourse of sameness:"[67]
"There is neither Jew nor Greek, there is neither slave nor freeman,
there is no male and female. For you are all one in Christ Jesus" (Gala-
tians 3:26–29). The physical kinship of genealogy was superseded by
a new identity based on a commonality of spiritual kinship. Translated
into contemporary terms, consent rather than descent became the main
term of societal relations, the concept which dominated the melting-
pot and to some extent also the pluralist ideology of American immigrant society. The American philosophy of re-creating and re-inventing onself, the making of Americans through volitional allegiance, is
thus a profoundly Christian, Pauline idea. Conversely, pluralism, and
especially multiculturalism, can also be seen as Jewish concepts.

To the Rabbis, Paul's egalitarian promise, his rejection of "an in-
appropriate doctrine of specialness" (723), meant a threat to Jewish
identity, just as his universalizing of the Torah was a dispossession of
their religion. Their solution to the cultural dilemma was the invention
of diaspora, even in the Land. They insisted on the importance of
genealogical lineage to keep their separate identity, but in turn gave up
all political claims: "The Rabbinic answer to Paul's challenge was to
renounce any possibility of domination over Others by being perpetually out of power" (722). This strategy of powerlessness, the Boyarins
argue, proved a very effective means of self-preservation in the dia-

---

[67] Boyarin & Boyarin, "Diaspora," 707.

sporic context of a hostile Christendom. In this sense, the Rabbinic idea of the diaspora provides an ideal model of coexistence beyond the nation-state even today: the "dissociation of ethnicities and political hegemonies [is] the only social structure that even begins to make possible a maintenance of cultural identity in a world grown thoroughly and inextricably interdependent" (723). In allowing for both Jewish (or, indeed, any particularist) cultural creativity and participation in the common cultural life, diasporic identity embodies a synthesis of the dialectic between Paul's and the Rabbis' approach, accepting Paul's critical challenge, but not his solution: a concern for all human beings, but without making them all the same.[68]

Elsewhere, Daniel Boyarin clarifies[69] that this dual cultural allegiance is not a version of the motto "Be a Jew at home and a human being abroad," which was propagated both by Emancipation and pluralism discourses. Rather than as an opposition between a particular and a universal identity, he regards Jewish identity as a "concatenation of two equally particular identities in the same polysystem." His own Jewish identity is not compromised by the fact that he is also "profoundly [...] American"; thus, he may go to the synagogue in the morning and in the evening attend a concert of the country singer Emmylou Harris. Yet the question remains what 'American culture', in

---

[68] Boyarin & Boyarin, "Diaspora," 713. Although the Boyarins usually treat diaspora and Rabbinic Judaism as synonyms, they conceive their ideal of the diaspora as a combination of the relative virtues of Rabbinic particularism and Pauline universalism. This inconsistency may reveal their idealization, or biased perception of Rabbinic Judaism, which also has a strong separatist and exclusivist side. The open multicultural society needs the universalist concern for all its members, and this, in their view, is also what constitutes Israel's only legitimation: as a hegemonic power Judaism has to renounce all exclusivism and "reimport a diasporic consciousness": ie, the consciousness of a Jewish collective sharing space with other groups. The Israel that they envision is thus based on the American model.

[69] Daniel Boyarin, *A Radical Jew: Paul and the Politics of Identity* (Berkeley & Los Angeles: U of California P, 1994): 244.

contrast to minority cultures, means; whether it is not inevitably an
expression of the dominant social group. To what extent can that
group, and 'white' country music, be ethnic when ethnicity is usually
associated with otherness? His particularization of universal identity,
or the 'othering' of mainstream culture, seems to be as much an
attempt to undermine its totalizing power as an observation of fact. On
the other hand, it also bespeaks the ease with which he, an American
Jew, can slip in and out of his ethnic and other social roles. Being an
insider as much as an outsider, he can access both systems, and from
his own privileged, double position the centre will indeed appear less
overpowering. For white ethnic groups, ethnicity, being largely invisible, is voluntary – a matter of personal choice rather than an exter-
nally enforced identity. This makes them the ideal representatives of a
diasporic identity that can fully participate in both cultures.

For instance, when Boyarin says the prayer for the sick in synagogue "because this is the way Jews express their solidarity with sick
people,"[70] he is enacting his ethnicity rather than practising his religion, and the enactment reveals the voluntary nature of his ethnicity. It
is a *cultural* practice which combines nostalgia ('homesickness') for
tradition with a critical, 'ethnographic' attitude. The nostalgic performance allows for a kind of (precarious?) homecoming at the same time
that the cultural critic's attitude establishes a distance and difference
from his ancestors (and from Modern Orthodox contemporaries).[71] It
thus prevents his nostalgia from ever becoming, as criticized by Stratton, the desire for a return to a romanticized or "imagined past time
[...] before the impact of [...] diasporic experience."[72] Being insiders

---

[70] Boyarin, *A Radical Jew*, 244.

[71] On the interplay of critical theory, or academic concerns, with a politics
of Jewish identity as developed in Jonathan Boyarin's concept of a "critical
post-Judaism," see Noah Isenberg, "'Critical Post-Judaism': or, Reinventing a
Yiddish Sensibility in a Postmodern Age," *Diaspora: A Journal of Transnational Studies* 6.1 (1997).

[72] Stratton, "(Dis)placing the Jews," 317–18.

and outsiders not only with regard to the mainstream, the Boyarins also choose to position themselves simultaneously within, and on the margins of, the Jewish community.

For other minorities, however, the situation presents itself differently. In their theorizing of the diaspora the Boyarins underestimate, or even neglect, race as a crucial factor in social relations. Their version of the diaspora is an idealization (as they themselves repeatedly admit) which reflects their own privileged experience of American-Jewish exceptionalism and ignores both the suffering caused by the diasporic condition throughout Jewish history, as well as that of contemporary non-Jewish minorities.[73] For most peoples of colour, in particular for African Americans, who are still largely excluded from power, American society as a 'polysystem' of equal particularisms, of multiple and voluntary allegiances, is still as far removed from reality as the vision of an ideally race-blind multicultural society.

If the contemporary Jewish diaspora is unable to provide a full model for all American diasporas, the dialectic between Paul and the Rabbis nevertheless has an important contribution to make to multiculturalism:

> When Christianity is the hegemonic power in Europe and the USA, the resistance of Jews to being universalized can be a critical force and model for the resistance of all peoples to being Europeanized out of their particular bodily existence.[74]

This formulation is interesting because American hegemony qua hegemony is here posited as essentially European, whereas 'true' Americanness is inherently multicultural. Calling Christianity a *European* legacy can again be seen as an effort to particularize and hence subvert it. If the Boyarins' diasporic model is Jewish, its ideal setting is

---

[73] Galchinsky considers class to be a further reason for an uncritical celebration of diaspora when he criticizes postcolonial theory for its "unconvincing claims for the privileged visionary potential of the diaspora intellectual" (Galchinksy, "Scattered Seeds," 187).

[74] Boyarin & Boyarin, "Diaspora," 720.

American; America is the society of diasporas par excellence. This is not equivalent to pluralism's judaization of Americanness and its americanization of Jewishness (which stresses the universalist trends in Judaism); on the contrary, this proposal simultaneously claims specialness and self-allegorization as the prototypical American(-as-diasporan).

"Moses in Reverse"

In their decidedly anti-Zionist postulations, the Boyarins do not even touch on the ultimate Zionist *raison d'être* of the Jewish state: the Holocaust, which made the creation of Israel absolutely necessary as a safe haven for the Jewish people. The Zionist proponents of American pluralism had already limited the necessity of the Zionist project to their persecuted fellow-Jews overseas, since America was different, and more than a safe haven to them. For the Boyarins, the problem of antisemitism and racism is solved; in their post-national ideal of diasporic societies, political power is shared between ethnicities. But also from the perspective of *Realpolitik*, recent political developments have, sadly, proved them right in their insistent warnings against state ethnicity, which not only undermines the Jewish nation's relation to its Others but ultimately also the Zionist enterprise itself. Thus, paradoxically, America may again (have) become a safe haven for Israeli Jews; for Israelis rather than the Jewish people as a whole: with the establishment of Israel, the problem has acquired a new dimension, one that concerns Jews less as Jews (the Jewish Other) than as members of the ethnic majority in an oppressive yet vulnerable Jewish state.

This situation is taken up by Philip Roth in his satirical novel *Operation Shylock*, which on many levels may be read as an intertextual dialogue with the Boyarins' diaspora essay and was coincidentally published in the same year. Roth's protagonist, Moishe Pipik, is afraid of a second Jewish Holocaust in the Middle East, sparked by an anti-Judaism which crucially emerges from the context of the nation-state (though the hatred of the oppressed for their oppressor may not be free of traditional antisemitic elements). As Pipik argues, Zionism, after fulfilling its historical role of "recover[ing] Jewish hope and morale" in the immediate postwar years, has exhausted itself and in turn become "the foremost Jewish problem."[75]

Following this insight, Pipik becomes an ardent promoter of Dia-sporism, impersonating (for publicity reasons) the famous author "Philip Roth," who also figures in the novel and turns into the fiercest opponent of this masquerading alter ego – though, as it *seems*, on personal rather than on political grounds. In any case, the whole text is a mirror maze of false identities and doubles, of feigned or real atti-tudes and affiliations too complex to disentangle here. When Roth's histrionic "Moses in reverse" envisions Diasporism as the ideology logically superseding Zionism as the solution to the Jewish problem, he does so for both ethical and existential reasons. First and foremost, he proposes a resettlement of his people in Europe as the necessary strategy to ensure their sheer survival, thereby employing a classical Zionist argument in reverse to plead for an exodus from Israel.

Pipik–Roth, moreover, again concurring with the Boyarins, stresses the historical foundations of his vision. Jewish history and identity, he claims, are inextricably bound up with the diasporic condition, which, on the same historical and cultural grounds, proves Zionist ideology wrong. By arguing that Europe is the most authentic Jewish homeland that his people ever had, and by maintaining that diaspora Judaism constitutes its most authentic mode of existence,[76] Roth's Pipik re-verses the traditional arguments, turning the centre–periphery relation-ships on their head. Thus, rather than challenging the authenticity of a properly Jewish existence in the diaspora (as did Zionism), Pipik–Roth deconstructs the nationalist myth of authenticity as a pure and un-

---

[75] Philip Roth, *Operation Shylock* (1993; London: Vintage, 1994): 44.
[76] Roth, *Operation Shylock*, 32.

adulterated cultural essence: "Cultures are not preserved by being protected from 'mixing' but probably can only continue to exist as a
product of such mixing."[77] Diasporic Jewish culture only highlights
this generally acknowledged fact, since, lacking a single national
space, it cannot be seen as a self-enclosed phenomenon. Thus, when
Pipik celebrates Europe as "the birthplace of Rabbinic Judaism
Hasidic Judaism, Jewish secularism and socialism" but also the cradle
of Heine and Einstein, he takes these movements and geniuses to have
grown out of an exchange with the surrounding culture, and to have
contributed in turn to the common culture. The fact of Jewish survival
through renewed and volitional dispersion is thus also crucially a
cultural issue. According to the logic of these insights, he demands the
"de-Israelization of Jews."[78]

From such a cultural emphasis, it follows that the "Diasporist
Herzl's" fantastical project, as Pipik–Roth calls it, does not concern
the entire Jewish nation, but only Ashkenazic: ie, European Jews, who
were also the protagonists of Zionist Israel, whereas "the Jews of
Islam have their own, very different destiny."[79] Instead of arguing
along national or religious lines, Pipik posits cultural space as a major
site of Jewish identity. As Arab cultural space, Israel/Palestine should
be the common home of Muslim, Christian and Jewish Arabs (or Arab
Jews). Pipik thus proposes an alternative notion of ethnicity, one that
cuts across the traditional dichotomies and instead gathers all local or
regional ethnicities into one cultural term. In a sense, this is also a
territorial approach, albeit a decidedly transnational one. It applies the
criterion of indigeneity as the Boyarins defined it in contradistinction
to the potentially devastating myth of autochthony.

---

[77] Boyarin & Boyarin, "Diaspora," 721.

[78] Roth, *Operation Shylock*, 32, 170–71. In his diasporist enthusiasm, Pipik
occasionally distorts some historical facts. Rabbinic Judaism *was* born in exile,
but its birthplace was not Europe, but Babylon and Palestine.

[79] Roth, *Operation Shylock*, 42.

The systematic ambiguities in *Operation Shylock*, not least its many tongue-in-cheek arguments reiterating anti-Israeli clichés of the un-cultured though strong and earthbound *sabra,* make easy identification with any position put forth in the novel impossible. Rather than seriously subverting the Zionist devaluation of the diaspora into a diasporist devaluation of Zion, its satirical mirror serves instead to expose Zionism's one-sided ideology. In contrast to the Boyarins, Roth thus ultimately argues for a Judaism with two centres. For Roth, however, as Galchinsky points out in reference to a scene in a Yiddish delicatessen back in New York, America, not Israel, is the true inheri-tor of and successor to European Jewish authenticity, though America provides only a static and romanticized version of it.[80] This prevailing nostalgia may explain Roth's uneasiness about a limitless multicul-turalism, which he voices through the figure of an Israeli secret agent:

> "Who will fall captive to whom in this city? The Indian to the Jew,
> the Jew to the Indian, or both to the Latino? Yesterday I made my
> way to Seventy-second Street. All along Broadway blacks eating
> bagels baked by Puerto Ricans sold by Koreans."[81]

Then again, this may just as well be read as Roth's celebration of America's multiculturalism, with all ethnicities metaphorically united through the culinary bond of ethnic food, here in the exemplary Yiddish bagel, Jewish symbol of prototypical American hybridity.

Summary

To take Roth's symbol one step further, the Yiddish bagel became "the bagel" only in America, and has since turned into the "daily bread" of common culture: Jews are figured as the prototypical minority in an ideal American society of diasporas and hence as the quintessential American, which simultaneously converts them into the privileged

---

[80] Galchinsky, "Scattered Seeds," 206.
[81] Roth, *Operation Shylock*, 382.

exception in relation to other minorities. With the current revaluation of diaspora, Jews are trying to reclaim the double position which they occupied in earlier theories of immigrant America and lost with the advent of multiculturalism. This complex and unique status has shaped the American-Jewish relationship with Israel. On the one hand, Jewish Americans have felt themselves to have the self-assured status of a diaspora throughout; on the other, America as a country of immigrants never defined itself in the European nationalist terms of 'one nation – one territory' (or a lack thereof).

While the three distinct contemporary voices on diaspora discussed in this essay are clearly to be perceived and understood against this background, they cannot be taken as representative of the common American-Jewish attitude towards Israel. Ozick and the Boyarins embody two extremes, Zionist and anti-Zionist, different cornerstones from which to stake out the middle ground where the majority of American Jews with their strong pro-Israel sentiments, or American Zionist attitudes, are located. Roth comes closest to the intermediary position, and from this perspective problematizes the consequences of an unqualified orthodox Zionism.

The discussion of these three authors also aimed at offering a re-reading of the conceptions of diaspora formed in the 1920s and 1930s. It raises the question whether there is a continuity or discontinuity with those earlier understandings, especially after 1945, 1948, and the Six-Day War of 1967. Quite clearly, Kallen's Americanism-as-Zionism resonates most prominently in *Operation Shylock*, whereas Ozick and the Boyarins in different ways represent versions of both continuity and rupture with regard to the formative years of American Zionism and its bipolar view of centre vs diaspora. Although the Boyarins' stance amounts to a subversion of the Israeli nation-state, it can also be read as a radicalized continuation of Kallen's Americanism-as-Zionism into the multicultural age, with American society as the model for Israel. In other words, the difference to Kallen arises from a changed, post-national approach to society, rather than from the decisive events of World War II and Israel's early years. At the same time, it is true that the Holocaust, though never mentioned, is always implicated in the Boyarins' general critique of state ethnicity as potential fascism.

Ozick's voice, though pragmatically sustaining the idea of a temporary double centre of Judaism, more clearly represents a rupture. Ozick, the American-born descendant of Russian Jews, displays an almost European sensitivity vis-à-vis the issue of antisemitism, being sceptical about the general conviction that "America is different." To her, the Holocaust is the crucial event, first and last cause of her pronounced political Zionism and even of her 'Zionist' poetic. Her essay on New Yiddish, first published in the wake of the Six-Day War, reflects a concern with the Holocaust (and the threat of another such catastrophe) which bears little relation to instrumentalization in identity politics.

The criticism of Western universalizing culture that is central to both Ozick's and the Boyarins' conceptions of diaspora introduces a new postcolonial (or old Rabbinic) note into American Jewish negotiations of diaspora and distinguishes them from the earlier proposals for a synthesis of American and Jewish or Zionist values. But while Ozick and the Boyarins share their critique of universalism – Ozick by dispraising the diaspora, the Boyarins by celebrating it – they disagree about the processes by means of which Jewish particularity can be asserted. Separatism from, or interaction with, the surrounding culture(s)? This is the question that will continue to preoccupy the Jewish-American diaspora.

✍

WORKS CITED

Antin, Mary. *The Promised Land* (1912; Harmondsworth: Penguin, 1997).

Auerbach, Jerold S. *Are We One? Jewish Identity in the USA and Israel* (New Brunswick NJ & London: Rutgers UP, 2001).

Biale, David. "The Melting Pot and Beyond: Jews and the Politics of American Identity," in Biale et al., ed. *Insider/Outsider*, 17–33.

——, Michael Galchinsky & Susannah Heschel, ed. *Insider/Outsider. American Jews and Multiculturalism* (Berkeley, Los Angeles & London: U of California P, 1998).

Boyarin, Daniel, *A Radical Jew: Paul and the Politics of Identity* (Berkeley & Los Angeles: U of California P, 1994).

——, & Jonathan Boyarin. "Diaspora: Generation and the Ground of Jewish Identity," *Critical Inquiry* 19 (Summer 1993): 693–725.

Cheng, Vincent. "Authenticity and Identity: Catching the Irish Spirit," in *Semicolonial Joyce*, ed. Derek Attridge & Marjorie Howes (Cambridge: Cambridge UP, 2000): 240–61.

Eisen, Arnold. *Galut: Modern Jewish Reflections on Homelessness and Homecoming* (Bloomington & Indianapolis: Indiana UP, 1986).

Galchinsky, Michael. "Scattered Seeds: A Dialogue of Diasporas," in Biale et al., ed. *Insider/Outsider*, 185–211.

Greenberg, Cheryl. "Pluralism and Its Discontents: The Case of Blacks and Jews," in Biale et al., ed. *Insider/Outsider*, 55–87.

Guttmann, Allen. *The Jewish Writer in America: Assimilation and the Crisis of Identity* (New York: Oxford UP, 1971).

Hall, Stuart. "Cultural Identity and Diaspora," in *Identity: Community, Culture, Difference*, ed. Jonathan Rutherford (London: Lawrence & Wishart, 1990): 222–37.

Howe, Irving. *World of Our Fathers* (1976; London: Phoenix, 2000).

Isenberg, Noah. "'Critical Post-Judaism'; or, Reinventing a Yiddish Sensibility in a Postmodern Age," *Diaspora: A Journal of Transnational Studies* 6.1 (1997): 85–96.

Mendes–Flohr, Paul. "Zion und die Diaspora: Vom babylonischen Exil bis zur Gründung des Staates Israel," in *Jüdische Lebenswelten. Essays*, ed. Andreas Nachama, Julius Schoeps & Edward van Voolen, tr. Jeanne A. Brombacher & Gennaro Ghirardelli (Frankfurt am Main: Jüdischer Verlag/Suhrkamp, 1991): 257–84.

Ozick, Cynthia. *Bloodshed and Three Novellas* (New York: Alfred A. Knopf, 1976).

——. "Innovation and Redemption: What Literature Means," in Ozick, *Portrait of the Artist as a Bad Character and Other Essays on Writing* (London: Pimlico, 1996): 126–36.

——. "Literary Blacks and Jews," in Ozick, *Art and Ardor: Essays* (New York: Alfred A. Knopf, 1983): 90–112.

——. *The Pagan Rabbi and Other Stories* (New York: E.P. Dutton, 1983).

——. "Toward a New Yiddish," in Ozick, *Art and Ardor*, 151–77.

Paley, Grace. "The Used-Boy Raiders," in Paley, *The Little Disturbances of Man* (1959; Penguin Contemporary American Fiction Series; New York: Viking Penguin, 1985): 127–34.

Roth, Philip. *Operation Shylock* (1993; London: Vintage, 1994).

Safran, William. "Diaspora in Modern Societies: Myths of Homeland and Return," *Diaspora: A Journal of Transnational Studies* 1.1 (1991): 83–99.

Schmidt, Sarah. "Messianic Pragmatism: The Zionism of Horace M. Kallen," *Judaism* 25.2 (Spring 1976): 217–29.

Spiro, Joanna. "Three Thousand Years of Your History … Take A Year For Yourself," in *The Schocken Book of Contemporary Jewish Fiction*, ed. Ted Solotaroff & Nessa Rapoport (New York: Schocken, 1996): 347–61.

Strandberg, Victor. *Greek Mind/Jewish Soul: The Conflicted Art of Cynthia Ozick* (Madison: U of Wisconsin P, 1994).

Stratton, Jon. "(Dis)placing the Jews: Historicizing the Idea of Diaspora," *Diaspora: A Journal of Transnational Studies* 6.3 (1997): 301–29.

Waxman, Chaim I. "The Centrality of Israel in American Jewish Life: A Sociological Analysis," *Judaism* 25.2 (Spring 1976): 175–87.

℘

BRYAN CHEYETTE

Diasporas of the Mind
British-Jewish Writing
Beyond Multiculturalism

Introduction

T
HE EXPERIENCE OF DIASPORA can be a blessing or a
curse or, more commonly, an uneasy amalgam of the two
states. It is not a coincidence that the Hebrew root for exile
or diaspora has two distinct connotations. *Golah* implies residence in a
foreign country (where the migrant is in charge of his or her destiny),
whereas *galut* denotes a tragic sense of displacement (where the
migrant is essentially the passive object of an impersonal history).[1]
Both words, in current usage, have a perjorative feel about them because they suggest an undesirable exile from an autochthonous 'homeland'. But the distinction between *golah* and *galut* is worth keeping
because it encapsulates a sense of differing historical possibilities
within the current idealization of an abstract diaspora.

The word 'diaspora' originally stems from the Greek *dia-speirein*
meaning 'to scatter' or 'to sow'. It was first used in the New Testa-
ment to indicate the dispersal of the disciples and the spreading of the

---

[1] Maeera Y. Shreiber, "The End of Exile: Jewish Identity and Diaspora
Poetics," *PMLA* 113.2 (March 1998): 273–87, and Phil Cohen, *Home Rules:
Some Reflections on Racism and Nationalism in Everyday Life* (London: U of
East London P, 1993): 34.

gospel. In the medieval period, it mainly referred to the resettlement of Jews outside of Israel and, more recently, has been applied to large-scale migrations of populations such as the African diaspora or the diaspora of the Irish or Palestinian peoples.[2] Today, however, the term 'diaspora' has effectively reverted to its original etymology indicating a universalized state of homelessness that is at the heart of the new gospel of postmodern and postcolonial theory.

Postmodern theory, especially as articulated by Philippe Lacoue–Labarthe, Emmanuel Lévinas and Jean–François Lyotard, conceives of "the jew" as the signifier of an ineffable alterity within Western meta-physics.[3] Lyotard's *Heidegger and "the jews"* (1988), for instance, constructs "the jew" to represent all forms of otherness, heterodoxy and nonconformity. At the beginning of the volume, Lyotard justifies the allegorization of Jews in the following terms:

> What is most real about real Jews is that Europe, in any case, does not know what to do with them: Christians demand their conversion; monarchs expel them; republics assimilate them; Nazis exterminate them. "The jews" are the object of a dismissal with which Jews, in particular, are afflicted in reality.[4]

While I have relied on the recent translation of Lyotard's text, Geoff Bennington has noted elsewhere that the phrase "'The jews' are the object of a dismissal" is more accurately rendered as "'The jews' are the object of a *non-lieu*." This latter juridical term carries a good deal of weight in *Heidegger and "the jews"* because, as Bennington points out, a '*non-lieu*' is literally a 'non-place' or 'noplace'. This sense of placelessness, of the inability to situate European Jews, above all

[2] Shreiber, "The End of Exile: Jewish Identity and Diaspora Poetics," 274–77.

[3] Gillian Rose, *Judaism and Modernity: Philosophical Essays* (Oxford: Blackwell, 1993): 1–24, 241–57.

[4] Jean–François Lyotard, *Heidegger and "the jews"*, tr. Andreas Michel & Mark S. Roberts (*Heidegger et "les juifs"*, 1988; tr. Minneapolis: U of Minnesota P, 1990): 3.

defines 'the jew' for Lyotard.[5] In this reading, the only place for "the jew" is within quotation-marks as the diasporist *par excellence* and, once again, the eternal victim.

What is ironic about the postmodern embrace of those who would wish "the jew" to be emblematic once more is that it reproduces the universalizing desire that has, historically, generated the violence that Lyotard is supposed to be writing against. The reconstruction of "the jew" as an ethnic allegory for postmodern indeterminacy – "at the end of the end of philosophy" – can be said to aestheticize, reify and de-historicize 'the Other'.[6] That is, the judaization of the site of 'the Other' elides the historical production of "the jew" within racial discourse. At the same time, Lyotard represents "real Jews" as nothing more than the effect of a hellenizing Christian culture. His abstracted account of Western antisemitism still leaves its trace in *Heidegger and "the jews"* which, once again, refigures "the jew" as the ineffable 'Other' of European postmodernity.

One need only glance at Sander Gilman's influential *The Jew's Body* (1991) to see the uncomfortable similarities between "the jew" as an ethnic allegory within postmodernity and as a racial allegory within modernity. Summarizing the physician–anthropologists of *fin-de-siècle* Germany, Gilman writes:

> It is circumcision which sets the (male) Jew apart. [...] The Jew in the Diaspora is out of time (having forgotten to vanish like the other ancient peoples); is out of his correct space (where circumcision had validity). His Jewishness (as well as his disease) is inscribed on his penis.[7]

---

[5] Geoff Bennington, "Lyotard and 'the Jews'," in *Modernity, Culture and "the Jew"*, ed. Bryan Cheyette & Laura Marcus (Cambridge: Polity, 1998): 192.

[6] Rose, *Judaism and Modernity*, 13.

[7] Sander Gilman, *The Jew's Body* (London & New York: Routledge, 1991): 91.

For Lyotard, "the jew" is out of space and time but this is deemed to make manifest a universalized absence of any grand narratives. At best, diaspora is embraced as an enabling *golah* or form of exile that contains within it a means of undermining racial and national absolutes. But, as Gilman demonstrates, Lyotard's ethnic allegory stems from the all-too-usable racial allegory of "the jew" as an irrevocable 'Other' within Western Christian culture. Diaspora, in these terms, is clearly an aspect of *galut*; the passive (male) body inscribed with an inexorable racial difference.

Diaspora as *golah* and *galut*, both a blessing and a curse, has been illustrated notably in the influential oeuvre of Zygmunt Bauman. Bauman is at pains to historicize the "conceptual Jew" in a number of volumes culminating both in his *Life in Fragments* (1995) and in his essay "Allosemitism." In these works, Bauman rethinks the historiography of antisemitism, which he renames "allosemitism" so as to utilize the Greek word for otherness when referring to the practice of representing "the Jews" as a radically different Other.[8] What Bauman argues is that the terms 'antisemitism' and 'philosemitism', which focus either on hostility or on sympathy toward "the jews," are two relatively distinct aspects of a much broader history of differentiating Jews from other human beings. The danger, for Bauman, consists in the fact that the conventional historiography continues to essentialize Jews as uniquely timeless, unchanging victims and thereby, as does Lyotard, positions the history of antisemitism outside of the social, political and historical processes which gave rise to this history in the first place.

Insofar as they essentialize and homogenize Jewishness, all Jewish racial representations are, on one level, ultimately 'antisemitic' or 'allosemitic' Jewishness. But instead of an aberrant hatred or a pro-

---

[8] Zygmunt Bauman, *Life in Fragments: Essays in Postmodern Morality* (Oxford: Blackwell, 1995): 207, and "Allosemitism: Premodern, Modern, Postmodern," in Cheyette & Marcus, ed. *Modernity, Culture and "the Jew"*, 143–56.

nounced affinity for "the Jews," Bauman highlights the prevalent constructions of Jewish 'difference' in wider historical terms. For Bauman, the conceptual or notional "Jew" is not just another case of 'heterophobia' – or the resentment of the different – but is, instead, a case study in 'proteophobia' (the apprehension or anxiety elicited by those who do not easily fall into any established categories). Bauman's "Jew" is "ambivalence incarnate," the alter ego emitting contradictory signals and undermining the orderly spatial and temporal boundaries of Christian civilization.[9]

The diasporic Jew as "ambivalence incarnate" relates Bauman's work to the representation of "the Jew" as outside of space and time in Gilman and Lyotard. Like them, Bauman locates modernity as the site par excellence which produced the ambivalent "conceptual Jew." He maintains that given the ordering, classifying nature of modernity – signified, above all, by the rise of the nation-state – the ambivalent "Jew" was particularly threatening because s/he made light of all modern social, political and cultural distinctions. In his Modernity and Ambivalence (1991), Bauman locates uncategorizable diasporic Jews, such as Kafka, Freud and Simmel, at the heart of modern culture. By contrast, in Modernity and the Holocaust (1989), Bauman shows that the confusion generated by this ambivalence resulted in a genocidal form of closure. The same diasporic ambivalence, in other words, produces modernist art and culture as well as quintessentially modern

---

[9] Bauman, Life in Fragments, 208, 211–12, and "Allosemitism," in Cheyette & Marcus, ed. Modernity, Culture and "the Jew", 146–48. "I propose that the proper generic phenomenon of which the resentfulness of the Jews is part is proteophobia, not heterophobia; the apprehension and vexation related not to something or someone disquieting through otherness and unfamiliarity, but to something or someone that does not fit the structure of the orderly world, does not fall easily into any of the established categories, emits therefore contradictory signals as to the proper conduct – and in the result blurs the borderlines which ought to be kept watertight and undermines the reassuringly monotonous, repetitive and predictable nature of all life world"; "Allosemitism," 144.

forms of racism. I will explore this negative dialectic throughout this essay.[10]

At this point, we can certainly learn from Paul Gilroy's *The Black Atlantic* (1993). Gilroy rejects both the essentializing racial modernity of afrocentrism and the postmodern anti-essentialism which reduces black history and culture to the by now familiar universalized alterity. In the last chapter of *The Black Atlantic*, Gilroy gestures towards the many points of connection between black and Jewish diasporic histories.[11] This is not merely to show the similarities between two of the most obvious victims of Western modernity. Gilroy also wishes to indicate the pitfalls, as well as the utter necessity, of making connections across obviously differing histories. By locating black and Jewish history within the diaspora it is therefore possible to move beyond the double bind of essentialism versus anti-essentialism or "the Jew's Body" versus "the jew." As Daniel and Jonathan Boyarin have shown, diaspora constitutes a space which both "disrupts the very categories of identity" and is the location of particularized histories and cultures.[12] This also corresponds to Gilroy's "anti-anti-essentialism" which enables him to re-memorialize and re-historicize black history and culture within the diasporic "Black Atlantic."

In his latest book, *Between Camps* (2000), Gilroy extends his critique of postmodernism to theories of multiculturalism especially as institutionalized in the USA. In general, Gilroy argues that "multicultural blackness" is attacked by the "advocates of absolute homogeneity" and defended by the "apostles of an equally absolute diver-

---

[10] See Bauman, *Postmodern Ethics* (Oxford: Blackwell, 1993) for a possible way out of this dialectic.

[11] Paul Gilroy, *The Black Atlantic: Modernity and Double Consciousness* (London: Verso, 1993): 205–23.

[12] Daniel Boyarin & Jonathan Boyarin, "Diaspora: Generation and the Ground of Jewish Identity," *Critical Inquiry* 19 (Summer 1993): 721.

sity."[13] It is the absoluteness on both sides of the "colour line" that results in a set of shared authoritarian assumptions with regard to race and culture. Multiculturalism, according to Gilroy, takes three main forms in the USA: "corporate, commercial and oppositional." He goes on to contend that "it has emerged [...] as a master signifier: as powerful today as justice, right, freedom, and reason must have been long ago."[14] As the editors of *Insider/Outsider* note, American multiculturalism is ultimately about "claiming public resources on behalf of [particular] groups."[15] But, as Stephen May, like Gilroy, has shown, this can be a rather conservative position which "revalorize[s] closed cultures, roots and traditions."[16]

American multiculturalism has become reified in particular laws, such as affirmative action and the distribution of public resources. It is in relation to such reification that the editors of *Insider/Outsider* locate the "postmodern" ambivalence of the Jew, neither black nor white, neither powerful nor powerless, a "boundary case" to challenge the institutionalization and commodification of American multiculturalism.[17] The main problem with this position, however, is that it assumes an equivalence between the American nation-state and the Jewish diaspora which reduces the issue of diaspora Jewry and multiculturalism to the national borders of the USA. As I have argued elsewhere, the americanization of the Jewish diaspora involves a false universalization of the American context, which has produced a parti-

---

[13] Paul Gilroy, *Between Camps: Race, Identity and Nationalism at the End of the Colour Line* (Harmondsworth: Penguin, 2000): 241.

[14] Gilroy, *Between Camps*, 244–45.

[15] David Biale, Michael Galchinsky & Susannah Heschel, "Introduction: The Dialectic of Jewish Enlightenment," in *Insider/Outsider: American Jews and Multiculturalism*, ed. Biale et al. (Berkeley: U of California P, 1998): 3.

[16] Stephen May, "Multiculturalism," in *A Companion to Racial and Ethnic Studies*, ed. David Theo Goldberg & John Solomos (Oxford: Blackwell, 2002): 131.

[17] Biale, Galchinsky & Heschel, *Insider/Outsider*, 5, 9.

cular brand of Jewish literature characterized by the received discourses of religion, roots, tradition and victimhood.[18]

In Europe, multiculturalism is less established in the market-place.
While one can be critical of such amorphousness, I prefer to make a
virtue of this imprecision. As Robert Lee's anthology *Other Britain,
Other British* (1995) unwittingly demonstrates, ethnicity in Britain is
founded neither in the hierarchy of victimhood nor in the institutional
power of a particular ethnic grouping. In stark contrast to the power-
politics underpinning *Insider/Outsider*, the editor of *Other Britain,
Other British* is happily uncertain about the value or status of the
multicultural ethnicities which make up his anthology:

> Culture, it will surely bear repeating, whether national or local, com-
> munal or individual, was ever so: ongoing, enactive, full of exception
> to any imagined rule [...] Have the post-war years, in fact, not seen a
> transition from an old coloniality (internal, indigenous), or [does this
> postcolonial model not] wholly meet the case? What, too, of yet other
> shaping ethnicities, among them Jewish, Irish, Chinese, or New
> Zealand–Australian?[19]

Gilroy contends that current theories of multiculturalism "do not assist
in capturing half the stories we need to consider."[20] What I want to
argue is that it is precisely the unprogrammatic nature of Jewish writing in Britain – neither wholly multicultural, nor ethnic, nor postcolonial – that resists delimitation within the received discourses that
make up American multiculturalism. Ironically, the heterodox and uncategorizable nature of British-Jewish writing is captured best by the
American painter R.B. Kitaj (who has lived in London for over three
decades) in his *First Diasporist Manifesto* (1989). Kitaj is at pains to

---

[18] For this argument in full, see my *Diasporas of the Mind: A Critical History of British Jewish Literature* (New Haven CT & London: Yale UP, forthcoming).

[19] A. Robert Lee, "Introduction" to *Other Britain, Other British: Contemporary Multicultural Fiction*, ed. Lee (London: Pluto Press, 1995): 2.

[20] Gilroy, *Between Camps*, 245.

point out that you need not be a "Jew to be a diasporist" and, by the same token, not all Jewish writers or artists are "diasporists."[21] He thus enacts the paradox of his "manifesto": when making a home out of his homelessness, he immediately has to redraw that which becomes "fixed," "settled" and "stable" (37). This is the "homeless logic" (41) of his "manifesto," which can only ever be provisional and capricious; his Jewishness "changes all the time," while simultaneously propelling him towards a "vision of Diasporic art" (49).

By contrast, the institutionalization of American multiculturalism fixes precisely that which should be fluid and unstable. At the same time, not all British-Jewish writing is, in these terms, diasporist. For the rest of this essay, I want to focus on three diasporist authors who write not only against the received discourses of the nation state but also against those of religion, race and ethnicity. As my three exemplars I have chosen (in chronological order) Muriel Spark, George Steiner and Clive Sinclair, but I could have opted for many other figures such as Elaine Feinstein, Eva Figes, Gabriel Josipovici or Harold Pinter.[22] But Spark, Steiner and Sinclair will, I believe, demonstrate sufficiently the extent to which diasporist writing in Britain challenges the very idea of a fixed diaspora. As David Cesarani has argued with reference to British Jewry, "diasporas are of many types and they are never static. As they change, so do diasporic identities and relations between Jews and non-Jews."[23] Because of the non-institutionalized nature of ethnic identity in Britain, we will see that it is especially in the cultural field that diasporic Jewish identities are

[21] R.B. Kitaj, *First Diasporist Manifesto* (London: Thames & Hudson, 1989): 71. Further page references are in the main text.

[22] For an account of Gabriel Josipovici in these terms, see Monika Fludernik, *Echoes and Mirrorings: Gabriel Josipovici's Creative Oeuvre* (Frankfurt am Main: Peter Lang, 2000).

[23] David Cesarani, "The Dynamics of Diaspora: The Transformation of British Jewish Identity," *Jewish Culture and History* 4.1 (Summer 2001): 62.

characteristically plural and in flux. I will now begin to explore this "homeless logic" with particular regard to the fiction of Muriel Spark.

Muriel Spark: The Gentile Jewess

Muriel Spark has for a long time been preoccupied with her upbring-ing in Morningside, Edinburgh, to parents of mixed national, ethnic and religious backgrounds. Her Calvinist-inspired education in the Presbyterian James Gillespie's Girls' School has, in particular, "bred within [her] the conditions of exiledom" which "has ceased to be a fate, it has become a calling."[24] In her essay "What Images Return" (1970) she is explicit about defining herself in opposition to the "Cale-donian Society aspect of Edinburgh which cannot accommodate me": "The only sons and daughters of Edinburgh with whom I can find common understanding are exiles like myself" (152). For this reason, she describes herself as "an exile in heart and mind" and as someone who is "moving from exile into exile" (151–52). Spark is reacting strongly against a predetermined Caledonian Scottishness, which she perceives as a determining cultural formation, and she thus places her-self beyond its reach. Appropriately enough, she thinks of her Jewish father, born in Edinburgh, as being akin to the Castle Rock or the "great primitive black crag" (153) which belongs to the heart of the city and is also strangely incongruous. Like her father, Spark is both part of, and out of place in, her home town.

Spark's hybrid background – part-English, part-Scottish, part-Protestant, part-Jewish – has enabled her to become an essentially dia-sporic writer.[25] Always shifting in time, from the 1940s to the 1990s, her fiction encompasses Zimbabwe, Edinburgh and Jerusalem and

---

[24] Muriel Spark, "What Images Return," in *Memoirs of a Modern Scot-land*, ed. Karl Miller (London: Faber & Faber, 1970): 151. Further page refer-ences are in the main text.

[25] For a longer version of this argument, see my *Muriel Spark* (Writers and their Work; Plymouth: Northcote House, 2000).

rotates, habitually, between London, New York and Rome. No one time, place or culture has been allowed to delimit Spark's imagination. The many and varied versions she has given her own biography have meant that she has refused to settle on a single account of her formative years. From this perspective, an unproblematic Jewishness (as opposed to an uncertain gentile Jewishness) could be said to be one of many predetermined national and cultural formations which are challenged in Spark's fiction. As with Kitaj, her "homeless logic" refuses to make a "home" out of her Jewishness.

As well as challenging any national narrative in her fiction, Spark also puts into question the religious discourses which surround her work. While Spark has been commonly marginalized as a 'Catholic Writer', due to her conversion to Roman Catholicism in 1954, it is clear that her fiction is driven not by a single unproblematic moralized identity but also by an ambiguous doubleness, as signified by her self-designation as a "gentile Jewess."[26] I would like to argue that, far from transfiguring her sense of difference, Spark's conversion to Roman Catholicism places her many contradictions in a sustained and creative dialogue. Spark's fiction displays a tension between an orthodox religious view of conversion which splits the self into old and new, before and after, pure and impure, and an aesthetic response to conversion, which most frequently focuses on the tensions and ties between these split identities. It is within this framework that I want to explore two different kinds of diaspora in Spark's novels and short stories.

Those critics who have noted Spark's double conversion to both Roman Catholicism and the art of the novel have argued mistakenly that these parallel transformations are somehow equivalent.[27] On the

---

[26] Spark describes her story "The Gentile Jewesses" as "nearly factual" in her memoir *Curriculum Vitae: A Volume of Autobiography* (Harmondsworth: Penguin, 1992): 81.

[27] For this widespread assumption, see Malcolm Bradbury, "Muriel Spark's Fingernails," in Bradbury, *No, Not Bloomsbury* (London: Arena,

other hand, instead of assuming that there is an organic coherence between her religion and art, Gauri Viswanathan has maintained that religious conversion, far from being a unitary form of exchange, is a model of "dissent." In her reading, conversion is primarily a form of doubleness which "destabilises" national cultures as it "crosses fixed boundaries between communities and identities."[28] According to this argument, the mixing of two different cultures inevitably creates a sense in which any one ideology can be viewed from an estranged and defamiliarized perspective. Far from merely superseding the past, conversion then constitutes an interpretative act which perceives one world through the eyes of another. Spark's fiction, in this reading, re-interprets the secular novel as a parodic form of spiritual transfiguration, at the same time viewing her Catholicism with an artist's sceptical eye. Rather than being an all-encompassing orthodoxy, Spark's Catholicism becomes, for Viswanathan, a form of heterodoxy which multiplies endlessly official discourse.

Although Viswanathan is correct to highlight conversion's subversive potential, she overstates her case by focusing only on the question of dissent, as opposed to religious assent, even in reference to a figure as contradictory as John Henry Newman.[29] Spark's fiction, crucially, illustrates both the authoritarian and the anarchic potential within the act of conversion, and shows how this ambivalence helps her maintain an abiding sense of cultural singularity. In fact, at the beginning of her career as a novelist, when most closely influenced by Newman, she was to reinforce the orthodox reading of conversion as a means of creating narrative and moral 'order' out of the waste and disorder of her early years. Here is Spark's much-cited 1961 interview, which she has since repudiated, in which she talks about her conversion and

---

1987): 268–78, and Peter Kemp, *Muriel Spark* (Novelists and Their World; London: Paul Elek, 1974): 158.

[28] Gauri Viswanathan, *Outside the Fold: Conversion, Modernity, and Belief* (Princeton NJ: Princeton UP, 1998): xvii, 3–43.

[29] Viswanathan, *Outside the Fold*, 44–72.

describes Catholicism as a "norm from which one can depart."[30] She goes on to relate her reasons for her conversion to a "breakdown" at the time:

> The first reaction I had when I became a Catholic was that my mind was far too crowded with ideas, all teeming in disorder. This was part of my breakdown. The oddest, most peculiar variety of themes and ideas of all sorts teemed in my head. I have never known such mental activity. It made me suffer a lot. But as I got better I was able to take them one at a time. ... It was like getting a new gift. (60)

Catholicism, in these conventional terms, becomes an ordering principle as well as an act of faith: "I used to worry until I got a sense of order, a sense of proportion. At least I hope I've got it now. You need it to be either a writer or a Christian" (63). Her conversion thus provided her with a renewed healthy identity and the ability to write in a controlled manner. Unlike Spark herself, who is much more ambivalent in her statements, critics have habitually tended to repeat these sentiments, as if they were writ in stone, in order to lend weight to her credentials as an entirely Catholic writer – in the great tradition of Ford Madox Ford, Graham Greene and Evelyn Waugh.

Far from destabilizing different religious perspectives, the Jewish religion at this stage in Spark's career tended to be constructed as a figure of confusion and ambivalence when compared to the sanity and clarity of Christian culture. But, as we have seen in the work of Bauman, diasporic ambivalence can result both in an authoritarian closure and in outstanding cultural creativity. In the case of Spark, authoritarian thinking at first helped fix her identity as a Catholic writer although such distinctions were then quickly disrupted in her

---

[30] Muriel Spark, "My Conversion," *The Twentieth Century* 170 (Autumn 1961): 60. Further page references to this work are in the main text. While Spark's "My Conversion" is referred to widely in many previous critical studies of her fiction, it has recently been repudiated by Spark herself. For an annotated version of the essay, in a bid to expose its inaccuracies, see the Muriel Spark Manuscript Collection in the McFarlin Library, University of Tulsa, item 53:3.

fiction. At the start of "My Conversion" Spark characterizes the "very peculiar environment" (58) of her childhood, which, she says, was "difficult to locate": "I am partly of Jewish origin, so my environment had a kind of Jewish tinge but without any formal instruction" (58). Later on, she reinforces this diasporic anxiety by speaking of the "very indefinite location" (59) of her childhood as opposed to the clarity of her later Catholic identity which enabled her to find "[her] own individual point of view" (61).

As in T.S. Eliot's *Notes Towards the Definition of Culture* (1948), which Spark had reviewed favourably, Christianity is seen as a means of imposing distinct boundaries on an excessively fluid and rootless identity. This incoherent and unstable Jewishness, along with a sense of alienation and ill-health, thus became a negative principle to set against received Christian aesthetics. It is in these authoritarian terms that Spark has been misguidedly seen as belonging to the neoclassical "Catholic novelists of detachment, like Joyce, whose God-like writer is indifferent to creation, paring his fingernails."[31] Spark's often cool aesthetic surface and the indifference of her narrators, coupled with her supposed commitment to a God-given truth, have persuaded many of her critics to classify her on the basis of her apparently secure identity and to view her as a Catholic writer. It is this classicist modernist tradition, which he calls "assimilationist modernism," that Kitaj is specifically battling with in his *First Diasporist Manifesto*. Many British-Jewish writers, such as Eva Figes, Gabriel Josipovici and Harold Pinter, have begun as classicist or assimilationist modernists and have gradually shaped and changed this tradition with reference to their own cultural difference.

[31] Bradbury, "Muriel Spark's Fingernails," 271; Spark, "The Poet in Mr. Eliot's Ideal State," *Outposts* 14 (Summer 1949): 26–28; and Cheyette, *Constructions of "the Jew" in English Literature and Society: Racial Representations, 1875–1945* (Cambridge: Cambridge UP, 1993): 264–67, for a discussion of *Notes Towards the Definition of Culture* in these terms.

There are, in other words, two different kinds of imaginary diasporas at play in Spark's fiction – on the one hand, the universalizing and unifying diaspora taken from Catholic orthodoxy; on the other, a disruptive and uncontainable diaspora as articulated through her heterodox Jewish background. Spark's critics have tended to underestimate the extent to which her conversion not only unified her but also enabled her to occupy more than one cultural and ethnic space in her fiction. Her faith in a universal higher authority, in other words, is thrown into disarray by a fictional practice which is plural and partial and embraces a multiple sense of self. Here the Joycean analogy is worth returning to. The Catholic authorial model, embodied in Stephen Dedalus, of the writer indifferent to creation, "paring his fingernails," is countered in *Ulysses* (1922) by the figure of Leopold Bloom. The Greek-Jewish Bloom, in this novel, represents ambivalence *in extremis*; the impossibility of imposing meaning on the world however much his God-like author might wish to.[32] The ordering of reality in Spark's experimental fiction is similarly provisional and always open to question. That which she wishes to transfigure invariably proves uncontainable and returns to haunt her.

Given the universalizing rhetoric that shapes the conventional representation of the convert, it is not surprising that Spark was to stress continually her radical singularity in relation to this generalizing and categorizing orthodoxy. In particular in her fiction of the 1960s, her acknowledged difference as a "Gentile Jewess" enables her to challenge the redemptive promise of conversion. She makes a point of not describing her characters as "Christian Jews" or "Jewish Christians" – which would have reinforced a traditional Catholic view of the founders of the Church. Instead, the term "Gentile" is deliberately open and suggests both a resonant paganism in relation to Judaism and a rather prim and comic Edinburgh gentility. *The Mandelbaum Gate*

---

[32] For this argument in full, see Cheyette, *Constructions of "the Jew" in English Literature and Society*, 206–34.

(1965), throughout its composition, was called "The Gentile Jewesses" although, in the end, only a short story emerged with this title. In that story, Spark is able to embrace her identity-less Jewishness in opposition to the strictures of religious orthodoxy.

Throughout the story, in fact, Spark's authorial voice stresses the extreme arbitrariness of her "Gentile Jewish" identity. When told that she did not "look like a Jew," she points to her small feet and claimed that "all Jews have little feet."[33] At another time, referring to her father's profession, she notes mischievously that "all Jews were engineers" (313). The grandmother, on the other hand, dismissed as "Pollacks" (313) a group of Polish-Jewish immigrants to Watford while embracing some Londoners of German descent as honorary Jews. Rather than acknowledging a sense of confusion which would need to be resolved, Spark's narrative voice defines her "Gentile Jewish" identity as a creatively disruptive force. Much to the chagrin of her grandfather, the narrator's grandmother was an active suffragette who participated in women's marches down Watford High Street.

By the end of the story, the narrator's mother yokes together Christianity, Buddhism and Judaism, and this all-embracing pluralism becomes a version of diasporic otherness. At the same time, "The Gentile Jewesses" concludes rather abruptly with Spark turning Catholic, as "with Roman Catholics, too, it all boils down to the Almighty in the end" (315). This rather limiting point of closure contrasts starkly with the narrator's childhood home, where "all the gods are served" (315). The unresolved tension between the freedom inherent in a displaced multiple identity and the universalizing power of the Catholic church was to be addressed at length in *The Mandelbaum Gate*.

Appropriately enough, the second chapter of *The Mandelbaum Gate* is called "Barbara Vaughan's Identity" and it is her self-confessed "state of conflict" that extends into the polarized history of the Middle

---

[33] Spark, "The Gentile Jewesses," *The Collected Stories of Muriel Spark* (Harmondsworth: Penguin, 1994): 313. Further page references to this story are in the main text.

East and the bisected city of Jerusalem.[34] The eponymous Mandel-baum Gate, which separates the Israeli and Jordanian sides of Jerusa-lem, makes it possible for Barbara to move within and between iden-tities. From the beginning, Barbara argues that "the essential thing about herself remained unspoken, uncategorized, unlocated" (28) and later she makes explicit an orthodox conversionism: "There's always more to it than Jew, Gentile, half-Jew, half-Gentile. There's the human soul, the individual. Not 'Jew, Gentile' as one might say 'autumn, winter'. Something unique and unrepeatable" (37). In *The Comforters*, Jewishness is dismissed as one of Caroline Rose's "half-worlds" which needed to be transfigured.[35] Barbara Vaughan, a gentile Jewess after Caroline Rose, also stresses her transcendent uniqueness, which goes beyond such racial or ethnic categories. But, unlike Caroline in *The Comforters*, Barbara is aware that the too-easy universalization of racial difference, especially in the Middle East, is an essentially fruit-less form of transformation.

By refusing to either territorialize her racial difference or to tran-scend it, Barbara Vaughan stands outside both dominant nationalism and orthodox religious conversionism. Instead, her gentile Jewishness becomes a model for an alternative non-national and supra-religious diaspora. *The Mandelbaum Gate*, in fact, teems with anarchic unplace-able characters, such as Abdul and Suzi Ramdez, who cannot be addressed in a conventional mode. In the end, these diasporic indivi-duals all seem to signal a breakdown of commonplace assumptions about nation, gender and class and can be said to form an alternative community of exiles. Spark is quite explicit about this in her account of the blue-eyed, dark-skinned Palestinian brother and sister, Abdul and Suzi Ramdez, who "belonged to nothing but themselves" (101) and yet, paradoxically, are part of a group made up of

---

[34] Spark, *The Mandelbaum Gate* (London: Macmillan, 1965): 23. Further page references are in the main text.

[35] Spark, *The Comforters* (London: Macmillan, 1957): 48.

lapsed Jews, lapsed Arabs, lapsed citizens, runaway Englishmen,
dancing prostitutes, international messes, failed painters, intellectuals,
homosexuals. Some were silent, some voluble. Some were mentally
ill, or would become so. (101)

The warning at the end of this passage reminds the reader of the price
that, as with Spark's own "breakdown," might be paid for such a
radically dislocated diaspora. At the same time, immediately after this
paragraph, the narrative voice intervenes to repeat unequivocally that
"others were not [mad], and never would become so; and would have
been the flower of the Middle East, given the sun and air of the mind
not yet available" (101). Such is the thin line between madness and
revolutionary change. Spark, throughout *The Mandelbaum Gate*, is at
pains to oppose orthodoxies of all kinds through her radically different
(Jewish and Palestinian) community of exiles.

In his *The Book of God* (1988), Gabriel Josipovici has usefully
placed the Pauline and Augustinian tradition of conversion at the
beginning of the rise of the modern novel. According to this argument,
the autobiographical narratives of both St Paul and St Augustine
demonstrate the need to "talk in order to fix the flux of inner turmoil
and objectify the crucial act of conversion."[36] Although Josipovici
reads Spark's fiction as opposing the Pauline and Augustinian confes-
sional traditions, I cannot think of a more apt description of her fiction
than as a "constant reiteration of the drama of conversion," as Josipovici puts it,[37] a reiteration that enables Spark to move in and out of
the dominant ideal of a universalizing diasporic identity within the
Catholic Church.

---

[36] Gabriel Josipovici, *The Book of God* (New Haven CT & London: Yale
UP, 1988): 252, 251–53.

[37] Josipovici, *The Book of God*, 253.

George Steiner: A Kind of Survivor

The next determinedly heterodox British-based author whom I want to consider is the writer–critic George Steiner. I want to concentrate on his fiction, which has been appearing at wide intervals, and which he keeps belittling as "scripts for thought" or "allegories of argument."[38] Steiner's complete fiction, recently published, subtly contests the valorization of single cultures, roots and traditions that characterizes much current American-Jewish writing. His multivocal fictions are written against his most sacredly held beliefs and can be considered to be an internal commentary on his more familiar critical writings.

Put briefly, Steiner's first and probably best volume of stories, *Anno Domini* (1964), was published at the same time as he was writing *Language and Silence* (1967) and imaginatively prefigured his life-long fascination with the slaughter which he managed to escape. The primacy of translation, fathomed at length in *After Babel: Aspects of Language and Translation* (1975), is, crucially, a structuring metaphor in *The Portage to San Cristobal of A.H.* (1981). In this latter novella, with an ambiguity that has always been present in his fiction, Steiner put into the mouth of an aged Hitler ("A.H.") words which he himself had used a decade earlier in his *In Bluebeard's Castle: Some Notes towards the Redefinition of Culture* (1971). His more recent novella and stories, *Proofs and Three Parables* (1992), continues this pattern of creative self-sustenance. Written at about the same time as his *Real Presences*, these fictions make human the "wager on transcendence" which Steiner has long since called for as an antidote to our current "post-cultural" nihilism.[39]

---

[38] George Steiner, "A Responsion," in *Reading George Steiner*, ed. Nathan A. Scott, Jr. & Ronald A. Sharp (Baltimore MD & London: Johns Hopkins UP, 1994): 279.

[39] George Steiner, *Real Presences: Is there anything 'in' what we say?* (London: Faber & Faber, 1989) and *In Bluebeard's Castle: Some Notes Towards the Redefinition of Culture* (London: Faber & Faber, 1971): 49–74.

On this level, Steiner's fiction might be said simply to dramatize the idea of a 'post-culture' and the impossibility of religious transcendence in his fictional work. If language is increasingly diffuse and muddled, and culture remains complicit with mass murder, then history becomes a form of catastrophe (from the crucifixion to the death camps). Robert Alter has argued persuasively that this lethal teleology gives us a simple reading of Steiner's fiction as a form of "negative transcendence" (a term which was first applied by Erich Heller to the fiction of Franz Kafka).[40] In a meaningless world, Steiner seems to be saying that what defines us is not culture but, as with Lyotard, the horrors which continue to overwhelm the century. The significance of his fiction is that it need go no further than this sense of futility and masochistic attraction, even desperate need, for that which lies beyond culture. In Steiner's imaginative world, the desire to experience the worst excesses of war and destruction make the received culture seem feeble by comparison. His post-Holocaust fiction therefore engages with diaspora as *galut*, a place of pain and torture made up of victimized Jews. As we will see, diaspora as *galut* is in constant tension in his work with the more benign version of diaspora as *golah*.

Steiner has described himself as "A Kind of Survivor," the title of his autobiographical 1965 essay, and he is understandably obsessed by his first eleven years in Paris before he was whisked off to America by his father in 1940. Of the Jewish boys and girls in his school class and circle of friends, he has often noted, only two, including himself, survived. Steiner's need to surround himself with words, however distrusted, cannot be separated from this history. With characteristic bombast, he has written of the "unmerited scandal of his survival" and goes on to note what he calls his "pathological bent toward some immediate sharing of his school-friends' fate – how would I have behaved, how abject would my fears have been," and states that this

---

[40] Robert Alter, "Against Messiness," *Times Literary Supplement* (12 January 1996): 23–24.

feeling is "with me always." This perversely envious sense of missing the "rendezvous with hell" is the subject of much of Steiner's early fiction.[41]

All of the stories in *Anno Domini* are about individuals or groups of individuals (whether German, American, French, or British) who, like Steiner, are both attracted and repulsed by the horrors which they have escaped. His protagonists finally make their "rendezvous with hell" and fatally embrace the terrors which, after the war, continue to obsess them. Many of the representative figures of this fatal attraction are non-Jews who place their "fearful envy" at the heart of their particular national culture. Here diaspora as *galut* unsettles all national cultures, replacing a humanizing imperative with the lure of death. Such death-obsessed individuals also echo Steiner's version of Franz Kafka, which stresses the "obscene collaboration between torturer and victim," of one who was not there, and its relation to the Holocaust. As he puts it in his memoir *Errata* (1997), "victimisation, ostracism, and torture are dialectic."[42] The only version of diaspora that Steiner allows in these early stories is as a place of "fearful envy."

This dialectic is given its most complete portrayal in "Cake," where an American graduate student from Harvard, the son of an elite family, decides to stay behind in Nazi-occupied France. He acts as a "courier" for the underground, and, after witnessing the torture of a young woman and her father, begins to fantasize about being captured by the Gestapo. Only under torture can he really know himself; otherwise, he fears, he will live "as spinsters do, in the brittle familiarity of mere

---

[41] Steiner, "A Responsion," 276, and "A Kind of Survivor," in Steiner, *Language and Silence: Essays 1958–1966* (London: Faber & Faber, 1967): 119–35.

[42] Steiner, "K," *Language and Silence*, 163, and *Errata: An Unexamined Life* (London: Weidenfeld & Nicholson, 1997): 52.

acquaintance."[43] Although his romantic masochism is soon squashed
when Steiner's narrator narrowly escapes capture, it also becomes the
driving force of the story. From the beginning, the American is "grip-
ped" by the image of the girl's abduction, which "brought a queer
warmth and drew [his] skin tight" (200). After this he wakes at nights
"shivering with an unclean sweetness" and his perverse jealousy of the
old man and the girl grows "like a cancer" (201). As he walks along
the deserted banks of the Loire, his overpowering envy becomes "the
thing worth living for. At any cost. So I spent my days between fear
and desire, between hysterical imaginings of pain, and a secret longing" (203). Evading torture by the Gestapo, he is smuggled to a sana-
torium, where he is entrusted with the family history of Rahel Jakob-
sen, with whom he falls in love, and whom he commemorates after the
war.

His role as a "courier" introduces him to experience *in extremis*
and, in Steiner's terms, makes him an allegorical or Kafkaesque Jew
who eventually internalizes Jewish history. The universalization of
diaspora as *galut* is, however, fraught with difficulties. In the story, the
American is also an antisemite who expresses his loathing for a
Steiner-like Jewish student in his Renaissance seminar – "He had been
educated in half a dozen countries ('Herr Hitler, you know') and spoke
English with flair; but he retained a sugary intonation, part-French,
part-German. I detested the fluent acrobatics of his mind" (219). He
goes on to argue that "by their unending misery, the Jews have put
mankind in the wrong. Their presence is a reproach" (219). This corresponds to Steiner's philosophy of antisemitism elaborated in his *In
Bluebeard's Castle*. "Cake," then, elides the distinction between Jew
and non-Jew, or even between Jews and antisemites. But this is the
imaginative 'dialectic' of one enraptured by the violence inflicted on
the victims of Nazism.

---

[43] George Steiner, "Cake," in Steiner, *The Deeps of the Sea and Other
Fiction* (London: Faber & Faber, 1996): 202. Subsequent references to this
work will be in parenthesis in the text.

Steiner's next fictional work, *The Portage to San Cristobal of A.H.*, differs from his earlier fiction in being explicitly judaized. Unlike the universalized "deeps of the sea," the title of his 1956 story, the search for ultimate meaning in *The Portage* is made manifest by a journey to San Cristobal, with Steiner's protagonists quite literally carrying the baggage of history on their backs. As with *Anno Domini*, Steiner in *The Portage* deliberately makes sense of the past in the language of a "babel" of national cultures – here Israël, Russia, America, Britain, Germany and France. This is a text, in other words, not about the Holocaust itself but about the effect that this history has produced on particular national cultures.

Ronald Sharp has rightly argued that the issue of translation, as formulated at length in *After Babel*, is at the heart of the novella – after all, a 'portage', like a translation, is a form of transportation, a carrying over from one place to another. In this spirit, the structure of Steiner's novella is a series of "congruent or discordant translations" of Hitler in the contemporary world by a chaotic variety of national interpreters.[44] The fact that the journey to San Cristobal is unfinished indicates Steiner's refusal to make his story conform to a reality principle or an ultimate translation (the name "San Cristobal" seems to point towards a Christian transcendence of Jewish suffering). Instead, Steiner offers a range of possible commentaries for the reader to engage with. The helicopters' hovering at the end indicates the open-endedness of the text, in desperate need of his reader's counter-interpretation, as we are asked to see which national narrative is about to be imposed on history.[45]

The outrageously disturbing voice of "A.H." represents the ultimate negative transcendence and the triumph of diaspora as *galut*. What the crudest readings of *The Portage* have done is to simply contrast

---

[44] Ronald Sharp, "Steiner's Fiction and the Hermeneutics of Translation," in Scott & Sharp, ed. *Reading George Steiner*, 208.

[45] Steiner, "Postscript" to *Language and Silence*, 193.

Leiber, a symbol of the cultural power of the diaspora as 'Golah,' and "A.H.," the failed messiah who despises diasporic culture. These critics argue that Leiber is moral and "A.H." is immoral and that Steiner has mistakenly given too much credence to the evil figure. For example, Alvin Rosenfeld contends somewhat over-generously that Leiber's fractured and partial testimony is as sophisticated as a Paul Celan poem while, on the other hand, the last speech of Steiner's Hitler is as kitschy and dangerous as a bad 'B' movie (he invokes *The Boys from Brazil* in this context).[46] But Steiner does not merely contrast Leiber and "A.H." but is portraying them as part of the same dialectic. Far from being easily containable opposites, these figures are, above all, two different aspects of George Steiner. Just as Leiber tells the story of the escape of Steiner's father from Paris and of the slaughter of his friends and family, the portrayal of "A.H." unites contradictory features: "A.H." has a "withered arm" like Steiner and he repeats verbatim much of his theory of antisemitism in *In Bluebeard's Castle*. The reference to *In Bluebeard's Castle* does not, however, make "A.H." the mouthpiece of Steiner's literary criticism – as those who condemned the text have argued – but is, more subtly, Steiner's most profound means of thinking against himself.

Both Steiner and "A.H.," above all, agree that "Jews are the conscience of the world" (in the guise of monotheism, Christianity and Marxism) and that this has caused a lethal resentment which culminated in the Shoah. In embodying the redemptive homeland of the text – at its most creative and lasting in an extraterritorial Central Europe – Jews, such as Leiber, personify an essential life-giving cultural transcendence. But the "blackmail of transcendence" could also take a catastrophic form and, as "A.H." argues, become a death-warrant for the Jews.[47] This unbearable dialectic between diaspora as *galut* and

---

[46] Alvin Rosenfeld, *Imagining Hitler* (Bloomington: Indiana UP, 1985): 83–102.

[47] This argument was first made in detail in Steiner's *In Bluebeard's Castle*, 40.

golah lies at the heart of *The Portage*, which is why this work explores these different versions of diaspora within Steiner himself.

On the one hand, Steiner can be considered as an assimilationist modernist who invokes the authority of tradition in relation to an apocalyptic present. In Walter Benjamin's words, he belongs in the front line of the traditionalists who recognize that, at any time, "everything can go wrong."[48] But his radical distrust of any form of cultural creation (especially his own) and his refusal to place tradition within a majoritarian context also undermine the authority and ordering principles of classical modernism. His Jewishness is crucial in this regard. At one point in his defining essay "Our Homeland the Text" (1985), Steiner speaks of the Jewish cleric "deranged by some autistic, otherworldly addiction to speculative abstractions and the elixir of truth"; and more recently he has described this "autistic ubiquity" to be the "very essence of Judaism."[49] His use of this term autism – which also includes, bewilderingly, God, chess-players, deconstructionists, and himself – as a form of "ubiquity" is ambiguously applied to the Jewish diaspora. All of Steiner's suicidal male protagonists (his "destructive characters," in Benjamin's terms) can be described as autists who are, in equal measure, deranged and redeemed by their yearning for the *galut*.[50]

For this reason, Steiner has a stake in the continuation of Western culture while also recognizing that it has completely "gone wrong." Such is his "wager on transcendence" where "diasporic Jews" are both the "elixir of truth" and embody all of the regimes of thought – monotheism, Christianity, and messianic socialism – which have supposedly led to their own destruction. In an early uncollected essay, Steiner sums up this "sinister and mendacious dialectic" that has made dia-

---

[48] Cited in Norman Finkelstein, *The Ritual of New Creation: Jewish Tradition and Contemporary Literature* (New York: SUNY Press, 1992): 100.

[49] Steiner, "A Responsion," 277, and "Our Homeland the Text," in Steiner, *No Passion Spent: Essays 1978–1996* (London: Faber & Faber, 1996): 324.

[50] Finkelstein, *The Ritual of New Creation*, 99–100.

sporic Jews both a "stranger among others" and also a "stranger" to themselves. It is, he argues, this "limbo of identity" – in an extra-territorial zone between "gentile acceptance" and "transcendental separateness" – which has led both to a "quantum leap" in Jewish creativity and also to the "venom of antisemitism."[51] This paradox and unresolved doubleness inherent in diasporic existence, most fully articulated by Zygmunt Bauman, lies at the heart of Steiner's fiction.

Clive Sinclair: Diaspora Blues

Whereas Muriel Spark is a voluntary exile from Britain, and George Steiner an enforced emigré to Britain, Clive Sinclair can be described as an inner exile within Britain's national borders. Steven Connor has recently distinguished between postwar British writers who write as "insiders" about a supposedly representable "condition of England" and those who write from the "outside in." Connor refers mainly to postcolonial writers who have previously been deemed to be "cul-turally and spatially at a distance" and have "returned and doubled back" to re-narrate the metropolitan centre.[52] But this formulation can also be applied to British-born Jewish writers such as Sinclair and Spark. However, one needs to make a distinction between doubleness and hybridity which, according to Salman Rushdie's ideal of an "imaginary homeland," characterizes the postcolonial diasporic writer:

> Let me suggest that Indian writers in England have access to a second tradition, quite apart from their own racial history. It is the culture and political history of the phenomenon of migration, displacement, life in a minority group. We can quite legitimately claim as our ancestors the Huguenots, the Irish, the Jews; the past to which we belong is an Eng-lish past, the history of immigrant Britain. Swift, Conrad, Marx are as

---

[51] Steiner, "A View From Without," *Jewish Quarterly* 16.4 (1968–69): 3–5, and 17.1 (1969): 3–9.

[52] Steven Connor, *The English Novel in History* (London & New York: Routledge, 1996): 85–86.

much our literary forebears as Tagore or Ram Mohan Roy. America,
a nation of immigrants, has created a great literature out of the phenomenon of cultural transplantation, out of examining the ways in which
people cope with a new world; it may be that by discovering what we
have in common with those who preceded us into this country, we can
begin to do the same.[53]

The danger with Rushdie's "imaginary homelands," however, is that
he simply aestheticizes the diaspora so that it becomes a 'great
tradition' of international writers and thinkers who are beyond any
historical or political contingency. By concentrating exclusively on
postcolonial writers, Connor also illustrates the dangers of ethnicizing
the diaspora so that it turns into an all-too-usable 'black and white' or
'colonial/metropolitan' allegory. Clive Sinclair can equally be said to
write from the 'outside in' about British national culture. Yet, as I
want to show, his work challenges both the aestheticization of the diaspora and its potential reduction to an ethnic allegory.

Sinclair's fiction creates a diasporic universe where language carries considerable weight, as opposed to history, which is merely a
function of language. From his earliest collection of short stories,
Hearts of Gold (1979) and *Bedbugs* (1982), Sinclair has attempted to
"write fiction that owes nothing to any English antecedents." He
therefore self-consciously locates his 'national' history as that of a Jew
in Israel, America and Eastern Europe. Sinclair describes his work as a
failed "attempt to distill the essence of other places. To make myself
temporarily at home."[54] Continuing this "homeless logic" in his *Diaspora Blues*, Sinclair defines himself as an "insider–outsider," who has
a "dual loyalty" to "the language of England and the history of Israel,"
and argues that, for a writer, there is "something to be gained from

[53] Salman Rushdie, "Imaginary Homelands" (1982), in Rushdie, *Imaginary
Homelands: Essays and Criticism 1981–1991* (London: Granta, 1991): 20.

[54] "'On the Edge of the Imagination': Clive Sinclair interviewed by Bryan
Cheyette," *Jewish Quarterly* 3.4 (1984): 26–29. Sinclair's stories have been
republished as *For Good or Evil: Collected Stories* (Harmondsworth: Penguin,
1991). Further page references are in the main text.

having a language but no history, a history but no language." Compared with his alienation from England, his unrequited love-affair with Israel has provided him with a 'narrative' in which to situate himself.[55]

The construction of an extraterritorial 'national' past beyond his English birthplace – which is displaced onto both the Jewish diaspora and Israel – has posed an interesting dilemma for Sinclair. As the story "Bedbugs" demonstrates, the history of the Holocaust is deemed to be outside the moral purview of his protagonists. When asked to teach First World War poetry to German students, Joshua, Sinclair's protagonist, fantasizes about teaching a parallel course called "Rosenberg's Revenge" which highlights, above all, Nazi atrocities. Isaac Rosenberg's poem "Louse Hunting" (1917) is evoked in this story as a metaphor for the Holocaust, with a parallel in Joshua and a German student burning the bedbugs which infect their living-quarters. But all of Sinclair's stories are about the dangers of turning such historical metaphors into reality. Joshua, finally, acts as if he has the right to exact "revenge" on behalf of the Nazi victims but, by the end of the story, he is clearly deranged.

Sinclair's protagonists are often made delirious by their impossible displacement of an "English" identity onto an extraterritorial diaspora. In the story "Ashkenazia," collected in *Bedbugs*, Sinclair takes such solipsism to its extreme limit by inventing an aestheticized "imaginary homeland" untouched by the Nazi genocide. Situated somewhere in central Europe, Ashkenazia, a fictitious Yiddish-speaking country, is defined exclusively as a language-community outside of history:

> Many of my fellow-countrymen do not believe in the existence of God. I am more modest. I do not believe in myself. What proof can I have when no one reads what I write? There you have it; my words are the limit of my world. You will therefore smile at this irony; I have been commissioned by our government to write the official English-language Guide to Ashkenazia. (238)

---

[55] Clive Sinclair, *Diaspora Blues: A View of Israel* (London: Heinemann, 1987): 50–53, 65, 202.

By the end of the story, all that remains of Ashkenazia is a "field of wooden skeletons" and Sinclair's demented persona truly becomes bounded by his words, "Now the world will listen to me, for I am the guide to Ashkenazia. I am Ashkenazia" (248). This conflation of self-hood with nationhood is, on one level, the necessary solipsistic response of an author who displaces the national culture of his birth-place onto a useful fiction. For the post-Holocaust writer, however, such aestheticized "imaginary homelands" cannot just be constituted by words alone. A purely textual Ashkenazia is an act of artistic megalomania precisely because Sinclair's narrator thinks that he can bring these "skeletons" to life.

Sinclair's first two novels, *Blood Libels* (1985) and *Cosmetic Effects* (1989), take to its logical conclusion the insane union of self-hood with nationhood which prevails in his stories. Both novels, that is, are personal histories which have national consequences. As in one of Sinclair's later stories, "Kayn Aynhoreh," hypochondria is the natural condition of those who place the imagination at the centre of nationhood. Jake Silkstone, the alter ego in this story, reappears in *Blood Libels* and describes his various Scriptophobic and Dermato-graphic ailments as "the psychosomatic approach to history":

> Just as the mind, knowing the symptoms, has no need of bacillus or virus to counterfeit an illness, so history does not need facts to proceed. What people believe to have happened is more important than what actually did.[56]

"The psychosomatic approach to history" has especially telling consequences in *Blood Libels*, resulting in the emergence of the fascistic "Children of Albion" in England and the 1982 Israeli invasion of Lebanon. In this novel, Sinclair deliberately undermines the idea of history as the "pseudo-scientific study of facts"[57] by, on the one hand,

---

[56] Clive Sinclair, *Blood Libels* (London: Allison & Busby, 1985): 188. Further page references are in the main text.

[57] Sinclair, *Blood Libels*, 188.

treating well-known political events in Israel as grotesque fantasy and, on the other, turning grotesque fantasy in England into seemingly plausible historical narrative.

In *Cosmetic Effects*, the centrality of the imagination in the creation of historical and political "facts" becomes the subject of the novel. This can be seen especially in the involvement of Sinclair's protagonist, Jonah Isaacson – a teacher of Film Studies at the University of St Albans – with the making of a Biblical Western in Israel called *The Six Pointed Star*. The producer of this film, Lewis Falcon (based on John Ford), is quite explicit about the fictionality of his "America":

> Every people has its story [...] which is not the same as its history. It is this story that roots them on the land, that sustains their sense of identity. It may not be the truth, but it is believed. I have lived all my life in the twentieth century, I am not ignorant of the importance of truth, but I am an artist and my first responsibility is to the story – the story of the American people.[58]

Sinclair's own short story called "America" anticipated Falcon by showing that the idea of America, based on puns and word-play, is always liable to inventive reinterpretation. The depiction in *Cosmetic Effects* of "America" as being not only a nation-state but a "state of mind" (61), not unlike Sinclair's Israel or "Albania" (named after St Albans), interestingly shows the dangers of a Lyotardian view of the world based exclusively on language-games. Sinclair's "America," in *Cosmetic Effects*, is a metaphor that eventually becomes real. Jonah Isaacson recognizes this when he proclaims: "give my imagination a metaphor and it'll have the *mise-en-scène* worked out in no time" (5). Isaacson, in fact, comes to embody the competing stories which, as he shows, are literally fighting it out to the death in the Middle East:

> Although I have only one arm I really feel like two people – a smooth man and a hairy man – two people in a single body, like the Israelis and the Palestinians are two people in a single land [...] (204).

---

[58] Clive Sinclair, *Cosmetic Effects* (London: André Deutsch, 1989): 163. Further page references are in the main text.

Cosmetic Effects deals with the situation that Jonah Isaacson might unwittingly be turned into a human bomb by his Palestinian doctor, Said Habash, who fits him with a prosthetic arm. Whether Isaacson is a "Son of Ishmael" (the name of a Palestinian guerrilla group) or the son of Isaac (an Israeli national hero) is deliberately left open. Isaacson loses his memory and for much of the novel has a number of competing national stories imposed on him. This terrorizing or civilizing quality of his dual nature is embodied in his animalistic desires and self-control respectively, but it can also symbolize a conscious narrative "pluralism" which encourages "a proliferation of stories and interpretations [so that] the future won't be fascistic" (45). For Sinclair, the imagination "bind[s] more strongly than kinship" and yet he is careful to locate his diasporic fiction within specific national stories.

In *Augustus Rex* (1992), Sinclair brings August Strindberg back to life. After half a century in the grave Strindberg is resurrected with the Faustian pact that he will once again become an all-powerful writer and unbridled lover of women. The novel is narrated by Beelzebub, Lord of the Flies, who tempts the resurrected Strindberg to over-reach himself (he is turned into a fly). Following on from the megalomanic storyteller of "Ashkenazia" – who thinks that he can breathe life into Europe's "skeletons" – *Augustus Rex* sets out to ironize the supposedly unlimited power of Strindberg's death-defying art. In this way, Sinclair is able to question the limits of an extraterritorial writing, displaced from space and time. His more recent collection of novellas and stories, *The Lady With the Laptop* (1996), continues to invent purely imaginary national homelands – such as "Ishmalaya" in his story "The Iceman Cometh" – while simultaneously subjecting his aestheticized diaspora to the contingencies of history. *Meet the Wife* (2002), his most recent novel, deliberately plays with the borders between life and death, past and present. Of all the writers considered, Sinclair's diasporas are the most constructed and artificial. At the same time, as with Spark and Steiner, Sinclair's diasporic imagination is essentially dialectical. He creates "imaginary homelands" precisely to show the limits of such an aestheticized view of history.

Conclusion

All of the writers under discussion have unsettled the notion of a fixed and idealized diaspora by constructing two radically antithetical imagined diasporas in their fiction. Spark's work contains both the ideal of a universalizing diasporic realm, taken from an assimilationist modernism and Catholic orthodoxy, which is disrupted by a more heterodox and uncontainable part-Jewish "community of exiles." Steiner is preoccupied with a post-Holocaust *galut*, which enraptures his self-destructive characters, while also upholding the cultural and humanizing ideals of the *golah*. Finally, Sinclair sets up a model of diaspora as a purely aestheticized or textual realm which he then challenges and undermines in his fiction. By rejecting a unitary model of diaspora, which revolves around the twin poles of nation and exile, all these writers go beyond the spatial and temporal constraints, fixed between empire and colony, beginnings and ends, inherent in much postcolonial theory.

Jonathan Boyarin has shown, in particular, the need to construct diasporic identities not merely spatially – where the other is perceived exclusively in relation to the centre and periphery – but also temporally. This temporal perspective enables an engagement with the Jewish dead of the *galut* who, in Europe at least, continue to unsettle received narratives of Western modernity. Instead of thinking of time and space as contrasting axes, Boyarin complicates the postcolonial stress on spatiality, as it tends to discount minority history *within* Europe. That is, spatial organization – the Spivakian stress on "other worlds" – denies the existence of more than one time-frame or more than one kind of Europe. Boyarin contends suggestively, in these terms, that one should begin to think of "different times [existing] in the same place" to account for the Jewish dead of the *galut*, who are not merely spatially but also temporally displaced.[59]

As Peter McLaren and Rodolfo Torres have rightly argued, many theories of the diaspora and multiculturalism have tended to focus on a "black–white paradigm" which has down-played or ignored "comparative ethnic histories of racism."[60] I would go further and note that the prominent place given to a dominant Euro-American "Judaeo-Christian tradition" within much postcolonial theory has perforce excluded Jews (and, for that matter, the Irish or Hispanics) from the realm of minority ethnic discourse. What is clear about the authors under consideration, however, is that by writing from within a self-consciously extraterritorial realm they refuse any simple opposition between nation and exile, power and powerlessness. As Sidra DeKoven Ezrahi has exhaustively demonstrated, this ambivalent identity-less identity is at the heart of much diasporic Jewish literature: "If exile is narrative, then to historicize the end of narrative [in Israel] is to invite a form of epic closure."[61] Not unlike Gillian Rose in *The Broken Middle* (1992), DeKoven Ezrahi is most concerned with those Jewish writers who go beyond the dialectic of ends and beginnings and she instead stresses those authors who express the "*middle* as an errant, meandering, endlessly deferred, never-ending story." Here we are close to Bhabha's work on the "inter" and "in-between," the liminal "third space" which carries the burden of postmodern and postcolonial culture.[62]

[59] Jonathan Boyarin, *Storm From Paradise: The Politics of Jewish Memory* (Minneapolis: U of Minnesota P, 1992): 82.

[60] Peter McLaren & Rodolfo Torres, "Racism and Multicultural Education: Rethinking 'Race' and Whiteness in Late Capitalism," in *Critical Multiculturalism: Rethinking Multicultural and Antiracist Education*, ed. Stephen May (London & New York: Routledge, 1999): 45–46.

[61] Sidra DeKoven Ezrahi, *Booking Passage: Exile and Homecoming in the Modern Jewish Imagination* (Berkeley: U of California P, 2000): 14.

[62] Ezrahi, *Booking Passage*, 10. May, "Multiculturalism," 132–34, discusses Homi Bhabha's work in these terms. See also Bhabha, "Foreword:

Along with the theoretical connections between postcolonial studies and Jewish cultural studies, there is an equally compelling link between Jewish and postcolonial writers in Britain. As I have shown elsewhere, the works of Anita Desai and Caryl Phillips explicitly utilize Jewish history in order to challenge the rootedness of a particular ethnic realm. Both writers utilize the Venetian Jewish Ghetto as a liminal space where Europe and Africa or the Occident and Orient meet.[63] Desai's *Baumgartner's Bombay* (1988) and Phillips's *The Nature of Blood* (1997) specifically embrace the unbounded and ghettoized territory of Venice so as to locate the Jewish diaspora within a postcolonial narrative. Not unlike their British-Jewish counterparts, these writers embrace a "cosmopolitan alternative" so as to write rootlessly outside of all national narratives.[64] Venice enacts Bhabha's liminal "third space" as well as the cosmopolitanism of many Jewish writers in Britain who represent the diaspora as a place without a beginning or end, a place that is always doubled and contested. This is a radically different construction of diaspora from that current within American-Jewish discourse, which stresses Jewish tradition and rootedness in Eastern Europe, an autochthonous 'homeland' of Israel, and the universalization of diaspora Jewishness in the USA.

∅

Joking Aside: The Idea of a Self-Critical Community," in Cheyette & Marcus, ed. *Modernity, Culture and "the Jew"*, xv–xx.

[63] Bryan Cheyette, "Venetian Spaces: Old–New Literatures and the Ambivalent Uses of Jewish History" in *Reading the "New" Literatures in a Postcolonial Era*, ed. Susheila Nasta (Cambridge: Boydell & Brewer, 2000): 53–72. See also Susheila Nasta, *Home Truths: Fictions of the South Asian Diaspora in Britain* (Basingstoke: Palgrave, 2002), for further comparisons.

[64] May, "Multiculturalism," 134–36, for the relationship between cosmopolitanism and multiculturalism.

WORKS CITED

Alter, Robert. "Against Messiness," *Times Literary Supplement* (12 January 1996): 23–24.

Bauman, Zygmunt. "Allosemitism: Premodern, Modern, Postmodern," in Cheyette & Marcus, ed. *Modernity, Culture and 'the Jew'*, 143–56.

——. *Life in Fragments: Essays in Postmodern Morality* (Oxford: Blackwell, 1995).

——. *Modernity and Ambivalence* (Oxford, Polity, 1991).

——. *Modernity and the Holocaust* (Cambridge, Polity, 1989).

——. *Postmodern Ethics* (Oxford: Blackwell, 1993).

Bennington, Geoff. "Lyotard and 'the Jews'," in Cheyette & Marcus, ed. *Modernity, Culture and 'the Jew'*, 188–96.

Bernstein, Michael André. *Foregone Conclusions: Against Apocalyptic History* (Berkeley: U of California P, 1994).

Bhabha, Homi K. "Foreword: Joking Aside: The Idea of a Self-Critical Community," in Cheyette & Marcus, ed. *Modernity, Culture and 'the Jew'*, xv–xx.

Biale, David, Michael Galchinsky & Susannah Heschel, ed. *Insider/Outsider: American-Jews and Multiculturalism* (Berkeley: U of California P, 1998).

Boyarin, Daniel, & Jonathan Boyarin. "Diaspora: Generation and the Ground of Jewish Identity," *Critical Inquiry* 19 (Summer 1993): 693–725.

Boyarin, Jonathan. *Storm from Paradise: The Politics of Jewish Memory* (Minneapolis: U of Minnesota P, 1992).

Bradbury, Malcolm. "Muriel Spark's Fingernails," in *No, Not Bloomsbury* (London: Arena, 1987): 268–78.

Cesarani, David. "The Dynamics of Diaspora: The Transformation of British Jewish Identity," *Jewish Culture and History* 4.1 (Summer 2001): 53–64.

Cheyette, Bryan. *Constructions of "the Jew" in English Literature and Society: Racial Representations, 1875–1945* (Cambridge: Cambridge UP, 1993).

——. *Diasporas of the Mind: A Critical History of British Jewish Literature* (London & New Haven: CT Yale UP, forthcoming).

——. *Muriel Spark* (Writers and their Work; Plymouth: Northcote House, 2000).

——. "Venetian Spaces: Old-New Literatures and the Ambivalent Use of Jewish History," in Nasta, ed. *Home Truths*, 53–72.

——, & Laura Marcus, ed. *Modernity, Culture and "the Jew"* (Cambridge: Polity, 1998).

Cohen, Phil. *Home Rules: Some Reflections on Racism and Nationalism in Everyday Life* (London: U of East London P, 1993).

Connor, Steven. *The English Novel in History* (London & New York: Routledge, 1996).

Desai, Anita. *Baumgartner's Bombay* (London: Heinemann, 1988).

Ezrahi, Sidra DeKoven. *Booking Passage: Exile and Homecoming in the Modern Jewish Imagination* (Berkeley: U of California P, 2000).

Finkelstein, Norman. *The Ritual of New Creation: Jewish Tradition and Contemporary Literature* (New York: SUNY Press, 1992).

Fludernik, Monika. *Echoes and Mirrorings: Gabriel Josipovici's Creative Oeuvre* (Frankfurt am Main: Peter Lang, 2000).

Gilman, Sander. *The Jew's Body* (London & New York: Routledge, 1991).

Gilroy, Paul. *Between Camps: Race, Identity and Nationalism at the End of the Colour Line* (Harmondsworth: Penguin, 2000).

——. *The Black Atlantic: Modernity and Double Consciousness* (London: Verso, 1993).

Harrison, Bernard. *Inconvenient Fictions: Literature and the Limits of Theory* (New Haven CT: Yale UP, 1991).

Josipovici, Gabriel. *The Book of God* (New Haven CT & London: Yale UP, 1988).

Kemp, Peter. *Muriel Spark* (Novelists and Their World; London: Paul Elek, 1974).

Kitaj, R.B. *First Diasporist Manifesto* (London: Thames & Hudson, 1989).

Lee, A. Robert, ed. *Other Britain, Other British: Contemporary Multicultural Fiction* (London: Pluto Press, 1995).

Lyotard, Jean–François. *Heidegger and "the jews"*, tr. Andreas Michel & Mark S. Roberts (*Heidegger et "les juifs"*, 1988; tr. Minneapolis: U of Minnesota P, 1990).

McLaren, Peter, & Rodolfo Torres, "Racism and Multicultural Education: Rethinking 'Race' and Whiteness in Late Capitalism," in May, *Critical Multiculturalism*.

May, Stephen. "Multiculturalism," in *A Companion to Racial and Ethnic Studies*, ed. David Theo Goldberg & John Solomos (Oxford: Blackwell, 2002): 124–44.

——, ed. *Critical Multiculturalism: Rethinking Multicultural and Antiracist Education* (London & New York: Routledge, 1999).

Nasta, Susheila. *Home Truths: Fictions of the South Asian Diaspora in Britain* (Basingstoke: Palgrave, 2002).

Phillips, Caryl. *The Nature of Blood* (London: Faber & Faber, 1997).

Rose, Gillian. *Broken Middle* (Oxford: Blackwell, 1992).

——. *Judaism and Modernity: Philosophical Essays* (Oxford: Blackwell, 1993).

Rosenfeld, Alvin. *Imagining Hitler* (Bloomington: Indiana UP, 1985).

Rushdie, Salman. *Imaginary Homelands: Essays and Criticism 1981–1991* (London: Granta, 1991).

Scott Jr, Nathan A., & Ronald A. Sharp, ed. *Reading George Steiner* (Baltimore MD & London: Johns Hopkins UP, 1994).

Sharp, Ronald. "Steiner's Fiction and the Hermeneutics of Translation," in *Reading George Steiner*, ed. Nathan Scott & Ronald Sharp (Baltimore MD & London: Johns Hopkins UP, 1994): 205–29.

Shreiber, Maeera Y. "The End of Exile: Jewish Identity and Diaspora Poetics," *PMLA* 113.2 (March 1998): 273–87.

Sinclair, Clive. *Augustus Rex* (London: André Deutsch, 1992).

——. *Bedbugs* (London: Allison & Busby, 1982).

——. *Blood Libels* (London: Allison & Busby, 1985).

——. *Cosmetic Effects* (London: André Deutsch, 1989).

——. *Diaspora Blues: A View of Israel* (London: Heinemann, 1987).

——. *For Good or Evil: Collected Stories* (Harmondsworth: Penguin, 1991).

——. *Hearts of Gold* (London: Allison & Busby, 1979).

——. *The Lady With the Laptop* (London: Picador, 1996).

——. *Meet the Wife* (London: Picador, 2002).

——. "'On the Edge of the Imagination': Clive Sinclair interviewed by Bryan Cheyette," *Jewish Quarterly* 3.4 (1984): 26–29.

Spark, Muriel. *The Collected Stories* (Harmondsworth: Penguin, 1994).

——. *The Comforters* (London: Macmillan, 1957).

——. "My Conversion," *The Twentieth Century* 170 (Autumn 1961): 58–63.

——. *Curriculum Vitae: A Volume of Autobiography* (Harmondsworth: Penguin, 1992).

——. "The Gentile Jewess," in Spark, *Collected Stories*, 308–15.

——. *The Mandelbaum Gate* (London: Macmillan, 1965).

——. "The Poet in Mr. Eliot's Ideal State," *Outposts* 14 (Summer 1949): 26–28.

——. *The Takeover* (London: Macmillan, 1976).

——. "What Images Return," in *Memoirs of a Modern Scotland*, ed. Karl Miller (London: Faber & Faber, 1970): 151–53.

Steiner, George. *After Babel* (London: Oxford UP, 1975).

——. *Anno Domini* (London: Faber & Faber, 1984).

——. *In Bluebeard's Castle: Some Notes towards the Redefinition of Culture* (London: Faber & Faber, 1971).

——. "Cake," in Steiner, *The Deeps of the Sea*, 197–234.

——. *The Deeps of the Sea and Other Fiction* (London: Faber & Faber, 1996).

——. *Errata: An Unexamined Life* (London: Weidenfeld & Nicholson, 1997).

——. "K," in Steiner, *Language and Silence*, 141–49

——. "A Kind of Survivor," in Steiner, *Language and Silence*, 119–35.

——. *Language and Silence: Essays 1958–1966* (London: Faber & Faber, 1967).

——. *No Passion Spent: Essays 1978–1996* (London: Faber & Faber, 1996).

——. "Our Homeland, the Text," in Steiner, *No Passion Spent*, 304–27.

——. *The Portage to San Christobal of A.H.* (London: Faber & Faber, 1981).

——. *Proofs and Three Parabels* (London: Faber & Faber, 1992).

——. *Real Presences: Is there anything 'in' what we say?* (London: Faber & Faber, 1989).

——. "A Responsion," in Scott & Sharp, ed. *Reading George Steiner*, 275–85.

——. "A View From Without," *Jewish Quarterly* 16.4 (1968–69): 3–5 & 17.1 (1969): 3–9.

Viswanathan, Gauri. *Outside the Fold: Conversion, Modernity, and Belief* (Princeton NJ: Princeton UP, 1998).

✆

BEATE NEUMEIER

Kindertransport
Memory, Identity and the British-Jewish Diaspora

T HE *KINDERTRANSPORT* IN 1938/9, a unique British rescue operation, saved ten thousand Jewish children from Germany and Eastern Europe, who were brought across the Channel and survived in British foster-homes and hostels. Surprisingly, this "act of mercy not equalled anywhere else" (to quote from the documentary film on the *Kindertransport, Into the Arms of Strangers*) has only recently gained international public attention. It was not until the 1990s that this endeavour was suddenly thematized in a variety of media ranging from the reissue of personal accounts such as Lore Segal's autobiography *Other People's Houses* (1958, 1994) to Diane Samuels' stage-play *Kindertransport* (1995) and the documentary film *Into the Arms of Strangers* (2000). A number of other texts could be mentioned in this connection, dealing with children's transports not only in the closely defined terms of this organized rescue operation, but in the wider sense of individually organized endeavours or even evacuations within England for safety reasons during the time of the air raids (see Eva Figes, *Little Eden*, 1978, Anita Brookner, *Latecomers*, 1988, Zina Rohan, *Sandbeetle*, 1993).

This rise of interest in the *Kindertransport* has to be seen as part of a remarkable "rise of British-Jewish literature"[1] during the past decade, which in turn can be linked to growing self-awareness of Britain as a multicultural society characterized by difference and plurivocality and to concomitant changing notions of 'Englishness'. From this perspective, current representations of the *Kindertransport* highlight a number of issues decisive for a discussion of diasporas at large: questions of identity-formation and diaspora consciousness, questions about the interrelation of past and future, as well as questions about culture-specific relations between diaspora and host-country, and – more generally – about forms of representing the past. Thus a discussion of representations of the *Kindertransport* in different media can be used to understand both the specificity of the historical context and the possibility of making connections between diasporas.

Diaspora(s)

For a long time, questions of the Jewish diaspora and the postcolonial diasporas have been kept distinctly apart.[2] The emergence of the concept of the diaspora as one of the dominant postcolonial paradigms in the 1990s, however, necessitates a reconsideration and re-evaluation of this separation.[3] The rise of diaspora not only marks a cultural shift away from notions of multiculturalism and hybridity, emphasizing the role of the diasporic subject as part of a diasporic community, but it also inevitably links "the diasporic imaginary with the prototype of the

---

[1] Bryan Cheyette, "Moroseness and Englishness: The Rise of British-Jewish Literature," *Jewish Quarterly* (Spring 1995): 22–26.

[2] Bryan Cheyette & Laura Marcus, "Introduction" to *Modernity, Culture and "the Jew"*, ed. Cheyette & Marcus (Cambridge: Polity, 1998): 2.

[3] See Robin Cohen, *Global Diasporas: An Introduction* (Seattle: U of Washington P, 1997).

Jewish diaspora."[4] Ironically, this development from first ignoring the Jewish diaspora as part of postcolonial studies to a later appropriation of the Jewish diaspora as a central paradigm proves indicative of the familiar oscillation between, on the one hand, universalizing Jewish experience and, on the other, excluding it from the discussion on account of its supposed difference and uniqueness.

In connection with this, a number of distinguished critics have argued that the exclusion of the study of antisemitism from studies of racism in Western civilization on the basis of the uniqueness of the Holocaust can also be read as an attempt at externalizing the Holocaust from a supposedly liberal humanist consensus, instead of acknowledging the centrality of the construction of Jewish difference for the concept of the modern European nation-state.[5] On the other hand, important critics have warned us that the tendency in postmodern theories to universalize Jewish diasporic existence as a paradigm of the postmodern condition ignores the specificity of Jewish history.[6] In this context, the rise of diaspora as a key concept within postcolonial theory can be seen as a chance to foreground the necessity of linking the history of Judaism "to other histories of oppression, but always with a difference," in an attempt "to make connections across differing histories, yet avoid the pitfalls of universalising."[7]

❡

---

[4] Monika Fludernik, "The Diasporic Imaginary: Postcolonial Reconfigurations in the Context of Multiculturalism," in the present volume, xxiv.

[5] See Zygmunt Bauman, *Modernity and the Holocaust*, 1989; *Modernity and Ambivalence*, 1991; *Life in Fragments*, 1995.

[6] See Gillian Rose, *Judaism and Modernity: Philosophical Essays* (Oxford: Blackwell, 1993): 1–24, 241–57.

[7] Cheyette & Marcus, "Introduction" to *Modernity, Culture and "the Jew"*, 13–14. See also Daniel & Jonathan Boyarin, ed. *Jews and Other Differences: The New Jewish Cultural Studies* (Minneapolis: U of Minnesota P, 1997).

(Collective) Identity, Memory and Representation

The identity-formation of diasporic communities involves the development and constant reconsideration of collective memory as well as the
definition and constant redefinition of the relation to the host country.[8]
The importance of remembering, of memory and its cultural representations, is decisive for all diasporas. But in contradistinction to the
sometimes playful revisions of the past discernible in a good deal of
postcolonial diasporic writing of the present, the Holocaust marks the
limits of plurivocal approaches to the past. The Holocaust radicalizes
questions about the tension between the necessity of remembering and
the impossibility of representing the past.

Since memory is crucial to individual, social, cultural and national
identity-formation, an analysis of individual, communicative and collective mechanisms of remembering can help to foreground the intricate relation of memory and history. It is thus precisely when living
memory is about to disappear that cultural forms of commemoration
and archival collecting gain intensified importance.[9] This is what is
happening at this moment, when the generation of Holocaust survivors
is slowly disappearing.[10] The recent interest in the stories of the
Kindertransport can therefore be explained as part of this effort to
save the past from oblivion.

Memory, however, is decisive not only for the identity-formation of
diaspora communities but also for that of the host-countries. The question of what and how the country at large remembers is particularly
important with regard to Jewish diasporas. Aleida Assmann and Ute
Frevert have analysed ways of remembering the Holocaust with regard

---

[8] See Cohen's nine categories defining diaspora in *Global Diasporas*, 26.

[9] See Jan Assmann, *Das kulturelle Gedächtnis: Schrift, Erinnerung und
politische Identität in frühen Hochkulturen* (Munich: C.H. Beck, 1992).

[10] See Aleida Assmann & Ute Frevert, *Geschichtsvergessenheit/Ge-
schichtsversessenheit: Vom Umgang mit deutschen Vergangenheiten nach
1945* (Stuttgart: Deutsche Verlagsanstalt, 1999): 28.

to the specific workings of the *Tätergedächtnis* (perpetrator's memory) in German society since 1945, foregrounding conflicting strategies of forgetting and remembering, and – in this context – of commemoration as a sign of responsibility, but also of unburdening, and of repression through manipulation and censoring.[11]

Linked to the vital question of how and by whom the past is represented are thus questions about "who receives it, under what conditions and to what ends."[12] Tony Kushner in particular has drawn attention to the question of "how the memory of the Holocaust impinges on present-day social and political agendas," applying his analysis of "the relationship between selective memory and state power with regard to the Shoah"[13] to the British context. The commemoration of the Holocaust can serve as a decisive indicator of the relation between the British-Jewish diaspora and British society at large.

The British-Jewish Diaspora: Diaspora-Consciousness and Cultural Visibility

The conspicuous lack of a visible tradition of British-Jewish writing in contrast to Jewish-American writing can be linked to notions of a "normative" or "monolithic Englishness," in the sense that "Jewish writers in Britain have been made to feel distinctly uncomfortable with their Jewishness. To succeed in the wider culture, authors such as Harold Pinter and Anita Brookner have had to write out virtually any

---

[11] "Zeichen der Mahnung und Verpflichtung, aber auch als Zeichen der Entlastung, des Vergessens durch Auslagerung und des Verdrängens durch Manipulation und Zensur"; Aleida Assmann, *Erinnerungsräume: Formen und Wandlungen des kulturellen Gedächtnisses* (Munich: C.H. Beck, 1999): 33.

[12] James Young, "Arts of Jewish Memory in a Postmodern Age," in Cheyette & Marcus, ed. *Modernity, Culture and "the Jew"*, 214. See also James Young, *Texture of Memory: Holocaust Memorials and Meaning* (New Haven CT: Yale UP, 1993).

[13] Cheyette & Marcus, "Introduction," to *Modernity, Culture and "the Jew"*, 15.

reference to their Jewishness."[14] But these notions of a normative
Englishness may also have hindered a stronger critical interest in, and
wider reception of, Jewish writing in Britain. The distinctive "rise of
British-Jewish writing" and a concomitant rise in academic and
general public interest in British-Jewish writing and culture, indeed,
coincides with the rise of postcolonial writings in Britain and with the
radical questioning and redefinition of notions of Englishness. Significantly, this thematization of Jewishness in literary works seems to
apply not only to a newer generation of writers like Clive Sinclair,
Gabriel Josipovici or Zina Rohan, but also to established writers like
Harold Pinter, Eva Figes or Anita Brookner.

Englishness and Antisemitism

The assumption of a predominant monolithic Englishness implies
questions about constructions of 'the Other' beyond the norm, and
thus raises the issue of racism and antisemitism in British history.
Significantly, although the term 'diaspora' may have been coined with
reference to the Jewish-American "success story – to be the same but
different,"[15] the interest in drawing connections between diasporas
seems to be particularly strong in the British context, where this normative Englishness has only recently given way to an acknowledgement of the plurivocality of Britain as a multicultural society. In contrast to this, the American concept of a multicultural society privileging the Judaeo-Christian tradition seems to have prevented the
drawing of connections between the "Jewish-American success story"
and stories of other diasporas.

The strategies of silencing and denial, discernible in earlier British
relations to the Jewish community, are linked to a denial of British
antisemitism and to an apparent absence of memory of the Holocaust

---

[14] Bryan Cheyette, "Moroseness and Englishness," 22–23.
[15] Fludernik, "The Diasporic Imaginary," xxi.

in British culture. Tony Kushner has described this phenomenon as a form of "constant amnesia to retain the special, mythical memory of Britain alone."[16] According to his analysis, "the Holocaust questioned the scale of British sacrifices and therefore the centrality of the war in the construction of postwar British (or more accurately) English national identity."[17] Kushner links the construction of a normative Englishness to the secret persistence of antisemitism in postwar British society. He not only notes striking examples of blatant antisemitism, but also points to examples of official policies to prevent Jewish visibility within British society. He instances the exclusion of Holocaust survivors from the Cenotaph ceremony to celebrating the twentieth anniversary of the end of the war in 1965, or the official negation of "the efforts of those of colour and the refugees from Nazism [...] in the British military effort."[18] According to Kushner, this attitude is still epitomized today in prevailing objections to a British Holocaust memorial: "Instead, a small, obscure rock in Hyde Park in a space that is both public and hidden (thus only known to a few Jews and neo-Nazis) remains Britain's *only* civic memorial to the victims of the Holocaust."[19]

In the light of Kushner's analysis, one can surmise that the long-time lack of public interest in the *Kindertransport* may be linked to the fact that this sensational endeavour was not only a sign of British humanism but inevitably also opened up questions about British–Jewish relations. Thus, only in the wake of a changing British self-image were questions of British-Jewish relations and aspects of anti-semitism finally allowed to surface, and led to a reconsideration and

---

[16] Tony Kushner, "Remembering to Forget: Racism and Anti-Racism in Postwar Britain," in Cheyette & Marcus, ed. *Modernity, Culture and "the Jew"*, 231.

[17] Kushner, "Remembering to Forget," 229.

[18] Kushner, "Remembering to Forget," 231.

[19] Kushner, "Remembering to Forget," 230.

redefinition of the relation between the British-Jewish diaspora and
their host country.

Kindertransport: Mediations

In the following, the focus will be on an analysis of the complex implications of these issues in Harris and Oppenheimer's film *Into the Arms
of Strangers* (2000), Lore Segal's novel *Other People's Houses*
(1958), and Diane Samuels' play *Kindertransport* (1995). The starting-point for all three textualizations is personal accounts of participants in the *Kindertransport*.

In this context, the various commemorations of the *Kindertransport*
can be recognized as part of a culture of memory – resistance to oblivion. Significantly, the texts discussed below do not attempt to represent the Holocaust *per se*, but focus on absence and silence, thema-
tizing haunting childhood experiences caused by the Holocaust. All
the examples chosen for discussion are characterized by ambivalences,
thematic ones with regard to identity and belonging, but also generic
ambivalences relating to the fact that these texts are situated on the
borderline between fact and fiction. Each of these life-writings about
the child as lonely migrant thematizes questions of memory, identity
and representation, drawing on the interrelation between past/ present
(and future), home/diaspora, assimilation/resistance, victim/perpetra-
tor. The central focus of each of these versions, however, differs in
terms of its genre/medium and context (of production and reception).

Screening the Escape:
Into the Arms of Strangers (Harris/Oppenheimer)

Among the representations of the *Kindertransport*, the film version
from the makers of the Academy Award-winning Holocaust documentary *The Long Way Home* undoubtedly had the most international

impact. The scriptwriter and director Mark Jonathan Harris was assisted by the producer Deborah Oppenheimer, whose mother Sylvia had been on the *Kindertransport*. The film blends documentary film material from the period, including old photographs and letters, with on-camera interviews with survivors, foster-parents, the adult escort Norbert Wollheimer, and the rescue organizer Nicholas Winton. The film presents the survivors in the static situation of a quasi photographic close-up, as they tell their childhood experiences. Changes from black and white to coloration and music are used to emphasize the difference between past and present, or alternatively to blend the past into the present, as the survivors tell their stories in an attempt to recapture their children's perspective.

The film opens on a nostalgic camera sweep over the paraphernalia of a child's world of the past: (old-fashioned) toys, children's books, and school things. Coloration and music add to the evocation of the familiar cinematic atmosphere of the fairytale happiness of a childhood from the past. The German language recognizable in book titles and handwriting is the only reminder of another story behind those images. When the picture of a child's suitcase changes into that of a contemporary train station, which in turn fades into an old-fashioned station shot in black and white, the actual story sets in, with Judi Dench as voice-over providing the factual information of the narrative, presented in chronological order.

The image of the train is used here to foreground the relation of past and present through association and dissociation. The shots of trains from different times foreground the lasting effects of the past on the present as well as the radical disruption of childhood bliss by Nazi atrocities. The train thus functions as a central symbol of escape and survival but also of loss and death, as during the Nazi terror trains left in both directions towards freedom as well as towards extermination. The ambivalence of the train symbol is apparent in many survivors' life-long difficulties in taking trains, mentioned in the film by the survivor Lori Cahn.

The first part of the film is dedicated to the depiction of a *happy childhood* set in 1934. The nostalgia created by the initial images is enhanced by documentary film material presenting an idyllic life in prewar times. This is emphasized by the background music of well-known children's songs. Scenes from birthday parties, playgrounds, skating in winter, fairs in summer and walks with doting parents re-create an atmosphere of love and warmth and happiness. This construction of happiness functions as a means of setting off childhood bliss from the atrocious realities of life which were to follow with Hitler's rise to power. However, this contrastive technique contains the danger of hiding the rise of Nazism and antisemitism beneath the surface of happiness. As the film does not thematize this impending threat – restricting itself to the child's perspective – audiences might feel invited to share that perspective. The depiction of a happy Jewish life in Germany and Austria before 1938 threatens to confirm the complacent assumption that antisemitism and the Holocaust were limited to Hitler and his immediate followers. Only rarely do we get some cautious hint of impending disaster, as in the memory of the doting father who provides "his little princess" with the gift of a model suit in adult fashion (Lori Kahn). The contrast between the words and the static setup and subdued voices in this scene contradicts this impression of unalloyed happiness by painfully foreshadowing the terror to come.

In keeping with well-known filmic conventions, an abrupt cut accompanied by an equally abrupt change of music signals the onset of the second part of the film, *Hitler's rise to power*, presenting in rapid succession documentary material on the annexation of Austria and Czechoslovakia, and on the Kristallnacht. The use of archival film material first focuses on Hitler himself as source and centre of National Socialism and moves from there to show how the social climate within the population changes along with Hitler's rise to power, represented by documentary sequences of marches, Hitler Youth, and Hitler's salute. The stories told by the survivors all mark the harsh awakening to a nightmarish Nazi reality. From a childhood perspective this change is often linked to seemingly trivial things like the story told by the survivor Ursula Rosenfeld of the child's birthday party to which no one came. Whereas in some reviews of the film this has been criticized as belittling the past, taking away the monstrosity of events, I would argue that, on the contrary, in this case the monstrosity (of Nazism) is heightened through the presentation of the child's perspective, particularly as the children's stories foreground the identification with Nazism among the population at large. The stories told by the survivors vary according to the age of the children at the time, and get darker and more directly threatening in the case of older children, like Alexander Gordon, who was thrown through a glass window by Nazi youths.

The film attempts to capture the growing Nazi threat in a succession of images, from balloons with swastika emblems to official measures against Jews and outbursts of violence against Jews by the people. At this point, the shot of a spiral staircase is used repeatedly to evoke emotions of fear and anxiety, of growing dizziness, of disequilibrium, of falling into an abyss. The camera follows the children's flight upstairs to hide in an attic wardrobe while Nazis storm the house. The blurred vision of these images emphasizes the terror and panic of moments too painful to remember (see Hedy Epstein's story). These cinematic means are certainly effective, but at the same time leave the viewer with an uncomfortable feeling. The use of the image of the spiral staircase, well-known from the film noir and thriller genres (as in Alfred Hitchcock's *Vertigo*), inevitably evokes this intertextual horizon of the fiction film. It is here that the limits of representation seem to become most obvious.

The third part of the film, dedicated to the *Kindertransport*, is situated precisely in the middle of the film. In this section, Judi Dench's voice-over gains prominence as she describes the preconditions and circumstances of the rescue operation, significantly setting off Britain from other countries deciding not to participate in the operation. Among these, the USA is noted in particular, where "a congressional bill voted against it on grounds of it being contrary to laws of God to send children on their own without parents." The obvious aim here is to underline the uniqueness of the British endeavour. The cinematic construction of Britain evoking the well-known nostalgic tourist image of Englishness and its continuity to the present day clearly functions in terms of gratitude towards the saviour country.

The heartbreaking stories of leavetaking between children and parents in this part of the film are accompanied by pictures of packing children's suitcases with teddy bears placed lovingly on top and by pictures of parents' farewell on the railway platform, with the camera gradually receding from the scene, thus underscoring the children's loneliness, increasing with the growing distance. One of the most haunting stories is that of the survivor Lori Cahn, who narrates how her father, unable to bear the separation, snatched his "Puppele," as he called her, out of the train at the very last moment before departure. (Later, Lori Cahn was deported to Theresienstadt, and then to Auschwitz.)

The fourth part concentrates on *life in England*, and on difficulties of adjustment and experiences of assimilation and rejection in the host-country. The film traces the various stages of arrival, from the port at Harwich to Liverpool station, on to provisional children's camps, and eventually to foster-homes. Lore Segal recalls her stay at the children's camp in strange images of snow on her English breakfast of frozen kippers and in the humiliating experience of the "cattle market," when prospective foster-parents visited the camp to choose from among the children. This part of the film emphasizes most vividly the plurality of experiences, positive and negative, of both children and foster-parents. The stories foreground the different expectations on both sides and the resultant difficulties in adjusting to one another.

Statements of survivors that they "should be grateful and happy" but "were not treated nicely" by cold und unemotional foster-parents capture the children's mixed feelings towards the host-country. More-over, there are the complex motivations of foster-parents to consider. Apart from humanitarian feelings, the decision to take in children from the *Kindertransport* was determined by hopes of finding a substitute child of their own or by the desire to provide themselves with a substitute servant. Sometimes religious denomination (the question of orthodoxy) or hair colour dec ided whether one would be taken in or refused. Thus the survivor Bertha Leverton describes how she tricked her foster-parents into taking on her little sister Inge as well, by changing Inge in her portrayal from a redhead into a more favourably received blonde. And Lore Segal describes how she was taken into a Liverpool family by inadvertently supporting their wrong assumption of her being orthodox. Lore Segal most poignantly captures the mixed feelings of the survivor between feelings of alienation and the obliga-tion to show gratitude. She describes her unhappy life in five foster-families, all of whom she experienced as not particularly warm, but – as the survivor emphasizes – who nevertheless "had the grace to take a Jewish child in." To picture the difficult relation between children and foster-parents, Segal uses the analogy of the bird with the broken wing which, instead of showing gratitude and love for those rescuing it, immediately struggles to break free.

However, there are also examples of positive adjustment and happi-ness: at school, for instance, with the library opening up a new world (Ursula Rosenfeld). And, most importantly, the film gives a voice to foster-parents, or – to be precise – to one foster-mother, who did be-come a second mother to her foster-child, Kurt Fuchel. But even in this case of growing attachment between child and foster-parent, the difficulties of adjustment are foregrounded in his rendering of the past, as he describes the cost of trying to be good all the time, to keep the anger in, which led once at the dinner-table to his groundlessly throw-ing a knife at his "brother."

Part five of the film is dedicated to the *End of War*, the ceasefire and the time after. Archival material centres on the victory celebra-

tions of the British public and its political leaders, Winston Churchill
and royals, with fireworks and dancing in Piccadilly Circus. This
sequence thus clearly points up the events as part of national identity-
formation. The film ends with a brief outlook on what happened to the
children afterwards, focusing on the decisive question of a reunion
with their real families. Although we are informed by voice-over that
in most cases such a reunion never eventuated, the end is dedicated to
the stories of the happy few whose parents survived and eventually
joined them. Even those positive examples, however, are proof of the
difficulties of a diaspora existence. Kurt Fuchel and his foster-mother
movingly describe the divided loyalties between two families and
homes, and the difficulty of the sixteen-year-old in being reunited with
the parents he had left at age seven. Consequently, Fuchel's statement
about the good luck of having two families is accompanied by tears.
Even Lore Segal's earlier reunion with her parents, who worked as
servants in British households till the end of the war, did not spare her
the consciousness of a divided identity. And only in retrospect can
Segal value her experiences as a "helpless member on the inside of
those [foster] families" as "good fortune" for a future writer, opening
up her mind to the plurality of existence. But she adds: "Of course it
didn't seem so at the time." Despite this complexity in the stories of
the members of the *Kindertransport*, the closing scenes of the film
overcome this notion of ambivalence by staging a happy ending which
focuses on present-day family pictures portraying the survivors' own
families and grandchildren, or showing their humanitarian involvement later on. The film ends with a visit to the British Parliament
today, undertaken by one of the survivors in the company of a young
woman, possibly a granddaughter, where a plaque commemorates the
Kindertransport as an "act of mercy not equalled anywhere else."

Critical reception of the film has been divided. It has been described
as "incredibly moving" and as commercial and superficial. Cinematic
representations of events linked to the Holocaust have always been
under particular critical scrutiny, as shown by the controversial – and

often polarizing – discussion of Stephen Spielberg's *Holocaust* and Claude Lanzman's *Shoah*.[20] The film *Into the Arms of Strangers* blends documentary material and interviews with a number of carefully fictionalized pictures and scenes. The structural pattern of the film tends to incorporate the different stories told into the coherent five-act narrative reminiscent of classical drama, with the most important fictionalized scenes linked to the motif of the spiral staircase situated at the centre of events. This reliance on a conventional cinematic pattern providing structural closure seems to facilitate audience empathy and identification. But this also implies the danger of belittling the monstrosity of what happened and failing to do justice to the fate of the survivors, since it leaves the audience's complacency intact. Consequently, Gillian Rose argues for films "foregrounding ambivalence and drawing attention to [their] own making," for films being "self-referentially sceptical about their own means and form of representation," thus pointing towards the limits of representation.[21]

The difficulty inherent in the conception of *Into the Arms of Strangers* seems to be related to its twofold aim of celebrating the British rescue operation and of probing into the complex effects on the survivors. This inevitably generates a (sometimes unbearable) tension between ambivalence and closure. Whereas the filmmakers' arrangement of images and scenes comes dangerously close to closure in the sense of a happy ending, this conciliatory effort is contradicted by the survivors' stories, which foreground the irreducible complexity of what happened to them. As long as this tension is felt in the process of reception, the film succeeds in keeping alive the ambivalence between belonging and alienation, home and diaspora, love and fear, assimilation and rejection, suggested in the title: *Into the Arms of Strangers*.

---

[20] Gillian Rose, "Beginnings of the Day: Fascism and Representation," in Cheyette & Marcus, ed. *Modernity, Culture and "the Jew"*, 247.

[21] Rose, "Beginnings of the Day," 247.

Life-Writing in *Other People's Houses* (Lore Segal)

Lore Groszmann Segal's autobiographical fiction, first published in 1958, was reissued twice during the following six years (1961 and 1964). She seems to have been among the first survivors to tell the story of the *Kindertransport* and of her successive struggles for identity.[22] This might be due to the fact that – like many other Jewish refugees – she did not stay in Britain after the war, but moved on to South America and eventually to the USA, to become a writer of children's books, translator, and editor of fairytales. Alan Isler has described this Jewish escape from the austerity of normative Englishness to the freedom of New York in the 1950s: "So in those early years I never felt homesick. [...] America had everything, and in abundance. [...] America was dynamic; Britain seemed then moribund."[23] Significantly, it is only in the 1990s that Isler returned to a Britain characterized by changed notions of Englishness accommodating different diasporas. And it was only in the context of this changed cultural climate of the 1990s, after a thirty-year period, that Lore Segal reissued her novel in 1994 and gained new acclaim in the context of a new perception of the *Kindertransport*.

Segal's life is told in two parts: the first part describes her childhood and adolescence up to college life in London. The second part depicts her move to South America and the USA. This life-writing thus follows (on formally conventional lines) the chronology of events from early childhood to married life. As her professed intention in this book is to save the past from oblivion for future generations, she uses the real names of those involved in her first-person narrative. Nevertheless. she calls her book a novel, thus self-consciously drawing

---

[22] See also the collection of personal accounts in Karen Gershon, *We Came as Children* (London: Victor Gollancz, 1966).

[23] Alan Isler, "A la Recherche du Cricklewood Perdu," *Jewish Quarterly* (Spring 1996): 21.

attention to the narrative process of ordering and remembering events. However, Segal tries to avoid structuring the events of her life into the quasi-teleological pattern of classical autobiography (as a kind of first-person *Bildungsroman* unfolding the development of the individual into fully integrated identity), but instead focuses on an exploration of the complexities and ambivalences involved in the formation of the diasporic subject.

Consequently, most of the *first part* of her novel explores the difficult implications of the *Kindertransport* (necessitated by the Holocaust) on the diasporic subject. Rather than concentrating on the idyllic bliss of childhood prominent in the film *Into the Arms of Strangers*, Segal captures the torn emotions of Jewish families in Austria between attachment to their homes and the necessity of making preparations to leave because of the approaching Nazi threat. The author uses the child's perspective to describe this tension between awareness and denial of what was happening in a brief episode starting with the sentence: "On the twelfth, Hitler took Austria and my mother called Tante Trude a cow."[24] These two seemingly unrelated events associated by the child are indeed directly related, as Aunt Trude is called a cow by Lore's mother because of her denial of the political reality of what is happening.

The child Lore becomes aware of the ensuing changes when she wants to join the children's game of pebble-skipping:

> There were some local children skipping flat pebbles across the water, and my father sat down on the crest of the bank and told me to go and play with them. [...] The biggest, a man-sized boy, turned and threw a little pebble. I thought it was a game and felt pleased; all the children were coming toward me up the bank. Then I saw that they had filled their mouths with Danube water, and I turned and ran, but they spat it down the back of my dress and called me 'Jew.' (22)

---

[24] Lore Segal, *Other People's Houses* (1958; New York: New Press, 1994): 4. Further page references are in the main text.

This episode not only captures the suddenness of the change from carefree happiness to fear, but also the irrationality and inexplicability of this transformation of seemingly friendly children into hateful enemies. If unpredictability appears as the most terrible threat to security, it is ambivalence that from now casts its shadow on Lore's self-esteem.

The depiction of this episode foregrounds the connections and differences across different diasporas. Jean Rhys, for instance, in her rewriting of the colonial novel *Jane Eyre* in *Wide Sargasso Sea* evokes a similar scenario where the protagonist Antoinette's identity-split is captured in the image of her childhood friend Tia hitting her with a stone at the very moment when Antoinette runs towards her. In both cases, radical experiences of alienation and unbelonging are linked to the unpredictability of the seemingly known being transformed into the unknown. In *Wide Sargasso Sea*, Jean Rhys uses this motif to explore conflicts of race, class and gender in a fictionalized nineteenth-century Caribbean context, foregrounding the destructive effects on identity-formation. In this context, Rhys's heroine is doomed from the start as a female – and racially doubtful – representative of an impoverished white colonizer's class on which the hatred and violence of the colonized black Other can focus ("white cockroach").[25] Consequently, the relationship between Antoinette and her friend Tia has always been cast in ambivalent terms. By contrast, the pebble-skipping episode in Lore Segal's autobiographical account of a Jewish childhood after Hitler's rise to power in Austria during the late 1930s, although depicted in less violent terms, appears as a more shockingly unprecedented event, foregrounding the fate of assimilated Jewish families who were harshly disabused of any assumptions about and cultural integration and social acceptance.

---

[25] Jean Rhys, *Wide Sargasso Sea* (1966; Harmondsworth: Penguin, 1997): 9, 24.

In the next section of the book, Segal focuses on the intricate ambivalences between fear and excitement, guilt and relief, about escaping
the Nazi terror through the *Kindertransport*. Leaving meant escape
from a home-country become deadly, hostile territory as well as
separation from loving parents and their uncertain fate. Again Lore
Segal resorts to vivid images capturing the way the child survivors had
to cut themselves off from their feelings in order to cope, as she puts
it. Their emotions are only are allowed to surface in relation to seemingly trivial circumstances. Consequently, the difficult emotional
situation linked to the children's transport is encapsulated in the image
of the knackwurst Lore's mother wants to give her daughter for the
journey. The desperation of mother and child about having to part
becomes evident in the mother's frantic attempt to purchase the
sausage Lore supposedly likes, and in Lore's later increasingly absurd
attempts to hold on to the knackwurst for memory's sake. In the end,
Lore only gets rid of this symbol of mother–child bonding and of an
assimilated Jewish life when her first foster-parents force her to drop
into a trash bin the by then badly smelling "guilty sausage," which
"isn't even kosher" (47). Following this enforced symbolic act, Lore
has to acknowledge that she is cut off radically from her own past, that
she has lost her home, and that she will now be living in other people's
houses.

Lore represents the paradigmatic outsider living successively in five
different houses in England with people with different cultural, social
and religious backgrounds. Segal's account, significantly, starts out
with the child's disappointment at the fairytale fantasy of rescue.
Instead of being taken in by "very special, very beautiful people," Lore
is introduced into a family whose foster-mother she experiences as
"frightening," "ugly" and "fat" (49–50). The disappointment, however, is on both sides, as the Levine family take her in on the assumption of a shared orthodoxy. Thus Segal succeeds in foregrounding the
clashes between expectation and reality on both sides. In retrospect,
Segal describes herself as a "difficult child," rather than "a grateful

survivor," and certainly not as a "happy and cheerful" new family member (ch. 3 passim). Here the communicational gap between child and foster-family seems unbridgeable, as neither gentile nor Jewish foster-families seem to be able to understand the dilemma of the child whose rescue is overshadowed by leaving her parents behind under immediate death threats, and whose desperate obligation and responsibility it is to rescue them by helping to bring them to Britain. All feelings of happiness are thus inevitably accompanied by a sense of guilt, provoking a strategy of self-punishment as Lore habitually refuses what she most desires. This goes along with the repression of emotions, which only come to the surface in the form of physical reactions (she frequently inadvertently wets herself).

Again this episode highlights the connections (and differences) between diasporic narratives. The body that refuses to be contained, that spills over enforced boundaries, that counters attempts at closure can be traced in many post/colonial novels. Particularly in stories about the female post/colonial subject, the body figures prominently as a site of resistance to control and oppression. The works of the Caribbean writer Joan Riley are a case in point: in *The Unbelonging*, for instance, the heroine's history of oppressive objectification goes hand-in-hand with various experiences of bodily fluids "spilling over" of: from incontinence to menstrual flow to nausea.[26] In Segal's autobiography, the body also speaks, but the context is not one of direct oppressive objectification but of well-intentioned gestures of assistance (against the threat of destruction).

In contradistinction to many other children on the *Kindertransport*, Lore Segal is reunited with her parents long before the war ends. In her autobiography, Segal describes the obstacles to be overcome by Jewish refugees, who – apart from having to get a permit from the Nazis – had to procure sponsors as well as a work-permit before they

---

[26] Beate Neumeier, "Crossing Boundaries: Joan Riley's No/Mad Women," in *Engendering Realism and Postmodernism: Contemporary Women Writers in Britain* (Amsterdam: Rodopi, 2001): 311.

were allowed to enter Britain, at that time – as in the case of Lore Segal's parents – mostly to "replenish a diminishing servant class." The next section of Segal's autobiography illustrates the refugees' experiences of a particularly class-based 'normative Englishness' and occasionally its association with antisemitism. In this section of the novel, the predominantly retrospective adult perspective secures the necessary satirical distance to the events. However, this section is dedicated not only to a critical portrayal of a normative Englishness, by which Lore's parents are put in their place as part of the servant class, but also to the intricate complexities of guilt and gratitude. Thus the English employers' expectations of gratitude are illustrated when they agree to Lore's visiting her parents. Mrs Willoughby even kindly allows Mrs Segal to get the linens "to make up your little girl's bed." But she sees to it that the mother does not use the "good sheets" but rather "rust-stained" ones from the back of the linen closet. "'How good you are,' said my mother, close to tears" (85–86). In these descriptions of British–Jewish relations, the connections to other diasporic histories of oppression become clear. Normative Englishness sets the rules: it is expected that foreigners take the place offered; they do not have the luxury of choosing their own.

The difficulties of establishing an identity when confronted with normative Englishness lead many survivors to move on to other regions of the world. The *second part* of the novel portrays diasporic life across the Atlantic, and ends in a multicultural New York, where Lore is finally able to settle as a wife, mother and writer. In this context, New York in the 1950s appears as "home" for different diasporas to such an extent that Lore at one point wants to meet "real" Americans: "All I've ever met in New York are Pakistanis, Indians, and Hungarians, and Israeli, German, and Austrian Jews" (302). Lore's answers to questions about her celebration of Thanksgiving are symptomatic of the in-betweenness of the diasporic subject:

> "We don't celebrate anything anymore. No Christmas because we're Jewish, and no Jewish holiday because we were assimilated

Austrians, and no Austrian holidays because we got thrown out for
being Jewish, and we haven't acquired the American holidays yet"
(303).

Segal describes her identity-formation as a confrontation with different expectations of Jewishness, Englishness, even Austrianness.
She foregrounds the complexity of the diaspora experience by pointing
out the differences and similarities between different Jewish and other
diasporas. This is highlighted in a conversation with an African-
American friend who tries to explain these differences to Lore:

> "And you also thought that because I'm a Negro and write bitter
> stories, you and I were going to sit here and make snide remarks
> about Thanksgiving together. I'm an American, you know. At any
> rate, there's nothing else I am." [...]
> "That's like a Pakistani friend of mine," I said. "He's lived in
> America for eleven years and he's no longer an Oriental, and yet he's
> not an Occidental, either."
> "No," Carter said. "It's not like that at all. I have not, like your
> friend, lost my culture, nor, like you, my country. My isolation is
> peculiarly American." (303)

When, after having lived in many other people's houses, the married
Lore can finally say "we made ourselves a home" (311), this does not
imply the erasure of differences. Lore's past, radically different from
that of her American-born Jewish husband, will always mark her
difference, as the very last words of the novel underscore: "but I [...]
walk gingerly and in astonishment upon this island of my comforts,
knowing that it is surrounded on all sides by calamity" (312).

Staging the *Kindertransport* (Diane Samuels)

"Remembering has to have a present and a future perspective," states
one of the survivors in the film version of the *Kindertransport*. Diane
Samuels' play centres on the importance of memory not only for the
present but – most decisively – for future generations. The published
version of the play opens with excerpts from Karen Gershon's collec-

tion of personal accounts, *We Came as Children*, as well as with references to interviews with survivors (Walter Fulop, Bertha Leverton, Paula Hill, Vera Gissing, and "Lisa"), serving as the autobiographical basis of the play. The play itself, however, focuses not only on the interrelation of past and present, but is most insistently concerned with the future. In this context the intricate interlocking of two different time-levels in this two-act drama (with four scenes) is used to foreground questions of memory and identity, home and belonging, which are linked to the mother–daughter relationships of two successive generations.

The play opens on an everyday – yet decisive – family situation, when the grown-up daughter is about to leave home in order to live on her own. This situation is played out in an attic in a London suburb, where the mother is sorting out things for the daughter to take with her to her new household. In the course of this activity, however, mother and daughter are increasingly confronted with memories of the past. The attic thus appears as the site of memories, carefully stored or, rather, hidden away by the mother, memories that are eventually unearthed by the daughter. The familiar image of the attic as a site of the repressed evokes genre expectations of the uncanny as alluding to family secrets linked to illicit love, intrigue and betrayal. In this context, however, very different notions of the past are associated with the uncanny. Whereas in the film version of the *Kindertransport, Into the Arms of Strangers*, the uncanny spiral staircase leading to the attic was linked to the fear of an impending loss of home and identity through Nazi invasion, in Samuels' play the motif of the attic is linked to the fear of a loss of present identity and home through the unearthing of another identity and home in the past. The use of the uncanny in both media signifies the difficulty of finding images and symbols representing the unrepresentable. As argued above, this reliance on familiar images and recognizable patterns can have the effect of belittling the past, but it can also function as a strategy of defamiliarization.

The play unravels a past unknown to the daughter, Faith. Her mother Evelyn, it turns out, is not the daughter of grandmother Lil, but was a child-refugee named Eva, who came to England on the *Kindertransport*. And another secret is finally revealed, unknown even to Grandma Lil – that Evelyn disclaimed her real mother, Helga, who survived the Holocaust and eventually came to London to take her daughter to America. Eva/Evelyn is thus presented as the prototype of total assimilation (into the British context) and even – most radically – of the annihilation of her Jewish origins. Whereas Lore Segal's novel explores the intricate but decisive effects of ambivalence and in-betweenness on the making of the diasporic subject, Diane Samuels' play traces the consequences of an attempt to erase ambivalence by blending completely into the new context. The play traces three stages in this development and reveals at what cost this new identity was achieved.

The memories surfacing during the play epitomize little Eva's desires and fears after her arrival in England, centering on her desperate attempts (knocking on rich people's doors for support) to get her parents out of Germany, and on her traumatic fear of being left alone and sent away. As the attachment between Eva and her foster-mother grows over the years, her attachment to her real parents seems to retreat, ending in her naturalization as a British citizen and her adoption by her foster-parents. Having been on the *Kindertransport* as a nine-year-old, Eva at the age of sixteen changes her name, and at eighteen gets baptised ("I was cleansed that day. Purified"[27]). This adoption of a new identity is, however, presented not as a smooth transition but as a very painful conscious decision, linked to gratitude and love towards her foster-mother Lil, as well as to feelings of anger towards her real mother Helga, who sent her away and left her to survive on her own.

---

[27] Diane Samuels, *Kindertransport* (London: Nick Hern, 1994): 82. Further page references are in the main text.

The difficulties inherent in Evelyn's self-fashioning have surfaced in the past in a climactic confrontation between Eva/Evelyn and her real mother, who, unbeknownst to Lil, returned to take Eva with her to a new world. In the course of her own confrontation with her daughter Faith, Evelyn remembers this encounter in a haunting scene. During the heated debate between Evelyn and her mother Helga, questions of identity and belonging are posed in increasingly painful ways, as the mother more and more urgently affirms the daughter's former identity: "Why have you lost yourself, Eva? [...] I want my daughter Eva with me. If you find her, Evelyn, by any chance, send her over to find me" (85). The confrontation ends in the daughter's outburst: "I wish you had died," followed by the mother's reply: "I wish you had lived" (86). Significantly, this scene is set in relation to another scene of heated debate, this time between Evelyn and Lil, where Evelyn accuses her foster-mother of also murdering part of her:

> EVELYN: You took ... too much of me. Took me away. You made me betray her.
> LIL   I saved you.
> EVELYN: Part of me is dead because of you. (61)

But even before this acknowledgment of an inner 'split,' Evelyn's obsession with cleaning and with "ordering" and storing things away has always indicated that the past cannot be discarded, but remains an absent presence threatening to surface at any time.

In the play it is the daughter Faith who finds the photos, letters and the diary belonging to the little Jewish girl that Evelyn once was, thus unearthing the buried past to find the truth. But, most importantly, it is through Faith that the implications of the denial of the past for the following generations are eventually thematized, when Faith describes her own feelings of guilt as a child at believing herself responsible for her mother's unhappiness:

> Do you have any idea what it's like having a mother who walks out on you the moment you begin to disagree with her? Who polishes and cleans like a maniac? [...] You're so paranoid you go stiff and sharp at

> every speck of dust or object out of place in your precious home [...]
> You can't go on a train without hyper-ventilating. You cross the road
> if you see a policeman or traffic warden. [...] I've watched your panic
> attacks. All that shaking and gulping like you're going to die. But
> always it's me who's getting things out of proportion because I felt
> scared by them. "So silly and neurotic, Faith." I've always thought it
> was my fault that you were so unhappy. (42–43)

The mutual accusations during this increasingly heated discussion
climax in an exchange reminiscent of the encounter between Evelyn
and her mother Helga (and – to a lesser extent – between Evelyn and
Lil) as Faith's outburst "I could kill you," is countered by Evelyn's
exclamation "I'll bloody kill you first" (44). This scene foregrounds
the similarities and differences between the two former scenes. Each
time it is the repressed feelings in an ambivalent mother–daughter
relationship that erupt violently. But in this second instance the trauma
of second-generation immigrants is revealed in the complex mechanisms of transference. The psychological dilemma repressed in one
family member surfaces in the difficulties of another. The play de-
fends the necessity of knowing and taking care of the past. There is no
identity without memory. Thus Faith's inability to leave her mother is
intricately connected with unknown past of her mother's, as the
latter's inability to let her go is linked with the repression of this past.
Only through the telling of the story of the past can the daughter be
freed to lead a life of her own, and the mother be freed from her
obsessions.

The favourite toys of mother and daughter, ironically, indicate their
owners' decisive difficulties in the process of individuation: The
favourite toy of the daughter, who is unable to leave, was a runaway
train. The favourite plaything of the mother, who has condemned herself to silence, was a mouth-organ. Throughout the play, toys function
as symbolic ties to the past. The only childhood reminders Evelyn
finally wants to pass on to her daughter (apart from the mouth-organ)
are two books: the Jewish Haggadah and the German Ratcatcher story
book. The Ratcatcher functions as a central symbol of ambivalence in

the play, associated with a range of very different situations. The children's story of the Pied Piper of Hamelin is presented in the play as a story of punishment of all children for ingratitude. Thus the story is intimately linked to feelings of guilt: naughty children are taken away by the Ratcatcher and led into an abyss of destruction. The intended educational effect is thus bound up with the fear of children of being sent away because they were bad. As a symbol linking the present to past guilt and future punishment, the Ratcatcher as dark figure haunts the childish imagination.

In the course of the play, Eva/Evelyn interprets a variety of disconcertingly different characters in terms of the ratcatcher. First it is the Nazi official who aptly appears as the menacing figure of the ratcatcher. However, after the arrival of the *Kindertransport* in England, the British officials leading them to their foster-homes are associated with the ratcatcher. In this context the symbol of the ratcatcher evokes the ambivalence of the children, between fear and anger at the parents who sent them away, and guilt because of that anger towards the loved ones staying behind under an immediate death threat. Still later, the foster-mother Lil ambivalently appears as both saviour and ratcatcher, rescuing Eva from Nazi terror but stealing her away from her real mother ("child stealer," 61). And still later, even more hauntingly, the real mother re-appears as a ratcatcher, a stranger with "razor eyes" trying to lure Evelyn into an abyss, away from her English home and seemingly safe identity-construction (86). Perhaps most darkly, at the very end of the play, when Faith leaves Evelyn, "the shadow of the ratcatcher covers the stage" (88), indicating the power of the past over the present as well as evoking fears of the future.

In contradistinction to the film version of the *Kindertransport*, the ambivalence of the toy as symbol of the past is radicalized. Whereas the images of toys and children's books in the film are used as part of a nostalgic flashback into a happy childhood, the figure and story of the ratcatcher are primarily linked to fear, guilt and punishment. Rather than merely invoking an image, Samuels uses a narrative pattern, producing stories of repetition with variation. Moreover, the ratcatcher's story itself is already inherently ambivalent. There are many different versions of the story of the ratcatcher. Some associate the plot with the revenge fantasy of an unpaid ratcatcher who had saved the medieval town of Hamelin from a rat plague; others with historical accounts of the medieval migration of dissatisfied young people away from home into the new (eastern) territories.[28]

At the core of the play are notions of ambivalence linked to the exploration of feelings of survivor *guilt* towards real parents and foster-parents (feelings of divided loyalty and love experienced as betrayal of both sides), as well as towards their own children for denying them a past. At the same time, there is an exploration of feelings of *anger* of survivors at their real parents, whose guilt it is to have sent them away, as well as at their foster-parents, whose guilt it is to want to take the place of their real parents. Consequently, it is only through an acknowledgement of these ambivalences that the diasporic subject can move on, as is shown in the play's exploration of the disastrous psychological effects of a denial of the past, and with it a denial of ambivalence in favour of seemingly clear-cut boundaries.

Diane Samuels' version of the *Kindertransport*, like the other two representations of this historical event, foregrounds the specificity of the Jewish diaspora. At the same time, it allows one to make connections with other diasporas. All representations of the *Kindertransport* stress the importance for the self-definition of the diasporic subject of individual and collective memory. These children experience their transport into alien territory as a diasporic microcosm of their larger macrocosmic affiliation with the Jewish diaspora. In the New York setting, in particular, Segal's depiction of diasporic existence merges with that of other refugees, exiles and expatriates. After the trauma of

---

[28] See Norbert Humburg, *Der Rattenfänger von Hameln: Die berühmte Sagengestalt in Geschichte und Literatur, Malerei und Musik, auf der Bühne und im Film* (Hameln: C.W. Niemeyer, 1990).

separation and the hostility of transit, New York offers a haven for those dispersed and recollected into the diasporic fold.

Works Cited

Assmann, Aleida. *Erinnerungsräume: Formen und Wandlungen des kulturellen Gedächtnisses* (Munich: C.H. Beck, 1999).

——, & Ute Frevert. *Geschichtsvergessenheit/Geschichtsversessenheit: Vom Umgang mit deutschen Vergangenheiten nach 1945* (Stuttgart: Deutsche Verlagsanstalt, 1999).

Assmann, Jan. *Das kulturelle Gedächtnis: Schrift, Erinnerung und politische Identität in frühen Hochkulturen* (Munich: C.H. Beck, 1992).

Bauman, Zygmunt. *Life in Fragments* (Oxford: Blackwell, 1995).

——. *Modernity and Ambivalence* (Ithaca NY: Cornell UP, 1991).

——. *Modernity and the Holocaust* (Ithaca NY: Cornell UP, 1989).

Boyarin, Daniel, & Jonathan Boyarin, ed. *Jews and Other Differences: The New Jewish Cultural Studies* (Minneapolis: U of Minnesota P, 1997).

Brookner, Anita. *Latecomers* (London: Jonathan Cape, 1988).

Cheyette, Bryan. "Englishness und Extraterritorialität: Britisch–Jüdisches Schreiben und die Kultur der Diaspora," in *Jüdische Literatur und Kultur in Grossbritannien und den USA nach 1945*, ed. Beate Neumeier (Wiesbaden: Harrassowitz, 1997): 1–24.

——. "'Ineffable and Usable': Towards a Diasporic British–Jewish writing," *Textual Practice* 10 (Spring 1996): 295–313.

——. "Moroseness and Englishness: The Rise of British-Jewish literature," *Jewish Quarterly* (Spring 1995): 22–26.

——, & Laura Marcus, ed. *Modernity, Culture and "the Jew"* (Cambridge: Polity, 1998).

Cohen, Robin. *Global Diasporas: An Introduction* (Seattle: U of Washington P, 1997).

Figes, Eva. *Little Eden* (New York: Persea, 1978).

Fludernik, Monika. "The Diasporic Imaginary: Postcolonial Reconfigurations in the Context of Multiculturalism," in the present volume, xi–xxxviii.

Gershon, Karen. *We Came as Children* (London: Victor Gollancz, 1966).

Humburg, Norbert. *Der Rattenfänger von Hameln: Die berühmte Sagengestalt in Geschichte und Literatur, Malerei und Musik, auf der Bühne und im Film* (Hameln: C.W. Niemeyer, 1990).

Into the Arms of Strangers. Dir. Mark Jonathan Harris & prod. Deborah Oppenheimer (2000).

Isler, Alan. "A la Recherche Du Cricklewood Perdu," *Jewish Quarterly* (Spring 1996): 20–23.

Kushner, Tony. "Remembering to Forget: Racism and Anti-Racism in Postwar Britain," in Cheyette & Marcus, ed. *Modernity, Culture and "the Jew"*, 226–41.

Neumeier, Beate. "Crossing Boundaries: Joan Riley's No/Mad Women," in *Engendering Realism and Postmodernism: Contemporary Women Writers in Britain*, ed. Beate Neumeier (Postmodern Studies 32; Amsterdam & New York: Rodopi, 2001): 303–16.

Rhys, Jean. *Wide Sargasso Sea* (1966; Harmondsworth: Penguin, 1997).

Rohan, Zina. *Sandbeetle* (London: Hodder & Stoughton, 1993).

Rose, Gillian. "Beginnings of the Day: Fascism and Representation," in Cheyette & Marcus, ed. *Modernity, Culture and "the Jew"*, 226–41.

——. *Judaism and Modernity: Philosophical Essays* (Oxford: Blackwell, 1993).

Samuels, Diane. *Kindertransport* (London: Nick Hern, 1995).

Segal, Lore. *Other People's Houses* (1958; New York: New Press, 1994).

Young, James. "Arts of Jewish Memory in a Postmodern Age," in Cheyette & Marcus, ed. *Modernity, Culture and "the Jew"*, 211–25.

Young, James. *Texture of Memory: Holocaust Memorials and Meaning* (New Haven CT: Yale UP, 1993).

∅

AMERICAN, BRITISH AND OTHER DIASPORAS: MULTICULTURALISMS AT PLAY

FEROZA JUSSAWALLA

Cultural-Rights Theory
A View from the US–Mexican Border

T
HERE IS A POEM by Barbara Kingsolver, based on an
actual incident along the US–Mexican border in Arizona,
that highlights some of the constant harassment of immigrants and the lack of 'cultural rights', even human rights, in US
courthouses:

Refuge

For Juana, raped by immigration officers and deported

Give me your hand,
He will tell you. Reach
Across seasons of barbed wire
And desert. Use the last
of your hunger
to reach me. I will
take your hand.
Take it.

First
He will spread it
Fingers from palm
To look inside,
See it offers nothing.
Then

With a sharp blade
Sever it.

The rest he throws back
to the sea of your
blood brothers.
But he will keep your hand,
clean, preserved in a glass case
under lights:
Proof
he will say
of the great
desirability
of my country.[1]

The intention of this essay is to show how contemporary "critical theory" betrays immigrants and people of colour in various situations. It will be argued that the 'cultural rights' of diasporic communities cannot be defended via such concepts as 'hybridity' or 'liberal multiculturalism'.

I live on the US–Mexico border in Las Cruces, New Mexico, and work in El Paso, Texas. From the classrooms in which I teach, I see the *colonias* across the river and sometimes even the *mojados*, the 'wet ones' (called "wetbacks" by the Americans), making their way across the dusty river, which often does not even have a teacup of water. The greatest danger is the stray bullet from the border patrol – or the US Marines patrolling the border – the kind that, in Redford, Texas, killed a young Hispanic goatherd called Esquivel Hernández, who was born in the USA. The atrocities of the Border Patrol and the immigration service are many, and often these are not even cases that make it to the courthouse. But when these atrocities are fuelled by other immigrants and theories written by people of colour that can be construed by the "white majority" as supportive of their positions, then we must pause

---

[1] Barbara Kingsolver, *Another America/Otra America* (Seattle: U of Washington P, 1991): 21–22.

and question. At the borders, there are subtle civil atrocities against people of colour, immigrants, minorities, and usually brown-skinned children of immigrants that too often do not make it to the courthouse.

The politics of race, in this, probably the most indigenously multicultural part of the USA, are intense and complicated. To obtain justice via legislation is difficult, because these politics of race do not really split across party lines. For instance, in the 2001 nomination of Linda Chavez as Labor Secretary, the *El Paso Times*, the newspaper most supportive of Hispanics and immigration, on 11 January 2001 lauded Chavez for having "a long track record of aiding immigrants, particularly to find employment, to learn to speak English etc." Linda Chavez, though on record as being against affirmative action, is seen as a victim of liberal democratic racism. After all, she was sheltering an immigrant and helping her, albeit possibly exploiting her. In fact, here in El Paso, where it is very common for most people at all levels to engage the assistance of a Mexican household worker as a way of helping their poor neighbors to the South, the Chavez case is clearly seen as the shutting-out of a person of colour. The *El Paso Times* feels that Zoe Baird's case was decidedly different from Chavez's.[2] But here, where the hiring of illegals by ASARCO, the now defunct copper-mining company, to counter a strike has always been seen as an opportunity for immigrants, particularly Hispanics, Chavez is seen as a victim in much the same way as Elián Gonzales, the little Cuban boy who was washed ashore in 1999 and returned by the Clinton administration to his Fidel Castro-supported father.

---

[2] Editorial, "Chavez did Right Thing," *El Paso Times* (11 January 2001). The questioning of the Linda Chavez nomination has drawn much fire from local Hispanics, except from the 'radical' columnists Patricia Gonzales and Roberto Rodriguez, who simply asked why Latinos were not asked by the national media to comment on the Linda Chavez case; see Patricia Gonzalez, "Hispanics forming Fifth Pillar," *Las Cruces Sun News* (13 January 2001): B-5. The *Las Cruces Sun News* runs a "Sound Off!" column where many women have called in to ask why male candidates are not questioned about their household help.

The Texas Democratic Representative Silvestre Reyes, as chief of the Border Patrol, on the other hand, was the initiator of "Operation Hold the Line." Under advisement by Janet Reno and the Clinton administration, he requested more border patrol agents, and this may have been directly responsible for the shooting of the American-born goatherd by the Marines patrolling the border. While Representative Reyes has done much to defuse Hispanic issues, in some minds there remains the lingering sense of a *vendido* – a sell-out who, once he gets his immigration papers, closes the door to others. The Republican Senator Phil Gramm, however, at the beginning of 2001, advocated more open immigration and the removal of background checks. Gramm, together with Pete Dominici, the Republican Senator from New Mexico, seems to be working with other Republican senators to make the Mexican President Vicente Fox's "dream" of an open border possible. The Clinton–Gore administration remained non-committal, approving expenditures for "1,300 miles of road and fence, [and to] rig up spy cameras and thousands of portable floodlights. The number of Border Patrol agents doubled from 4,000 to 8,000 between 1993 and 1999."[3] Of course, this is a classically 'capitalist' move, since immigration helps American enterprise. This in itself divides Marxist and Labor supporters. Megan Stack's article presents both points of view, saying, on the one hand, that "legal migration could redeem millions of undocumented workers squeezed out of their homelands by blistering poverty and sparse jobs," and on the other that "Economists say that the unfettered flow of Mexican workers could drive labor wages lower and strain social services to the breaking point, particularly in the border states." However, Stack shows that this has not always been true. The Roosevelt–Bracero programme brought in Mexican workers to help replenish the dwindling US labour pool, and the (Republican) Eisenhower government drove them out in 1954.

---

[3] Megan K. Stack, "Pledges of Open Border draw skepticism," *Las Cruces Sun News* (3 December 2000): A-12.

So border politics have a particularity that is hard to pin down, in much the same way as 'multicultural liberalism' and its effects on legislation and the making of laws to uphold in the courthouse are hard to pin down in our increasingly pluralistic society. Here on the border, the Clinton administration was seen as the most xenophobic, as I shall be indicating, particularly in the case of Elián González. Here the Republican Governor of neighbouring New Mexico, also of "legalize drugs" notoriety, is seen as a hero on account of his legislation to allow the Native American gambling industry, the casinos, to stay legal.

Here, in New Mexico–West Texas, the Native American, the Hispanic and white (mostly Texan or, as the Hispanics put it, Tejano) cultures meet. Into this mix comes the daily steady stream of Mexican immigrants and illegal workers whom most of the Hispanic Americans disavow. There are as many cultures to Hispano-Americana here as there are local cultures. Some Hispanics see themselves as descendants of Castilians and intend to keep their race pure. Others see themselves as Hispanic Americans, born in the *Estados Unidos*, to which they owe their allegiance and from which they expect rights, the birthright of all Americans.[4] Yet others see themselves as *Chicano*–chico–Mexicano, US residents with allegiance to the mother country, seeking power for oppressed Hispanic US citizens. Yet all three of these Hispanic-American groups, together with the tri-culture of the region, harbour resentments against all other immigrants: Mexican, Guatemaltecans, and even South Asians like myself, or the boatloads of Chinese arriving on Mexican and Central American shores and then, by sealed boxcars and half-dead, into the Spanish-style squares or *plazas* of these US border towns. No one wants a piece of the all-

---

[4] I use the term 'American' throughout this essay as referring to the citizens of the USA rather than as *norteamericanos*, for example, only because both the British and the Mexicans from whom my examples are drawn refer to them as such.

American pie made of milk and honey taken away from them, however resentful of the US government they may be.

On Sunday, 13 February 2000, the *El Paso Times* intervened with a review of Susan Moller Okin's *Is Multiculturalism Bad for Women?*.[5] The book, of course, immediately became fodder for those who would block immigration and curtail the rights of women and people of colour, perpetuating the stereotype that Third-World women are trapped in cultures which promote the veiling of women, marriage by capture, clitoridectomy, and other barbarous Muslim rituals. In a recent case, Britain, for instance, is planning to charge parents who force arranged marriages on their children with abduction or to prevent the immigration of the spouse. Britain's Junior Home Minister, Mike O'Brien, said: "Multicultural sensitivity is not an excuse for moral blindness."[6] The review of Okin's collection then turned to the Rushdie controversy and to the burning of the *Satanic Verses*, to point out that "certain cultures accept and practice [the] belief that people are not owed equal respect and concern," without making any mention of whether Rushdie or the present reviewer showed the same concern for people of cultures and contexts other than their own. Homi Bhabha ends his essay in Okin's collection with what seems to be a plea for his usual cause, hybridity:

> An agonistic liberalism questions the "foundationalist" claims of the metropolitan, "western" liberal tradition with as much persistence as it interrogates and resists the fundamentalisms and ascriptions of indigenous orthodoxy. An awareness of the ambivalent and "unsatisfied" histories of the liberal persuasion allow "us" – postcolonial critics,

---

[5] Paul K. Haeder, "The Problem with Diversity," *El Paso Times* (20 February 2000). See also Susan Moller Okin and respondents, *Is Multiculturalism Bad for Women?*, ed. Joshua Cohen, Matthew Howard & Martha C. Nussbaum (Princeton NJ: Princeton UP, 2000).

[6] Richard Ford, "Abduction Charges to Halt Forced Marriages," *The Times* (London; 30 June 2000): 12.

multiculturalists, or feminists – to join in the unfinished work of creating a more viable, intra-cultural community of rights.[7]

What such an intracultural community of rights would entail, we are not told, and in this specific case, in El Paso, what it would do for the uneasily resting "cultural diversity" was unclear. Bhiku Parekh, while seeming to counter Okin and Will Kymilicka, sounded an even more ominous note:

> If minority cultures are to be required to conform to fundamental liberal values there is no reason to stop with the equality of the sexes. One could equally consistently require them to respect such other fundamental liberal values as autonomy, individualism, choice and open internal debate.[8]

This could easily be misread in a community with a growing Muslim presence, a new mosque, and a plea to allow their children to observe Ramadan in a horrified school system. An ordinary reader picking up this book upon reading the newspaper review could easily interpret this as an injunction to make culturally or religiously different people conform to Western liberalism, if not to Western values *per se*. This is a position very similar to that of the conservative fundamentalist Christians, whether Baptists or charismatic Catholics, who knock on our doors almost every day in this part of the country. Soon after the review appeared, both my students and people I knew asked if I'd had a clitoridectomy, how I had managed to get out of an arranged marriage and being in purdah, etc. The most dangerous result was that the reviewer began to subject an Hispanic female graduate student in the department to email invective.

I am a lighter-skinned Parsi from India, who is often mistaken for Hispanic or Latino. Being mistaken for Hispanic, I am often subject to the racism and exclusion that target Hispanic peoples. Often I am

---

[7] Homi K. Bhabha, "Liberalism's Sacred Cow," in Okin, *Is Multiculturalism Bad for Women?*, 84.

[8] Bhikhu Parekh, "A Varied Moral World," in Okin, *Is Multiculturalism Bad for Women?*, 72.

embraced by Hispanics. But, when I am addressed in Spanish and am
unable to reply, a chill pervades the air. "*Soy de la India, pero también
de Nuevo Mexico*," I explain. But at least I am able to explain myself.
Every day, as I see more immigrants like Barbara Kingsolver's Juana
flailed in the name of upholding the USA's laws, mostly because of
their race or difference and only because they attempted to make their
lives the slightest bit better, or more *chicanas* denied jobs and the
rights and privileges afforded to working "white" men and women,
particularly in the universities, where radical ideologies are supposed
to prevail, I get more *chicana*, more militant, and more angrily assertive of my individual and particular rights, and of my cultural indigeneity, and feel less of a 'curry'-mixed hybrid (though I suppose the
very act of getting more *chicana* is a hybridization). I move increasingly towards recognizing particularities and indigeneities based on
the particular 'contexts of situation' that determine 'rights', that are
valid in the courthouse, that provide the ability to work, that provide
accessibility to educational opportunities, etc. I don't say here 'equal
accessibility', only because I know from the experience of losing an
administrative position based on pregnancy disability, an issue not
supported either by feminists or by unions, that 'equality' can end up
re-affirming the 'rights' of white males. In particular, culture- and
gender-based rights need to be recognized and created for legislative
purposes so that individuals can count on those rights being available
to them rather than seeing what the court does on an ad-hoc basis.
Increasingly I feel that 'radical ideologies', Marxist theories like those
of the cultural critics, particularly those that are anti-multiculturalism,
collude with standard conservatism, exclude the needy and the 'different' from the mainstream, shut the door on immigrants and *différance*,
and exploit rather than protect from exploitation those who most need
protection and rights. It is this collusion that I am most interested in
uncovering, to show how contemporary 'cultural-rights theory' betrays
immigrants and people of colour in various situations. The many and
diverse examples are necessary to the case I make, for they show that

the theory merely theorizes and as usual fails to consider the particularities of the actual 'human' situations. When I questioned Homi
Bhabha about this in 1998, he replied point-blank that he was interested in "high theory," not in actualities.

I realize that particularities of 'race' are complicated as society
itself gets hybridized racially. As college affirmative-action admission
gets increasingly contested in the courthouse, one asks: What are the
rights, for instance, of 'mixed race' individuals? Does a child of a
mixed-immigrant-'white' American background qualify for the same
minority rights? College counsellors go out to geographical areas like
mine, looking for the minority entrant, and admit someone with a 900
SAT [Scholarly Aptitude Test] score, while a child of mixed race with
a 1425 SAT score, going to the same public school, with the same resources, is not seen as qualifying for minority status. At my own
campus, in the University of Texas system, the Hopwood legislation
seeks to ban affirmative-action legislation precisely to protect the
rights of such individuals, but, at the same time, this policy is seen as a
conservative backlash against allowing minorities into the mainstream.

Living in El Paso, an area of culture-contact and of an admixture of
diaspora peoples, is rather like living in London. The parallels with the
UK are many, and I will refer to them in a moment to show how the
overwhelming presence of nativized diasporic peoples draws one's
attention constantly to *cultural rights* being invoked and countered.
But first here are some examples again from New Mexico. Five years
ago, a Native American driver, Gordon House, returning from a
Christmas ritual on a *pueblo* road, off 1–40 between Albuquerque and
Grants, New Mexico, crashed into a white family traveling on Christmas Eve. The defence claimed a genetic proclivity for alcohol together
with the necessity of imbibing alcohol in Native American religious
rituals.[9] Such a defence only leads to stereotyping and further dis-

---

   [9] Stanley Fish, "Boutique Multiculturalism, or Why Liberals Are Incapable
of Thinking about Hate Speech," *Critical Inquiry* 23 (Winter 1997): 378–95.

tancing of Native American peoples from the mainstream. Again, for instance, when Mothers against Drunk Drivers attempted to pass a law against driving with an open container of alcohol, LULAC, the League of United Latin American Citizens, countered that this law would occasion the violation of Hispanic civil rights, since it would tend to expose large percentages of Hispanics to search and seizure. This only led to the outcry stereotyping Hispanics as "murderous drunk drivers."

Homi Bhabha, in a lecture given at an NEH Institute in London during the summer of 1998, talked about how, in the wake of "politics of identity," "multiculturalism" had become a "new kind of holding term," for very specific issues, such as "cultural defense cases" where "minority individuals and multi-cultural and multi-ethnic societies" who have criminal charges against them for what seemed to be criminal acts, say "Well I'm very sorry. It might seem to you that I was performing a criminal act, but in my culture, this is precisely acceptable." Bhabha felt that such notions of rights invoked very specific notions of subjectivities. These, of course, do not fit into his framework of hybridity. He raised the question of "Who is one of us?" Who does belong in what culture? Can we really define that today?

However, as the world changes and although we come together in migrations and metropolitaneity, the denying of specific cultural rights or needs, based on culture and origin (another extremely problematic term to define), needs such as that of an immigrant on the border for shelter and work, that s/he cannot find in his or her home country, becomes an issue of denying human rights. Hybridity occurs with culture contact; culture contact presumes migrations and movement. But if, in the name of hybridity, we deny cultural rights, we in effect shut the door on the migration and movement that make hybridity happen. We therefore deny, for instance, the right of a black person to move to

---

Fish talks here, for instance, of the Native Americans' right to use peyote in their rituals.

a dominant white culture and live there safely, despite the colour of his skin.

Take, for instance, the situation recently under discussion in Britain following the murder of Stephen Lawrence, a black youth aged sixteen, who was waiting for a bus with a friend when he was assaulted by five white youths on 22 April 1993. Clearly, Stephen Lawrence was "not one of us," and there was no Conradian Marlow among the five white youths, asking "who is one of us?" of that unthinking gang murder of a boy who was simply looking out for the bus, whether it was coming or not. I mention Conrad's Marlow because Bhabha used him as his literary example to show that we cannot identify "who is one of us" any more – there are no specificities of race. In this one instance, we can see what Stanley Fish means when he says in his essay "Boutique Multiculturalism" that "we have to make special adjustments to the specific requirements of distinctive groups."[10] We have to recognize the particularities of black skin and the reaction it produces within some "white dominant" groups. Fish's notion of multiculturalism (though Bhabha would say it is the same position as his, where he simply does not want liberals to nod towards "cultural diversity") is actually one that we can apply to the theories of post-colonial cultural critics. Fish describes his multiculturalist as resisting

> the force of the culture he appreciates at precisely the point at which it matters most to its strongly committed members, the point at which the African American tries to make the content of his culture the content of his children's education, the point at which a Native American wants to practice his religion as its ancient rituals direct him to, the point at which anti-abortionists directly confront the evil that they believe is destroying the moral fiber of the country, the point at which Mormons seek to be faithful to the word and the practices of their prophets and elders.[11]

---

[10] Fish, "Boutique Multiculturalism," 382, summarizing Charles Taylor's position.

[11] Fish, "Boutique Multiculturalism," 379.

This is actually a very interesting definition, because one could accuse Bush's cabinet of having been formed by a boutique multiculturalist. In the light of what we have seen of the Linda Chavez controversy, we could accuse Bush of being embarrassed by what seems a standard "Hispanic" practice – hiring illegal Latino help. We could apply this to our "liberals" and feminists unable to accept Ashcroft. But we could also apply this to our cultural critics who want acceptance for themselves as "third worlders or people of colour" in the white academic worlds of America and Britain, yet do not want to accept those persons, from their own background, whose religious beliefs conflict with their "supposed gut feeling" for Salman Rushdie's freedom of speech. Should the postcolonial theorists not want to be the "third worlders" or "subalterns" of "white academia," then surely they are committing Linda Chavez's and Dinesh D'Souza's mistake of disavowing their identities in their success. It is a very interesting circular trap/corner that "cultural criticism" has backed itself into. It is the phenomenon that I have christened the "How Homi Bhabha became Dinesh D'Souza" syndrome.

Hybridity is meant to escape "binaristic Manichaeanism." It is meant to get past the "essentialism of binaries," or the essentialism of identity origins such as "Indianness" for people from India, for instance. Bhabha suggests that there is an "irreducible element to identity."[12] Tell that to Stephen Lawrence's parents! Hybridity does not escape the essentialisms of racial features and in fact begins to sound an awful lot like Fish's citation of Stephen Rockefeller arguing for our universal identity as human beings. Even "boutique multiculturalism," granting the superficial right to protection, is better than arguing that the specific right not be invoked because it focuses on particularities. In this case, in focusing on particularities of race, the British conservatives have capitalized on the situation. The London Metropolitan

---

[12] Bart Moore–Gilbert, *Postcolonial Theory: Contexts, Practices, Politics* (London: Verso, 1997): 126.

police, found racist in not conducting the Lawrence enquiry properly, are supposedly demoralized and not stopping and searching enough black people. According to the Conservative William Hague, they are thereby causing more crimes against blacks such as the murder of Damilola Taylor.[13] Mr Hague's implication, focusing on particularities, of course, sounds like that of the majority "white" perspective in the Southwestern USA about "drunk-driving Hispanics and Native Americans": that "blacks" are murderous people killing each other and therefore have to be protected by the white government from each other – the same argument as in the Rushdie Affair, where Rushdie, himself probably seen as "a barbarian," had to be protected from "barbarians of his own type," both by himself and his supporters, the postcolonial critics, and the dominant British and American "white" hegemony. According to Mr Hague, "A conservative government would not allow 'political correctness' to come in the way of law enforcement. And it would have an honest debate about crime, policing and race relations."[14]

What Hague is arguing, Stanley Fish would see as Charles Taylor's "inspired adhoccery," each situation-of-crisis as an "opportunity for improvisation."[15] In his talk given at the NEH Institute on Postcolonial Literatures, Bhabha said that issues of globalization, multiculturalism, and the politics of identities raise particular matters of subjectivities:

> These were the very specific issues which invoked the notion of subject, which invoked the notion of identity, which invoked the notion of right, which invoked the notion of justice, which invoked the notion of choice.[16]

---

[13] Bagehot, "Playing the Race Card Again," *The Economist* (23 December 2000): 88.

[14] Bagehot, "Playing the Race Card Again," 88.

[15] Fish, "Boutique Multiculturalism," 386.

[16] All quotation are taken from Homi Bhabha's lecture given at the Stuart Hall Conference of the Centre for Sociological and Social Anthropological Studies at the Open University in London in 1998.

But, Bhabha said, "because culture is translational and transitional and because culture is in a process of change, these categories that migrants and minorities identify with, cannot be hard and fast." This leads to a new term in Bhabha's work, "jurisdictional unsettlement," which, as I said before, is a kind of "inspired adhoccery,"[17] the type we see in William Hague. Black British citizens have come to see Hague as a political "ambulance chaser."[18] While Tony Blair has accused Mr Hague of playing the race card, the latter's rhetoric of "one nation" sounds incredibly like the rhetoric not only of Stephen Rockefeller, whom Fish criticizes, but also of our postcolonial theorists who celebrate "hybridity" – one nation as a melting-pot of "cultural difference" – where the difference can be recognized, but is subsumed under "cultural diversity." To speak up for "cultural diversity" – a certain component of Native American ritual – or a Hispanic "right" would consist in the "recognition of pre-given cultural contents," according to Bhabha.[19] Cultural diversity for Bhabha is a radical rhetoric of separation which he, together with several theorists, ascribes to the "liberals" who position themselves as though they were radicals. Through recognizing "cultural difference," Bhabha would like to move to a place of "hybridity, figuratively speaking, where the construction of a political object that is new, *neither the one nor the other*, properly alienates our political expectations" and changes "the moment of politics."[20] It is uncannily like Mr Hague's position, where difference between black and white is recognized but subsumed under some new protective, policed space rather than allowed to coexist independently and peaceably, everywhere, rooted in epistemologically

---

[17] Charles Taylor, "The Rushdie Controversy," *Public Culture* 2 (Fall 1989): 118–22.

[18] Black Information Links, "Hague's Hate from a Black Perspective," www.blink.org.uk.

[19] Homi K. Bhabha, *The Location of Culture* (London & New York: Routledge, 1994): 34.

[20] Bhabha, *The Location of Culture*, 34.

recognized cultures. It is the similarities in rhetoric between Bhabha and the dominant conservative position that make me argue that the politics of hybridity and "anti-multiculturalism," so espoused by our critical theorists, is a dangerous politics of subsuming conservatism, the old-fashioned American melting-pot, or, like Shaw's Professor Higgins, of asking "Why can't *they* be like *me*?" Ironically, Hanif Kureishi in his essay "Bradford" quotes a Sir Michael Shaw, MP for Scarborough, speaking to the Muslim community of Bradford:

> You have come into our community, [...] and you must become part of that community. All branches must lead to one trunk, which is the British way of life. We mustn't retire to our own communities and shut ourselves out. Yet you have felt you have needed schools of your own [...] [21]

The Rushdie Affair and the Elián Gonzales Case

It was in Britain with the so-called Rushdie Affair, the Muslim protests over the publishing of the *Satanic Verses*, that 'cultural-rights theory'[22] came to the forefront. Ironically, it is misnamed, because the theorists who most write about "cultural-rights theory" are normally against the cultural rights of specific groups such as the Muslims. This is because, as Kureishi pointed out so long ago in his essay on Bradford, the word "culture" had become a "dirty" word, one that in Britain was being bandied about in places like Southall and Bradford by the "New Right" in order to marginalize those seen to be outside the culture. This we need to rectify, making it a term *for* our "cultural rights,"

---

[21] Hanif Kureishi, "Bradford," *Granta* 20 (Winter 1986): 156.

[22] Charles Taylor, Will Kymlika, Michael Walzer, Stanley Fish and Bikhu Parekh all ascribe the beginning of "Cultural Rights Theory" to the Rushdie Affair. For an overview both of the Rushdie Affair and of cultural rights theory subsequent to the Rushdie Affair, see Daniel O'Neill, "Multicultural Liberals and the Rushdie Affair: A Critique of Kymlicka, Taylor and Walzer," *Review of Politics* 61 (Spring 1999): 219-50.

our right to be different and yet *not* marginalized and stereotyped. Postcolonial critics, including the usual defenders of Islam such as Edward Said, decried the "rights" of the Muslims in Bradford and Brick Lane to protest against the book and to invoke Britain's outdated blasphemy laws in order to ban the book. Supposedly, "Multicultural Liberalism," in the name of tolerance and acceptance of a multicultural society, promulgated the rights of the Muslims who objected to *The Satanic Verses*. Daniel O'Neill, in his article entitled "Multicultural Liberals and the Rushdie affair," quotes from Will Kymlicka:

> It was this case, perhaps more than any single event, which has led people in the West to think carefully about the nature of 'multiculturalism' and the extent to which the claims of minority cultures can or should be accommodated within a liberal democratic regime.[23]

Muslim demands to have the book banned clashed with the views of those very liberals who had spoken up not only for Rushdie but also for Muslims' rights, and who also did not believe in censorship. The protesting Muslims were therefore seen as barbaric. In pushing this position, Rushdie's friends, postcolonial critics like Edward Said[24] and Homi Bhabha writing in his support, further bolstered the image already created by Rushdie, in his book, of Muslim immigrants as uncouth, uncivilized and basically unfit to immigrate to the metropole. Rushdie, for instance, portrayed the immigrants Gibreel Farishta and Saladin Chamcha as unable to dress like the British, stuffing their mouths with bacon so that it and its grease are dripping out the sides, when as Muslims they were not supposed to be eating pork, and as behaving crudely towards British women. He painted a dismal picture of Muslim communities in Britain. This is an image no different from

---

[23] O'Neill, "Multicultural Liberals," 220.

[24] I have discussed this at length in my article "Resurrecting the Prophet: the Case of Salman, the Otherwise," *Public Culture* 2 (Fall 1989): 106–17. See also Feroza Jussawalla, "Rushdie's Dastan-e-Dilruba," *diacritics* 26.1 (Spring 1996): 50–73.

that portrayed by the British school principal Honeyford in Bradford.[25] In fact, the whole stance in the book is that of the Rugby-educated Rushdie looking down on the crude Bangladeshis of East London. Ironically, Rushdie and his postcolonial supporters had previously criticized metropolitan communities and governments as racist and exclusionist, when even individuals like them were not embraced inclusively. Witness, for example, Kureishi's essay "Bradford." Now the metropole was held up as the bastion of civilization, a binary opposite to the Manichaean Iran of the Ayatollah. Allan Bloom best characterized this when he wrote that Rushdie, Said et al. were criticizing the Western cultural establishment, but when threatened "came running back like a herd of elephants to the principles of Milton and Locke."[26] Stanley Fish distinguishes between "boutique multiculturalism" and "strong multiculturalism" by saying that strong multiculturalists can and will maintain their support for multiculturalism even when it encounters something that threatens what "constitutes the core of our identities."[27]

Ironically, then, postcolonial theorists supporting Rushdie became "boutique multiculturalists" because they could not take seriously the "core values of the cultures" they had been speaking for, because the cultures, like those of the Asian immigrants they had been speaking for, drew a line against blaspheming against and criticizing their religious leaders. In the *Satanic Verses*, Rushdie calls the Ayatollah and the Prophet Mohammed "haramzadas" or "bastards," perhaps presuming that the principle of freedom of speech would allow this to pass jokingly. What he didn't realize was that, when the core values of those immigrant cultures clashed with the core values of his British public-school education, which taught him freedom of speech, he

---

[25] Kureishi, "Bradford," 156.
[26] Alan Bloom, "A Cultural Critic Answers his Own," *Wall Street Journal* (30 March 1989): A12.
[27] Stanley Fish, "Boutique Multiculturalism," 378–83.

would come out the loser and the whole issue of who should tolerate whom, or, as Bhabha would put it, "who is one of us," was threatened.

∅

Daniel O'Neill's division of multiculturalism into "strong multiculturalism" and "weak multiculturalism" is an interesting one. He associates "strong" multiculturalism with the work of Will Kymlicka, Charles Taylor, and Michael Walzer. O'Neill writes:

> Strong multiculturalists are committed, in certain circumstances, to the defense of differential (or special) citizenship rights for multicultural groups based on their culture. The second level of multicultural argument I refer to (for lack of a better term) as 'weak' multiculturalism. Weak multiculturalists do not argue for differential citizenship rights, but seek a range of different goals. In the USA, these have included for example, expanding the academic curriculum to reflect more fully the contributions of minorities.[28]

This last has definitely been true of the postcolonial theorists who are now writing about cultural rights. While they fought the fight to expand the curriculum multiculturally, in the shape and form of radicalism, they took away the rights of certain cultural groups, especially immigrants. It is interesting here to note that now, after consolidating themselves in high academic positions in the name of expanding their curriculum and exploring the Orientalist bias in academia, individuals like Edward Said are also shutting the door on future teachers of the expanded curriculum by calling for a return to the teaching of the canon, especially Swift.

Their radical critiques of immigrant groups such as the Bradford Muslims, in works such as *The Satanic Verses*, helped to feed the paternalistic stereotypes of "liberal democrats" about some cultural groups practising barbarianisms from which they need to be saved.

---

[28] O'Neill, "Multicultural Liberals," 220.

Every time there is an article in *Glamour*[29] on the Taliban's excesses against women refusing to wear the chador or burkha in Afghanistan, or in *Redbook* about female genital mutilation, it becomes a cultural-rights issue in the USA with repercussions that limit the rights of innocent foreigners, foreign-born nationals, and immigrants. The tone is usually the same as in the UK: "Why don't they go back to where they came from?" Patricia Gonzales and Roberto Rodriguez attest to this.[30] Kureishi makes yet another important point: "Americans, Australians, Italians and Irish are not immigrants. It isn't Rupert Murdoch, Clive James, or Kiri Te Kanawa who will be in their way: it is black people."[31] Interestingly, this is not just a class issue, or an assimilation issue, or a hybridity issue either. Witness the repeated refusal to give Mohammed Al Fayed, the owner of Harrod's, an immigrant visa, long before his son's involvement with Princess Diana.

All this, of course, fed into the already existing American fear of Muslims as fundamentalists, who, for some reason, unlike the US Christian fundamentalists, were seen as terrorists. The Reagan government and the Bush government in their "Desert Storm" fever bought all this. By the time the Clinton government was in office, an innocent Egyptian professor going home was arrested at the Oklahoma City airport for the Oklahoma City bombing when in fact it was a "good" "white" "conservative" Christian fundamentalist with his rather uncivilized mix of fertilizer who was the culprit. Echoes of the pre-9/11 World Trade Center bombings rang in Janet Reno's ears as she still enforced background checks on foreigners, despite evidence to the contrary. These background checks have, as of 8 June 2000, taken the shape of vigilance over foreign students. John Ritter's news story in *USA Today*, "Students Decry Idea of Monitoring," reports on "a

---

[29] For instance, "I could have been executed for...," *Glamour* (March 2000): 286–300.

[30] Patricia Gonzales & Roberto Rodriguez, "Keeping the Barbarians at Bay," *Las Cruces Sun News* (9 January 2001): B4.

[31] Hanif Kureishi, "Bradford," 168.

government commission's recommendation that they (foreign students) be more closely monitored for ties to terrorism." Fortunately, it is at my university in the University of Texas system that international students are most resisting this effort. Ritter reports and quotes Jerry Wilcox, our director of International Students:

> University officials point out that the only student terrorist connection uncovered so far was that one of the World Trade Center Bombers, had attended college in Kansas before dropping out. To use that rationale for monitoring 500,000 plus students because they might be wanting to do something similar seems to be stretching the point.[32]

The same *USA Today* article quotes Ron Sexena, a twenty-three-year-old Indian graduate student saying, about the Clinton administration's background-checks programme, that, yes, "the government should be able to investigate the origin and past history of U.S. visa applicants," but that it makes it harder for "legitimate candidates to get legitimate papers processed." In India, where a small bribe of even twenty dollars can stop somebody's visa for going overseas, or where such a bribe can stop someone's passport from being issued, where the trade on Colaba Causeway for false passports is intense and heated in the desperation of engineers and doctors to get out of the country, this poses immense problems and inequities.

In the Rushdie Affair, postcolonial critics would not or could not support the Muslim fundamentalists, the binary opposite of themselves. They viewed these Muslims as models of those who follow the practices of their local cultures to the point of failing to respect the practices of other cultures – by calling for the death of an author "whose work was seen as blasphemous."[33] In fact, as Charles Taylor put it in his essay "The Rushdie Controversy," what people were doing who were upholding Rushdie's freedom of speech was "endorsing the

---

[32] John Ritter, "Students Decry Idea of Monitoring," *USA Today* (8 June 2000): 03A.

[33] Fish, "Boutique Multiculturalism," 379.

superiority of some cultures over others"[34] – in fact, that of Western culture, which upheld freedom of speech in the face of deep-rooted religious feeling among the Muslims. Such endorsement of Western culture's superiority is really very un-postcolonial, especially for those who have written against colonial oppression:

> The acute problem arises from the fact that international migration is making all societies less culturally uniform. There are large Muslim minorities in "Christendom." We are going to need some *inspired adhoccery* in years to come.[35]

Taylor is actually suggesting a compromise; but it is from here on – from the Rushdie Affair and its cultural critique onward – that we see the suspicions of immigrants who adhere to their cultures begin to multiply. Dr Tariq Madood, a Senior fellow at the Policy Studies Institute in Britain, has coined a phrase for this – "cultural racism":

> Cultural Racism is the willingness of white working class youths to incorporate young black men and women into their culture, and even emulate them, while hardening their attitudes against groups not seen to be assertively different and not trying to fit in, such as Asians and Muslims. Religion and individual ethnic identities should be the new touchstones. We need a more pluralized conception of racial equality in Britain and one from which Americans may learn something.[36]

Rushdie's right to "blaspheme" has been protected, but irreparable damage has been done to the image of the immigrant and the Muslim. Indeed, we in the USA could learn from this, particularly as several South Asians discover that we really do not have the privileging rights of Hispanics and blacks, and as we increasingly see Muslims and individuals with "differing" religions discriminated against. This was exacerbated during the Clinton administration, for not only did the Mexican immigrant groups see his administration as xenophobic but

---

[34] Charles Taylor, "The Rushdie Controversy," 119.
[35] Taylor, "The Rushdie Controversy," 121.
[36] Stuart Wavell, "Wrestling for an Equal Share," *Sunday Times* (26 March 1995), Report: 8-10.

(as pointed out before in the case of the Muslim faculty member being stopped at the Oklahoma city airport and in the case of Janet Reno's special institution of background checks for immigrants) the Clinton administration was seen as the most xenophobic administration the USA has ever had. No comment is necessary on developments since 11 September 2001. The rights of all the rest of us, from immigrants to women of colour to, most recently, the foreign students on the Berkeley campus of the University of California have been taken away in the belief that multiculturalism is bad for democracy and leads to terrorism. It was and is in the name of supporting freedom of speech, Salman Rushdie against censorship, that "cultural-rights theorists" (who should really be called "anti-cultural-rights theorists") have fueled an anti-immigrant fervour that Rushdie seems to have escaped in *his* immigration to the USA at the expense of the British taxpayer. The Clinton administration's record on cultural rights took a further interesting turn in the Elián Gonzales case, which was the unmaking of the US Democrats. Anti-immigrant fever, and again here a kind of radical support of Fidel Castro, in fact became a very conservative, anti-immigrant position. It simply required and insisted upon the deportation of a simple little six-year-old whose mother risked her life to bring him to "the Land of the Free and the Home of the Brave." It also demonized, as the Rushdie Affair had demonized the immigrant Muslims, the Hispanic, Cuban-American population of Florida, who became the deciding electorate in the 2000 election, for attempting to speak out against a Communist regime; a regime that Americans had once wanted to see wiped out. Of course, for postcolonial Marxists this was a wonderful opportunity to uphold the communism of Fidel Castro against the Disney consumerism of America, but in this they sold out on the rights of the Hispanic minority not only in Florida, but of those immigrants, the *trabajadoras* and the *trabajadores*, who do in fact come seeking the same economic opportunities that postcolonial theorists, and in Said's case his father, came seeking in this great land of opportunity. So our postcolonial theorists in their cultural-rights theories have in fact literally become the "Stalinist elite" supposed to speak for the people, but are the oppressors of the people! And those who would speak for "the people," "workers" or "immigrants" are dubbed "paternalistic multicultural liberals".... Ruben Navarette, a nationally syndicated columnist for the *Dallas Morning News*, put the whole situation in an interesting perspective. He described how the 1990s were the great decade of immigration to the USA. Ten million immigrated to the USA – more than in any other decade. Yet, in this decade, it was the "greens," the environmentalists, the most radical fringe group, who became the anti-immigrant lobby. Playing on this same irony of "liberals having turned conservatives," Navarette writes of Elián Gonzales' supposed "rescue": "What was sold by democrats as the rescue of a Cuban boy actually was an effort to rescue Al Gore from a possible political nightmare in Florida. How well that turned out."[37]

The Hispanic columnist Roger Hernandez, in a wonderful column entitled "Elian giveth and Elian taketh away," laid out the appeal of George W. to Hispanic voters:

> In Florida, with its incredibly close race, the Hispanic vote was more decisive than in the other Hispanic-heavy states. Because Cuban Americans were angry at the Clinton administration for the raid that forcibly removed Elian Gonzales from his relatives' Miami home, George W. expected to win upwards of 80% of the Cuban vote...[38]

Elián Gonzales did, in fact, cost the Democrats the election. *Newsweek* reported that Miami–Dade county's Hispanic Democratic mayor, Alex Penelas, refused to support Al Gore, to show up at any rallies or to help with the election recount. Although Cuban Americans are historically Republican and in most cases may not hold the position of other Hispanics, particularly Chicanos, they did highlight in a very

---

[37] Ruben Navarette, "Anti-immigrant bias continues," *El Paso Times* (10 November 2000): A4.

[38] Roger Hernandez, "Elian Giveth and Elian Taketh Away," *El Paso Times* (10 November, 2000): A4.

dramatic way their particular cultures' rights to be upheld. Like other immigrant groups, they too wanted Janet Reno, who seemed so much to buy into the notion that "multiculturalism is bad for democracy," out.

✆

The greatest impact of the portrayal of multiculturalism as being bad for democracy is on immigration and the restriction of immigration. For Charles Taylor, as stated before, this is a problem – a problem that arises from the definitions of culture. The question of cultural rights arises because "international migration is making all societies less culturally uniform." So what do you do? Restrict immigration? These restrictions affect South Asians, but most particularly Mexican immigration. This is interesting in that US industry has long depended on Mexican legal and illegal labour for its success. Navarette, in "Anti-immigrant bias," puts this interestingly:

> Gatekeepers disguised as greens might be right about the growth issue. In almost any suburb in America, there are new rows of houses, restaurants and hotels. Immigrants pound nails, cook short orders and change beds, all amid the ringing of cash registers.
>
> Get rid of immigrants, and it will all come to an end.[39]

Of course, our postcolonial theorists would call this exploitation; but most seeking immigration prefer this exploitation to their conditions at home, as I imagine do the postcolonial critics living and writing in this country. In his article "The Politics of Recognition," Charles Taylor, whom Kymlicka and O'Neill label a strong multiculturalist, argues "for a type of liberalism grounded very much on judgement of what makes a 'good life'."[40] "The good life" is what Edward Said tells us

---

[39] Ruben Navarette, "Anti Immigrant bias continues," A4.
[40] Charles Taylor, "The Politics of Recognition," in *Multiculturalism and The Politics of Recognition*, ed. Amy Gutman (Princeton NJ: Princeton UP, 1994): 61.

his father came for, in his most recent memoir. It is the image of America that is held up everywhere, the reason why postcolonial critics are not just content to live and work in Britain. But, with Kymlicka, I would question Taylor when he, like Homi Bhabha, claims that the political expression of one range of cultures is quite incompatible with other ranges. On the Rushdie issue he writes, "'how we do things' covers issues such as the right to life and to freedom of speech."[41] But in protecting the right to life of Salman Rushdie, now in New York City, and his right to freedom of speech, we are now restricting the rights of several others. If we had to send back Elián Gonzales, on the bogus issue of paternal right, to please Fidel Castro, why don't we send Salman Rushdie back to England so that we can repair US–Iran relations, especially at this time of an energy crunch? But Iran doesn't really care about the Rushdie matter any more and, probably, as a whole nation, never really cared enough even to carry through on the *fatwa* injunction of the Ayatollah.

All the reactions against the restrictions of immigration cannot be blamed on cultural-rights theorists. Indeed, there is a definite "white" backlash and there always has been a white conservative, particularly Christian, resistance. But it is the cultural-rights issues that fan the flames of the fear individuals feel about the 'Other', the different. An old passage from Fredric Jameson comes to mind:

> So from the earliest times, the stranger from another tribe, the 'barbarian' who speaks an 'incomprehensible' language and follows 'outlandish' customs, but also the woman, whose biological differences stimulates fantasies of castration and devoration, or in our own time, the avenger of accumulated resentments from some oppressed class or race, or else that alien being, Jew or Communist, behind whose apparently human features a malignant and preternatural intelligence is thought to lurk: these are some of the archetypal figures of the Other, about whom the essential point to be made is not so much that he is

---

[41] Taylor, "The Politics of Recognition," 63.

feared because he is evil; rather he is evil because he is Other, alien, different, strange, unclean, and unfamiliar.[42]

But how is it that the Arizona and New Mexico ranchers, despite their entrenched senses of otherness and whiteness, ranchers who long used Mexican hands on their properties, have suddenly threatened to shoot immigrants if they should trespass?[43] How is it that my institution, the University of Texas at El Paso, which long relied on Mexican students for funding, has suddenly allowed plainclothes immigration police to question students and faculty on campus?

Perhaps foreign students, albeit quiet and law-abiding, threaten American citizens as an incursion or invasion, as it were, into the realm of jobs and opportunities. Perhaps the Indian computer engineers arrested and deported from Houston on J–1 visas were in fact taking American jobs. But the evidence fails to corroborate these allegations. There are just not that many qualified Americans to fill those jobs, as there are not enough American doctors who are willing to go out to deliver health care to Americans in Portales, New Mexico, or in Roswell. It is the exercise of cultural rights that highlights difference, the particularities of race and culture that instil fear in the "white" Americans and British who would prefer to see immigrants mainstreamed.

Mainstreaming can only be done to a limit. You can't mainstream your facial features or the colour of your skin. The more our own theorists write against our cultural rights, the more suspicious white Americans and British become on behalf of our *"weird" cultures*.

∅

---

[42] Fredric Jameson, *The Political Unconscious* (London: Methuen, 1981): 115.

[43] Mark Stevenson, "Arizona Ranchers try to spark anti-immigrant movement," *Las Cruces Sun News* (30 May 2000): A9.

One of US? Towards the Utopia of True Globalization

Now, the issue is: do our postcolonial theorists who have originated from the subcontinent or Middle Eastern countries consider themselves to be "one of us?" Do they consider "us" – those of us who speak for indigeneity, those of us who presume to speak (Who Should Speak? Gayatri Spivak would ask) for the Muslim immigrant's freedom of expression exercised in burning a book, for instance, or speak for the Mexican immigrants, albeit illegal – do they consider us "one of them"? Maybe not; maybe we are too deep in the trenches muddying ourselves, while they as Marxists inhabit the luxury glass towers of "high theory." When, in his London talk, Homi Bhabha raised the issues of 'cultural rights', 'multiculturalism', and 'the politics of identity' in terms of his framework of hybridity, in which culture is a 'translational' and 'transitional' entity, he said: "The question we have to ask is, 'Who is one of us?' It's the proximity, the closeness of the other that is the real challenge, never the distance. That's the ethical moment."

One's notion of home is itself in the process of change, he said. As someone coming from the town of Hyderabad, now renamed after Clinton's visit and the big electronic chip industry "Cyberabad," I realize that home is in the process of change. But I also know that my very best friend, Vaseema Aziz, an architect, who rides a Lambretta scooter to her work with a chador around her head, spits on me at the very mention of Rushdie, even if I am criticizing him, and has a deep unchanging Muslim self within her; much in the same way the Indian Brahmin writer Raja Rao, living in Texas, says, "My India, I carry with me." As Daniel O'Neill would say in his critique of Kymlicka, Taylor and Walzer, here "there is no Gadamerian fusion of cultural horizons."[44] Bhabha claims that "*radical nationalism*" can only be achieved through blood feuds. Yes, this is true. Bhabha, of course, is

---

[44] O'Neill, "Liberals and the Rushdie Affair," 244.

referring to the nationalism of the Serbs in Bosnia; he does not, however, take into account the backlash against multiculturalism generated
by the rhetoric of our theorists and the bloodbath against Mexican
immigrants.

However, Bhabha says, "the question of the rights of a culture" and
"who is one of us" turns on the ethical and political freedom of choice.
It is next to impossible to "choose a cultural affiliation." You can
'choose' the cultural affiliation of the "white Christian" majority –
say, as a Methodist in an American suburb – but, by the colour of your
skin and your past experience, you will *never* be one of them. Though
you can 'choose' to be British, as *The Satanic Verses* ironically shows
in the experience of Gibreel Farishta, if the British don't want to
accept your 'bowler-hatted' self, you cannot choose British cultural
affiliation or have the rights in the courthouse that belong to that specific group. You will always be an outsider, "a Paki," "a nigger." Basically, then, a woman opposed to clitoridectomy can quit her culture.
But what is the alternative, when cultural rights are denied in the
immigrant's new culture? A woman could often flee Afghanistan if
she was opposed to the Taliban, but can she flee the essential Muslim
self – maybe even a spiritualism inside her that calls out to her traditional religion when beset by racism in the country immigrated to?
'Quitting' a culture is really not possible for those raised under a
specific set of circumstances and beliefs. When individuals are immersed in a practice and are socialized into it, much as many white
fundamentalist Christians are socialized into believing that anyone not
Christian is Satanic, quitting is not a choice. This is a different kind of
quitting from legal and political exiting, which can also be very
difficult.

∅

In his critique of Susan Moller Okin's *Is Multiculturalism Bad for
Women?*, Homi Bhabha points out that, yes, Okin is reproducing
"monolithic cultural stereotypes." But, by saying that individuals can

opt out of such a society, one is complicit in condemning that society and its action. To Muslims burning Rushdie's book, the action, as Daniel O'Neill points out, is one that could have been condoned by "The Prophet." Bhabha said in his lecture:

> Nobody can force you against your better interest to belong to a cultural group if you feel that your best interests as a woman, for instance, are served by wanting to leave that group and its particular jurisdiction.

Conversely, nobody can force a society into accepting you. Several Parsi and Indian legislators, such as Dadabhoy Naoroji, went to Britain, followed all the mores, were completely assimilated, even like Nirad Chaudhuri, the Indian writer who was living and teaching in Oxford, but essentially remained "white oriental gentlemen" – wogs.

Though Bhabha claims that he is deeply sceptical of globalization via "technophilia," he also sees the global or transnational as emerging as a new "conceptual category." I mean, I am deeply sceptical of the discourse of cultural rights, proved in large part by the pressure of minorities, multiculturalism, immigration and the "communities of interest." Bhabha, of course, has been always, as he says, sceptical of mere approximations or distortions of some essentialist sense of authentic roots. "Both forms of identification, both forms of recreating a home, whether it is the authentic version or whether it is the cosmopolitan version, are indeed precisely that, they are creations." And so, because we cannot understand "what authorizes a judgement in one space or another because we are somehow standing on the boundaries of both spaces," this is why Bhabha moves towards the term "*jurisdictional unsettlement.*" Accordingly, you cannot say, "sorry, I come from somewhere else, my behaviour must not be judged."

Is *globalization* possible? I believe that globalization is a worthy goal. I hope for it, like Carlos Santana and Jacques Derrida, who articulated a dream at a talk which was given at the ICA and widely quoted on the postcolonial net, where Vietnamese refugees were falling past his window and he hoped the world would not need to have refugees and borders – a world where, as Carlos Santana put it, "there will be no borders, no boundaries, no flags, and no countries, and the only passport will be the heart." Such a worthy goal would make un-necessary background checks, immigrant abuses, electrified fences that make barbecued meat of aspiring immigrants and early a.m. raids with battering-rams on tiny six-year-olds. A "globalized placeless culture" such as Jean Baudrillard proposes seems absolutely distant from my position on the border, where I drive to work past an elec-tronic sign that says how many immigrants were deported during that day, where Arizona ranchers threaten to shoot Mexican immigrants, where Mexicans offer rewards for murdered Border Patrol agents, and where xenophobia is the order of the day. Post-nationalist societies will only emerge when "white" elite hegemony allows cultures with their particular rights to coexist and be recognized as equally valuable.

I am afraid that as long as white protectionism is in force, as long as white people want the world to turn in their direction, on their terms, theories like hybridity, like the refusal to empower individual particu-larities, end up doing away with cultures and even peoples whom "they," the dominant, white, conservative, elite, deem barbaric. In this, they are led on by our own images that "our" cultural practices are barbaric. As long as we are "re-thinking multiculturalism," *they* are "re-thinking multiculturalism" also, in the light of what we have said. It doesn't take much for someone like Britain's Conservative ex-MP Charles Wardle not only to resign over immigration's "open door," "Europe without Frontiers," but to shut that door because we ourselves describe ourselves as unworthy to enter that door. Yes, our Juanas, *violadas y deportadas*, will continue to have their hand cut off as theorists stand and watch and even encourage it.

I would like to end with a small poem of my own which shows, I hope, that cultural rights have to be protected in order to protect global human rights:

La Migra

We play a game, he and I
the battle of 1–10, I call it.
I drive almost up to him
wanting to look in to
the back of the van,
white
with a green stripe,
the green logo, "U.S. Border Patrol."
The standard regulation bars
protect the driver
from the criminals,
"Which ones are they?"
But there, in the back, is a cage.
I strain to look in.

My eyes glaze over, transported
to a distant land, a land said to be
A friend of democracy, of our nation
settled by people like "our" people,
where, in such a van, beaten, bruised
eyes bulging and glazed over,
shoes stuffed in his mouth,
my brother, a common student,
who, when he worked,
to fill his belly, an act disallowed
of immigrants everywhere,
was transported, in such a cage.

As I strain to look in, I see
a hand, straining towards me.
I edge my car closer, try to catch up
with the speeding van, read its number,
take down an 800 number while he
pulls over and takes down
my license plate,
while the 800 number refuses
to take my call,
and amnesty international
will not take my call.

Dark bushy hair
continues to strain towards me
a dark mustache, a man
caught in a man-cage.

And we, Estados Unidos,
want to fight for the human rights
of Kosovars and East Timorians.
Twenty five years of my
tax dollars at work.

WORKS CITED

Bagehot. "Playing the Race Card again," *Economist* (23 December 2000): 88.

Bhabha, Homi K. Lecture given at the Stuart Hall Conference of the Centre for Sociological and Social Anthropological Studies at the Open University in London in 1998.

——. "Liberalism's Sacred Cow," in Moller Okin, ed. *Is Multiculturalism Bad for Women?*, 79–84.

——. *The Location of Culture* (London: Routledge, 1994).

Black Information Links. "Hague's Hate a Black Perspective," www.blink. org.uk.

Bloom, Alan. "A Cultural Critic Answers his Own," *Wall Street Journal* (30 March 1989): A12.

Borden, Tessie. "Hispanic Agents Face Inner Struggle," *Las Cruces Sun News* (10 June 2000).

Gonzales, Patricia, & Roberto Rodriguez. "Hispanics forming Fifth Pillar," *Las Cruces Sun News* (13 January 2001): B5.

Gonzales, Patricia & Roberto Rodriguez. "Keeping Barbarians at Bay," *Las Cruces Sun News* (9 January 2001): B4.

Fish, Stanley. "Boutique Multiculturalism, or Why Liberals Are Incapable of Thinking about Hate Speech," *Critical Inquiry* 23 (Winter 1997): 378–95.

Ford, Richard. "Abduction Charges to Halt Forced Marriages," *The Times* (London; 30 June 2000): 12.

Hale, Charles. "Travel Writing: Elite Appropriations of Hybridity, Mestizaje, Antiracism, Equality, and Other Progressive Sounding Discourses in Highland Guatemala," *Journal of American Folklore* 112.4 (Summer 1999): 297–314.

Haeder, Paul K. "The Problem with Diversity," *El Paso Times* (15 February 2000).

Hernandez, Roger. "Elian Giveth and Elian Taketh Away," *El Paso Times* (10 November 2000): A4.

Jameson, Fredric. *The Political Unconscious* (London: Methuen, 1981).

Jussawalla, Feroza. "Resurrecting the Prophet: the Case of Salman, the Otherwise," *Public Culture* 2 (Fall 1989): 106–17.

——. "Rushdie's Dastan-e-Dilruba," *diacritics* 26.1 (Spring 1995): 50– 73.

Kingsolver, Barbara. *Another America/Otra America* (Seattle: U of Washington P, 1991).

Kureishi, Hanif. "Bradford," *Granta* 20 (Winter 1986): 149–70.

Moore–Gilbert, Bart. *Postcolonial Theory: Contexts, Practices, Politics* (London: Verso, 1997).

Navarette, Ruben. "Anti-Immigrant Bias Continues," *El Paso Times* (10 November 2000): A4.

Okin, Susan Moller, ed. *Is Multiculturalism Bad for Women?* (Princeton NJ: Princeton UP, 2000).

O'Neill, Daniel. "Multicultural Liberals and the Rushdie Affair: A Critique of Kymlicka, Taylor and Walzer," *Review of Politics* 61 (Spring 1999): 219–50.

Parekh, Bhikhu. "A Varied Moral World," in Moller Okin, ed. *Is Multiculturalism Bad for Women?*, 69–75.

Ritter, John. "Students Decry Idea of Monitoring," *USA Today* (8 June 2000): 03A.

Stack, Megan K. "Pledges for Open Border Draw Skepticism," *Las Cruces Sun News* (3 December 2000): A–12.

Stevenson, Mark. "Arizona Ranchers Try to Spark Anti-Immigrant Movement," *Las Cruces Sun News* (30 May 2000): A9.

Taylor, Charles. "The Politics of Recognition," in *Multiculturalism and the Politics of Recognition*, ed. Amy Gutman (Princeton NJ: Princeton UP, 1994).

——. "The Rushdie Controversy," *Public Culture* 2 (Fall 1989): 118–22.

Wavell, Stuart. "Wrestling for an Equal Share," *Sunday Times* (26 March 1995), Report: 8–10.

℘

Roy Sommer

"Simple Survival" in "Happy Multicultural Land"?
Diasporic Identities and Cultural Hybridity in the Contemporary British Novel[1]

MULTICULTURALISM HAS BECOME one of the key concepts in English studies in recent years. Its popularity may be seen as a reaction to the ongoing ethnic and cultural transformation of Britain. Thus, according to the *New York Times*, by the end of this decade Leicester may become the first British city with a non-white majority. Besides this topical relevance, the term multiculturalism serves as an umbrella for a wide variety of practices and approaches within literary and cultural criticism. It is therefore hardly surprising that, in the words of Cynthia Willett, "multiculturalism has not yet been fully theorized"[2] and continues to be a controversial issue.

This essay explores the complex relationship between multiculturalism, hybridity and the diaspora, both in current cultural theory and in contemporary British fiction. The first section is devoted to a discus-

[1] I would like to thank Conor Geiselbrechtinger, Monika Fludernik, Ansgar Nünning and Bruno Zerweck for their valuable comments on earlier versions of this essay.

[2] Cynthia Willett, "Introduction" to *Theorizing Multiculturism: A Guide to the Current Debate*, ed. Willett (Oxford: Blackwell, 1998): 1.

sion of Stanley Fish's recent reply (1997) to Charles Taylor's (1994) dialectical model of multicultural identity. It will be argued that Fish's critique of Taylor is based on a wrong assumption – that multicultural- ism should be regarded as a philosophical concept rather than a dis- course: ie, a heterogeneous grouping of statements produced under the constraint of certain power relations. This assumption, which allows for dismissal of the multicultural debate as academic talk, is necessary in the context of Fish's argument, as he merely uses the concept of multiculturalism as a pretext for an attack on the failure of American liberals to come to terms with racism and other forms of illiberalism and fundamentalism.

The second section of my essay analyses the concepts of diaspora and cosmopolitan hybridity as two opposed visions of a multicultural society. Both of these visions have been explored in contemporary British fiction, which is the focus of the third section. It will be shown that the multicultural novel in Britain gives voice to the diasporic experience as well as to the notion of hybrid identities. This develop- ment within multicultural literature calls for a revaluation of current literary and cultural theory with its emphasis on cultural hybridity.

Why Multiculturalism Should be Regarded as a Critical Discourse Rather Than as a Philosophical Concept

In his introduction to a special issue of *Narrative* on "Multiculturalism & Narrative," Herman Beavers states that

> *multiculturalism happens*. Or to put it another way, *multiculturalism* is not just a term we use to refer to the multiracial and multiethnic dimensions of the United States and its population, but also some- thing that has effects and consequences in the world.[3]

This unspecific use of the term, Beavers goes on to claim, may lead to misunderstandings: "*Multiculturalism happens*," as he says, yet what

---

[3] Herman Beavers, "Editor's Column," *Narrative* 7.2 (1999): 129.

really 'happens' is, strictly speaking, not multiculturalism but multi-ethnicity. While ethnic diversity is a demographic phenomenon that can be observed almost everywhere in the world today, multicultural-ism more aptly refers to a variety of legal, political, philosophical and literary discourses.[4] According to Manfred Titzmann, discourses have subject-matter in common and are related to other discourses.[5] The subject-matter of multicultural discourse is multi-ethnicity or, more precisely, ethnic and cultural difference. Multiculturalism is closely related to discourses on national or cultural identity: eg, Englishness, Americanness and so on, colonial and postcolonial discourses and a number of emancipatory discourses such as feminism and afro-centrism.

The philosophical response to multi-ethnicity is based on the assumption that in a democratic society no one must be deprived of fundamental rights such as freedom of opinion, freedom of speech and religion, nor of their right to their cultural tradition. The majority is morally obliged to ensure that minorities are neither marginalized nor forced to assimilate completely to the dominant culture. This moral obligation to abide by the principles of the Enlightenment has been defended in Charles Taylor's highly influential essay "The Politics of Recognition," which, ever since its publication in 1994, has been at the centre of a controversial debate. The starting-point of Taylor's theory is a dialectical model of personal identity which assumes that the

---

[4] Stanley Fish makes a similar point, proposing "the introduction of a new distinction between multiculturalism as a philosophical problem and multi-culturalism as a demographic fact"; Fish, "Boutique Multiculturalism, or Why Liberals Are Incapable of Thinking about Hate Speech," *Critical Inquiry* 23 (1997): 385. (Where clear, further page references are in the main text.) How-ever, Fish's argument that multiculturalism is, or should be treated as, a philo-sophical concept rather than a critical discourse leads to a set of wrong conclu-sions, as will be shown below.

[5] Manfred Titzmann, "Skizze einer integrativen Literaturgeschichte und ihres Ortes in einer Systematik der Literaturwissenschaft," in *Modelle des literarischen Strukturwandels*, ed. Titzmann (Tübingen: Max Niemeyer): 406.

behaviour of one's 'significant others' such as parents and friends towards the 'self' is of vital importance to the constitution of individual identity.[6] As the denial of recognition may lead to self-deprecation and even self-hatred, recognition has to be considered as a "vital human need" (26). Having established this moral principle, Taylor, whose main interest lies not with the individual migrant but, rather, with cultural or collective identities of diasporic minorities, transfers the problem of recognition from the private to the public sphere. The principles of the Enlightenment, on which modern democracies are based, demand that all citizens are treated as equals: "What is to be avoided at all costs is the existence of 'first-class' and 'second-class' citizens" (37). The adherence to the "ideal of authenticity" (38) and society's duty to avoid "other-induced distortions" (37) form the basic rules of a multicultural society, which is required not only to give status to "something that is not universally shared" (39) but also to acknowledge the "equal value of different cultures" (64). This conflict between equality and difference leads us down a blind alley, a dilemma which cannot be solved theoretically but has to be dealt with in a pragmatic way:

> There must be something midway between the inauthentic and homogenizing demand for recognition of equal worth, on the one hand, and the self-immurement within ethnocentric standards, on the other. There are other cultures, and we have to live together more and more, both on a world scale and commingled in each individual society. (72)

Precisely this Taylorian notion of a politics of difference has been the target of Stanley Fish's attack against multiculturalism and its aca-

---

⁶ See Charles Taylor, "The Politics of Recognition," in *Multiculturalism: Examining the Politics of Recognition*, ed. Amy Gutman (Princeton NJ: Princeton UP, 1994): 25: "The thesis is that our identity is partly shaped by recognition or its absence, often by the *mis*recognition of others, and so a person or group of people can suffer real damage, real distortion, if the people or society around them mirror back to them a confining or demeaning or contemptible picture of themselves." Further page references are in the main text.

demic proponents, "who believe, on the model of the world-as-philo-sophy seminar, that any differences between 'rational' persons can be talked through."[7] Fish distinguishes between two versions of multi-culturalism – 'boutique' and 'strong'. The former is characterized by a patronizing attitude towards those who belong to a different culture or hold different beliefs:

> A boutique multiculturalist may enjoy watching Native American reli-gious ceremonies and insist that they be freely allowed to occur, but he will balk if those ceremonies include animal sacrifice or the use of a controlled substance. (379–80)

'Strong' multiculturalism is Fish's synonym for Taylor's politics of difference. Its proponents are more seriously committed to tolerance than the 'boutiquers', yet they ultimately face a serious dilemma, as "the trouble with stipulating tolerance as your first principle is that you cannot possibly be faithful to it because sooner or later the culture whose core values you are tolerating will reveal itself to be intolerant at that same core" (382–83).

One may wonder why Fish chooses to portray such a negative image of 'other' cultures, portraying them as necessarily intolerant. After all, the *fatwa* against Salman Rushdie, Fish's prime example of cultural intolerance, cannot really be regarded as typical of the prob-lems that multi-ethnic societies have to cope with day by day. Given that he is not 'against' ethnicity, "whose existence Fish not only recog-nizes but would aggressively defend,"[8] the most plausible explanation is that his polemic is directed against the shortcomings of universalist liberalism rather than multiculturalism itself:

> Fish is interested in multiculturalism only insofar as it gains him access to another subject, namely, academic liberals' inadequate and

---

[7] Fish, "Boutique Multiculturalism," 391.

[8] Donald E. Pease, "Regulating Multi-Adhoccerists, Fish('s) Rules," *Critical Inquiry* 23 (1997): 398.

to his mind hopelessly muddled effort to address the matter of hate speech.[9]

Thus, the inconsistency of both 'strong' and 'boutique' multicultural-ists, whose attitudes are grounded in liberal beliefs, only serves as an example for liberalism's failure to come to terms with the fact that "in a fundamental disagreement, basic assumptions are precisely what is in dispute."[10]

An example where basic assumptions are indeed in dispute is the debate on the genital mutilation of women, which has been con-demned as a violation of human rights by its opponents, whereas its practitioners claim the practice as their right to cultural tradition. This highly controversial issue has recently received a lot of attention, per-haps in response to the best-selling book *Desert Flower* (1999) by the former Ethiopian top model Waris Dirie. Since this practice, which is often euphemistically referred to as 'female circumcision', often results in irreversible physic damage and even death, there should be no debate on whether or not it may be allowed to happen: this is a clear case of a fundamental conflict between basic values, and one where a democratic society needs to defend its own principles. As the intercultural debate following the publication of *Desert Flower* has shown, there is growing opposition to this form of patriarchal oppres-sion even in those countries in which genital mutilation is still legal or at least tolerated as a traditional practice. Thus it can be argued that although we face a fundamental conflict, it is not really a cultural but a political one: what is at stake is not cultural tradition and religious beliefs, but power and control.

The example of genital mutilation supports Fish's thesis that there are conflicts in which an intercultural dialogue is no longer possible.

---

[9] Pease, "Regulating Multi-Adhoccerists," 396.

[10] Fish, "Boutique Multiculturalism," 388. Cf Pease, "Regulating Multi-Adhoccerists," 411: "According to Fish, it is in recognizing the difference between another culture's values and their own that boutique multiculturalists rediscover the philosophical dilemmas of universalist liberalism."

However, its applicability to the multicultural situation needs to be reviewed: Is it true that multicultural conflicts always amount to fundamental disagreements between the open society and its ethno-centric opponents? If one looks at multi-ethnic European nations such as Britain or Germany, it seems that most conflicts arise over everyday issues such as the building of mosques or the question of whether Muslim women teachers and civil servants should be allowed to wear head scarves at work. While these issues reveal considerable differences of attitude towards the respective roles of religion and the secular state, they do not really threaten the basic assumptions of a pluralistic society: ie, the belief that its values and norms must be based on a democratic consensus. In Britain and Germany, at least, anti-democratic fundamentalism among Islamic minorities is a rare exception rather than the rule.

Not only does Fish's central attack on academic "faith in talk"[11] depend on exceptional examples like the Rushdie Affair, thereby exaggerating the nature of multicultural conflicts, but it also relies on a clever use of rhetoric in order to hide theoretical inconsistencies. Fish's argument is based on the assumption that multiculturalism is a philosophical concept. A critical concept, of course, needs to be clearly defined in order to be useful. As multiculturalists cannot escape the dilemma of the equality vs difference debate and therefore need to resort to "inspired adhoccery," Fish concludes "that multiculturalism is an incoherent concept that cannot be meaningfully either affirmed or rejected" (388). In order to come up with the kind of essentialist concept which Fish seems to have in mind, multiculturalists would have to define and defend "core values" (379) or "general principles" which would allow them "to come to terms with difference" (384). As this is not possible, Fish claims that "no one could ever *be* a multiculturalist in any interesting and coherent sense" and that "every one of us always is [...] a uniculturalist" (384). Fish's alter-

---

[11] Fish, "Boutique Multiculturalism," 391.

native to this dilemma is quite simple: admit to being a uniculturalist, stop thinking in terms of therapy, and take up effective strategies instead; ask "real questions" (393), continue engaging in "distinctly illiberal actions" (395), and do so "with less anxiety" (395).

Fish's 'solution' to the 'problem' of multiculturalism may appeal to those who are fed up with endless debates about political correctness. From a theoretical perspective, however, it makes little sense to dismiss multiculturalism as an incoherent and therefore useless concept. It should, rather, be regarded as a discourse which accommodates "a multiplicity of diverging perspectives outside of dominant traditions."[12] As discourses always embrace heterogeneous positions, multiculturalism cannot seek "to reconcile the claims of difference and community in a satisfactory formula."[13] This view is supported by those critics who argue that multicultural thinking is not yet advanced far enough to allow for a philosophical system,[14] or even that multiculturalism represents a different kind of theorizing that explicitly refuses to operate within a systematic framework. The fact that there are more multiculturalisms around than anyone could sensibly hope to reconcile – "critical multiculturalism,"[15] "critical democratic multiculturalism,"[16] "mainstream multiculturalism,"[17] "ludic multicultural-

---

[12] Willett, "Introduction," 1.

[13] Fish, "Boutique Multiculturalism," 385.

[14] Cf Bill Martin, "Multiculturalism: Consumerist or Transformational," in Willett, ed. *Theorizing Multiculturalism*, 121: "The reflections presented here are not yet integrated into any kind of 'system'. In fact, I'm not sure that we are ready for that yet, and, in any case, the whole issue of multiculturalism raises the question of difference in a way that would seem to run against inherited forms of philosophical or social theoretical system building."

[15] Chicago Cultural Studies Group, "Critical Multiculturalism," *Critical Inquiry* 18 (1992): 553.

[16] Judith Green, "Educational Multiculturalism, Critical Pluralism, and Deep Democracy," in Willett, ed. *Theorizing Multiculturalism*, 440.

[17] Nancy Fraser, "From Restribution to Recognition? Dilemmas of Justice in a 'Post-Socialist' Age," in Willett, ed. *Theorizing Multiculturalism*, 34.

ism,"[18] "corporate multiculturalism,"[19] "imperial multiculturalism,"[20] "'consumerist' multiculturalism"[21] and "Hollywood multicultural-ism,"[22] to name but a few – makes it even more unlikely that a quest for a 'formula' would ever yield convincing results.

If multiculturalism is such a heterogeneous affair, what, then, should multicultural theory be about? First of all, it should be about learning how to tolerate difference, ambiguity and ambivalence. With regard to the situation in multi-ethnic Britain, Paul Gilroy warns us that "the temptation to evaluate and assess contemporary London as though it could be a simpler, more homogeneous and less irreducibly diverse place, is something we should regard with the utmost suspi-cion."[23] A multicultural society needs to learn how to cope with diver-sity rather than how to get rid of it. Secondly, multicultural discourse analysis needs to fulfil the "productive task of reconceptualizing the central components for social, political, and ethical theory."[24] Al-though it has been argued that, considering the multicultural trans-formation of Britain, one should speak of British cultural identities or 'Englishnesses' in the plural form rather than of one national identity to which the cultural status of a master-narrative can be ascribed,[25] one

---

[18] Martin J. Matuštík, "Ludic, Corporate, and Imperial Multiculturalism: Impostors of Democracy and Cartographers of the New World Order," in Willett, ed. *Theorizing Multiculturalism*, 101.

[19] Matuštík, "Ludic, Corporate, and Imperial Multiculturalism," 102.

[20] "Ludic, Corporate, and Imperial Multiculturalism," 106.

[21] Martin, "Multiculturalism," 121.

[22] Carole Boyce Davies, *Black Women, Writing and Identity: Migration of the Subject* (London: Routledge, 1994).

[23] Paul Gilroy, "A London Sumting Dis...," *Critical Quarterly* 41.3 (1999): 57.

[24] Willett, "Introduction," 2.

[25] See Silvia Mergenthal, "Englishness/Englishnesses in Contemporary Fiction," in *Unity in Diversity Revisited? British Literature and Culture in the 1990s*, ed. Barbara Korte & Klaus Peter Müller (Tübingen: Gunter Narr, 1998): 53.

should not forget "how much work there is still to do in demystifying racial differences and reconfiguring Britishness."[26]

Maybe the most difficult task for the critical project of multiculturalism, however, is to avoid creating its own master-narratives in this process of reconfiguring Britishness. That this really is a danger becomes apparent when one looks at the omnipresence of the term 'hybridity' in multicultural literary criticism. Since its introduction into postcolonial theory by Homi Bhabha, this cosmopolitan concept has become almost synonymous with multiculturalism. The vast majority of the growing number of multicultural novels and stories in Britain, however, cannot be described as hybrid in any meaningful way. A survey of multicultural fictions of migration, which can be defined as literary representations of ethnic identity and cultural alterity, proves that the notion of multicultural pluralism (Taylor's politics of difference) is much more widespread than the cosmopolitan or transcultural representation of hybrid identities à la Rushdie. The difference between multicultural and transcultural representations of identity is crucial to an understanding of contemporary 'black' British literature, which is much less homogeneous than this convenient label implies: it accommodates both diasporic pluralism and hybrid cosmopolitanism. Before I turn to some literary examples to illustrate this, however, I would like to contrast the utopian vision of newness and intercultural intermingling that has come to be associated with hybridity with another concept that presents a more realistic version of multiculturalism – the concept of the diaspora.

⌀

---

[26] Gilroy, "A London Sumting Dis …," 59.

Conflicting Versions of Multiculturalism:
The Pressures of the New Diaspora
and Cosmopolitan Hybridity

Traditionally, 'diaspora' refers to the dispersion of the Jews among the gentiles and their belief in an eventual return to the (lost) homeland. In current (multi)cultural theory, the term has been applied to all expatriate groups who chose, or were forced, to leave their native countries for a variety of reasons including indentured labour and the slave trade. In their new countries, these diasporic subjects form ethnic or cultural minorities while still retaining strong affiliations with their – or, more often, their ancestors' – homelands.

Despite the considerable differences in their respective histories, self-concepts and relationships with the dominant cultures, diasporic groups also share similarities. The two main characteristics of the diasporic imaginary as defined by Vijay Mishra are its grounding in the communal rather than the individual experience and a strong sense of displacement shared by all members of the "ethnic enclave" in question.[27] The loss of cultural, religious and national roots enforces collective mythmaking, "as imaginary homelands are constructed from the space of distance to compensate for a loss occasioned by an unspeakable trauma" (424). While Mishra recognizes that the image thus created is a cultural construct, he also points out that the members of the diaspora themselves certainly do not always regard their homeland and cultural heritage as a fiction. Diasporas generally preserve an essentialistic world-view and tend to be exclusivist, presenting their own culture as the desirable norm.

---

[27] See Vijay Mishra, "The Diasporic Imaginary: Theorizing the Indian Diaspora," *Textual Practice* 10.3 (1996): 423: "The diasporic imaginary is a term I use to refer to any ethnic enclave in a nation-state that defines itself, consciously, unconsciously or because of the political self-interest of a racialized nation-state, as a group that lives in displacement." Further page references are in the main text.

This idealization of the distant homeland has been explained
psychologically and politically, Mishra argues, as a reaction to the diaspora's "particular condition of displacement and disaggregation"
(442) and as a token of resistance to the pressures of assimilation to
the dominant culture. The notion of an ideal homeland also has a
normative effect within the diasporic community, as it creates the impression of homogeneity that seems to dominate the self-image of
many diasporas. This unity, however, is often the result of internal
oppression, especially of women, who can be subjected to "the collective horror of a double oppression" (435), the combined pressures of
'race' and gender.

This tension between external and internal oppression is illustrated
by *Circle of Light* (1997), the autobiography – rather, biography[28] – of
Kiranjit Ahluwalia, an Indian immigrant who came to Britain in 1979
to marry a man unknown to her. During the ten years of her marriage
she suffered constant physical and mental abuse by her violent husband Deepak, whom she finally killed in 1989. Ahluwalia was subsequently found guilty of murder and sentenced to life imprisonment.
However, after a nationwide campaign for her re-trial organized by an
ethnic women's group called the Southall Black Sisters, the case was
re-opened. The prosecution accepted the plea of manslaughter on the
basis of diminished responsibility, and Ahluwalia was released in
1992.

The relevance of this biography to a theory of the diaspora lies in its
emphasis on the difference between 'real' and imagined Indianness or,
rather, the functioning of the social structure of the extended family in
India and its failure to survive abroad: "There was a unity you don't

---

[28] The book, named an autobiography, is really a biography, as Ahluwalia's
story was actually written by her confidante, the black women's rights cam-
paigner Rahila Gupta.

see in our communities in Britain."[29] Although "the Indian circle is quite tightly knit" (90) and offers a sense of protection in the face of white racism (115), it fails to prevent domestic violence. Divorce was never an option for Ahluwalia, as this would violate the reputation and honour of the family (*izzat*) – held in very high esteem[30] – and thus effectively exclude her from the community:

> If I became single again, [...] I would be accused by my community of being a woman without character. These chains of character, divorce, *izzat*, family were tying me down. (95)

In his statement before the court of appeal, Deepak's uncle Tayaji confirms "that the system in the Indian community failed Kiranjit" (299).

Circle of Light thus illustrates the deficiencies of the diaspora that cuts itself off from the rest of society. Although one has to bear in mind that Ahluwalia's story is a subjective account and may well glorify the situation in India, her portrayal of the diaspora as a static microcosm trying to continue the Indian way of life in the new country cannot be dismissed too easily. It supports the view that, despite its essentialist self-concept as an 'outpost' of the allegedly homogeneous culture of the homeland, the diaspora is really as heterogeneous as any other imagined community. In the case of the Indian diaspora described by Ahluwalia, the price for unity is paid by the community's Others, its internal scapegoats, battered women who are denied divorce in a patriarchal family system which leaves them with little or no choice: "It was like looking at life through a microscope" (200).

Ahluwalia's experiences mirror a different (and perhaps more common) reality than the kind of cosmopolitan freedom evoked by postcolonial notions of hybridity, "a key concept of cultural diversity in which racist 'impurity' has been reinscribed as subversive multiplicity

---

[29] Kiranjit Ahluwalia & Rahila Gupta, *Circle of Light: The Autobiography of Kiranjit Ahluwalia* (London: HarperCollins, 1997): 42. Further page references are in the main text.

[30] See Ahluwalia, *Circle of Light,* 49, 50, 68, 109, 112.

and as progressive (but not unidirectional) agency."[31] Homi Bhabha's
conception of hybrid identities is characterized by a continuous
attempt to overcome the binary opposition of 'us' vs 'them,' expressed
in his frequent reference to the liberating 'beyond,' the 'in-between'
space in which difference loses its menacing connotations: "This interstitial passage between fixed identifications opens up the possibility of
a cultural hybridity that entertains difference without an assumed or
imposed hierarchy."[32] Although Bhabha claims that there is "overwhelming evidence of a more translational and transnational sense of
imagined communities" (5), he also admits that his "third space" is a
rather utopian concept which

> may reveal that the theoretical recognition of the split-place of enun-
> ciation may open the way to conceptualizing an *inter*national culture,
> based not on the exoticism of multiculturalism or the *diversity* of
> cultures, but on the inscription and articulation of culture's *hybridity*.
> (38)

The multicultural recognition of difference (Bhabha's use of the negative term 'exoticism' in this context echoes Fish's 'boutique multiculturalism') gives way to a liberating 'postculturalism' in which identities are no longer dictated by a politics of representation but can be
chosen freely.

While this liberating vision certainly seems appealing to many, it
has also been questioned for two reasons. First, Edward Said points to
the considerable gap between "the optimistic mobility, the intellectual
liveliness, and 'the logic of daring'" that characterizes current theories
of migrancy and the actual experience of migrants, who suffer "mas-

---

[31] Monika Fludernik, "The Constitution of Hybridity: Postcolonial Interventions," in *Hybridity and Postcolonialism: Twentieth-Century Indian Literature*, ed. Fludernik (Tübingen: Stauffenburg, 1998): 21.

[32] Homi Bhabha, *The Location of Culture* (London & New York: Routledge, 1994): 4. Further page references are in the main text. For a detailed
critique of Bhabha's concept of hybridity, see Fludernik, "The Constitution of
Hybridity."

sive dislocations, waste, misery, and horrors."[33] This difference is particularly obvious in current literary criticism, where hybridity has almost become a synonym for postcolonial multiculturalism as a whole. According to Raimund Schäffner, there is a widespread preference "for a processual, hybrid concept of culture and identity" among British left-wing intellectuals who view "the mutual fertilization and mixture of different cultures as an enrichment of society."[34] With the exception of Salman Rushdie and a few other literary proponents of a transcultural world literature, however, the majority of contemporary 'black' British authors are rather sceptical regarding the chances offered to the migrant by his or her 'hybrid' position.

Secondly, Bhabha's transfer of the concept of hybridity from its colonial context to the postcolonial scenario has to be regarded as problematic for paying too little attention to the specific circumstances that influence the diasporic experience.[35] In his article on the history of

---

[33] Edward Said, *Culture and Imperialism* (London: Vintage, 1994): 403.

[34] Raimund Schäffner, "'Identity is not in the past to be found, but in the future to be constructed': History and Identity in Caryl Phillips' Novels," in *Unity in Diversity Revisited? British Literature and Culture in the 1990s*, ed. Barbara Korte, Klaus Peter Müller (Tübingen: Gunter Narr, 1998): 122. The desire for a liberating vision of cultural hybridity is evident in the following quotation from Salman Rushdie: "To migrate is certainly to lose language and home, to be defined by others, to become invisible or, even worse, a target; it is to experience deep changes and wrenches in the soul. But the migrant is not simply transformed by his act; he also transforms his new world. Migrants may well become mutants, but it is out of such hybridization that newness can emerge"; Rushdie, "John Berger" (1987), in Rushdie, *Imaginary Homelands: Essays and Criticism 1981–1991* (London: Granta, 1992): 210.

[35] See Ania Loomba, *Colonialism/Postcolonialism* (London & New York: Routledge, 1998), 180-81: "while there are of course themes in common across different kinds of diasporic experiences and exiles, there are also enormous differences between them. The experiences and traumas generated by the single largest population shift in history – the division of India and Pakistan – are quite different from another enormous movement, that of immigrants from once-colonised nations to Europe or America. The experience of diaspora is also marked by class, and by the histories that shape each group that moves."

the Indian diaspora, Mishra convincingly distinguishes between the
"old," colonial diasporas, which consisted of indentured labourers
migrating from India to the various British colonies, and the "new"
diasporas of the late-twentieth century.[36] This differentiation takes into
account that diasporic identities are historical phenomena which need
to be addressed within their specific cultural contexts, a notion that
Monika Fludernik supports with her distinction between colonial and
postcolonial hybridity. Fludernik stresses the fact that racism in a
multicultural society has little immediate connection with colonial
domination, so that "the more precise shape and quality of migrants'
hybridity remains to be determined."[37]

As suggested above, a more specific approach to hybridity requires
a distinction between the two major discursive responses to multi-
ethnicity that have come to dominate multicultural theory in the 1990s.
On the one hand, the postcolonial concept of hybridity that emancipates the term from its racist connotations has contributed valuable
insights to theories of colonial agency as well as to the postcolonial
critique of eurocentrist and neo-imperialist mentalities. On the other,
there is a growing awareness among critics as well as novelists that
ethnocentrism is here to stay – not only within the cultural majorities,
which continue to call for assimilation and integration, but also within
the diasporic communities, which prefer to cling to idealized versions
of their homelands and cultural traditions.

Both visions of the multicultural society, the optimistic notion that
fixed, stable identities are a thing of the past while the future belongs
to hybrid, shifting constellations of 'self' and 'Other', and the diasporic insistence on ethnic identities and cultural roots, can be found

---

[36] Mishra, "The Diasporic Imaginary," 422.

[37] Monika Fludernik, "Colonial vs. Cosmopolitan Hybridity: A Compari-
son of Mulk Raj Anand and R.K. Narayan with Recent British and North
American Expatriate Writing (Singh Baldwin, Divakaruni, Sunetra Gupta)," in
Hybridity and Postcolonialism: Twentieth-Century Indian Literature, ed.
Fludernik (Tübingen: Stauffenburg, 1998): 262.

in contemporary British literature. In the remaining section of this essay I want to turn to such fictions of migration – novels that explore the tension between diasporic and hybrid conceptions of multicultural identities.

Making Sense of the Diaspora: Multicultural Literature between the Celebration of Hybridity and the Mediation of Diasporic Experience

If one looks at the variety of migrant, diasporic and cosmopolitan experiences depicted in contemporary British literature, two major tendencies can be distinguished.[38] First, there is the large body of multicultural writing that is concerned with what Mark Stein has aptly termed the "burden of representation."[39] These texts traditionally give voice to the world-views and interests of migrant communities, often also highlighting the internal tensions within diasporas. Secondly, there is a much smaller yet enormously influential number of what I would like to call 'transcultural' novels, promoting a kind of cultural hybridity compatible with Bhabha's vision of the third space.[40]

---

[38] For a typological review of British fictions of migration in the 1980s and 1990s, see Roy Sommer, *Fictions of Migration* (Trier: Wissenschaftlicher Verlag Trier, 2001).

[39] Mark Stein, "The Black British 'Bildungsroman' and the Transformation of Britain: Connectedness Across Difference," in Korte & Müller, ed. *Unity and Diversity Revisited?*, 93.

[40] The euphoria that welcomes authors like Rushdie and, now, Zadie Smith, should not obscure the fact that their cosmopolitan, hybrid multiculturalism is an exception rather than the rule. Moreover, it has been observed that in his more recent works Rushdie actually seems to distance himself from his earlier optimistic version of hybridity: "More pessimistically than Rushdie's former novels, *The Moor's Last Sigh* recognizes that the dream of cultural hybridity is little more than a soothing illusion (not only) in twentieth-century India"; Sabine Schülting, "Peeling Off History in Salman Rushdie's *The Moor's Last Sigh*," in Fludernik, ed. *Hybridity and Postcolonialism*, 241. This observation is supported by the interpretation of Rushdie's second-latest novel, *The*

The first type of multicultural literature includes the tradition of
migrant narratives going back to the 1950s whose gloomy titles signal
what the first generation of hopeful immigrants encountered in the
streets of racist London: loneliness, second-class citizenship and unbelonging. Although the protagonists of the novels of Sam Selvon,
Buchi Emecheta and Joan Riley come to Britain from different parts of
the world (the West Indies, Nigeria and Jamaica), their experiences of
poverty, hostility and outright racism are very similar. A more optimistic kind of second-generation writing has emerged since the late
1980s with the works of authors such as Hanif Kureishi, Farhana
Sheik, Meera Syal and Diran Adebayo. Their second-generation
Bildungsromane, whose protagonists have been born and brought up
in Britain, document the changes that the tight diasporic communities
of their parents have undergone.

The second type of contemporary multicultural fiction includes
authors such as Salman Rushdie or Zadie Smith who are less concerned with the politically correct, authentic representation of ethnic
diasporas than with the collective perception and construction of cultural alterity and fictions of racial or ethnic purity. Their cosmopolitan,
often ironic approach to culture and tradition questions the very notion
of stable identities. The following interpretation of novels by Courttia
Newland and Zadie Smith tries to illustrate the scope of contemporary
intercultural fiction which ranges from affirmative, multicultural approaches to identity on the one hand to a transcultural critique of
identity on the other.

Courttia Newland's novel *Society Within* (1999), a sequel to his
best-selling novel *The Scholar* (1997), explores the fringes of multi-
ethnic society. Like its predecessor, the novel is set in Greenside, a
fictional South London estate which can be regarded as the prototype

---

Ground Beneath Her Feet (1999), in Bruno Zerweck, *Die Synthese aus Realismus und Experiment: Der englische Roman der 1980er und 1990er Jahre
aus erzähltheoretischer und kulturwissenschaftlicher Sicht* (Trier: Wissenschaftlicher Verlag Trier, 2001): 226–48.

of the suburban ghetto.[41] *Society Within* consists of twelve interwoven
and overlapping short stories which are told from the perspectives of
several youths growing up on the estate. This episodic structure with
its recurring characters and loosely connected plot-lines illustrates one
of the main themes of the novel: the vital importance of social net-
works to the young Greensiders, whose everyday life is dominated by
a vicious circle of unemployment, drugs and crime.

The first chapter or story describes an arrival scene: the newcomer
Elisha, who has moved to Greenside after her council flat in Fulham is
destroyed by fire, on her first day makes friends with Valerie and
Leonora. When the two girls learn that Elisha has lost all her personal
possessions, including a much cherished "cris' pair ah Versace jeans
dat got bun up,"[42] they offer to share some of their clothes with her
(60), help her find a job at a local take-away (62) and even introduce
her to her later boyfriend Orin and his friends (216). Elisha's "official
Greenside welcomin' committee" (60), as Valerie and Leonora call
themselves, thus makes it easy for her to settle down in the new neighbourhood.

Friendship and solidarity become even more important when the
Greensiders are faced with external threats, such as raids by the police
or attacks by gangs from outside the estate. When Orin steals a kilo of
hashish, he and his friend Malcolm are chased by professional dealers.
While Orin manages to get away, Malcolm is caught and beaten up by

---

[41] The narrator of Newland's debut novel *The Scholar* (London: Abacus,
1997), which is also set in Greenside, describes the estate as follows: "When
West Indians started immigrating to the 'Motherland' in large numbers, the
estate was more than ready. Many black families found themselves housed in
Greensides all over England, tucked away with the lower-class whites, where
the middle and upper classes didn't have to see them" (37). Most of the people
who live in Greenside have accepted that they have no option to get away, as
Teresa and Marcus who "had wanted to be buried in Dominica, their homeland, but they'd never been able to afford to return home" (7).

[42] Courttia Newland, *Society Within* (London: Abacus, 1999): 11. Further
page references are in the main text.

his attackers. In order to help his friend, Orin approaches a group of
children who readily offer their assistance: "The next minute, stones,
pebbles and rocks were raining down on them [Malcolm's attackers],
like some freak weather system"; Malcolm shows his respect for the
kids' support by "touching every available little fist, including the
girls" (37).

In this climate of poverty and violence, friendships and alliances
offer at least some sense of security. The vital importance of solidarity
and the implicit insistence on unity and conformity, however, leave
little room for ambition and improvement. This is revealed when the
drug dealer Maverick decides to turn his back on crime, a scene which
is reminiscent of Sean's firm, yet ultimately futile resolutions in *The
Scholar*.[43] Maverick tells Orin and Malcolm that he would like to open
a fast-food restaurant selling "a whole range ah West Indian pizzas."[44]
Instead of encouraging him, Orin and Malcolm make fun of him. Later
Malcolm regrets his negative reaction and even starts arguing with
Orin:

> "Wha' d'you reckon of Maverick's pizza idea den?" Malcolm asked
> Orin seriously. "Nigga's crazy." "You reckon?" "Yeh man. Dem
> pizzas soun' disgustin'! I wouldn't fuckin' well eat 'em anyway!" [...]
> "Dat's the trouble wid us man," Malcolm started snidely. "We don't
> support each other's ideas...." (34–35)

Orin's rejection of Maverick's idea brings to mind the adherence to
tradition that is typical of closed communities such as migrant dia-

---

[43] Newland's protagonist Sean Bradley, affectionately nicknamed "the
scholar" by his friends, tries hard to improve the situation for himself and his
girlfriend Sonia: "Other boys smoked weed, ash and worst of all crack; Sean
didn't even touch Benson & Hedges. Other boys spent nights robbing and
chatting up girls; Sean was always studying or relaxing with a lager when he
had no work. Other boys were materialistic, wanting cars, mobile phones and
jewellery now; Sean was working towards his long-term future – *their* long-
term future – so they could leave Greenside behind forever"; Newland, *The
Scholar*, 14.

[44] Newland, *Society Within*, 32.

sporas. The youths from Greenside as well as the minorities they represent favour exclusive notions of identity which are characterized by the strict opposition of 'us' to 'them' rather than by liberal notions of social mobility and cultural change.[45] Among the Greensiders, the social and ethnic boundaries marking off 'them' not only exclude the white English society symbolized by the expensive West End shops where the kids buy the latest sportswear with stolen credit cards from the 'black' suburb. The cultural 'Other' also includes social climbers from Greenside and their new values. It seems that a new way of life without drugs and crime is only possible outside the estate: the former crack addict Art even decides to emigrate to America.

If examined closely, however, the ostensible unity of the neighbourhood quickly turns out to be a construct. The various ethnic minorities in Greenside form separate communities that hold prejudices against each other. There are several instances of intercultural stereotypes and even ethnic racism among the kids of West Indian and Jamaican parentage. This becomes most apparent in the scene when the fourteen-year-old Clive argues with Sammy about his ethnic roots: "'Hey Sammy. I'm Jamaican man.' 'You ain' bin Jamaican in yuh life!' 'My parents are Jamaican den!'"[46] While Sammy ridicules Clive, whose parents come from Barbados, Clive tries in vain to convince him that members of ethnic minorities shouldn't argue among themselves:

> I don't even know why you're coming with all dis bullshit! Don't you feel say we shoulda lef' all dat wid our parents? We're stuck on this one island [Britain] now, all goin' through the same shit no matter where we come from. Do you think *they* [the British] give a fuck which island, which country we're from? (222)

---

[45] This phenomenon is, of course, not only restricted to ethnic diasporas but can also be observed in other closed communities such as the traditional English working class of the post-war period. See Richard Hoggart, *The Uses of Literacy: Aspects of Working Class Life* (London: Chatto & Windus, 1957).

[46] Newland, *Society Within*, 222.

Sammy, however, is not convinced by this appeal to political correctness, and Clive has to learn that the notion of united minorities is a
political fiction rather than multicultural reality, at least in Greenside:
"He [Clive] didn't see what difference it made, but in the last three
months he'd realised some people took their roots very seriously; even
if they weren't actually born there" (226). Clive finally realizes that
ethnic racism is indeed an issue on the estate when the Jamaican
mother of his girlfriend Carolyn rejects him because of his origin. She
tells her daughter: "'Fin' yuhself a Jamaican bwoy...' [...] 'Yuh cyaan
get nowhere wi' dem small-island people. Jamaican an' Barbadian ...
Dem jus' not compatible'" (233–34).

Thus, despite the numerous chance encounters and friendships
among drug dealers and their customers there is no real unity among
most youths living on the estate. This may be due to the generation
gap, as Garvey suspects, when he watches two young kids beating up
and robbing a third one: "'You see that? Thatcher's kids man. Money,
money, money, fuck yuh community, go out fuh youself. *Individualism*. The kids even rob off each other nowadays, y'get me...'" (286).

These illustrations of the variety of relationships portrayed in this
novel serve to demonstrate the complexity of diasporic identities. On
the one hand, the ubiquitous violence and prejudice on the estate show
that unifying concepts of the diaspora as a homogeneous group fail to
take account of multicultural realities: Greenside is a synonym for a
social patchwork of minorities with conflicting beliefs, interests and
opinions. On the other hand, the West Indian, Bajan, Jamaican and
African minorities share the experience of poverty and the sense of
exclusion from the cultural centre of society. In this respect, Greenside, a place that even cab drivers try to avoid (209), appears as a
multicultural microcosm.

The characterization of Greenside as the prototype of the 'black'
suburban ghetto is underlined by the choice of characters. The
majority of the few white characters in *Society Within* represent the
'official' Great Britain, as the two BBC employees in the initial take-

away scene: "A brown-skinned woman sat on one of the stools by the right-hand counter, humming softly to the beautiful child on her lap. Two white men in suits stood beside the woman, arms crossed, holding clipboards bearing the letters 'BBC'" (8). The clothing (suits) and 'official' status (BBC) of the only white customers in the restaurant as well as the fact that the notes on their clipboards are invisible to the locals, which implies that the visitors hold a rather powerful position – all this symbolizes the gap between them and the Greensiders, while their posture (crossed arms) can be interpreted as a sign that they themselves are not entirely at ease in their present situation.

Then there is Trisha, the white social worker. She serves as a bridge between the 'white' and 'black' worlds. Being from a working-class background herself, she knows the problems the youths are faced with and is generally accepted among them. However, when it comes to solving racial conflicts, her advice to ignore the insults rather than to respond in kind is rejected by the West Indian kids. They assume that as a white person she isn't able to understand their situation:

> "It's easy for you to talk about ignorin' things," Robby commented as he joined them. "You're white innit?" Everybody looked pained, as though Robby had touched on a sore subject. He started speaking quickly to cover himself. "Not that you're *her* type of white person, but you can't understand how it feels to be in our shoes, I don't see how you can." (71)

Intercultural understanding, which is taken for granted by cosmopolitan visions of transculturalism proposing the transgression of ethnic and cultural borders, is not possible from the point of view of Newland's main characters. The white social worker may plead for patience and understanding, but Stacey, Robbie and Benji live in a different world where different rules apply: the ignorance and insults of white people cannot be easily dismissed. Their experience makes the three youths distinguish between two sets of white people:

> "Far as I'm concerned dere's two sets ah white people in this worl' – the safe ones an' the racis' ones. You're one ah the safe ones Trish,

> but I'm sorry to say it, the racis' ones outweigh the safe ones by nuff, y'get me?" (72)

Trisha herself realizes that she has lost her credibility:

> Trisha watched them go, thinking that no matter how close she got to them, she'd always be an outsider. Her age, her way of life and her skin colour practically guaranteed that. (72)

The distance between the way of life in Greenside and the world of the 'white' majority is further illustrated by the extensive use of 'black' accents and street slang in the dialogues that dominate this novel: "yout' man" (youth, 15), "ki" (a kilo of hashish, 15), "cat" (crack-head, 105), "drum" (flat, 26), "Met men" (police, 24), "bucky" (gun, 38), "wong" (money, 38), "Yard" (Jamaica, 230) and so on. There is also a lot of 'specialist' vocabulary designating drugs (weed, E and whizz, bone, 13) or brand-names from the fields of sound recording and fashion like "TDK D90" (2), "Calvin Klein" and "Dolce & Gabbana" (28), "Nike" (155), "Armani" (223), "Karl Kani" (223), "Ericson" (29), "Seiko" (68), "Kenwood" (98), "Technics" (223), "twelve tens" (282), and "Gemini" (282). The repetitive use of this kind of 'technical' language gives the speech of Newland's characters the authentic street credibility for which he is praised in numerous reviews, and also implicitly characterizes the values and interests of the youths in Greenside.

Intelligibility (hence compatibility with a wider audience) is ensured by narratorial explanations and comments. Although *Society Within* is a dialogue-driven heterodiegetic narrative without a personalized narrator, we can identify a narrative instance trying to mediate between the world of the characters and the world outside the estate. Two kinds of narrative comments can be distinguished: explanations for those readers who are not familiar with culture-specific items, and didactic comments. Examples of the former are the narrator's description of a 'roti pan' used in a take-away —"She was placing them [thin circles of dough] on a roti pan – a large metal skillet that looked like a flattened frying pan" (211) – and the synonyms offered for the various forms and kinds of drugs featuring in the novel: "Hashish. Cannabis. Ash. Rocky. Pox. Call it what you like" (27). Besides these narratorial explanations there are also some examples of rather didactic comments which justify the 'bad' behaviour of the non-white characters:

> An old white woman was heading the youths' way, shuffling at a snail's pace, shopping bags in hand, head down. The youths were laughing, shouting and play fighting with each other uproariously, oblivious to her presence. The old woman didn't see them until they were almost on top of her; when she did, she jumped halfway out of her skin, almost dropped her bags, and shakily crossed the road as quick as her skinny legs would carry her. Responding in kind, the three youths instantly turned nasty. They began shouting insults at the woman, which scared her even more. (70)

Despite such narratorial descriptions, explanations and comments, the distance between the world of the characters and the world outside the estate cannot be ultimately bridged by the narrator as a mediating instance. This is underlined by the fact that traditional poetic justice does not apply – the bad guys, violent drug dealers and notorious thieves, do not get punished in the end. There remains a gap between insiders and outsiders, a gap that reminds Orin of the difference between the virtual world of television and his experience of reality:

> He felt as if he was an actor playing a part, and he'd just stepped off-camera. Now it was all over. He felt weak, and his mind refused to accept what had happened – things that happened to him on this estate gave him that kind of feeling. He supposed it was his way of dealing with things that most people only saw on a cinema or TV screen. (44)

℘

Let us now turn to our second type of multicultural fiction. An outstanding example of the transcultural novel is *White Teeth*, Zadie

Smith's fictional account of "Happy Multicultural Land."[47] Smith's
successful debut novel tells the story of three families from very different ethnic backgrounds and a "friendship that crosses class and
colour" (83); Archie Jones, a white English veteran of the Second
World War, is married to the Jamaican immigrant Clara; Archie's best
friend Samad Iqbal and his wife Alsana are originally from Bangladesh; and the Chalfens are a secularized Jewish family in which
"therapy had long supplanted Judaism" (270). They all share the
ability to adapt to the new country and culture. As the narrator reflects,
"And it goes to prove what has been said of immigrants many times
before now; they are resourceful; they make do. They use what they
can when they can" (398).

There is no such thing as ethnic purity in Smith's novel. Not only
do her characters favour interracial relationships, they also exploit
English stereotypes to make the most of their 'exotic' ethnicity. Thus,
Samad's cousin Ardashir revives "the simple idea of an Indian restaurant (small room, pink tablecloth, loud music, atrocious wallpaper,
meals that do not exist in India, sauce carousel)" and makes a fortune
"in the biggest tourist trap in London, Leicester Square" (51), while
Samad himself takes advantage of the fact that his sons' attractive
music teacher admires his alleged Eastern virtues, by having an affair
with her. Samad's sons, the twins Millat and Magid, have also learnt
to adapt to different cultural contexts from an early age: "To the black
kids he [Millat] was fellow weed-smoker and valued customer. To the
Asian kids, hero and spokesman. Social chameleon" (232–33).

The reference to the chameleon which changes its colour as circumstances demand underlines the novel's attitude towards identity: its
characters adapt themselves to the situations in which they find themselves. Their presumed ethnic identity does not prevent them from
(re)inventing themselves. This becomes clear when Samad decides to

---

[47] Zadie Smith, *White Teeth* (London: Hamish Hamilton, 2000): 398. Further page references are in the main text.

send Magid back to Bangladesh, where he is supposed to be educated
"properly." Magid returns as a perfect example of the postcolonial
'mimic man', "more English than the English" (348), while Millat,
who stays in London, joins a fundamentalist Islamic group that is too
radical even for his father's liking: "'The one I send home comes out
a pukka Englishman, white suited, silly wig lawyer. The one I keep
here is fully paid-up green bow-tie-wearing fundamentalist terrorist'"
(349). In the end, Samad has to accept that he cannot turn back the
clock. As Irie's reflections near the end of the novel affirm, ethnic
roots, however painful they are, will soon be a thing of the past:

> In a vision, Irie has seen a time, a time not far from now, when roots
> won't matter any more because they can't because they mustn't
> because they're too long and they're too tortuous and they're just
> buried too damn deep. She looks forward to it. (450)

While Newland's novel relies heavily on dialogue and street language
to characterize its protagonists and to create the impression of authenticity and spontaneity, Smith's extensive use of irony creates, rather, a
distance between the readers and her characters. Not unlike Rushdie's
The Satanic Verses, White Teeth plays with the functions of a (heterodiegetic) narrator who not only openly comments on the events of the
story as well as the actions, thoughts and decisions of the characters
but also addresses the readers and plays with their expectations, creating an atmosphere of suspense. The following quote, which describes
Archie's and Samad's favourite pub, O'Connell's, is a good example
of this:

> You need to *know* the place. For example, there are reasons why
> O'Connell's is an Irish pool house run by Arabs with no pool tables.
> And there are reasons why the pustule-covered Mickey will cook you
> chips, egg and beans, or egg, chips and beans, or beans, chips, eggs
> and mushrooms but not, under any circumstances, chips, beans, eggs
> and bacon. But you need to hang around for that kind of information.
> We'll get into that later. (159)

The ironic comments of the narrator are, for one, directed against exaggerated political correctness, embodied by the good-natured school principal and the naive music teacher Burt–Jones ("'I don't think it is very nice to make fun of *somebody else's culture*'," 135), for whom his pupils' ethnic backgrounds serve as excuses for almost any offence committed at school. Thus, when Millat is caught consuming drugs, the director goes out of his way to find an explanation in Millat's favour: "'You're going to have to give me a little more to work on, Millat. If there's some religious connection here, it can only work in your favour, but I need to know about it'" (259). Moreover, the students' ethnic background constitutes an ideal prerequisite for applying for public funding. Secondly, the narrator ridicules homogenizing notions of Englishness or Britishness. This becomes apparent in the chapters dealing with Archie's and Samad's experiences in World War II. Their captain, Dickinson–Smith, who commits suicide towards the end of World War II, thus becoming "the only Dickinson–Smith to die by English hands" (80), is characterized as the prototype of the English imperialist:

> Killed by the Hun, the Wogs, the Chinks, the Kaffirs, the Frogs, the Scots, the Spics, the Zulus, the Indians (South, East and Red) [...], traditionally the Dickinson–Smiths were insatiable in their desire to see Dickinson–Smith blood spilled on foreign soil. (77–78)

Again and again, the narrator emphasizes that the ethnic identity of second-generation immigrants has given way to a universal youth subculture: "'*Cha*, man! Believe, I don't *want* to tax dat crap,' said Millat with the Jamaican accent that all kids, whatever their nationality, used to express scorn" (145). Cultural hybridity thus replaces ethnic boundaries, at least among the younger generation, who – at least in Smith's novel – have no historical or political consciousness whatsoever. While their fathers, "makeshift historians" (218), dwell on their memories of the war, Irie and her friends are used to growing up between two or more cultures. Their predicament is the result of a "century of the great immigrant experiment" (281):

you can walk into a playground and find Isaac Leung by the fish
pond, Danny Rahman in the football cage, Quang O'Rourke bouncing
a basketball, and Irie Jones humming a tune. Children with first and
last names on a direct collision course. Names that secrete within
them mass exodus, cramped boats and planes, cold arrivals, medical
checks. (281)

In *White Teeth*, the transcultural present has superseded the monocultural past which was guided by xenophobic notions of national
identity and racial purity. Samad's wife Alsana sums it up nicely:

you go back and back and back and it's still easier to find the correct
Hoover bag than to find one pure person, one pure faith, on the globe.
Do you think anybody is English? Really English? It's a fairy tale!
(204)

Concluding Remarks

Ethnic minorities have to meet at least two challenges: the external
pressure of assimilation to the traditions of the cultural majority and
internal tensions between different generations within the diaspora
itself. They may respond to these challenges by adapting to the new
way of life or by holding on to the traditions and beliefs of their homelands. These two attitudes may be labelled 'transcultural' and 'diasporic'. Of course, I am not suggesting that there are only two ways to
respond to multi-ethnicity. Diasporic and transcultural multiculturalism can, rather, be considered as two opposite ends of a scale that
includes various combinations of essentialist notions of 'race' and
collective identities, pragmatic approaches to cultural pluralism and
cosmopolitan visions of free choice between different cultural roots
and traditions.

The proposed distinction between diasporic and transcultural multiculturalism reveals a shortcoming of current multicultural theory:
owing to the widespread preoccupation with cultural hybridity, multiculturalism and hybridity have almost become synonyms, especially
among those literary critics who take the novels of Salman Rushdie as

multicultural paradigms. However, multicultural fiction includes affirmative constructions of ethnic or social identity as well as their ironic dismissal as essentialist fictions.

The two novels discussed above, Zadie Smith's *White Teeth* and Courttia Newland's *Society Within*, represent two opposed literary responses to multi-ethnic London. While Newland depicts the grim realities of everyday life of second-generation immigrants in the suburban estates, Smith's novel can be read as a cosmopolitan celebration of transcultural hybridity. The obvious differences in the treatment of ethnicity, identity and community illustrate the broad spectrum of fictional responses to multi-ethnicity in contemporary Britain. They also emphasize that multicultural fiction is not as homogeneous as the commonly used label 'black fiction' implies.

This takes me back to the main argument of this essay. Multiculturalism is not a homogeneous concept but a discourse on multi-ethnicity that accommodates conflicting voices. Some of these voices call for the cultural assimilation of minorities, others for the recognition of difference; some support the postmodern concept of patchwork identities, others endorse essentializing notions of ethnicity. Multicultural discourse offers no 'solutions' to the 'problems' resulting from multi-ethnicity, but allows different voices to be heard, different opinions to be expressed. A look at the multicultural texts, moreover, demonstrates that multiculturalist scenarios need not be confined to a setting that negotiates the relationship between the dominant white population and the immigrant minorities as diasporas. Multi-ethnicity and ethnic clashes are observable precisely among the immigrant communities. This poses once again the question of recognition between and within diasporic communities, leaving the white world outside as a powerful but largely irrelevant frame for the ethnic immigrant experience.

Stanley Fish is right when he reminds liberal academics that even an open society has to resort to decidedly illiberal "acts of ungenerosity, intolerance, perhaps even repression"[48] if its values and principles are in danger. He is also right when he condemns hate speech. However, it is theoretically invalid, morally questionable and politically dangerous to imply that cultural differences always lead to fundamental disagreements and that ethnic minorities should therefore be compared with racist, sexist or homophobic hate speakers. Moreover, these arguments ignore the actual problems and positive perspectives afforded by diasporic multi-ethnic and transcultural communities as described in literary texts.

WORKS CITED

Ahluwalia, Kiranjit, & Rahila Gupta. *Circle of Light: The Autobiography of Kiranjit Ahluwalia* (London: HarperCollins, 1997).

Beavers, Herman. "Editor's Column," *Narrative* 7.2 (1999): 129–30.

Bhabha, Homi K. *The Location of Culture* (London & New York: Routledge, 1994).

Chicago Cultural Studies Group. "Critical Multiculturalism," *Critical Inquiry* 18 (1992): 530–55.

Davies, Carole Boyce. *Black Women, Writing and Identity: Migrations of the Subject* (London: Routledge, 1994).

Dirie, Waris. *Desert Flower* (London: Virago, 1999).

Fish, Stanley. "Boutique Multiculturalism, or Why Liberals Are Incapable of Thinking about Hate Speech," *Critical Inquiry* 23 (1997): 378–95.

Fludernik, Monika. "Colonial vs. Cosmopolitan Hybridity: A Comparison of Mulk Raj Anand and R.K. Narayan with recent British and North American Expatriate Writing (Singh Baldwin, Divakaruni, Sunetra Gupta)," in Fludernik, ed. *Hybridity and Postcolonialism*, 261–90.

——. "The Constitution of Hybridity: Postcolonial Interventions," in Fludernik, ed. *Hybridity and Postcolonialism*, 19–53.

——, ed. *Hybridity and Postcolonialism: Twentieth-Century Indian Literature* (Tübingen: Stauffenburg, 1998).

Fraser, Nancy. "From Redistribution to Recognition? Dilemmas of Justice in a 'Post-Socialist' Age," in Willett, ed. *Theorizing Multiculturalism*, 19–49.

---

[48] Fish, "Boutique Multiculturalism," 390.

Gilroy, Paul. "A London Sumting Dis...," *Critical Quarterly* 41.3 (1999): 57–69.

Green, Judith. "Educational Multiculturalism, Critical Pluralism, and Deep Democracy," in Willett, ed. *Theorizing Multiculturalism*, 422–48.

Hoggart, Richard. *The Use of Literacy: Aspects of Working Class Life* (London: Chatto & Windus, 1957).

Korte, Barbara, & Klaus Peter Müller, ed. *Unity in Diversity Revisited? British Literature and Culture in the 1990s* (Tübingen: Gunter Narr, 1998).

Loomba, Ania. *Colonialism/Postcolonialism* (London & New York: Routledge, 1998).

Martin, Bill. "Multiculturalism: Consumerist or Transformational?" in Willett, ed. *Theorizing Multiculturalism*, 121–50.

Matuštík, Martin. "Ludic, Corporate, and Imperial Multiculturalism: Impostors of Democracy and Cartographers of the New World Order," in Willett, ed. *Theorizing Multiculturalism*, 100–17.

Mergenthal, Silvia. "Englishness/Englishnesses in Contemporary Fiction," in Korte & Müller, ed. *Unity in Diversity Revisited?*, 51–61.

Mishra, Vijay. "The Diasporic Imaginary: Theorizing the Indian Diaspora," *Textual Practice* 10.3 (1996): 421–47.

Newland, Courttia. *The Scholar* (London: Abacus, 1997).

——. *Society Within* (London: Abacus, 1999).

Pease, Donald E. "Regulating Multi-Adhoccerists, Fish('s) Rules," *Critical Inquiry* 23 (1997): 398–418.

Riedel, Wolfgang. "Black and/or British. Writing in a Multicultural Society," *anglistik & englischunterricht* 48 (1992): 65–77.

Rushdie, Salman. *The Ground Beneath Her Feet* (London: Jonathan Cape, 1999).

——. *Imaginary Homelands: Essays and Criticism 1981–1991* (London: Granta, 1992).

Said, Edward. *Culture and Imperialism* (London: Vintage, 1994).

Schäffner, Raimund. "'Identity is not in the past to be found, but in the future to be constructed': History and Identity in Caryl Phillips' Novels," in Korte & Müller, ed. *Unity in Diversity Revisited?*, 107–26.

Schülting, Sabine. "Peeling off History in Salman Rushdie's *The Moor's Last Sigh*," in Fludernik, ed. *Hybridity and Postcolonialism*, 239–60.

Smith, Zadie. *White Teeth* (London: Hamish Hamilton, 2000).

Sommer, Roy. *Fictions of Migration: Ein Beitrag zur Theorie und Gattungstypologie des zeitgenössischen interkulturellen Romans in Großbritannien* (Trier: Wissenschaftlicher Verlag Trier, 2001).

Stein, Mark. "The Black British 'Bildungsroman' and the Transformation of Britain: Connectedness Across Difference," in Korte & Müller, ed. *Unity in Diversity Revisited?*, 89–105.

Taylor, Charles. "The Politics of Recognition," in *Multiculturalism: Examining the Politics of Recognition*, ed. Amy Gutman (Princeton NJ: Princeton UP, 1994): 25–73.

Titzmann, Manfred. "Skizze einer integrativen Literaturgeschichte und ihres Ortes in einer Systematik der Literaturwissenschaft," in *Modelle des literarischen Strukturwandels*, ed. Manfred Titzmann (Tübingen: Max Niemeyer, 1991): 395–438.

Willett, Cynthia. "Introduction" to Willett, ed. *Theorizing Multiculturalism*, 1–15.

——, ed. *Theorizing Multiculturalism: A Guide to the Current Debate* (Oxford: Blackwell, 1998).

Zerweck, Bruno. *Die Synthese aus Realismus und Experiment: Der englische Roman der 1980er und 1990er Jahre aus erzähltheoretischer und kulturwissenschaftlicher Sicht* (Trier: Wissenschaftlicher Verlag Trier, 2001).

✍

MINOLI SALGADO

Nonlinear Dynamics
and the Diasporic Imagination

> If the criteria of knowledge defining centre and margin change,
> in a very real sense the structure of knowledge changes as well.[1]

THE LITERATURES AND CULTURES of migrancy are
invariably complex, contradictory, and unstable, drawing as
they do upon a migrant experience that is "structured and
open, continuous and interrupted."[2] And yet the analysis of diasporic
migrant flows has until recently been dominated by a monologic
discourse of spatial fixity and temporal and geographic linearity. In his
analysis of modernity and migrancy, Nikos Papastergiadis has argued
that while such a discourse may well have suited the earlier patterns of
migrancy when destinations were knowable and journeys were predominantly a one-way enterprise, the increasingly complex flows of
migrant movement demand a corresponding paradigm shift from the

---

[1] N. Katherine Hayles, *Chaos Bound: Orderly Disorder in Contemporary
Literature and Science* (Ithaca NY: Cornell UP, 1991): 144.
[2] Ian Chambers, "Migrancy Culture, Identity," in *The Postmodern History
Reader*, ed. Keith Jenkins (London: Routledge, 1997): 80.

linear to the multidirectional. Drawing on chaos theory, he argues that, whereas earlier

> [...] movement was generally mapped in linear terms, with clear co-ordinates between centre and periphery, and definable axial routes, the current phase can best be described as turbulent, a fluid but structured movement, with multidirectional and reversible trajectories.[3]

Papastergiadis is not alone in drawing on the structural and ideological paradigms of chaotics for evaluating modern migration. Antonio Benítez–Rojo has used the metaphor of recursive flux to order his study of Caribbean culture in *The Repeating Island*,[4] and Arjun Appadurai has argued that modern cultural forms of hybrid identities and deterritorialisation are "fractally shaped [and ...] polythetically overlapping in their coverage of terrestrial space."[5] All three cultural critics use the language and rationale of chaotics as a "bridging concept,"[6] to formulate a critical language responsive to the cultural conditions created by modern migrancy. In their bold and wide-ranging analyses, chaos theory – and the related science of complexity theory – on the one hand are analytical tools for understanding a social and cultural condition, and, on the other, are in their turn expressive of this condition.

My own analysis is differently angled. Exploring the imaginative and structural affinities between the emergent sciences of chaos complexity theory and the theoretical and literary paradigms of the diasporic experience, I go on to draw correspondences between key concepts in the fields of science and postcolonial studies. It will be

---

[3] Nikos Papastergiadis, *The Turbulence of Migration: Globalisation, Deterritorialisation and Hybridity* (Cambridge: Polity, 2000): 7.

[4] Antonio Benítez–Rojo, *The Repeating Island: The Caribbean and the Postmodern Perspective*, tr. James E. Maraniss (Durham NC: Duke UP, 1992).

[5] Arjun Appadurai, *Modernity at Large: Cultural Dimensions of Globalisation* (Minneapolis: U of Minnesota P, 1996): 46.

[6] Papastergiadis, *The Turbulence of Migration*, 5.

seen that the fundamental principle of chaos, that of generative disorder, lies at the unstable core of the diasporic experience and has a variety of divergent repercussion in the texts of postcolonial writers. These will be illustrated from the work of Salman Rushdie and Michael Ondaatje. My aim is not simply to present and promote a chaotic reading of the diasporic condition or reflect upon the ways in which complexity manifests itself in migrant culture, but, more specifically, to explore the ways in which chaotics intersects with, and informs, diasporic literary practice and the production of knowledge of diasporic experience. In the process it will be seen that the principles of chaotics – sensitivity to initial conditions (popularly known as 'the butterfly effect'), generative disorder, nonlinearity, irreversibility, and exponential bifurcation – are not merely a convenient critical paradigm for evaluating diasporic experience, but are systematically embedded within this experience and internal to the logic of the diasporic imagination. Chaotics provides a means of analysing the links between the global and the local in processual and emergent terms. The implications for literary analysts are, in my view, far-reaching. Chaotic readings serve not to regularize but to reveal, and insist on the rich complexity of diasporic texts; they describe a dynamic in which contradictory and conflictual readings become not only possible but also necessary.

The Chaos of Diaspora

Diaspora. To sow, disperse or scatter; a term first used in Deuteronomy to describe the dispersal of the Jews. Diaspore. A native hydrate of aluminium, so named from its strong decrepitation when heated.[7]

---

[7] *The Shorter Oxford English Dictionary* (Third Edition) rev. G.W.S. Friedrichsen (London: Guild, 1983), vol. 1: 542.

In this dictionary entry the scientific and the religious converge, aligning the popular notion of the diasporic as a collective dispersal with
the notion of disintegration under pressure. This connection between
coercion and collectivity lends itself to comparison with the causal
language of energy flows found in the physical sciences – a language
which can, often unwittingly, influence theorists of diaspora; the correspondence between migrant movement and 'pressure points' can be
seen, for example, in Robin Cohen's observation that in enforced
migration "there is an inverse relationship between the amount of
compulsion involved and the likelihood of anticipatory socialization to
the new environment."[8]

Diasporas are fluid, fluctuating systems determined by energy flows
and the pressures of globalization and migrant labour. They interrupt,
unsettle, connect with and transform existing cultural formations.
They correspond to what the Belgian physicist Ilya Prigogine has
described as open systems that exist far from equilibrium and fluctuate
non-linearly.[9] Prigogine's research – concisely outlined by Katherine
Hayles in her seminal work on chaotics and literature – reveals how
entropic disorder creates new kinds of order, jumping to a new level of
order, a moment described as a 'bifurcation point', resulting in increasing complexity in the macroscopic world.[10] Chaos is a form of
generative disorder that has structural correspondences with the diasporic condition of flow, flux and entropic disintegration, encoded
with the power for generative complexity. Thus, in terms of chaotics,
the migrant group's contact with a host community constitutes a temporal and spatial bifurcation point that generates cultural complexity

---

[8] Robin Cohen, *Global Diasporas: An Introduction* (Seattle: U of Washington P, 1997): 195.

[9] See David Porush, "Fictions as Dissipative Structures," in *Chaos and
Order: Complex Dynamics in Literature and Science* ed. N. Katherine Hayles
(Chicago: U of Chicago P, 1991): 70.

[10] See N. Katherine Hayles, "Introduction" to *Chaos and Order*, 13.

and diversity that are irreversible. The creation of hybrid identities is central to this dynamic.

The chaotic model of diaspora draws on what Harriet Hawkins has described as the two central characteristics of chaotic systems: nonlinearity and irreversibility.[11] The first correspondence with nonlinearity is self-evident. Diasporic trajectories are multidirectional and composed of endless motion. As Nikos Papastergiadis has shown, such migrational flows are difficult to trace to a stable, originary point – they replicate chaotic processes in which original causes are hidden and consequences are unpredictable.[12] As will be seen, this rupturing of causality has specific and unpredictable effects in the temporal and spatial configurations of migrant writers. Nonlinearity is also replicated in the lateral cultural transferences found in the intertextual legacy of the migrant artist, in which texts such as Rushdie's deliberately foreground their dialogic relationship to the work of other writers.

The second characteristic – that of irreversibility – has a more uneasy relationship to diasporic aesthetics and is often problematized and contested by migrant writers. In chaotics, the principle of irreversibility is predicated on Prigogine's and Stenger's' observation that "time can only go forward because an infinite information barrier divides past and present."[13] For time to go backward, it would require "a massive correlation of information to have [for example] collisions on every level, from subatomic particles to cars on a California freeway to meteorites striking Jupiter, reverse themselves"[14] – every event would have to reverse itself precisely in every detail.

---

[11] Harriet Hawkins, *Strange Attractors: Literature, Culture and Chaos Theory* (Hemel Hempstead: Prentice–Hall/Harvester Wheatsheaf, 1995): 131.

[12] Papastergiadis, *The Turbulence of Migration*, 1.

[13] N. Katherine Hayles, *Chaos Bound: Orderly Disorder in Contemporary Literature and Science* (Ithaca NY: Cornell UP, 1990): 97.

[14] Hayles, *Chaos Bound*, 98.

Yet a form of temporal reversal is a key feature of the diasporic imagination in its quest for wholeness and connection with the past. While the lived reality of the writer undeniably affirms the violent temporal rupture that migration enforces – "of his present being in a different place from his past"[15] – this very dislocation creates the conditions for the imaginative desire to negate time, reverse it and enact an endless return to the past. It is as if the irreversible "wholesale transition"[16] involved in the act of migration and settlement opens up imaginative possibilities for the migrant writer who wishes not so much to reverse time but to step back in time, embarking on a journey or, in the discourse of chaotics, enacting a 'feedback loop'. It is this impulse that guides Ondaatje's return to his native land in his travel memoir *Running in the Family*, as he creates the intimate imaginative landscape that allows him to enter into dialogue with his dead father.[17] In some cases, while the desire for such connection may be strong, no reconciliation is possible, and the migrant writer is unable to overcome imaginatively the information barrier that divides the past from the present. In such cases, the disjuncture marked by spatial and temporal dislocation results in a bifurcated perspective (what Rushdie has described as a "stereoscopic vision")[18] such that, as John McLeod has claimed in his critique of Naipaul, "the idea of the home country splits from the experience of returning home."[19] This divided perspective results in irreversible ontological instability for the migrant, for whom home (the perceived point of origin) becomes displaced into a condition of possibility located in the future, creating a site of endlessly deferred desire. As Avtar Brah observes, "'home' is a mythic space of

[15] Salman Rushdie, "Imaginary Homelands," in *Imaginary Homelands: Essays and Criticism 1981–1991* (London: Granta, 1991): 12.

[16] Hawkins, *Strange Attractors*, 160.

[17] Michael Ondaatje, *Running in the Family* (London: Picador, 1983).

[18] Rushdie, "Imaginary Homelands," 19.

[19] John McLeod, *Beginning Postcolonialism* (Manchester: Manchester UP, 2000): 209.

desire in the diasporic imagination. [...] It is a place of no-return even if it is possible to visit the geographical territory that is seen as the place of 'origin'."[20] This uncertainty punctuates the linearity of diasporic writing, creating, as will be seen, spatially transversive texts.

The migrant writer is situated on the edge of cultural exchange and negotiation, experiencing the contingency and crisis of travel and displacement. Migrancy enacts a nonlinear trajectory that, in Paul Gilroy's formulation, challenges the certainty of "roots" with the contingency of "routes."[21] Drawing on bifurcation theory, which posits that "at each forking the number of possible flow paths doubles,"[22] Harriet Hawkins has argued that nonlinearity results in the exponential diversification of language and culture[23] – a model analogous to the complex trajectories and subject formations that result from the diasporic encounter. For migrant writers, the crisis of travel involves an act of dislocation that positions them at a point of perpetual emergence – a "phase space": ie, "a place or instant of transition" of a dynamic system.[24] Poised on the edge of order and instability, their work not only reflects but also actively explores the conditions that create wholesale transition, often replicating the structures of chaotics. For example, causality gives way to casualty in Rushdie's *Midnight's Children*, in which small changes in one variable have disproportionately large effects on another. Exponential bifurcation can be found in the digressive narrative form of *Midnight's Children*, in which stories multiply exponentially in time – what Rushdie has aptly ascribed to India's capacity for "non-stop self-generation" in the face of disinte-

---

[20] Avtar Brah, *Cartographies of Diaspora: Contesting Identities* (London: Routledge, 1997): 192.

[21] Paul Gilroy, *The Black Atlantic* (London: Verso, 1993), cited in McLeod, *Beginning Postcolonialism*, 215.

[22] Thomas P. Weissert, "Representation and Bifurcation: Borges' Garden of Chaos Dynamics," in Hayles, *Chaos and Order*, 235.

[23] Hawkins, *Strange Attractors*, 41.

[24] Hawkins, *Strange Attractors*, 155.

gration[25] – and, in a different form, in the self-conscious use of exaggeration in Michael Ondaatje's *Running in the Family*, in which each re-telling of a story serves to "swell" the narrative.[26] Finally, dissipative structures, in which disorder generates new forms of order, punctuate Ondaatje's *In the Skin of a Lion*.[27]

All these literary articulations of the dynamics of chaos and emergence deserve fuller consideration. My aim here is to focus on just one element in the system and reveal its connection to the dynamics of diasporic emergence. By considering the ways in which randomness and accident influence the formal and ideological imperatives of migrant literature, I will reveal some of the implications that these chaotic replications of causality have on formulations of agency and 'free will'.

Rushdie and Ondaatje: Textual Chaos

The work of Salman Rushdie and Michael Ondaatje is symptomatic of the complex diversity of migrant writing, in that it demarcates two very different trajectories of chaotic order. Rushdie's work follows a totalizing impulse, a desire to "swallow the world."[28] He draws on a holistic model of action, interaction and reaction, and foregrounds the determinism of cause and effect. *Midnight's Children* affirms a deductive logic in which apparently random events are framed and given meaning by a larger pre-existing whole. Rushdie repeatedly draws attention to this method of constructing meaning through enforced correspondences and, in exilic reclamation of his former home, locates this method as archetypally 'Indian':

---

[25] Rushdie, "Imaginary Homelands," 16.

[26] Ondaatje, *Running in the Family*, 26.

[27] For a detailed consideration of this, see Minoli Salgado, "Complexity and the Migrant Writer: Chaotics in Michael Ondaatje's Fiction," *Angles on the English Speaking World* 1 (2001): 98–105.

[28] Salman Rushdie, *Midnight's Children* (London: Picador, 1981): 109.

As a people we are obsessed with correspondences. Similarities between this and that, between apparently unconnected things, make us
clap our hands delightedly when we find them out. It is a sort of
national longing for form – or perhaps an expression of our deep
belief that forms lie hidden within reality; that meaning reveals itself
only in flashes. Hence our vulnerability to omens.[29]

This obsession with correspondences is directly linked with the desire
to give shape to the past (metafictionally deployed in the ridiculous
and overtly random connections made by Saleem in constructing his
version of events)[30] and predict the future (evident here in the reference to omens). Rushdie's work reveals the difficulties involved when
the nonlinearity of diasporic experience encounters the hegemonic,
historicizing, linear logic of cause and effect.

This self-reflexive emphasis on the constructed nature of causality
draws on a chaotic model of generative disorder that is both deterministic and unpredictable.[31] (Saleem's telepathy is retrospectively
inscribed – his predictions are simultaneously historically determined
and predictive.) Rushdie's work highlights the paradox of deterministic chaos, in which action can be seen as both determined and
haphazard,[32] but does so in order to lay bare the mechanics of chaotics,
to expose its complexity and exploit its paradoxes. He is a self-
conscious exponent of chaotics whose formulations of generative
disorder are, at one level, extrinsic to the events described. "How does
newness come into the world?" asks the narrator of *The Satanic
Verses*, "of what fusions, translations, [...] is it made? How does it
survive, extreme and dangerous as it is? What compromises, what
deals, what betrayals of its secret nature must it make to stave off [...]
the exterminating angel? Is birth always a fall?"[33] The question that
dominates the novel is thus encoded within the rationale of emergence

---

[29] Rushdie, *Midnight's Children*, 300.
[30] Rushdie, *Midnight's Children*, 279.
[31] Hawkins, *Strange Attractors*, 30.
[32] Hawkins, *Strange Attractors*, 114.
[33] Salman Rushdie, *The Satanic Verses* (London: Vintage, 1988): 8.

and generative disorder, as the birth of a new order is shown to be predicated upon elective but unpredictable change, upon transformative
disintegration and collapse. In keeping with this deterministic logic,
Rushdie's novels are overtly schematized – none more so, perhaps,
than *The Satanic Verses*, in which the complementarity of the contrastive hybrid identities of the two main characters is inverted in the
course of the novel.[34]

Rushdie's trajectory thus presents us with a paradoxical model of
agency and intentionality, revealing how "the unpredictable and the
predetermined unfold together to make everything the way it is."[35] His
work is teleologically constrained and follows a dialectical reasoning
in which polarized forces (for example, democracy and dictatorship in
Midnight's Children; monologic fixity and dialogic instability in *The
Satanic Verses*) struggle for supremacy. Yet, in foregrounding the
dynamics of power, Rushdie can be seen to reinforce the very logic of
difference and duality through which dominant systems gain legitimacy. By reconciling free will with determinism (in the case of
Saleem's telepathy, for instance), chance with fate, Rushdie highlights
the constraints rather than the indeterminacy of emergence. This
understanding of determinism is in line with the claims of Medd and
Haynes, who argue that "apparent indeterminacy is [...] the consequence of epistemological, not [...] ontological limits." As 'the butterfly effect' (in which small causes can have disproportionately large
effects) is based on the irrecoverability of the initial conditions (rather
than their indeterminacy), "indeterminacy is the consequence of the

---

[34] Minoli Salgado, "Migration and Mutability: The Twice Born Fiction of
Salman Rushdie," in *British Culture of the Postwar: An Introduction to
Literature and Society 1945–1999*, ed. Alistair Davies & Alan Sinfield (Lon-
don: Routledge, 2000): 40–41.
[35] Tom Stoppard, *Arcadia* (London: Faber & Faber, 1993), cited in
Hawkins, *Strange Attractors*, 2.

limitations of observation rather than creativity generated by the model."[36]

While determinism functions as an overarching principle structuring the teleological narrative drive in many of Rushdie's novels (such as *Midnight's Children, Shame* or *The Moor's Last Sigh*), generative disorder is explored intrinsically through the creative potential of language. Metaphoric analogy and rich semantic play, evidenced, for example, in the nasal leitmotif in *Midnight's Children*, generate the (apparently) spontaneous self-organization of meaning, propelling the narrative onto new levels of order. A chaotic reading of Rushdie's texts thus foregrounds this paradoxical alignment of historical determinism with linguistic unpredictability that underpins his narrative mode and provides a systemic understanding of the structuration of deterministic emergence and generative disorder in his work.

In contrast to Rushdie's deterministic, deductive model of chaotic emergence, Michael Ondaatje's work explores the unpredictability of chaotic systems inductively, presenting the haphazard process of textual creation.[37] The 'slippages' and 'shifts' that are forms of spatial and temporal compression in his work[38] are also bifurcation points that open multidirectional, labyrinthine pathways in which multiple potentiality is explored. A key example of the textual inscription of such multiple potentiality can be found in the lyrical passage describing the

---

[36] Will Medd & Paul Haynes, "Complexity and the Social," ESRC Complexity Workshop, http://www.keele.ac.uk/depts/stt/cstt2/comp/medd.htm.

[37] In interviews, Ondaatje himself has repeatedly drawn attention to the fact that he has no clear sense of direction when writing. See Linda Hutcheon's interview in *Other Solitudes: Canadian Multicultural Fictions* (Oxford: Oxford UP, 1999): 196–202, in which he acknowledges that he composes in a "random [...] accidental way [...] going down roads that end up nowhere"; Sam Solecki's interview in *Spider Blues: Essays on Michael Ondaatje* (Montreal: Véhicule, 1985): 321–32; and the Salon Interview, http://www.salon1999.com/nov96/ondaatje961118.html.

[38] Rufus Cook, "'Imploding Time and Geography': Narrative Compressions in Michael Ondaatje's *The English Patient*," *Journal of Commonwealth Literature* 33.2 (1998): 110.

lovemaking of Gianetta and Caravaggio in *In the Skin of a Lion*. Here
Ondaatje repeats the opening lines (referring to Caravaggio drinking
some milk and Gianetta's perception of its whiteness) at the end,[39]
effectively taking the reader back to the beginning of the scene and
thus repeating and erasing the original in a way that projects an experience of simultaneity and multidirectionality. The movement replicates
the "virtual transitions" described by Danah Zohar in her presentation
of motion at the quantum level, in which "there exist [...] myriad
possibilities of countless actualities" such that things "happen simultaneously in every direction at once."[40] Similarly, when Hana in *The
English Patient* dislodges a glass in one country and Kip is shown to
simultaneously pick up a fork in another,[41] cause and effect are
"replaced by the notion of correlation across gaps in space and time."[42]
Ondaatje's emphasis on multiple potentiality, temporal simultaneity
and spatial contiguity undermines not only a teleological narrative
drive but also, in my view, promotes a fluid co-optive notion of 'free
will' that is at variance with the more deterministic notion of indivi-
duated agency found in Rushdie's texts.[43]

Nonlinearity in Ondaatje's work thus serves to disrupt and subvert
rational explanation. It takes many forms, from disturbance on a
spatiotemporal (and ontological) level through to the formal irregularity of line structures in poems such as "Sweet Like a Crow" and
"Women Like You" in *Running in the Family* (76–77; 92–94). It can
be seen in the interrupted journeys that structure *Running in the
Family* and *In the Skin of a Lion*, which do not so much reveal

[39] Michael Ondaatje, *In the Skin of a Lion* (London: Picador, 1988): 204, 206.

[40] Danah Zohar, *The Quantum Self* (London: Flamingo, 1991): 15.

[41] Michael Ondaatje, *The English Patient* (Toronto: Vintage, 1993): 301–302.

[42] Zohar, *The Quantum Self*, 21.

[43] Ondaatje's presentation of agency and his mobile structuration of self-
hood are discussed in more detail in Salgado, "Complexity and the Migrant
Writer," 99–100.

ruptured linearity as give rise to generative disorder: the nonlinear trajectory of the train journeys of his drunken father and his mother's search for him in the darkness of the tunnel replicating the former's turbulent state of mind and the latter's loss of bearings. It is also evident in his subtle use of prolepsis – or predictive narration – which is used not so much to foreground a deterministic logic and promote suspense (as in Rushdie's *Midnight's Children*) as to disturb the causal dynamic and show how the future implodes on the present,[44] creating uncertainty and unpredictability. Whereas Rushdie's *Midnight's Children* stresses the way in which small changes in one variable can have disproportionately large effects in another, Ondaatje dispenses with linear paths and instead privileges indeterminate process through the juxtaposition of apparently unconnected events, casting what J. Hillis Miller has described as a "self-generated web."[45]

This is especially evident in the section "A Fine Romance" in *Running in the Family*. Here key events such as the courtship, wedding and honeymoon of Ondaatje's parents signpost individual passages in chronological order (subscribing to an evolutionary logic) but are dismantled by the content of these passages themselves. "Courtship," for example, focuses on the peripatetic romantic trajectories of Mervyn and Doris, whose paths cross, bifurcate and collide again without any clear moment of connection. "April 11, 1932" (the day of the wedding and one signposted again in "Wilpattu") does not describe the wedding at all but a frustrated journey that preceded it, and in "Honeymoon" unrelated historical events are brought into bizarre juxtaposition (emphasizing the randomness of historical process) and the newly-weds themselves are notably absent.[46] The haphazard

---

[44] Salgado, "Complexity and the Migrant Writer," 96.

[45] J. Hillis Miller, *Fiction and Repetition: Seven English Novels* (Cambridge MA: Harvard UP, 1982), cited in Rufus Cook, "Being and Representation in Michael Ondaatje's *The English Patient*," *Journal of Commonwealth Literature* 30.4 (1999): 37.

[46] Michael Ondaatje, *Running in the Family*, 31–38.

trajectory delineated by Ondaatje invites the reader to reflect on the unpredictable way in which individuals negotiate and interact with the currents of accident and chance, and make it a wonder that his parents got married at all. This pattern of repeated and random spatiotemporal regression and circumlocution has led Rufus Cook to claim that Ondaatje's work "evolves backwards."[47] A chaotic reading, however, helps re-situate such nonlinearity in a punctuated (rather than evolutionary) dynamic, in which random connections serve as an attractor for crisis and change.

What is more, this section of the memoir reveals how *Running in the Family* also foregrounds the uncertainty of initial conditions and the indeterminacy of causal connections by using dates and key events as markers of connective crisis rather than continuity. The reader is propelled into the stochastic and heuristic world of probability, in which meaning is rendered indeterminate, provisional and processual. Ondaatje's work thus actively invites different readings from the same reader, revealing the way in which interpretation itself is sensitively dependent upon conditions that cannot be readily traced or determined. Hence, unlike Rushdie, whose paradoxical alignment of historical determinism and linguistic unpredictability works in the interests of a dialectical, totalizing teleology, Ondaatje privileges the provisional in order to foreground fragmentation, dispersal and the isolated image or moment, thereby unsettling the possibilities for monumentalizing historical inscription.

Further Trajectories

Through the work of Rushdie and Ondaatje, it is possible to trace two different but interconnected paths followed by writers who have been

---

[47] Cook, "Being and Representation in Michael Ondaatje's *The English Patient*," 38.

subject to "the turbulence of migration."[48] My brief literary analysis has, inevitably, been somewhat reductive, charting the general direction that each writer has taken; each of their texts deserves closer consideration, as each follows its own complex trajectory, expressing different forms of nonlinearity, unpredictability, determinism, iteration and irregularity. Other migrant writers trace other paths. Collectively, they form part of the dynamic continuum of the diaspora which – in its recursive consideration of the rupture of migration and the violence of realignment with new cultural formations – allows us to see how the diaspora itself forms part of a complex system, the evolution of which "cannot be followed in causal detail because such systems are holistic; everything affects everything else."[49] This anti-causal mode of analysis dismantles the situated determinism of autonomy and agency by investing it with provisionality of purpose and the unpredictability of historical contingency. As John Berger has succinctly pointed out, "the migrant's intentionality is permeated by historical necessities of which neither he nor anybody he meets is aware."[50] The challenge, it therefore seems, is to relish the opportunities generated by this crisis and to embrace the difficult freedom that such uncertainty grants us.

WORKS CITED

Appadurai, Arjun. *Modernity at Large: Cultural Dimensions of Globalisation* (Minneapolis: U of Minnesota P, 1996).

Benítez–Rojo, Antonio. *The Repeating Island: The Caribbean and the Postmodern Perspective*, tr. James E. Maraniss (Durham NC: Duke UP, 1992).

Brah, Avtar. *Cartographies of Diaspora: Contesting Identities* (London: Routledge, 1997).

Chambers, Ian. "Migrancy Culture, Identity," in *The Postmodern History Reader*, ed. Keith Jenkins (London: Routledge, 1997): 77–83.

---

[48] The term is borrowed from Papastergiadis' *The Turbulence of Migration*.

[49] Hawkins, *Strange Attractors*, 160.

[50] John Berger, quoted in Papastergiadis, *The Turbulence of Migration*, 21.

Cohen, Robin. *Global Diasporas: An Introduction* (Seattle: U of Washington P, 1997).

Cook, Rufus. "Being and Representation in Michael Ondaatje's *The English Patient*," *Journal of Commonwealth Literature* 30.4 (1999): 35–49.

——. "'Imploding Time and Geography': Narrative Compressions in Michael Ondaatje's *The English Patient*," *Journal of Commonwealth Literature* 33.2 (1998): 109–26.

Hawkins, Harriet. *Strange Attractors: Literature, Culture and Chaos Theory* (Hemel Hempstead: Prentice–Hall/Harvester Wheatsheaf, 1995).

Hayles, N. Katherine, ed. *Chaos and Order: Complex Dynamics in Literature and Science* (Chicago: U of Chicago P, 1991).

——. *Chaos Bound: Orderly Disorder in Contemporary Literature and Science* (Ithaca NY: Cornell UP, 1990).

McLeod, John. *Beginning Postcolonialism* (Manchester: Manchester UP, 2000).

Medd, Will, & Paul Haynes. "Complexity and the Social," ESRC Complexity Workshop, http://www.keele.ac.uk/depts/stt/cstt2/comp/medd.htm .]

Ondaatje, Michael. *The English Patient* (Toronto: Vintage, 1993).

——. *In the Skin of a Lion* (London: Picador, 1988).

——. *Running in the Family* (London: Picador, 1983).

Papastergiadis, Nikos. *The Turbulence of Migration: Globalisation, Deterritorialisation and Hybridity* (Cambridge: Polity, 2000).

Porush, David. "Fictions as Dissipative Structures: Prigogine's Theory and Postmodernism's Roadshow," in Hayles, ed. *Chaos and Order*, 54–84.

Rushdie, Salman. *Imaginary Homelands: Essays and Criticism 1981–1991* (London: Granta, 1991).

——. *Midnight's Children* (London: Picador, 1981).

——. *The Satanic Verses* (London: Vintage, 1988).

Salgado, Minoli. "Complexity and the Migrant Writer: Chaotics in Michael Ondaatje's Fiction," *Angles on the English Speaking World* 1 (2001): 89–105.

——. "Migration and Mutability: The Twice Born Fiction of Salman Rushdie," in *British Culture of the Postwar: An Introduction to Literature and Society 1945–1999*, ed. Alistair Davies & Alan Sinfield (London: Routledge, 2000): 31–49.

Weissert, Thomas P. "Representation and Bifurcation: Borges' Garden of Chaos Dynamics," in Hayles, ed. *Chaos and Order*, 223–43.

Zohar, Danah. *The Quantum Self* (London: Flamingo, 1991).

⌀

VERA ALEXANDER

Postponed Arrivals
The Afro-Asian Diaspora
in M.G. Vassanji's *No New Land* [1]

HOW LONG DOES IT TAKE to complete the process of arriving in a foreign country? M.G. Vassanji's second novel *No New Land* (1991) describes the adjustment struggles of an Afro-Indian family who settle in Canada after decolonization has deprived them of their foothold in Tanzania.[2] While the narrative focuses on middle-aged Nurdin Lalani and his family, their experiences are interspersed with anecdotes illuminating the parallel difficulties undergone by fellow immigrants of different generations. *No New Land* in this manner creates a kaleidoscope of an immigrant community's attempts at negotiating their individual and collective responses to dislocation and change.

In depicting the trials and errors of his protagonists, M.G. Vassanji can draw on autobiographical material. He is of South Asian origin and grew up in East Africa. Having lived and studied in the USA from 1970 onwards, he came to Canada in 1978 as a physicist. In his novel

[1] The essay has been condensed and the order of paragraphs has been slightly rearranged by the editor. Thanks also go to Anne Herlyn for her comments on an earlier draft version.

[2] Details on the situation of Asians in Tanzania before and after Independence are taken from Thomas P. Ofcansky & Rodger Yeager, *Historical Dictionary of Tanzania* (Lanham MD & London: Scarecrow, 2nd ed. 1997).

he narrates parts of his own itinerary, even though he stresses that he never hailed from within the walls of the immigrant ghetto described in *No New Land*.[3]

The Afro-Asian network of immigrants to which the protagonists belong plays an important but ambivalent role in their trials of initiation. In practical terms, the community facilitates their access to the 'new land' by providing help-lines and familiar social structures. The safety in numbers alleviates the newcomers' sense of inadequacy and insecurity. On the other hand, the modern life-style in Canada exposes the immigrants to problems for which they have no traditional panacea. In this respect, the all-embracing community acts as an impediment rather than as a help, because it prevents its members from entering into a dialogue with Canadian culture and society – or, as the case of Nurdin Lalani shows, affects the necessary processes of negotiation. In this sense, 'arrival' is more than just the physical touchdown in a new country. It refers to the entire stage of settling down in there. The protagonist is faced with a double problem of how to manage his integration into a new culture: on the one hand, his personal ambitions need to be re-evaluated. On the other, he has a responsibility towards his community, whose reactions to the new situation often differ from his personal ones. Torn between allegiances to the past, present and future, the novel's protagonist takes some seven years to really cross the threshold to the 'new land'.

As the title of this essay indicates, immigration in *No New Land* is depicted as a drawn-out process which involves an intensive negotiation of change, in the sense both of progress and of degeneration (or regression). In this essay, after a survey of the plot, I will examine the interaction of individuality and collective identity in *No New Land*. Vassanji's novel outlines the ambivalent processes of cultural negotiation undergone by characters who aim to make their home in a new

---

[3] Chelva Kanaganayakam, "'Broadening the Substrata': An Interview with M.G. Vassanji," *World Literature Written in English* 31.2 (1991): 29–30.

country without giving up their own traditions. Strategies for upholding imported traditions and for preserving memories and customs
relating to a past homeland are often summarized as 'diasporic'. I start
out by characterizing the specific community portrayed and examine
the use of discursive diaspora concepts in an interpretation of *No New
Land*. While the concept of diaspora is interesting from an anthropological or sociological point of view, one also needs to ask what the
function of this concept is in the discussion of a fictional text in which
different layers of imaginative constructions overlay one another. The
novel uses the concepts of diaspora and especially of the 'diasporic
imaginary' to present variations on the recurring theme of immigrant
suffering prevalent in many postcolonial works of fiction. Earlier
criticism of Vassanji's novel has declared his portrayal of individual
and collective immigrant reactions to be problematic. Some critics
indict him for allowing the community to suffocate the individual. By
interpreting some key scenes which illuminate the problems of the
novel's protagonist, Nurdin Lalani, I offer an alternative reading of
these observations by aligning the problem of individuality in *No New
Land* with the collective phenomenon of the diasporic pattern of
identification.

Nurdin's Problems with Homelands Old and New

Nurdin Lalani and his family emigrate to Canada in the 1970s as the
nationalization of their property renders their position in East Africa
precarious and job prospects are bleak. Canada offers the comforts of
a modern 'first world' state as well as promising the social security
and friendly climate of its multicultural policies. However, while some
of the protagonists' optimistic expectations of a prosperous future are
fulfilled on arrival, manifested by such surface luxuries as an electro-
nically equipped modern apartment, it gradually dawns on them that
life in Canada holds many unexpected setbacks as far as their social
rise and recognition are concerned.

At the stage of initial dislocation, it seems to Nurdin and his family that they have not actually entered a new country. They are plagued by a sense of *déjà vu*. Toronto strikes them as the mirror-image of multicultural Dar es Salaam, where their minority struggled for a foothold among Africans, Britons, Germans and Indian Hindus. In Toronto the Lalanis find accommodation in a block of flats which bears puzzling similarities to their former home in Dar es Salaam: "you step out into the common corridor with its all too real down-to-earth sights, sounds, and smells, and you wonder: *This*, Sixty-nine Rosecliffe? And you realize that you've not yet left Dar far behind you."[4] Rosecliffe Park represents an "upright village" (69) in which several ethnic groups live beside each other. The all-purpose high-rises merely turn their familiar world into a vertical position, or upside down. Altogether, life in Toronto for Nurdin reproduces many of the demoralizing living conditions known to him in Tanzania: he and his family still belong to a minority group floating in a multicultural melting pot, except that the oppression of the majority culture is now exerted by white Canadians and takes a less avowedly aggressive approach.[5]

Three years into his stay, Nurdin is humiliated by his failure to land an adequate job. When at last he finds permanent work, his colleagues, who hail from outside his narrow community, introduce him to liberated Canadian life: from eating pork in secret, Nurdin moves on to tasting beer, and allows himself to be dragged to a peep-show. For him, all practical transgressions result in a moral dilemma: "Eat pig and become a beast. Slowly the bestial traits – cruelty and promiscuity, in one word, godlessness – overcame you. And you became, morally,

---

[4] M.G. Vassanji, *No New Land* (Toronto: McClelland & Stewart, 1991): 60. Where the context is clear, further page references are in the main text.

[5] The discrepancy between Canada's official policy of multiculturalism and concrete manifestations of racism and xenophobia has been explored in many literary works of Canadian writers ever since the publication of Joy Kogawa's groundbreaking novel *Obasan* (1981), which deals with the sufferings of Japanese Canadians in the tense post-Pearl Harbor climate.

like *them*. The Canadians" (127). Finally, Nurdin encounters his strongest temptation in Sushila, an attractive Hindu widow who used to live in his neighbourhood in Dar. Just as their friendship is about to ripen into an affair, Nurdin's life reaches a dramatic nadir when he is accused of attempting to rape a girl at his work-place – a grossly exaggerated account of him putting a hand on her shoulder in the attempt to help her to her feet and, in the act, sneaking a glimpse into her shirt. In the hullabaloo surrounding Nurdin's disgrace, Missionary, their religious leader, joins his followers in Toronto. His arrival marks the happy close to Nurdin's drama: the charges against him are dropped thanks to the machinations of Jamal, a wily lawyer; moreover, Missionary helps Nurdin to finally make his peace with his confused allegiances.

The novel's somewhat implausible 'happy ending' (Amin Malak speaks of a "deus ex machina" solution[6]) contradicts the pessimism suggested by both the novel's title and its first epithet (taken from the poem "The City" by the Greek-Egyptian poet Constantine P. Cavafy). Cavafy's poem predicts that the sinful addressees cannot escape their tribulations by moving to a new place of residence. Part of people's self, problems will always re-emerge in any new location, and thus people will be doomed to a hopeless nomadic search for peace. Fortunately, this gloomy prediction is not Vassanji's last word: Cavafy's 'curse' is followed by a rather more pleasing image taken from an "old Gujarati hymn." This second epithet evokes the myth of 'Amarapur', the city of the "deathless,"[7] a destination of immortals where there are "Walls of gold, pillars of silver and floors that smell of musk." Page

---

[6] Amin Malak, "Ambivalent Affiliation and the Postcolonial Condition: The Fiction of M.G. Vassanji," *World Literature Today* 67.2 (1993): 280.

[7] R.N. Saletore, *Encyclopaedia of Indian Culture* (New Dehli: Sterling, 1985), vol. 1: 57. There is, in fact, a village of the name of Amarapur in the Indian state of Gujarat, but the novel makes it clear that for the diasporic community, Amarapur is not a concrete location but a point in the geography of the mind.

One of *No New Land* thus opens on an ambivalence as two contrasting concepts of place and identity clash from the very start, illustrating the conflicts which beset Nurdin's situation in Canada. Even though the near-magical solution to all problems at the end of the novel suggests that the optimistic view prevails, Cavafy's prediction dominates the tone of the novel.

The tension between the two epithets seems to pose the question: how can one escape the vicious circle of wanderings and reach Amarapur? The novel's offhand reply suggests that in order to find their dream destination, the immigrants must come to terms with the baggage they carry from one place to the next. However, *No New Land* is far from providing such a facile solution. For instance, the text's moralizing tendency throughout the novel keeps being fractured by Vassanji's irony. As a means of exploiting ambivalence to a comic effect, irony is an appropriate device for describing the conflicting ambitions of a protagonist and a community situated on a fence between two cultures. An early example of Vassanji's irony occurs in his unexpected passage of authorial comment at the end of the novel's exposition:

> We are but creatures of our origins, and however stalwartly we march
> forward, paving new roads, seeking new worlds, the ghosts from out
> pasts stand not far behind and are not easily shaken off. (9)

Since the novel is dominated by reflector-mode narration, the butting-in of an omniscient narrator comes as a startling turn at this point. As a result of this Dickensian tour de force, readers are left unsure about how to assess the novel's dramatis personae: are they a cast of flat characters exemplifying different immigrant generations and their attitudes to life, or are they to be taken for authentic and reliable individuals? Nurdin Lalani and his community's problems are thus approached from an ironic distance which modifies the immediacy of their experiences just as their portrayal balances on a tightrope between tragedy and comedy.[8]

Nurdin's alleged rape attempt is a good illustration of this: in danger of being classified as a criminal – the only one negative label he has been spared so far, after experiencing racism, ageism and sexism – circumstances still combine to make him look silly rather than a villain. Harold Barratt is not entirely unjustified in describing the episode as having "a rather contrived and gratuitous atmosphere."[9] It seems very much in line with Nurdin's image as an anti-hero that his moment of greatest shame is cast as a somewhat botched series of burlesque misunderstandings. This is in line with the fact that Vassanji's immigrants, no matter of which age and generation, undergo processes which are familiar from initiation fiction. Immigrants like Nurdin are not only geographically but also temporally displaced, as their advanced age does not match their immaturity of competence. This comparison with fictions of initiation underlines the fact that an immigrant's 'arrival' must be conceptualized less as a specific moment than a drawn-out development.

Taken together, the novel's epithets, which relate the problems of migrants to mytho-religious concepts of *navigatio vitae*, elucidate that there is a teleological dimension to the protagonists' emigration. Indeed, Vassanji's immigrants, whose multiple migrations have led them from India to Africa and now to North America, are not simply frozen in displacement; they participate in a shared quest for little less than paradise on Earth. By introducing the quest motif, *No New Land* presents us with a variation on the theme of mythic 'homelands' which

---

[8] Vassanji much deplores naive readings of *No New Land* which completely ignore his ironic treatment of the people displayed and take his novel for a mere documentary on, as he puts it, "Wow. Is this how they live?" See Kanaganayakam, "Broadening the Substrata," 32.

[9] Harold Barratt, "M.G. Vassanji," in *Writers of the Indian Diaspora: A Bio-Bibliographical Critical Sourcebook*, ed. Emmanuel S. Nelson (Westport CT: Greenwood, 1992): 447.

has repeatedly been used in recent discussions of the diaspora.[10] The
homeland towards which the activities of Vassanji's community are
geared is to be found – or to be constructed – in the future and is not
strictly tied to any specific region.

Diasporic Existence in *No New Land*

Does the Afro-Asian community depicted in *No New Land* constitute a
fictional representation of a diaspora? If so, what are the implications
of Vassanji's response to diaspora discourse as far as the critical
evaluation of the novel is concerned?

No New Land continues Vassanji's description of the fictional
Shamsi sect which he had first presented to the reading public in his
first novel, *The Gunny Sack* (1989).[11] Rosemary M. George describes
their function as follows: "The Shamsi sect [...], though invented by
Vassanji, is similar to existing religious organizations. The sect has a
world-wide network that serves as a support system for wanderers or
immigrants who need to be made at home in an unfamiliar place."[12]

---

[10] James Clifford lists "myths/memories of the homeland" among his
central items in recent definitions of diaspora. See Clifford, "Diasporas,"
Cultural Anthropology 9.3 (1994): 305.

[11] The Shamsis have been identified as "Vassanji's fictional representation
of the Isma'ilis, a sub-sect of Shi'ism, one of the two great branches of Islam";
Frank Birbalsingh, "South Asian Canadian Writers from Africa and the
Caribbean," *Canadian Literature* 132 (1992): 103; Amin Malak, "Ambivalent
Affiliation and the Postcolonial Condition," 281). In refutation of this identification, one could cite a passage in which the "Shamsis" are mentioned in a
line-up of sects *alongside* the Ishmaelis. This seems to contradict the view that
the two are meant to be identical (M.G. Vassanji, *The Gunny Sack* [London:
Heinemann, 1989]: 146). I will therefore respect Vassanji's pseudonym,
accept the "purely coincidental" nature of any resemblance with existing
groups claimed in the book jacket, and refer to the community as the Shamsis.

[12] Rosemary Marangoly George, "Travelling Light: Immigration and Invisible Suitcases in M.G. Vassanji's *The Gunny Sack*," in *Memory, Narrative*

The Shamsis are indeed "similar to existing religious organisations," given that their portrait is based on autobiographical material. Vassanji remembers:

> I was brought up in a community of Muslims who had been converted in medieval times but who quite unembarrassedly kept many of their 'Hindu' beliefs and made sense of them. Thus Allah was a form of Vishnu, Muhammad simply Brahma, and weren't the Vedas nothing but the Quran? Ordinary middle-class Muslims and Hindus alike are aghast upon hearing this, but it was a creative response to conversion and to the schism between religions with purportedly humanistic and spiritual ideas.[13]

Vassanji's protagonist sect thus straddles several cultural divides as it yokes together Muslim and Hindu beliefs and, in colonial Tanzania, acts as a border between the colonizers and the colonized native population of East Africa. The Shamsis are "a community that has sat on the fence (or rather that has a history of literally being the fence that divided colonizer from the colonized)."[14] Altogether the sect is self-consciously hybrid as the experience of creatively transgressing traditions and boundaries is as crucial to their collective memory as their history of uprooting. They practise their own culture in partial segregation from the mainstream and entertain contacts with their former homeland as well as with relatives and acquaintances who migrated to other parts of the world. Ambivalent towards all majority cultures alike, and preventing their blending into one another, they nevertheless create a point of contact between cultures, places and communities. Removal to Canada transfers the Shamsis into a third multicultural context, where technological progress and globalization have heigh-

---

and Identity: New Essays in Ethnic American Literatures, ed. Amritjit Singh, Joseph T. Skerrett & Robert E. Hogan (Boston MA: Northeastern UP, 1994): 285.

[13] M.G. Vassanji, "Life at the Margins: In the Thick of Multiplicity," in *Between the Lines: South Asians and Postcoloniality*, ed. Deepika Bahri & Mary Vasudeva (Philadelphia PA: Temple UP, 1996): 119.

[14] George, "Travelling Light," 292.

tened the challenges they face, as facilitated communication with other dispersed groups is measured up by the multitude of distractions and disruptions caused by the new media and the greater degree of liberty, social mobility and choice regarding religion and social opportunities.

Diaspora is a concept which much engages with the imagination (Benedict Anderson's "imagined communities"), with maintaining utopian hopes of a return but also identifying with a dispersed virtual community most of whose members one does not know personally but who rely on similar traditions and beliefs. In *No New Land*, Vassanji draws particular attention to the importance of the imagination in constituting identity by portraying a character whose imagination bars him from coming to grips with real life: that is, a character who becomes the victim of his own imagination.

The question of what diasporas are and how the term may be used has been debated since the early 1990s. To the consternation of some critics who try to delimit the over-use of the term 'diaspora', there is no accepted or normative model of what a diaspora has to be like. Societies and communities are subject to change and may have diasporic features at some stage and lose them at another. Which of the criteria listed in diaspora discourse can apply to the Shamsis in Vassanji's fictional community portrait?

We have already noted Paul Clifford's definition of the diaspora, which takes up Safran's categories and posits several criteria:

1   history of dispersal [= Safran (1)];
2   desire for an eventual return to the homeland [= Safran (4)];
3   ongoing support of the homeland [= Safran (5)];
4   the existence of myths and memories of the homeland [= Safran (2)];
5   a collective identity defined by the community's relation to the homeland [= Safran (6)];

6   a feeling of alienation from the host country [Safran (3)].[15]

The diaspora is thus a collective phenomenon and can only operate in contexts where emigrants create a community abroad that relies on the feelings, experiences and myths noted in Clifford's definition. Safran's list has been expanded by Cohen,[16] who added a distinction between enforced and voluntary dispersals, thereby downtoning the trauma of the original dislocation which Mishra focused on.[17] Rather than the traumatic rupture that has to be healed by the founding myth of the return to the homeland as visionary prospect, Cohen under-lines the recent positive revaluation of diasporic existence and extends category (e) to include "the establishment of inter-diaspora contacts" in which the two-way relationship between diaspora and homeland is enriched by interaction between dispersed communities. Finally, Cohen also notes the centrality of "a time lag between dis-persal and the development of a diaspora." This last criterion militates somewhat against the positive evaluation of dispersal which may seem to support the insight that the time lag is not always mandatory.

It has already been observed that the Shamsis are not a straight-forward case; after all, this is the story of a double diasporic repatria-tion. They have suffered expulsion from their country of origin (Guja-rat, India) and split into several communities (Safran's criterion 1[18]); they continue to identify vicariously with their original culture both in practical terms (eg, linguistic and religious idiosyncrasies, food restric-tions, intermarriage) and as far as their cherishing of myth and religion

---

[15] See Clifford, "Diasporas," 305. See William Safran, "Diasporas in Modern Societies: Myths of Homeland and Return," *Diaspora: A Journal of Transnational Studies* 1.1 (1991): 83–99.

[16] Robin Cohen, *Global Diasporas: An Introduction* (Seattle: U of Wash-ington P, 1997): 23–26.

[17] Vijay Mishra, "The Diasporic Imaginary: Theorizing the Indian Dia-spora," *Textual Practice* 10.3 (1996): 423.

[18] Safran, "Diasporas in Modern Societies," 83.

is concerned (criterion 2). All these practices combine to ensure that they keep a degree of distance from the local culture(s) of whatever new country of residence they migrate to (category 3 in Safran). However, regarding Safran's points 4 to 6, which are all concerned with a future return as well as preservation of the homeland (4., envisaging a later return to the original homeland, 5., commitment to the maintenance of the homeland, and 6., continued identification with it[19]), it can be observed that the concept of home undergoes drastic re-evaluations in Vassanji's Shamsi community. Place and related concepts, such as Safran's homeland, are conceived of as an extremely shifty category. Vassanji portrays a group whose sense of national allegiance has been watered down by multiple migrations. The Shamsis believe in a portable culture as their community-constitutive common basis. The older generation of Missionary and Haji Lalani, who remember India, carried the conviction that "After all, we've brought India with us" (39). The concrete location of origin is not one which any of Vassanji's Shamsis dream of returning to. Quite on the contrary, as we will see further below. They cling to notions of a utopia, a no place, or an abstract future paradise which is to be sought and aspired to in terms of life's journey. They consequently project their energies and ambitions (in correspondence with Safran's categories 5 and 6) into the future. Concrete memory is thus replaced by a (potentially utopian) concept of an imagined country, and it appears that their strategy for achieving this destination consists in knitting the community more closely together and forming a social and religious centre in lieu of a spatial one. Missionary, the religious leader of the Dar community, is thus invested with a special aura of authority to create such a centre during his visit to Toronto, however temporary even this identity-enforcing encounter is.

Evidently, among the Shamsis some are 'more diasporic than others'. Of the many generations portrayed in *No New Land*, the older

---

[19] Safran, "Diasporas in Modern Societies," 83–84.

members tend to be more interested in preserving their imported traditions than the younger ones. For the Lalanis, the degree of diasporic
zest in keeping up traditions develops into a bone of contention between the different generations and sexes. Antagonism marks their
home: while Nurdin's wife Zera compensates for her own sense of
dislocation by dogmatically practising her religious traditions, the two
children reject everything associated with their Third-World past.
Nurdin himself applies his community's syncretic strategies of multicultural integration and compromises which the Shamsi faith and
tradition seem to be based on when he wavers between seeking the
comfort of his community and a timid curiosity to explore Canadian
ways of living.

While Vassanji's protagonist community has no concrete desire to
return home, an abstract and ambivalent preoccupation with the concept of home is certainly crucial to their sense of community.
Throughout the novel this is ironically underlined by the auspicious
name of their former hometown, Dar es Salaam, which is consistently
translated as 'Heaven of Love'.[20] Their exodus from the third world is
thus aligned with an expulsion from paradise while all the flashbacks
to their lives in Dar point to quite a different reading of Tanzania.
Even more obviously, a double entendre of 'Dar es Salaam' is exploited when Nurdin strays into a peep-show bearing this name. The
novel's play with the omnipresence of Dar underlines the immigrants'
ambivalent identification with a 'not quite home'-land whose continuing hold on them the Shamsis try to deny. Geographically far
removed from Toronto, Dar es Salaam retains a partial presence both
in the vertical village of Rosecliffe Park and in Toronto's red light
district: although the real home-town is out of reach, it cannot quite be
escaped from or forgotten. By contrast, locations which are closer in
terms of physical distance may prove inaccessible (for instance, the

---

[20] Less pointed translations from Arabic tend to render the name as "Haven
of Peace" (eg, Ofcansky & Yeager, *Historical Dictionary of Tanzania*, 59),
and so does Vassanji himself in *The Gunny Sack*, 84.

Lalanis are not allowed to step out of the customs area for a sight-seeing tour of London during their stopover at Heathrow airport). Spatial distances are deceptive, and the impact of places does not necessarily diminish with distance. So how can immigrants tell where they stand? And if they cannot tell that much, how to move on?

In *No New Land* there is no indication that any of the members of the African Indian community are in contact with their original home-land, India. They do, however, correspond with Dar, especially Zera, who confers with Missionary over orthodox Shamsi responses to incidents of everyday life in Toronto and pleads with him to join them in the West. Some diaspora members entertain contacts with other Shamsi communities in the West: when Nurdin's rape allegation be-comes public, he visualizes how "it must have gone out in waves to the remainder of the community – Don Mills, Willowdale, Scarborough, Mississauga, Brampton ... perhaps even Kitchener–Waterloo and soon Calgary–Vancouver" (195–96).

The community members have an unspoken agreement to describe their former place of residence as a hopeless dump: "[...] they would go up to the eighteenth floor to the open house, to watch people play-ing cards and to chit-chat over tea, to find out the news in Dar – the status of roads and food prices and the dollar price – all, reassuringly, bad" (69). Similarly, when their religious leader finally arrives,

> they talked in the Lalanis' living room, of food prices and currency values 'there', of who was 'in' (for black-marketing and passport violations) and who 'out'. Food prices were rising, there were queues for bread, garbage was not being picked up regularly. It was as if they had to justify living here by proving to themselves how progressively worse it was getting there. (187)

The only member of their group who indeed goes back in order to pur-sue an artist's career in Tanzania is regarded as somewhat eccentric. Altogether, the immigrants are haunted by the experience that while they have left Dar, Dar has not really left them and continues to make claims on their conscience.

Vassanji thus subtly demonstrates that the act of looking back, which is often wrapped in nostalgia and a longing to return, forms part of a complex psychological negotiation of guilt and sensationalism. Nurdin is not the only member of his community who regards the past as a burden that he would like to shed. To look back means to face the shame of one's desertion of a Third-World land. At the same time, hearing about Tanzania's problems gives the disillusioned diaspora members a lift and provides much-needed reassurance that they have done the right thing in emigrating, no matter how downtrodden they may feel as a result. Their guilty enjoyment of 'horror stories' about the living conditions in Africa is symptomatic of their love–hate relationship with their former home where they used to live in a state of repressed guilt about their relative wealth compared to the poverty of many Africans.[21] But far from making them appreciate their present home, their memory of poverty in Africa only feeds their longing for a 'perfect' paradise in which they can be comfortable without feeling guilty. By talking about Dar they collectively appease their bad consciences.

In one of his interviews with the Canada-based critic Chelva Kanaganayakam, Vassanji admits that much of his writing is born out of this sense of guilt: "Every time you hear of problems in that part of the world, and every time you feel that something should be done, you wonder what you have done, and realize that there is essentially a lack of courage."[22] The Shamsis' utopian homeland is neither in India nor in Africa; nevertheless, it bears an Indian name, Amarapur, thus constituting a linguistic bridge to a country which is only kept alive in the shape of oral tradition. A permanent return home, however, is certainly no avowed aim: given that one remembers the everyday discomforts of a Third-World residence, the concept of home had best be kept

---

[21] For example, Vassanji, *No New Land*, 169.
[22] Kanaganayakam, "Broadening the Substrata," 25.

as abstract as possible and tied to fantasies about an imaginary location such as Amarapur.

Relating to the concept of spatial allegiance, it is important to note that the collective identity of the Shamsis is not tied to any particular country or nationality. Owing to their hybrid, hyphenated identity, they cannot be assigned any clear-cut category in terms of religion or nationhood. It is one sign of their alienation that even their concepts of identification are different from those prevalent in their new surroundings. Vassanji explains:

> From the 'South Asian' [...] perspective, 'community' is the more pervasive identity. For the most part I avoid the word 'nation' in its European connotation and complexity, using it only in the sense in which it had meaning for us when I was growing up, to denote an independent country or state as in 'United Nations'.[23]

It is an important fact that the focal generations portrayed in the novel have in fact been born 'in exile' and none of them have even seen India. 'Indianness,' if such a concept can be defined, for them makes sense only in relation to other social strata: ie, in relation to Tanzania, to German and British colonizers and to the native African communities.[24] Characteristically, when Nurdin is unexpectedly accosted by

---

[23] Vassanji, "Life at the Margins," 112. Even umbrella terms such as "South Asian" are problematic since they suggest a sense of group identity while being an artificial term created in academia: "South Asians do not exist as a concrete community." See introduction to *South Asians Overseas: Migration and Ethnicity*, ed. Colin Clarke, Ceri Peach & Steven Vertovec (Cambridge: Cambridge UP, 1990): 170. While at first equally unhappy with the terminological properties of 'South Asian' ("Life at the Margins," 116), Vassanji has come round to accepting this umbrella term as the lesser evil, and since becoming chief editor of the *Toronto South Asian Review* he has been instrumental in remedying the term's lack of "imaginative force."

[24] Nationality is a background problem throughout the novel. It is a silent fact that the Lalanis must have retained their Indian passports throughout their lives in Tanzania; by becoming African citizens they could have escaped some of the discrimination they suffered, such as the nationalization of their property and career disadvantages – at the cost, presumably, of losing their status within

an Indian man from Guyana, he is at a loss about how to define
himself:

> "You Indian, man?" he said to Nurdin.
> He didn't know what to answer. India or Pakistan, what differ-
> ence? [...]
> "I am from East Africa," Nurdin said finally. (117)

If characters with shared Asian roots have trouble agreeing among
themselves about such concepts, how much more difficult is the act of
translating from Shamsi concepts into Canadian categories.

Although the Shamsis have few or no nostalgic longings associated
with India or Africa, they construct new myths to furnish their "Canadian Dream." By depicting a group which defines itself according to
religious parameters, Vassanji revives an important aspect which has
been neglected in recent anthropological and sociological debates on
the subject of diasporas: ie, that their minority status is determined by
their religion rather than their nationality or ethnicity. The religious
element in *No New Land* enforces the community's hermetic structure
and occlusive attitude towards outsiders. It furthermore explains the
significance of myth and justifies the search for hidden meanings
which is so characteristic of Nurdin's struggles. And finally, the
group's identification with an imaginary future paradise is all the more
powerful owing to its eschatological dimension.

One can therefore conclude that the representation of diasporic existence in Vassanji's work extends the current paradigm to include
double diasporization and its reshaping of the diasporic imaginary.
Thus the Shamsis create an imaginary homeland that is Indian from a
religious and cultural background that – owing to their previous assimilation to the East-African diaspora – eschews national identifications. Vassanji, moreover, introduces the fraught relationship with the
country of origin (Tanzania) not as, merely, a traumatic experience of

---

the Asian community (see Ofcansky & Yeager, *Historical Dictionary of Tanzania*, 23).

wrenching away from home to hostile exposure abroad, but as a liberation from poverty and chaos that has to be disavowed within the leading victimization myth of the diaspora.

In all of his works of fiction, Vassanji has portrayed the diaspora in such a way as to imply a criticism of any homogenizing tendencies displayed in lists such as the ones put forward by Safran or Cohen. While Vassanji's Shamsis are clearly not a model diaspora obeying any discursive pattern, their portrayal takes into account the imaginary force of diasporic identification. Altogether, Vassanji's diasporic group strains against the limitations of the discursive catalogue. As with regard to so many other cultural categories, the Shamsis sit on the fence circumscribing the diaspora concept, and they are scattered across several fence-posts to boot.

The Aesthetics of Community and the Hazards of Individuality

Having stated that the diasporic label can be cautiously applied to the community depicted in *No New Land*, the next question to be raised is: what are the implications of Vassanji's portrayal of a diasporic group for the novel? In the critical debate on Vassanji's work, it has severally been observed that the diasporic community in *No New Land* vies with Nurdin for the role of protagonist. Entire sequences of chapters mainly deal with other members of the Shamsi community. Is this polyphony a deliberate device, or is it a case of poorly managed characterization which endangers the cohesion of the novel? Even though *No New Land* has on the whole received friendly criticism, a few negative responses have been aimed at Vassanji's efforts at portraying collectivity. Neil Bissoondath, a fellow writer of Asian-Caribbean background, lists the novel's flaws as follows:

> Vassanji's ambition – to present community – is frequently unmatched by his ability. He often fails to present his background material with sufficient subtlety, so that community submerges character

(i.e. the individual). Fiction works best when it presents the viewpoint
of the singular and not of the plural, the I or (s)he, not the we or they.
It is, in other words, through individual lives that we best approach
alien outlook and experience. Yet a pressure faced by many writers,
not least by those writing from an 'ethnic' or 'immigrant' perspective,
is a need to present the whole, to be a kind of literary ringmaster for
the community circus.[25]

Bissoondath concludes his review with a piece of prescriptive advice:
"it is a mistake for any novelist [...] to *set out* to write a portrait of a
community."[26] Is that really so? While many critics endorse parts of
Bissoondath's criticism, his arguments have on the whole been merely
replicated, rather than being questioned, nor have alternative interpretations of the novel's alleged weaknesses been proffered so far.

Bissoondath criticizes the author's conception of the central character, unkindly arguing that "Nurdin shimmers on the page before us but
never quite comes into focus. He cannot coalesce amidst all the communal static."[27] However, taking into account the novel's characterization of the protagonist, this corresponds with Nurdin's self-image.
From the outset, Nurdin is portrayed as having rather a weak personality: self-conscious and mediocre in his intellectual and other
capacities, he is an anti-hero. In Tanzania, his main ambition in life
was to escape his formidable father, by travelling overland as a sales
agent. Somebody like Nurdin who is experienced at making himself as
inconspicuous as possible easily drowns in the masses. In addition to
Nurdin's general sense of inadequacy and lack of willpower, his self-
confidence is eroded even further in the course of immigration. He
feels that his personality dissolves, and his community is of no help in
his reconstruction of himself. Owing to his inexperience and, possibly,
immaturity, both Canadian people and his own community add to
Nurdin's irritation by belittling and patronizing him: many exploit his

---

[25] Neil Bissoondath, "True Expatriate Love," *Saturday Night* (June
1991): 44.

[26] Bissoondath, "True Expatriate Love," 45.

[27] Bissoondath, "True Expatriate Love," 45.

ignorance of Western ways, and even Missionary treats him like a child, however jocular and helpful his intentions. A neat, orderly, chronological sequence of narration focusing exclusively on Nurdin would fail to bring alive a character who feels that his social surroundings are in a process of erasing his identity. Due to the fact that Nurdin's point of view is usually adopted throughout the novel, the narrative must follow the distractions from his person and shift between himself and prominent acquaintances.

Among the novel's cast, other characters who acquire semi-protagonist status include Nanji the romantic intellectual, the brash and ambitious lawyer Jamal, and Esmail the novel's token victim of overt racism, all of whom exemplify alternative immigrant fates. The interspersion of their stories complements and sharpens the picture of possible extremes towards which Nurdin can only aspire without much success, in short: romantic love, a spirit of enterprise, publicly confirmed victimhood. These characters serve as foils in relation to the protagonist. Especially the views of Nanji, who has more insight into the immigrant predicament than Nurdin while sharing his sense of paralysis complement Nurdin's limited views.

In contrast to Jamal and his children, Nurdin is too old to gain a proper foothold in Canadian life: he fails to speak Canadian English without an accent, and he lacks the youthful power to make an entirely fresh start like his daughter and other younger initiates. At the same time, owing to his late entry into Canadian society he must needs submit to orientation and, in a way, education processes normally undergone by young people learning to understand the workings of social and linguistic codes. Psychologically, Nurdin finds himself, in many ways, on a par with young recipients of such an orientation. In a philosophical attempt to trace the role of education in what he terms the "post-metaphysical world," Lawrence J. Biskowski aligns young recipients of education with other new arrivals: ie, migrants: "Children are new arrivals, newcomers to this joint project of ours, and must be introduced to it."[28] In Nurdin's case this immigrant predicament is a particularly dire one, Nurdin labours under his perpetual failure to assert himself against his father. He never stood up to him during his life-time and even posthumously tries to run away from him.

While Nurdin's anti-heroic stance is uncontested, is he really as indefinite as Neil Bissoondath would have him? Although surrounded by "communal static," Nurdin does not allow himself to be swallowed up by it. After all, he successfully shields his dearest private concerns from his fellow Shamsis. Significantly, his only real friends, Sushila and his former assistant back in Dar, the African Charles, are not members of his community and unknown to any of the other Shamsis. More or less the same is true for his liberated friend Romesh from Guyana. Nurdin thus leads a double life in his community: one in which he performs the role prescribed by tradition, however poorly, and a secret one in which he dreams of liberation, education and sophistication (as personified in a smart, westernized "dream girl," 20, 26). None of his fellow Shamsis is privy to these wishes and thoughts. Therefore, the crisis which is triggered by his migration culminates in the question of whether to stay with the often oppressive body of his native Shamsi community or to leave them in order to choose his own company elsewhere.

Since this is the most crucial decision which the novel's protagonist has to make, it is clear that the portrayal of community must take up some space in order to do justice to its formidable role. *No New Land* thus differs from other postcolonial immigration novels such as Bharati Mukherjee's *Jasmine* (1989). Here, by contrast, the portrayal of a diasporic community of Indians in New York is embedded in the story of an exceptionally powerful heroine. They are little more than a foil to Jasmine's purposeful actions. In *No New Land*, by contrast, the

---

[28] Lawrence Biskowski, "Education and the Self in a Postmetaphysical World," in *Alternative Identities: The Self in Literature, History, Theory*, ed. Linda Marie Brooks (New York: Garland, 1995): 154.

Don Mills Shamsis represent a collective antagonist with whom Nurdin must interact and against whom he must define himself.

The importance of this constellation becomes clear in several instances where Nurdin is in disagreement with the mainstream opinion of his peers. The community's function of protecting its members comes across most forcefully in the confrontation of the Shamsis with Canadian society. Multicultural Canada as viewed from the Shamsi perspective is at best a superficially welcoming environment. The euphemistically named Rosecliffe Park underlines the fact that multicultural policy establishes a friendly façade behind which exploitation of newcomers and xenophobia are present but become increasingly harder to detect. When, however, in some key scenes, the mask of political correctness slips, the discovery of the hostility behind it comes as a shock. One such scene takes place shortly after the Lalanis' arrival to Toronto, when they are invited to a welcome 'party' but where the "new Canadians" (50) are trapped by a belatedly mounted cash-desk barring their exit. Similarly, while the racially motivated bashing of the Afro-Asian baker Esmail leads to effusive demonstrations of outrage against the perpetrators and public support for the victim community, the hype of patronizing philanthropy is likewise revealed to be motivated by commercial and publicity interests. Discrimination turns into its verbal opposite and the Shamsis are indiscriminately thrown in with the dominant Asian diaspora. The clash with other diasporic groups reveals the dark underside of Canadian "multivulturalism" (11), which is complemented by an aggressive ethnic rights movement that defines itself in perpetual accusatory opposition to the mainstream culture. Vassanji's novel is thus one of the few diaspora texts to actively position diasporic existence within a multicultural paradigm, exposing the ruptures between theory and practice and the hazards of cultural-rights dynamics arising from the well-meant theoretical models such as Charles Taylor's.

Not surprisingly, therefore, many Shamsis do not think much of "the Canadians," nor most of the other groups living in Canada,

because they consider them appallingly ignorant of all matters African
or Asian as well as regarding them as irreligious, amoral, and vulgar.
Many Shamsis share the outrage of Nurdin's neighbour who exclaims,
in a particularly fierce debate on their marginalization, "Why doesn't
someone tell these Canadians we are not Pakis. I have never been to
Pakistan, have you ever been to Pakistan? Tell them we're East
Africans!" (103–104). In a vicious circle, their negative assessment of
Canadian people enhances their insular segregation from mainstream
society, with the result that prejudices are reinforced and all contacts
channelled to confirm rather than alter the picture. In fact, some of the
more ardent religious Shamsis decide early on that they have a 'mission' to set the Canadians a good example. At a commercial fashion
show, the Shamsi ladies draw their own conclusions from what they
see:

> "This is the kind of thing we have to steer our kids from," Zera said ...
> "Precisely, sister," said Roshan. "We have something to give too to
> this country. Morals, I say." (55–56)

Nurdin, in contradistinction to these orthodox Shamsis, is compara-
tively open to the Canadian way of life and eager to make contact with
Canadian society. In moments of crisis he occasionally rebels against
his community's self-sufficiency and pride, even if at merely a small
scale. Thus, when a family quarrel threatens to escalate, he argues
back:

> But the women said no, hush-hush, don't wash your dirty linen in
> public. Well, hadn't they heard, that is precisely what you do, there
> are laundromats here. This is Canada, he told Roshan, giving back her
> own. (137)

The example shows that Nurdin differs from the hard-liners of his
community and argues creatively against pre-set dogmas and tradition.
Since progress (which is what the laundromat symbolizes) is associated with westernization, it is both a temptation and a menace to the
Shamsis' group identity. Collective responses take a longer time to

redefine themselves than individual ones, and thus the community delays Nurdin's privately longed-for rapprochement to Canada.

Diasporic Lethargy and the Challenges of Syncretism

By aiming for an interactive approach to Canadian life, Nurdin reveals himself as a progressive member of the Shamsi community who fights against xenophobic fear in his own camp. However, he is by no means free of these concerns himself. Change and the necessity to adapt to new living circumstances are at odds with the Shamsis' diasporic ambition of preserving their traditions. The Shamsi community endeavour to shield their members against foreign elements but they can never fully block out the influence of Canadian life. By maintaining traditional, partially obsolete views and tenets, the mainstream diaspora becomes alienated from many questions besetting its individual members. The ambition to preserve their old customs and beliefs not only resists change but moreover increases the fear of change. What things can or need to change? Does change jeopardize one's identity?

Vassanji's immigrants have a heightened perception of imminent disaster after having experienced radical change of government in Tanzania. This shift from an old era to a new one has had predominantly negative consequences on their lives: change can cause insecurity and fear. Despite initial high hopes, their change of place has led to disappointments. But all these are external changes. What bothers Nurdin most is the way in which these transformations affect the personalities of people around him. His children, Fatima in particular, who looks down on the "Paki-shitty-stan" she lives in, are a source of endless worry to him: "this country had taken his children away, and he felt distanced, rejected by them. Especially the girl. There were times when, he was sure, she despised him" (166–67). Zera's transformation into a near-ascetic religious maniac is largely an intensification and expansion of her former preferences (significantly, she also grows very fat). She is a teacher of religion; back in Dar she enjoyed nothing better than to debate theological issues with Missionary and her father-in-law. Deprived of such outlets for her fervour, she turns fanatic and rejects her less dogmatic husband. It is only on the day of Nurdin's rape-accusation that Zera becomes aware of a change in Nurdin: "She felt he was changing. She did not like change" (6). In fact, she is among the first to combat change wherever she spots it, accepting only such developments as accrue from education.

Nurdin is acutely aware of the changes in himself which his frustrating existence in Canada has brought about. He is frightened of Canada's power to transform people: "There must be something in the Canadian air that changes us, as the old people say" (136–37). In one of his gloomier moments of introspection, he interprets the process as one of degeneration:

> "When does a man begin to rot?" Gazing at the distant CN Tower blinking its signals into the hazy darkness, Nurdin asked himself the question. He sat in his armchair, turned around to look out into the night. [...] Pleased with the sound of his silent question, he repeated it in his mind again, this time addressing the tower. The lofty structure he had grown familiar with over the months, from this vantage point, and he had taken to addressing it. "When does a man begin to rot?" he asked. Faithful always, it blinked its answer, a coded message he could not understand. (82–83)

Exposed to double pressure from his community and his Canadian surroundings, Nurdin is especially susceptible to obsessions and paranoia. His imagination is heightened to the extent that he expects mysterious significations from the most unlikely sources, such as Toronto's most prominent landmark. The CN tower, one of the world's tallest freestanding structures and symbol of communication and commerce, epitomizes Canada's unreachable possibilities.[29] It becomes to Nurdin an inscrutable eye of a godhead 'looking down' on him as it seems to blink messages which he fails to decipher, in line with his general ignorance of Canadian codes and manners.

---

[29] Kanaganayakam, "Broadening the Substrata," 33.

Nurdin's symbolization of the CN tower is compounded by the fact that he must skulk past a picture of his father, Haji Lalani, whenever he goes out to the balcony to look at the tower:

> He liked to keep the room darkened when alone. Somewhat vaguely he was aware of the photograph on the wall, on his right. Vaguely, because he rarely looked at it, and when he did, by accident, he tried as much as possible to block his father's face on it from his mind. [...] The photograph on the wall, its face, intruded into his consciousness at this moment, eyes boring into him from the side, and he shuddered. His father's photograph, taken in the 1940s, was one of the prized possessions Zera had brought from Dar. [...] Sometimes when she lighted incense sticks and went around the apartment consecrating it, she would stand before the photograph and hold the incense to it – as one would to a real person – thus giving it a real presence. (83)

Of course, Haji Lalani has at best a partial presence, but his potentially disapproving gaze carries criticism beyond the grave. Even in such reduction he is a powerful super-ego on whom Nurdin projects his frustrations and feelings of inadequacy. Nurdin's paranoid imagination complements his already crowded surroundings by metonymically preserving fear-inducing objects from his past, most notably his father's picture. As a result, Nurdin is caught in a vicious circle of fear which keeps him at an irrational distance from the objects that cause it, and which prevents him from approaching them in a rational way: degeneration meets regression. The constant irritation of Haji Lalani's stern gaze and the CN tower thus stand for the combined pressures of past and present. Like two sphinxes, they fix Nurdin in their midst, leaving him unable to move either forward or back until all riddles are solved.

The sense of being watched and the compulsion to read meanings into looks or other visual signs is a significant over-reaction on Nurdin's part. Looking or being watched are activities which imply a certain distance between the agent and the object that is being observed. By transmitting judgement and control across a distance, looks exert an intangible kind of power. Nurdin's fear of looks has a psychological basis in his family history: in colonial Tanzania, his father once jeopardized his reputation by ogling a German lady in his shop (14). This event led to Haji Lalani's public disgrace and to his being hurriedly married off. In reparation, he subsequently spent his life as an arbiter of morals and fiercely puritan defendant of modesty in his vicinity. Despite his endeavours, he failed to eradicate indecency in his family: years later, he expelled his eldest son from the family because the boy looked at (and wrote to) the daughter of a Hindu neighbour, Sushila. Now, Nurdin ends up with a court order for indecent assault because of taking a lewd look into the shirt of a distressed female. While it was the concrete act of his touching the girl's shoulder that caused her to call for help, Nurdin is conscious that the visual liberties he has taken are his real transgression.

The experience of the power of looks forms a leitmotif throughout the novel as looks are associated with racism and xenophobia. En route to North America, the Lalanis have a traumatic encounter with an "imperial gaze" of this kind: stopping at Heathrow airport, they find that they are not allowed to leave the Customs for a sightseeing tour of London while waiting for their connecting flight because they are *regarded* as *personae non gratae*:

> London was not a foreign place, not really, it was a city they all knew in their hearts. [...] At London airport normal *eyes* would have *seen*, at the end of a long queue, a somewhat dowdy couple with puffed faces and two children practically asleep on their feet. What the immigration officer *saw*, apparently, was a pack of skilled and rehearsed actors from the former colonies out to steal jobs from hard-working English men and women. (33; my emphases)

Looks can inscribe difference and transmit hostility. In Canada where tactile contact is less accepted than in his former home, Nurdin learns that looks map out a Western brand of untouchability. The impediments encountered in London are a key experience overshadowing the Lalanis' arrival in Canada where they are held up in a differently constructed arrivals lounge fashioned by the stereotypes of various communities and hampered by their own difficulties at defining their identity.

The power of looks is dramatically dismantled at the ending of the novel. This forms part of the demystifying programme by which Missionary settles his community's problems. On his arrival at Nurdin's apartment, the religious leader uses his authority to elect Canada to become the earthly equivalent of paradise:

> He sat back with a satisfied sigh. Canada to him was a veritable Amarapur, the eternal city, the land of the West in quest of which his community had embarked some four hundred years ago. This was the final stop. He was very happy. (198)

In rendering this paradise concrete he first of all turns the CN Tower into a tangible location: "Ah, the CN Tower. I have been to the top of it, many years ago. Excellent restaurant" (186). Then he proceeds to exorcise the ghost of Haji Lalani's picture. He playfully proffers the "old red fez" which Nurdin's father was wont to wear, thereby cutting Haji Lalani's metonymic authority to size:

> he brought out the fez from a bag and put it on his own head. 'Well, Nurdin,' he said, [...] 'what punishment do you deserve?' – Nurdin recoiled, flitting his eyes from his father's hat on the Master's head to his father's picture on the wall, back and forth, several times. [...] But the Master gave a hearty laugh ... He removed the hat from his head, holding it irreverently like the dead object it was, and he laughed some more and they couldn't help laughing with him. That instant the red fez was exorcized. In one stroke that photograph on the wall had lost all potency, its once accusing eyes were now blank, its expression dumb. Suddenly they were here, in the modern world, laughing at the past. (96–97)

The momentary catharsis achieved by Missionary is part of a fairytale denouement: not only does Missionary dispel Nurdin's fear of his father, he furthermore curbs Zera's fanatism and knits the family together once again. These stunts are topped by a significant 'fairy king gesture' as Missionary bestows the hand of his daughter on Nanji. This paradigmatic happy ending reinforces the immigrants' sense of community, since intermarriage is evidently one of the crucial strategies for keeping a community intact.

This ending, fairytale-like and ambivalent, confirms that the strategy of cordoning oneself off against all foreign elements and living for an unreachable past is unprofitable. An exaggerated orientation towards the past (and its authority, as personified by Haji Lalani or his portrait respectively) are harmful to integration. Similarly, to turn away from one's tradition likewise endangers the community. This is exemplified by Nurdin's and Nanji's tentative aspirations to form relationships that will lead them away from the community and turn them into outcasts, or by Fatima's blind rejection of everything connected with her Third-World past. Neither a total abandonment of traditions nor a rigid clinging to them can be a productive reaction to the pressures of alienation. For Missionary, the problem of preserving the community's tradition and of immersing oneself in the ocean of a new country are not an inflexible either–or choice. He reminds his followers of the fact that integration of opposites and a combination of various cultural heritages are central to the Shamsi identity, and that when one approaches a culture more closely it will reveal itself to be less frightening and menacing than it appears from a distance. Vassanji's community is called upon to modify its more rigidly diasporic forms of behaviour so as to keep in mind their real aspirations. In order to find Amarapur or heaven anywhere on earth, the concept of a mythical homeland needs to be adapted to the circumstances. Missionary therefore calls for another round of multicultural compromises. The diasporic Shamsis need to recognize the need to reinvent themselves in response to their new surroundings. Missionary's magic reconciliation of opposites tells the Shamsis that it is time for another set of syncretic approaches to their surroundings to be developed.

Physical arrival is therefore less significant than the changes in the minds of the immigrants: the unpacking of mental luggage involves a process of initiation into the workings of a society which professes multicultural amity but remains steeped in racial prejudice, a society that makes use of economic tricks and mechanisms in order to turn ignorant immigrants into victims of exploitation. In the case of Nurdin, mental adjustment depends on his acceptance of the fact that the 'new land' is not as different from the old as he would like it to be: it still takes an effort to turn it into an earthly paradise.

However, the ironic fairytale ending also means that the novel ends in an enigmatic blurring of imagination and real life. *No New Land* shows that the diasporic imagination is in conflict with practical issues of adaptation and assimilation to a new culture. The novel proposes that most strategies which can be labelled diasporic are in fact unproductive and obstructive to personal and communal development. The Shamsis are consequently faced with the task of reinventing themselves and of reconstructing their identity in their new surroundings. The fairytale ending is really a beginning.

WORKS CITED

Barratt, Harold. "M.G. Vassanji," in Nelson, ed. *Writers of the Indian Diaspora*, 445–49.

Birbalsingh, Frank. "South Asian Canadian Writers from Africa and the Caribbean," *Canadian Literature* 132 (1992): 94–106.

Biskowski, Lawrence J. "Education and the Self in a Postmetaphysical World," in *Alternative Identities: The Self in Literature, History, Theory*, ed. Linda Marie Brooks (New York: Garland, 1995): 141–60.

Bissoondath, Neil. "True Expatriate Love," *Saturday Night* (June 1991): 44–45.

Clarke, Colin, Ceri Peach & Steven Vertovec, ed. *South Asians Overseas: Migration and Ethnicity* (Cambridge: Cambridge UP, 1990).

Clifford, James. "Diasporas," *Cultural Anthropology* 9.3 (1994): 302–38.

Cohen, Robin. *Global Diasporas: An Introduction* (Seattle: U of Washington P, 1997).

Freese, Peter. "Über die Schwierigkeiten des Erwachsenwerdens: Amerikanische stories of initiation von Nathaniel Hawthorne bis Joyce Carol Oates," in *Die Short Story im Englischunterricht der Sekundarstufe II: Theorie und Praxis*, ed. Peter Freese, Horst Groene & Liesel Hermes (Paderborn: Schöningh, 1979): 206–55.

George, Rosemary Marangoly. "Traveling Light: Immigration and Invisible Suitcases in M.G. Vassanji's *The Gunny Sack*," in *Memory, Narrative and Identity: New Essays in Ethnic American Literatures*, ed. Amritjit Singh, Joseph T. Skerrett & Robert E. Hogan (Boston MA: Northeastern UP, 1994): 278–304.

Heller, Arno. *Odyssee zum Selbst: Zur Gestaltung jugendlicher Identitätssuche im neuen amerikanischen Roman* (Innsbruck: Institut für Vergleichende Sprachwissenschaft, 1973).

Kanaganayakam, Chelva. "'Broadening the Substrata': An Interview with M.G. Vassanji," *World Literature Written in English* 31.2 (1991): 19–35.

——. "Don Mills and Dar es Salaam: *No New Land* by M.G. Vassanji," in *Floating the Borders: New Contexts in Canadian Criticism*, ed. Nurjehan Aziz (Toronto: TSAR, 1999): 200–203.

Kogawa, Joy. *Obasan* (Toronto: Lester & Orpen Dennys, 1981).

Malak, Amin. "Ambivalent Affiliation and the Postcolonial Condition: The Fiction of M.G. Vassanji," *World Literature Today* 67.2 (1993): 277–82.

Mishra, Vijay. "The Diasporic Imaginary: Theorizing the Indian Diaspora," *Textual Practice* 10.3 (1996): 421–47.

Mukherjee, Bharati. *Jasmine* (London: Virago, 1990).

Nandy, Ashis. *The Intimate Enemy: Loss and Recovery of Self Under Colonialism* (Delhi: Oxford UP, 1983).

Nelson, Emmanuel S. *Writers of the Indian Diaspora: A Bio-Bibliographical Critical Sourcebook* (Westport CT: Greenwood, 1993).

Ofcansky, Thomas Press, & Rodger Yeager. *Historical Dictionary of Tanzania* (Lanham MD & London: Scarecrow, 1997).

Safran, William. "Diasporas in Modern Societies: Myths of Homeland and Return," *Diaspora: A Journal of Transnational Studies* 1.1 (1991): 83–99.

Saletore, Rajaram Narayan. *Encyclopaedia of Indian Culture*, vol. 1 (New Delhi: Sterling, 1985).

Vassanji, M.G. "Foreword" to *Floating the Borders: New Contexts in Canadian Criticism*, ed. Nurjehan Aziz (Toronto: TSAR, 1999): vii–viii.

——. *The Gunny Sack* (London: Heinemann, 1989).

——. "Life at the Margins: In the Thick of Multiplicity," in *Between the Lines: South Asians and Postcoloniality*, ed. Deepika Bahri & Mary Vasudeva (Philadelphia PA: Temple U P, 1996): 111–20.

——. *No New Land* (Toronto: McClelland & Stewart, 1991).

✍

MAKARAND PARANJAPE

Writing Across Boundaries
South Asian Diasporas and Homelands

T
HIS ESSAY EXPLORES THE WAYS in which diasporas, specifically the Indian (or South Asian) diasporas, relate to the mother country. It begins by trying to define the relationship between retreating empires and advancing diasporas. While European settlers spread across the world as colonizers and conquerors, the natives of Africa and Asia were sent across the dark waters initially as slaves and indentured labourers. After the end of the imperial period, many more coloured people occupied their former masters' countries, thus creating a new kind of diaspora. Part of this process was the creation of the diaspora of the affluent, upwardly mobile, professional Indians emigrating to improve their prospects. How do these older and newer Indian diasporas relate to one another in terms of their literary creativity? Are there, in other words, two kinds of literatures that these two diasporas spawn? This essay seeks to show that diasporas and homelands are locked in peculiar, dialectical relationships, which need to be explored in greater detail. More specifically, I propose to examine the culture of this diaspora in Australia. For illustration, I will turn to the work of two women writers of the South Asian Australian diaspora.

☙

The South Asian Diaspora

The South Asian diaspora is more than eleven million strong.[1] Though smaller than the African or the Chinese diasporas – supposed to number approximately 200 million and 30 million respectively – it is more widely spread across the world and more varied. People of Indian origin now reside in over seventy countries, across all the continents, from Surinam to Singapore, from Canada to Australia. Its members come from several regions of India; they profess about a dozen religions and belong to hundreds of castes and sub-castes. What interests me most is the relationship of this diaspora to its motherland, India. More specifically, I would like to examine how India is imagined, defined, and narrated in the texts of the South Asian diaspora in Australia.

It might be useful at this point to offer a brief overview of the South Asian diaspora. With the abolition of slavery in the nineteenth century, cheap labour was required to service sugar, rubber, tea, and other plantations in the colonies. To this end, two systems for the export of Indian labour were devised. The first, contract labour, with fixed wages and a guaranteed return passage, was limited to Burma, Malaysia, and Sri Lanka. Most of the labourers were Tamils or Telugus. This system flourished for over a hundred years, from 1832 to 1937. The indentured-labour system was much more inequitable. The labourer was contracted for a period, usually five years, during which he was a virtual captive on the plantation. At the end, he could return, get himself re-indentured, work elsewhere, or, in very rare cases, buy a plot of land and settle down. Several impoverished Indian peasants were

---

[1]   Bhikhu Parekh, "Some Reflections on the Indian Diaspora," *Journal of Contemporary Thought* (1993): 105–107. Benedict Anderson puts the strength of the South Asian diaspora at nine million; Anderson, "Exodus," *Critical Inquiry* 20.2 (Winter 1994): 326–27. Recent estimates consider the number to be as high as twenty million.

shipped abroad under this system to work for meagre wages, plus room and board.

Indentured labour was introduced in 1829. Despite much opposition, it continued until 1924. In all, about 1.4 million Indian labourers were sent abroad to over fifteen colonies including – among others – Martinique, Kenya, Tanzania, South Africa, Singapore, Burma, Australia and Canada.

Since this essay will go on to discuss immigration to Australia as reflected in recent Indo-Australian literature, I start with a brief history of Australian contacts with India. Indians first impinged on the Australian psyche during the Great Revolt of 1857–58, when gory reports of heathens slaughtering Englishmen, raping their wives, and murdering their children were printed daily in all Australian newspapers.[2] Later, South Asians arrived in person. There are various accounts of the first South Asians in Australia. According to one version, there were Indian camel drivers in Australia from 1860, though they were all called "Afghans." There were also Indian, mostly Punjabi, farmers in Queensland and New South Wales since the first decades of the twentieth century. When they returned to India, they brought back stories of unlimited stretches of land waiting to be farmed. Several of these early immigrants, who came to be known as Afghans, were actually Indians. The large stock of wild camels in Australia has in fact descended from Indian camels taken there by these early farmers and traders. Even the number of these first South Asian immigrants is very uncertain. In the early decades of the twentieth century, it is estimated to have been anywhere from 1,000 to 7,000.[3]

[2] J.V. D'Cruz, "White Australia and the Indian Munity," in *The Asian Image in Australia: Episodes in Australian History* (Gloucestershire: Hawthorn Press, 1993): 11–13.

[3] David Walker, *Anxious Nation: Australia and the Rise of Asia, 1850–1939* (St Lucia: U of Queensland P, 1999): 36. See also S.P. Awasthi & Ashoka Chandra, "Migration from India to Australia," *Asian and Pacific Migration Journal* 3.2–3 (1994): 393–409.

The fiction of this period, which lasted up the 1960s, may be better characterized as orature than as literature.

The first bigger wave of Indian migration to Australia was triggered off by the boom of the software industry in the late 1970s and early 1980s. Today it is hard to find a software company that does not have one or more Indian employees. The most recent influx of Indians to Australia is a consequence of Australian higher education policy. Lacking government funding, Australian universities have started to look for full fee paying oversea students. Many Australian education institutes have permanent representatives in South Asia in order to recruit those who are able to pay the fees.[4] The University of Canberra alone recruits about 500 Indian students every year.

Immigration to the USA took place in two phases, from 1907 to 1924, and from 1965 up until the present. Prior to 1965, there were only about 6,500 Indians in the USA, while in 1990 the number of South Asian residents in the USA was estimated to be one million. Many of them are professionals – doctors, teachers, and so on. The diaspora in Canada follows a similar pattern. The first wave was made up mostly of Sikh and Punjabi labourers employed in blue collar jobs. By 1908 they numbered around 5,000. With the liberalization of the Canadian immigration laws after World War II, the number of South Asian immigrants strongly increased. Today there are about 1.5 million Indians in Canada.

Immigration to Europe started as a consequence of Indian independence. South Asians began to immigrate to the UK after 1947. Most of them were working-class people who moved to ethnic neighbourhoods. Today more than half a million South Asians live in Britian. The South Asian communities in the rest of Europe are much smaller. Germany granted asylum to Tamil refugees in the wake of the violent conflicts in Sri Lanka, some Indian professionals found jobs in Switz-

---

[4] See, on the Indian diaspora in Australia, http://indians.australians.com/indexIndians.htm.

erland, Austria and France. From the 1970s onwards, a wave of migration to the Gulf was triggered off by the boom in oil prices. As a result, Indians outnumber the native Arabian population in Dubai and Kuwait. What especially concerns us here, however, is the influx of South Asians to Australia.

The South Asian diaspora constitutes, as Amitav Ghosh puts it, "an important force in worlds culture" but "also increasingly a factor within the culture of the Indian subcontinent."[5]

Theorizing the Diaspora: Some Issues and Problems [6]

At the beginning of the "Diasporas" double issue of *SPAN*, Vijay Mishra, the guest editor argues that the definition of the diaspora as stated in the *OED* is completely outdated.[7] Even the examples of the usage of the word cited in the dictionary stop in the year 1889. In all these sentences, barring the first one, diaspora refers exclusively to the Jewish experience. But already, as far back as 1876, the word diaspora was used in a wider sense to refer to the dispersion of the Moravians among the national Protestant Churches of the continent.[8] At any rate,

---

[5] Amitav Ghosh, "The Diaspora in Indian Culture," *Public Culture* 2.1. (1989): 73. For accounts of the Indian diaspora, see: Colin Clarke et al. ed., *South Asians Overseas* (Cambridge, Cambridge UP, 1990); Hugh Tinker, *The Banyan Tree: Overseas Emigrants from India* (London: Oxford UP, 1997); Peter von der Veer, *Nation and Migration: The Politics of Space in the South Asian Diaspora* (Philadelphia: U of Pennsylvania P, 1994); and Parekh, "Some Reflections on the Indian Diaspora," 105–52.

[6] A portion of this essay has been published in my Introduction to *Diaspora: Theories, Histories, Texts*, ed. Makarand Paranjape (New Delhi: Indialog Publications, 2001): 1–15. Another portion was first presented at the Association of Commonwealth Literature and Language Studies 12th Triennial Conference. July 2001, Canberra, Australia.

[7] Vijay Mishra, "Introduction" to *SPAN* 34–35 (special double issue: "Diasporas"; November 1992–May 1993): 1–2.

[8] Mishra, "Introduction," 1.

after "the voice of authority from the Metropolitan Centre," Mishra wryly observes, "it appears that there is a 100-year gap of citations to fill to connect this word with the complex history of 20th century capitalism."⁹ As a corrective he offers the following definitions:

> 1. Relatively homogeneous, displaced communities brought to serve the Empire (slave, contract, indentured, etc.) co-existing with indigenous/other races with markedly ambivalent and contradictory relationship with the Motherland(s). Hence the Indian diasporas of South Africa, Fiji, Mauritius, Guyana, Trinidad, Surinam, Malaysia; the Chinese diasporas of Malaysia, Indonesia. Linked to high (classical) Capitalism.
> 2. Emerging new diasporas based on free migration and linked to late capitalism: post-war South Asian, Chinese, Arab, Korean communities in Britain, Europe, America, Canada, Australia.
> 3. Any group of migrants that sees itself on the periphery of power, or excluded from sharing power.¹⁰

Although Mishra's definitions do not address the African diaspora, I find them very apt for describing the Indian or South Asian diasporas.

In this context, it might be instructive to compare Mishra's account with Benedict Anderson's classic study, *Imagined Communities*.¹¹ Anderson distinguishes nations from two earlier types of polity, religious empires and imperial dynasties. There are communities at the margins of nations, says Bhabha, whose counter-narratives "continually evoke and erase" the totalizing boundaries of the modern nation-state.¹² These equivocal narratives are supplementary to those of the nation-state: "We must always keep open a supplementary space for the articulation of cultural knowledges that are adjacent and adjunct but not necessarily accumulative, teleological or dialectical."¹³ Ac-

---

⁹ Mishra, "Introduction," 1.

¹⁰ Mishra, "Introduction," 1.

¹¹ Benedict Anderson, *Imagined Communities: Reflections on the Origin and Spread of Nationalism* (London: Verso, 1983).

¹² Homi Bhabha, *The Location of Culture* (London: Routledge, 1994): 149.

¹³ Bhabha, *The Location of Culture*, 163.

cording to Chris Berry, beyond the horizon of nations a fourth kind of imagined community is taking shape: "it is a discordant and dynamic conjuncture, constituted when different cultures (themselves maybe less unified than we think) with different histories and different trajectories meet, intersect, overlay, fragment and produce hybrid forms within a certain geographic space."[14] Another way of expressing this unfolding would be as follows:

Religious Empires   Nations

$\rightarrow$ Global Empires $\rightarrow$

Imperial Dynasties   Diasporas

Of course, we need to remember that nations, empires, and diasporas evolve simultaneously. There is an overlap and slippage between these categories.

I have deliberately mentioned the work of the above critics, especially that of Vijay Mishra, because it marks a considerable advance over the earlier formulations of writers such as William Safran.[15] Safran's model, which he illustrates by listing six features of diasporas – dispersal, collective memory, alienation, respect and longing for the homeland, a belief in its restoration, and self-definition in terms of this homeland – are more applicable to the Jewish than the South Asian diaspora. Mishra considers Safran's characteristics of the Indian diaspora – middlemen role, long history, integrationist and particularist foci – to be "oversimplified."[16] While this essay relies extensively on Mishra's work, it also diverges from it to a considerable extent. Mish-

---

[14] Chris Berry, "These Nations Which Are Not One: History, Identity and Postcoloniality in Recent Hong Kong and Taiwan Cinema," *SPAN* 33–34 (special double issue: "Diasporas"; November 1992–May 1993): 38.

[15] William Safran, "Diasporas in Modern Societies: Myths of Homeland and Return," *Diaspora: A Journal of Transnational Studies* 1.1 (1991): 83–99.

[16] Vijay Mishra, "The Diasporic Imaginary: Theorizing the Indian Diaspora," *Textual Practice* 10.3 (1996): 443.

ra seems to suggest that the diasporic is a special epistemology which
can be used to define postcoloniality itself. For instance, in "New
Lamps for Old: Diasporas Migrancy Border," Mishra, carried away by
his enthusiasm for "diasporic analysis" over "a vague 'postcolonial'
theory,"[17] considers his essay to be, among other things, "a celebration
of diasporas as the exemplary condition of late modernity."[18] Mishra
contrasts the diasporic consciousness with older, primordial, ethnic
identities, arguing that "diasporic epistemology locates itself squarely
in the realm of the hybrid, in the domain of cross-cultural and con-
taminated social and cultural regimes."[19] In this, Mishra is akin to
Bhabha, who also elevates the hybrid to the level of a new consciousness:

> the colonial hybrid is the articulation of the ambivalent space where
> the rite of power is enacted on the site of desire, making its objects at
> once disciplinary and disseminatory – or [...] a negative trans-
> parency.[20]

Even though Mishra acknowledges the danger that "diasporas may
well become romanticized as *the* ideal social condition,"[21] in effect,
that is what the theoretical stance of critics like Mishra and Bhabha
amounts to. Neither refers to the fact that diasporic communities are
known, at times, to support the most rabidly violent and fanatical of
causes, not just ideologically but financially. In South Asia, for
instance, it is well-known how Sikh, Hindu, Muslim, Tamil, and other
militants have been supported by overseas communities.

---

[17] Vijay Mishra, "New Lamps for Old: Diasporas Migrancy Border,"
Interrogating Post-Colonialism: Theory, Text and Context, ed. Harish Trivedi
& Meenakshi Mukherjee (Shimla: Indian Institute of Advanced Study, 1996):
70.
[18] Mishra, "New Lamps for Old," 67.
[19] Mishra, "New Lamps for Old," 71.
[20] Bhabha, *The Location of Culture*, 112.
[21] Mishra, "The Diasporic Imaginary," 426.

The problem lies in equating the diaspora with every form of migration or with every perception of powerlessness. True, those who migrate, say, from villages to cities or those who are excluded from the structures of power do indeed experience something akin to the sense of diasporic displacement. On the other hand, there is nothing alienating or dispossessing about a South Asian's sudden burst of stupendous success in Silicon Valley, where she has relocated to better her prospects. Such a person's success is celebrated the world over and not invoked to illustrate the misfortunes of forced, cross-continental traffic in human beings. I shall dwell on such distinctions in greater detail later, but what I wish to emphasize immediately is that the diasporic experience, to my mind, must involve a significant crossing of borders. These may be borders of a region or a language, but more often are multiple borders such as the loss of homeland would suggest.

To me, the whole importance of the diaspora and its potential for creating a new kind of culture arises out of such a crossing of boundaries. The diaspora, then, must involve a cross-cultural or cross-civilizational passage. It is only such a crossing that results in the unique consciousness of the diasporic. In other words, there has to be a source country and a target country, a source culture and a target culture, a source language and a target language, a source religion and a target religion, and so on. Also, the crossing must be forced, not voluntary; otherwise, the passage will only amount to an enactment of desire-fulfilment. Or, even if voluntary, the passage must involve some significant tension between the source and the target cultures. It is through this displacement and ambivalence that what we consider the diasporic is engendered.

I started my essay with theories of the diaspora. I could just as well have used theories of (post)colonialism as a convenient point of departure. In their seminal *The Empire Writes Back*, Bill Ashcroft, Gareth Griffiths and Helen Tiffin provide a typology of postcolonial literatures. They assert that one of the key themes in this literature "is the concern with place and displacement": "the special post-colonial crisis of identity comes into being with the development or recovery of an effective identifying relationship between self and place."[22] This relationship, which ordinarily might be reasonably secure is radically eroded in the postcolonial experience because of "*dislocation* resulting from migration, [...] enslavement, transportation, or 'voluntary' removal for indentured labour" (8). Citing the work of D.E.S. Maxwell, the authors identify two broad groups of postcolonial societies: those springing from settler colonies, and those from invaded colonies; examples of the former are the USA, Canada, New Zealand and Australia, "where land was occupied by European colonists who dispossessed and overwhelmed the indigenous populations" (25). Invaded colonies include India and Nigeria, where native populations had their own languages and cultures, but these were "marginalized by the world-view which was implicated in the acquisition of English" (25).

One of the chief arguments of this essay is that, in the wake of such imperialistic expansion, there was also a reverse process of migration, which might, in fact, inversely mirror the spread of European colonialism. For the sake of convenience, let us call this reverse spread the postcolonial diaspora. We might call it postcolonial because it was a direct result of colonialism and imperialism, but I use this phrase in the manner in which Ashcroft et al. use it. Thus, the term 'postcolonial diasporas' would include all those diasporas which arose "from the moment of colonization to the present day" (2). In other words, I would like to theorize the diaspora as a sort of dialectical Other of colonialism. The latter was the dominant, assertive, masculine thesis of which the former is a submerged, apparently passive, feminine antithesis. We might be able to detect a sort of inverse symmetry between these two movements of populations, between empires and their diasporas. In addition, this takes us to the illuminative manner in which empires and diasporas reflect and interpenetrate one another.

---

[22] Bill Ashcroft, Gareth Griffith & Helen Tiffin, *The Empire Writes Back: Theory and Practice in Post-Colonial Literatures* (London: Routledge, 1989): 8. Further page references are in the main text.

One problem with trying to understand these interpenetrations is that we do not have a word to describe former empires which now must play host to their colonial chicken that have come home to roost. The former colonies give rise to postcolonial societies, but the metropoles, supposedly, continue as before, unaffected by a history they imagine happened *elsewhere*. The myopia of this imperial myth of self-sufficiency is eloquently demonstrated in the writings of Salman Rushdie.[23] The problem is that what happens at the peripheries of the empire not only produces, in the words of Eric Stokes, "a disturbing force, a magnetic power placed at the periphery tending to distort the natural development,"[24] but something much more material and tangible. Just as Gibreel Farishta crash-lands into Rosa Diamond's self-enclosed, well-ordered, and verdant garden, the milling crowds of diasporic people gatecrash their way into metropolitan centres of the once glorious imperium. These diasporas, displaced, alienated, excluded and oppressed, create their own kind of epistemic disjunction at the heart of the metropolis. What was formerly an empire has become the host to a new kind of colony, a colony made up of diasporic peoples from the various parts of the world that it once ruled.

The nature of the diaspora, its cultural location and politics, consequently, depend on the nature of the host, not just on that of the diaspora. Diasporas, despite their common origin, may behave in a totally different manner depending on their country of relocation. A host country like the USA, for example, ostensibly does not distinguish between immigrants and diasporic people. Officially, all are the same to her; and all those who enter have the opportunity of instant assimilation, of fashioning themselves anew. As Susan Koshy points out, it is myths such as these that inform Bharati Mukherjee's grossly oversimplified and celebratory narratives of triumphant, if postmodernist, feminism. What Mukherjee, in her enthusiasm, ignores is

---

[23] Bhabha, *The Location of Culture*, 166–169.
[24] Cited in Bhabha, *The Location of Culture*, 89.

that the USA treats legal and illegal immigrants very differently, as it does white as opposed to coloured immigrants, or modern European versus other cultural constructions of subjectivity.[25]

On closer examination of the entire South Asian diaspora, we notice that it falls into two distinct phases. To begin with, let us call them settler and visitor diasporas, taking our cue from *The Empire Writes Back*, which identifies settler and invader colonialists. Of course, both these labels are not entirely appropriate, but may serve for the time being. To the first category belong all those forced migrations on account of slavery or indentured labour, while the second would encompass the voluntary migrations of businessmen and professionals who went abroad for career purposes. These two distinct groups may be defined not just by the causes and patterns of their migration, but also by the historical period in which the migrations took place. Further, these two diasporas may also be contrasted by their destinations and class backgrounds, attitude to the mother country, economic status, language of creative expression, market access, and so on. As Mishra puts it,

> This narrative of diasporic movement is, however, not continuous or seamless as there is a radical break between the older diasporas of classic capitalism and the mid- to late-twentieth-century diasporas of advanced capital to the metropolitan centres of the Empire, the New World and the former settler colonies.[26]

He calls these two "interlinked, but historically separated diasporas" as "old ('exclusive') and the new ('border')" diasporas. I shall argue that these two diasporas produce two different kinds of literatures. The object here is to offer a preliminary map of these differences.

∅

---

[25] Susan Koshy, "The Geography of Female Subjectivity," *Diaspora: A Journal of Transnational Studies* 3.1 (1994): 79.

[26] Mishra, "The Diasporic Imaginary," 422.

The Motherland in Diasporic Narratives

How do diasporas construct homelands? It seems to me that they do so in accordance to their own needs and compulsions. In the case of the older diaspora, we see a certain break with the motherland. This break was not voluntary, but enforced by the distances between the motherland and the diasporic settlement, the older, much slower modes of travel, and, above all, the lack of economic means to make frequent journeys. In fact, the labourers who were shipped out rarely had enough money to make the journey back to India; for most, it was a one-way ticket to another land. In other words, the distance – physical, but more so psychological – was so vast that the motherland remained frozen in the diasporic imagination as a sort of sacred site or symbol, almost like an idol of memory and imagination. The poverty of the homeland, which was responsible for the dispersal of peoples in the first place, forgotten or overwritten with the *feeling* that it was home, a place where the present alienation of the diasporic person did not exist. Because a physical return was virtually impossible, an emotional or spiritual renewal was an ongoing necessity. As Mishra puts it, "the old Indian diaspora replicated the space of India and sacralized the stones and rivers of the new lands."[27] In other words, the old diaspora carried with it a sort of "Hindu toolbox" to indianize its new surroundings:

> [...] their homeland is a series of objects, fragments of narratives that they keep in their heads or in their suitcases. Like hawkers they can reconstitute their lives through the contents of their knapsacks: a Ganapati icon, a dog-eared copy of the *Gita* or the *Quran*, an old sari or other *deshi* outfit, a photograph of a pilgrimage or, in modern times, a videocassette of the latest hit from the home country.[28]

---

27 Mishra, "The Diasporic Imaginary," 442.
28 Mishra, "New Lamps for Old," 68.

But it is also important to remember that the old diaspora, made up largely of subaltern and underprivileged classes, hardly produced any literature at all. Theirs was still mostly an oral culture. It consisted of stories, narratives, songs, and texts which, by and large, did not enter into the print medium. This rich archive of orature and para-literature is yet to be explored.

Mishra calls V.S. Naipaul "the founding writer of the old diaspora."[29] By the same token, Salman Rushdie would be Naipaul's most visible and logical counterpart as far as the new diaspora is concerned. But I am not sure if we can accept such a formulation. If we read the recently published correspondence between Naipaul and his father, it is clear that Naipaul belongs, in fact, to the new diaspora. He finds himself breaking free from the old diaspora, almost on behalf of his father and the latter's unfulfilled aspirations. And he does so via Oxford and the publishing opportunities of the metropolitan capital, London. While the writings of the old diaspora are utterly marginalized, they find a new currency when they re-enter the world of discourse via the new diaspora. In some ways, then, the relationship between the two diasporas can be represented by the relationship between Naipaul and his father. It is the story of the thwarted ambitions of the father finding fruition in the celebrated literary triumph of the son. Naipaul's books are now part of English literature syllabi the world over, while his father's writings are remembered only because of their association with the son's. The subordinate culture of the old diaspora can only be recognized if it re-invents itself in the image of the dominant culture of the metropolis.

The manner in which the new diaspora imagines India is therefore to be understood in terms of the logic of this dominant culture, of which it is an ambivalent or unwilling part. While the old diaspora was cut off from the motherland, the new diaspora has unprecedented access to it by virtue of its privileged Non-Resident Indian status.

---

[29] Mishra, "The Diasporic Imaginary," 442.

What we see, then, is a narrative logic of continuous incorporation and appropriation which reinforces the self-validating logic of the new diaspora. Not forced to leave the motherland, these writers have chosen to relocate themselves in the metropolitan centres chiefly for economic reasons. This breeds in them a certain anxiety, if not guilt towards the homeland. In the international literary marketplace there is, and has always been, a niche market for fictional representations of India. Earlier, this Anglo-Indian slot was occupied by writers from Europe, the UK and the USA; now the South Asians have moved in.[30]

The texts of the new diaspora not only describe the motherland, but also justify why it has to be left behind; as Rushdie puts it, "Literature is self-validating."[31] The narratives of the new diaspora, then, are elaborate and eloquent leave-takings, often elegiac in tone. Like Rohinton Mistry's *A Fine Balance* [32] they construct the motherland as not only an area of darkness, confusion, violence, but also as a hopeless and doomed country which must be rejected. In this novel, however, the protagonist doesn't leave, but, instead, commits suicide. The trend-setting text of this type of representation of India was, of course, Rushdie's *Midnight's Children*.[33] In Rushdie's novel, India literally cracks up. Furthermore, the narrator–protagonist Saleem Sinai is himself a 'fragmented' personage; his digressive and disjointed narrative cannot encapsulate the chaos that is India. *Midnight's Children*, then, is about the de-composition of India, about its disintegration and dispersal. I would argue that this deconstructive narrative is an outcome of the new diasporic consciousness which, because it lacks internal

---

[30] Makarand Paranjape, "Indo-Anglian as Anglo-Indian: Ideology, Politics, and Cross-Cultural Representation," in *Postcolonial Perspectives on the Raj and Its Literature*, ed. Vrinda Nabar & Nilufer Bharucha (Bombay: U of Bombay P, 1994): 41–52.

[31] Salman Rushdie, *Imaginary Homelands: Essays and Criticism 1981– 1991* (1992; New Delhi: Vision, 1996).

[32] Rohinton Mistry, *A Fine Balance* (London: Faber & Faber, 1996).

[33] Salman Rushdie, *Midnight's Children* (London: Jonathan Cape, 1981).

coherence, cannot see any cohesion in the object that it describes. All that it can do is to try to incorporate its fictional India into a border-less, deterritorialized, but yet commercially lucrative marketplace whose multiple sites are scattered across the most advanced nation-states of the world. In a way, Mishra's own privileging of the diasporic imaginary legitimates his own (dis)location, while my essay may be seen as being grounded in a nationalist space. As a corrective to this view, I myself have argued that "there is no 'pure' belonging; there is no 'pure' diaspora. What we must contend with, instead, are types of belonging and uprooting, affirmations and denials of identity, same-ness and difference."[34]

Finally, I would argue that the lines dividing the older and newer diasporas are fast disappearing. The old diaspora can now be theorized primarily in chronological terms. Ideologically, its descendants are more akin to the new diaspora. This merger of the most privileged members and therefore the most articulate members of the old dia-spora – what we might call the literature-producing elite – into the new one takes place through a variety of processes. Chiefly, it is by a second migration from, say, the Caribbean to North America or West-ern Europe, from East Africa to Britain, from Malaysia and Sri Lanka to Australia. Through this second wave of relocation, the old diaspora incorporates itself into the new one, sharing its economic and cultural privileges. There is also a less dramatic, but quite persuasive process of reverse osmosis in which the values, beliefs, and consciousness of the new diaspora find their way into that of the old, largely through a process which we call globalization today. The gap between metro-politan and sub-metropolitan cultures is thus diminishing. Global access to cultures also means multiple choices of identities. What it

[34] Makarand Paranjape, "What about those who stayed back home? Inter-rogating the Privileging of Diasporic Writing," in *Shifting Continents / Colliding Cultures: Diaspora Writing of the Indian Subcontinent*, ed. Ralph J. Crane & Radhika Mohanram (Cross/Cultures 42; Amsterdam & Atlanta GA: Rodopi, 2000): 225–46.

does not mean is that cultural or civilizational differences, rooted as they are in thousands of years of history of material production will be erased or easily forgotten. But what we see is a complex pattern of overlaying whereby older cultures acquire the veneer and appearance of newer ones. This veneer may be a surface without substance, but it has a certain power and eloquence. Like a mask or a disguise it smuggles older mentalities into the brave new digital world of virtual reality. The tensions between surface textures and deep structures often result in curious and complex cultural tropes in which the old and the new contend or compromise in unusual ways. In a new global environment, diasporas and homelands may, paradoxically, come much closer to each other than ever before. Yet, this closeness will not necessarily camouflage their divergent interests or politics of representation.

Resistance and Reconciliation:
South Asians in Australia

I will now analyse the specific features of the South Asian diaspora in Australia and its literary representations. Of course, it is far from my purpose to suggest that the fissures or contradictions mentioned above are peculiar to Australia, though they may indeed have a special Australian manifestation. The fact is that all nation-states are built upon such contradictions and schizoid tendencies. Indeed, the project of modernity itself, of which the nation is just part, is itself ridden with such paradoxes and fault-lines. In fact, the diasporan or the immigrant may not be entirely innocent of such ambivalences himself. He may claim equality under the general dispensation of democracy while also, on the contrary principle, seeking and securing special privileges by capitalizing on his difference. If Hodge and Mishra characterize the typical Australian as a figure who "masks an unlimited ambiguity under his excessive simplicities,"[35] I would argue that the diasporan, the immigrant, and the underprivileged Aboriginal also hide a complex ambiguity of privileged victimhood under the mask of straightforward oppression or deprivation.

The literary output of South Asian Australians is neither vast nor especially impressive, at least for now; the secondary material on it is equally scanty. The best-known writers can be counted on the fingers of two hands – in alphabetical order: Mena Abdullah, Chitra Fernando, Yasmine Gooneratne, Adib Khan, Chandani Lokuge, Ernest MacIntyre, Christine Mangala, Satendra Pratap Nandan, and perhaps a few others. My purpose here is not to offer a detailed analysis of these authors or texts but to assess this body of work so as to detect its shape, direction, and quality. I am especially interested in understanding South Asian attitudes to Australia as evident in these writings. My method here is try to single out one text each from two distinct phases of this writing to identify patterns of diasporic consciousness in this literature, especially as they pertain to perceptions of Australia. My choice of these two texts is not entirely arbitrary. Both are texts by women and therefore offer a sense of double dispersal; both are also stories of growing up, though in different ways. But, more importantly, both represent the complexities of the diasporic experience, its refusal to yield to simple formulas of explanation or understanding. Specifically, the experience of expatriation is perhaps unpacked with much greater poignancy by women writers.

But before actually discussing these texts, it might be instructive to propose a periodization. The fiction of the early period of South Asian immigration to Australia, which lasted up until the 1960s, may be characterized as orature rather than literature. That is why I call it the pre-literary phase. The next phase may be said to begin in the late 1950s or early 1960s and last well into the 1980s, before the recent

---

[35] Bob Hodge & Vijay Mishra, *Dark Side of the Dream: Australian Literature and the Postcolonial Mind* (North Sydney: Allen & Unwin, 1990), xvi.

burst of South Asian creativity in Australia. This is what I would call the "quiet" phase, to borrow a term from Paul Sharrad's excellent essay on Mena Abdullah.[36] The contemporary phase, however, will give rise to a subsequent period in which really significant writing is likely to emerge. It is tempting to suggest a major shift or progression from the quiet to the contemporary phase. For instance, we could make a plausible case for considering the quiet phase to be basically assimilationist whereas the contemporary phase begins to show signs of a more openly critical engagement with Australia. I intend to show that any such categorization runs the risk of ending up as a reductionist simplification.

The most obvious candidate for a representative text of the quiet phase is Mena Abdullah's *The Time of the Peacock* (1965).[37] Abdullah's stories started appearing in periodicals as early as 1953. They were first collected in book form in 1965, before the Aborigines got their vote or before multiculturalism became an official policy in Australia. The manner in which the book was reviewed shows that it met with a largely positive, if condescending reception. The intriguing thing about the book was that it was published as jointly authored by Abdullah and Ray Matthew, though many of the stories were first published individually as Abdullah's. Matthew was a reasonably well-known poet and journalist of the period. The extent to which he indeed co-authored or contributed to the stories needs to be examined. This requires a comparison of the original manuscripts and the various versions of the stories until they appeared in book-form under joint authorship. My conjecture is that – like the first slave narratives, which always appeared with several authenticating documents by white writers – Abdullah's early diasporan text in Australia also

---

[36] Paul Sharrad, "Mena Abdullah's Untranslatable Diasporic Identity," in *The Literature of the Indian Diaspora: Essays in Criticism*, ed. A.L. McLeod (New Delhi: Sterling, 2000): 252.

[37] Mena Abdullah & Ray Matthew, *The Time of the Peacock* (1965; Sydney: Angus & Robertson, 1995).

needed a similar method of legitimation and validation. As a strategy
for gaining entry into a dominant culture, it had to disguise itself and
also to mask its own radical difference. At any rate, under their jointly
authored version, the stories did very well indeed, even being prescribed as school texts, presumably because they showed how good
immigrants behave when they come to a new country. Sharrad shows
how, to all appearances, this is a text of collusion and conformity:

> From the politicised perspective of Australian multiculturalism and
> minority discourse theory, the book looks to be an old-fashioned
> work, collaborating uncritically with the white settler nationalist pro-
> ject. The book, for example, features a child narrator with innocent,
> sometimes naive, ideas on life, and allows the white adult reader to
> feel benignly condescending towards all kinds of difference repres-
> ented.[38]

However, such a facile reading would do injustice to the complexity of
the narrative:

> Identity remains very much a conflictual and central issue across *Time
> of the Peacock* in ways that can be read productively from a contem-
> porary viewpoint. If it is not stridently oppositional, it is nonetheless,
> not simply or passively converting to assimilation. The co-authorship,
> for example, can be read not as capitulation to the mainstream so
> much as a strategic means of intervention into it and a resistance to
> exclusivist notions of ethnicity. The troubled intersections of national,
> ethnic, linguistic, religious, class and gender identities fragment
> homogenising essentialist constructions.[39]

In the end, Abdullah's stories, while seeming to offer comforting
visions of cultural translation and accommodation of identity under the
sign of religion and land, pick up Bhabha's challenge "to think of the
question of community and communication without the moment of
transcendence" of either.[40] Amid the tensions of history and the social
contradictions of the present, the family asserts its incommensurable

---

[38] Sharrad, "Mena Abdullah's Untranslatable Diasporic Identity," 253.

[39] "Mena Abdullah's Untranslatable Diasporic Identity," 253.

[40] Bhabha, *The Location of Culture*, 153.

identity that is part of, but not homogenized into, the new nation.[41] As the conclusion of the story "Mirbani" demonstrates, the situation is best described as belonging to the South Asian diaspora. The diasporic space is neither India nor Australia, though it has strong connections with both:

> 'It is not India,' said Father. 'And it is not the Punjab,' said Uncle Seyed. 'It is just us,' said Ama.[42]

Invoking Homi K. Bhabha, Sharrad calls this third space "untranslatable" because it is not a simple re-rendering of the South Asian home in the transplanted space of the Australian nation, but a secret time, the time of the peacock, that signifies private experiences and illuminations.

The Time of the Peacock, then, is not merely a straightforward prescription for assimilation, offered through the device of a child-narrator, that recommends how immigrants should leave their old cultures behind and adjust themselves to their new environment. It suggests, rather, a more complex engagement with a new land that calls into question inherited values and cultural mores. In the resultant conflicts and tensions, characters learn how to grow and cope with the complexities of a diasporic existence. I would, however, admit that the dominant culture of the host country is not interrogated as consistently or rigorously as that of the homeland.

This reluctance to criticize Australia changes in the contemporary phase. In one of the most eloquent and moving accounts of this predicament, Chandani Lokuge, in her first novel, *If the Moon Smiled* (2000),[43] shows the isolation, alienation, and loneliness of her female protagonist, Manthri, as she negotiates the difficult journey from Sri

---

[41] Sharrad, "Mena Abdullah's Untranslatable Diasporic Identity," 260.

[42] Mena Abdullah, "Mirbani," in Abdullah & Matthew, *The Time of the Peacock*, 29.

[43] Chandani Lokuge, *If the Moon Smiled* (New Delhi: Penguin India, 2000). Further page references are in the main text.

Lanka to Australia. In this novel from the contemporary phase, it is as if Nimmi, Mena Abdullah's child protagonist in *The Time of the Peacock*, had grown up. In Manthri's case, there is literally a double expatriation. First she has to leave the safe, secure, and idyllic home of her father, the place of her artless fantasies for self-fulfilment, a green and innocent world, to go to her husband's home. Her husband, Mahendra, on utterly flimsy grounds, suspects her of infidelity, or, should I say, "impurity." He thinks that she is not a virgin because the white bed-sheet remains unstained; she has not bled on their wedding night as he expects a virgin to do. Her crime, in her husband's eyes, is severe, because she hasn not been faithful to her husband-to-be. Manthri, though blameless, feels guilty partly because on her wedding night she has fantasized making love to the handsome and virile Thilakasiri, a farm-hand who works on her father's estate. The unstained bed-sheet, crumpled but utterly white, continues to haunt Manthri's marriage, even when she and her husband emigrate to Australia. This journey symbolizes her second expatriation. First she has left her father's home; now she has left her fatherland.

Manthri's passivity and propensity to suffer stoically may be attributed to her traditional upbringing. The weight of the ancient Buddhist traditions combined with centuries of patriarchy make her more acted upon than acting. Several rites of purification and penance have marked even her transition from girlhood to womanhood, her first menstruation. Every such rite of passage comes with its own trials and traumas. If marriage brings her continual coldness and disapproval on the part of her husband, motherhood brings her a disobedient and delinquent son. Devake is unable to live up to his father's expectations, while Nelum, the daughter, who is a brilliant student, also rebels. Refusing to marry the "boy" chosen for her by her father, she runs away from home. Shattered, Manthri returns to her father and to Sri Lanka, teaches in a school for some time, trying to recover, but has to return to Australia. What choices does she have? Adultery? A furtive but passionate relationship, as dangerous as it is alluring? Unable to do even that, unhappy and distraught, she suffers a nervous breakdown and has to be institutionalized. Her fate always to be in the hands of others, she seems like a doomed creature without choices. Despite its lyrical passages and evocative prose, Lokuge's novel paints a very grim picture of Manthri's life.

Moving back and forth between Sri Lanka and Australia, the novel grounds the diasporan experience in older cycles of karma, dukkha, and transmigration. After years in Australia, when Manthri returns to Sri Lanka, she finds a country under siege:

> Home at last. To set foot on Lankan soil. Each time I come back, I know I have been away too long. It is a tranquil night. I walk the short distance to the terminal. The security if frightening. I have to avoid walking into a bayonet. They all seem pointed at me. (153)

The tropical paradise of her childhood has been turned into an army camp bristling with guns. It is here that Nelum runs away the night before her arranged marriage to an eligible upper-caste groom. Home, as it used to be, offers no solace to Manthri. Her later return to Australia is not that much better:

> I face Australia once more. Like the first time, in the whitening dawn. But alone. The breeze fondles my neck and stiffens it. I pull the collar of my overcoat tightly across my body. My knees seem encased in ice. I seem to be losing control of my legs. I cling to my trolley. (190)

The bayonets of the army are here replaced by the icy chill, the numbness of abandonment and isolation. It is not as if Mahendra, the husband, is much better off in the end. After Manthri has been hospitalized and both children are gone from their home, he finds himself lost and disoriented: "He pauses now and then, feeling frail and grey," but "he will not admit to loneliness"; what is worse, despite all the years that have passed, "He has not forgiven himself, nor her" (204). Unforgiving and unforgiven, he lives in his own kind of hell.

The story that Lokuge's novel tells is one of disintegration and dispersal, not of the movement from one home to another. Once the homeland is lost, it cannot be retrieved, not just because no return to the past is possible, but also because the homeland itself is war-torn. The parents who represented solidity and solace for Manthri are now old and weak; the expensive Pajero in which she is picked up from the airport to be taken to their country estate cannot protect either Manthri or her family from the ravages of time. Australia, despite its prosperity and opportunities, does not give Manthri the freedom to develop a new self. Instead, its relentless pressures shatter the fragile unity of her beleaguered nuclear family. Both the children grow up only to drift away. The icy barrier between husband and wife neither melts nor is it overcome. Both end up isolated and empty.

To say the least, attitudes to both the homeland and to Australia are ambivalent in this novel. Both countries and systems come under criticism, for different reasons. The rigid and hidebound traditions of Sri Lanka are seen to constrict lives and limit human happiness, just as the independence and individuality of modern Australia draw people apart and render them lonely and isolated. The novel does not offer any solutions, but instead shows characters to be severally handicapped in what they can do to obtain their own happiness. Neither Manthri's passivity nor Mahendra's assertiveness saves either of them from the existential pain and suffering that seems to be their fate. Their move from Sri Lanka to Australia, in this sense, cannot be considered a progression or even an evolution from one state to another, but a transition that does not reduce their susceptibility to emotional and psychic distress. The void and futility at the heart of life's journeys are highlighted in a poignant but wordless exchange between Manthri and her mother-in-law. The latter, too, has lost her son, it would seem, for nothing, because Manthri hasn't really gained a husband either:

> But how can there by such easy solutions? Her last words, so swollen with unspoken accusations, hurl me into silence: 'It is too late, I think, Manthri, to make amends. I thought that by crossing the seas he would begin a new life. So I gave him my blessings. But how can we cross the chasm that estranges us from ourselves?' (126)

The estrangement of the diaspora, the sorrow of the passage across the black waters, is only a part of the larger alienation of human beings from themselves. Certainly, traditions, customs, practices, the false expectations and values that people adhere to, the hardness and coldness of hearts, the pressures of living in a new country, the clash of the new and the old worlds, the independence and self-assertiveness of children – all contribute to this essential self-estrangement. But the sense of doom seems to run deeper and is irreducible. Speckled with fleeing passages of beauty though it may be, the novel is elegiac in tone, moving forwards, yet into an inexorable gloom.

Conclusion

It will not suffice to end this essay by leaving unchallenged the notion of ambivalence itself. Clearly, "ambivalence" as the ubiquitous/generic/global disaporic response to both homelands and countries of residence is unsatisfactory. Taking recourse to a generalized sense of ambivalence to explain South Asian diasporic attitudes to Australia would, thus, be tantamount to replacing older false clarities with newer, perhaps equally false, indeterminacies. Instead, I propose to sketch, albeit briefly, the specificities of these ambivalences.

The ambivalence of the South Asian diaspora in Australia is linked with the crisis of nationalism, but from the post-national end, as it were. As deterritorialized and dislocated communities, diasporas have a special need to forge their own sense of location wherever they are. While older diasporas fetishized the homeland, the new diasporas commodify it. That is why I have argued elsewhere that, though Indo-Canadian writers seem to be harkening back to India in their work, their real target or focus is Canada.[44] These "passages to India" are

---

[44] Makarand Paranjape, "One Foot in Canada and a Couple of Toes in India: Diasporas and Homelands in South Asian Canadian Experience," in *Diaspora: Theories, Histories, Texts*, ed. Paranjape (New Delhi: Indialog, 2001): 161–70.

actually 'away-from-India and toward Canada' narratives. In the case of the Indo-Australian texts, a clear pattern is yet to emerge, though I definitely sense a pervasive and unresolved biculturalism in most of them. Many of the authors resort to a generational divide or progression to resolve the contrary pulls of the homeland and country of residence. On both sides, then, there are resistance and reconciliation at work, even if the resistance is vigorous and the reconciliation reluctant.

The two texts that I have chosen illustrate, in other words, two different kinds of ambivalence. Each of them tries to create its own unique sense of locality in face of the experience of displacement. To my mind, Abdullah's stories are less threatening, because they succeed in creating a sense of neighbourhood as a concrete, material reality in the new country, Australia. I use the word neighbourhood as an actual and situated community, in a definite spatial context, in contrast to 'virtual' communities of various kinds. Lokuge's book, on the other hand, illustrates what Arjun Appadurai has termed the "growing disjuncture between territory, subjectivity, and collective social movement."[45] In that sense, locality does lose its "ontological moorings" in *If the Moon Smiled*, becoming, instead, inverted and introverted. It is no longer spatial and social, but assumes a complex phenomenological dimension, mediated through the anguished inscape of Manthri's mind. None of the relief of a virtual neighbourhood enabled and produced through Internet or electronic media is offered here, nor solace in larger projects of transnational identity and solidarity, but only the solitude and anomie of subjectivities under stress. Unlike Bharati Mukherjee, there is no release here into postmodern free play where the self can gloriously and continuously re-invent itself, depending on context and contingency. Instead, we see only withdrawal and breakdown.

---

[45] Arjun Appadurai, *Modernity at Large: Cultural Dimensions of Globalization* (Minneapolis: U of Minnesota P, 1997): 189.

But whether the diasporic passage is successful, as in Abdullah, or unsuccessful as in Lokuge, its trajectory is marked by a unique provocation to produce new localities. That these localities cannot be easily absorbed or subsumed by the existing nation state, whether of the homeland or the host country, is, I am sure, obvious. In fact, neither of the two texts that I have chosen is in this respect typical of the literature of the South Asian diaspora in Australia. If anything, each is rather unusual and challenging. Yet I have made a case to consider them as representative texts of the two periods of this literature, the earlier quiet period and the more loquacious contemporary one. My purpose has been to show that the experience of diaspora is marked by a series of ambivalences and indeterminacies, and constitutes an interstitial site that is somehow untranslatable into either the dialect of the homeland or the language of the adopted country. Instead, the diasporic experience mirrors the ambivalence that the host country feels towards its minorities and racial Others, even as it questions the certitudes and solaces of the irretrievable homeland that it has left behind. It is this tenuousness that gives the diasporic text its rich ambiguity and complexity. The relationship of diasporas with their homelands provides an area of fertile cultural possibilities.

WORKS CITED

Abdullah, Mena, & Ray Matthew. *The Time of the Peacock: Stories* (1965; Sydney: Angus & Robertson, 1995).

Anderson, Benedict. "Exodus," *Critical Inquiry* 20.2 (Winter 1994): 314–27.

——. *Imagined Communities: Reflections on the Origin and Spread of Nationalism* (London: Verso, 1983).

Appadurai, Arjun. *Modernity at Large: Cultural Dimensions of Globalization* (Minneapolis: U of Minnesota P, 1997).

Ashcroft, Bill, Gareth Griffiths, & Helen Tiffin. *The Empire Writes Back: Theory and Practice in Post-Colonial Literature* (London & New York: Routledge,1989).

Australian Nationalism Information Database. www.ozemail.com.au/~natinfo.

Awasthi, S.P., & Ashoka Chandra. "Migration from India to Australia," *Asian and Pacific Migration Journal* 3.2–3 (1994): 393–409.

Berry, Chris. "These Nations Which Are Not One: History, Identity and Post-coloniality in Recent Hong Kong and Taiwan Cinema," *SPAN* 34–35 (special double issue: "Diasporas"; November 1992–May 1993): 37–49.

Bhabha, Homi K. *The Location of Culture* (London: Routledge, 1994).

Cannadine, David. *Ornamentalism: How the British Saw Their Empire* (Harmondsworth: Penguin, 2001).

Clarke, Colin et al., ed. *South Asians Overseas: Migration and Ethnicity* (Cambridge: Cambridge UP, 1990).

D'Cruz, J.V. "White Australia and the Indian Munity," in *The Asian Image in Australia: Episodes in Australian History* (Gloucestershire: Hawthorn Press, 1993): 11–31.

——, & William Steele. *Australia's Ambivalence Towards Asia: Politics, Neo/Postcolonialism, and Fact/Fiction* (Kuala Lumpur: National U of Malaysia P, 2000; Melbourne: Monash UP, 2001 forthcoming).

Fernando, Chitra. *Between Worlds* (Calcutta: Writers Workshop, 1988).

——. *The Golden Bird & Other Stories* (Calcutta: Writers Workshop, 1987).

——. *Kundalini and Other Tales* (Calcutta: Writers Workshop, 1986).

——. *Three Women* (Colombo: Lake House Investments, 1983; Calcutta: Writers Workshop, 1984).

——. *Women There and Here: Progressions in Six Stories* (Sydney: Wordlink, 1994).

FitzGerald, Stephen. *Is Australia an Asian Country? Can Australia Survive in an East Asian Future* (St. Leonards, NSW: Allen & Unwin, 1997).

Ghosh, Amitav. "The Diaspora in Indian Culture," *Public Culture* 2.1 (1989): 73–78.

Gooneratne, Yasmine. *A Change of Skies* (1991; New Delhi: Penguin, 1992).

——. *The Pleasures of Conquest* (New Delhi: Penguin India, 1995).

Hodge, Bob, & Vijay Mishra. *Dark Side of the Dream: Australian Literature and the Postcolonial Mind* (North Sydney: Allen & Unwin, 1990).

Khan, Adib Zaman. *Seasonal Adjustments* (St. Leonards, NSW: Allen & Unwin, 1994).

——. *Solitude of Illusions* (St. Leonards, NSW: Allen & Unwin, 1996).

Koshy, Susan. "The Geography of Female Subjectivity: Ethnicity, Gender and Diaspora," *Diaspora: A Journal of Transnational Studies* 3.1 (1994): 69–84.

Lepervanche, Marie de. "Sikh Turbans in Resistance and Response: Some Comments on Immigrant Reactions in Australia and Britain," *Population Review* 36.1–2 (January–December 1992): 29–39.

Lokuge, Chandani. *If the Moon Smiled* (New Delhi: Penguin India, 2000).

——. *Moth and Other Stories* (Sydney & Hebden Bridge: Dangaroo, 1992).

MacIntyre, Ernest. *Let's Give Them Curry: An Austral-Asian Comedy in Three Acts* (Richmond, Victoria: Heinemann Educational Australia, 1985).

Mangala, Christine. *The Firewalkers* (Sydney: Aquila, 1991).

Mishra, Vijay. "Introduction" to *SPAN* 34–35 (special double issue, "Diasporas"; November 1992–May 1993): 1–2.

——. "The Diasporic Imaginary: Theorizing the Indian Diaspora," *Textual Practice* 10.3 (1996): 421–47.

——. "New Lamps for Old: Diasporas Migrancy Border," in *Interrogating Post-Colonialism: Theory, Text and Context*, ed. Harish Trivedi & Meenakshi Mukherjee (Shimla: Indian Institute of Advanced Study, 1996): 67–86.

Mistry, Rohinton. *A Fine Balance* (London: Faber & Faber, 1996).

Moore, Jean Gloria. *The Anglo–Indian Vision* (Melbourne: AE Press, 1986).

Naipaul, V.S. *Between Father and Son: Family Letters*, ed. Gillon R. Aitkin (New York: Alfred A. Knopf, 2000).

Nandan, Satendra. *Faces in a Village* (New Delhi: Printox, 1976).

——. *Lines Across Black Waters* (New Delhi: Academy Press & Adelaide: CRNLE, 1997).

——. *The Wounded Sea* (East Roseville, NSW: Simon & Schuster/New Endeavour Press, 1991).

Nandy, Ashis. *The Tao of Cricket* (New Delhi: Penguin India, 1989).

Paranjape, Makarand. "Indo-Anglian as Anglo-Indian: Ideology, Politics, and Cross-Cultural Representation" in *Postcolonial Perspectives on the Raj and Its Literature*, ed. Vrinda Nabar & Nilufer Bharucha (Bombay: U of Bombay P, 1994): 133–42.

——. "One Foot in Canada and a Couple of Toes in India: Diasporas and Homelands in South Asian Canadian Experience," in *Diaspora: Theories, Histories, Texts*, ed. Makarand Paranjape (New Delhi: Indialog, 2001): 161–70.

——. "What About Those Who Stayed Back Home? Interrogating the Privileging of Diasporic Writing," Afterword to *Shifting Continents/ Colliding Cultures: Diaspora Writing of the Indian Subcontinent*, ed. Ralph J. Crane & Radhika Mohanram (Cross/Cultures 42; Amsterdam & Atlanta GA: Rodopi, 2000): 225–46.

Parekh, Bhikhu. "Some Reflections on the Indian Diaspora," *Journal of Contemporary Thought* (1993): 105–52.

Rao, Raja. *The Meaning of India* (New Delhi: Vision Books, 1996).

Rushdie, Salman. *Imaginary Homelands: Essays and Criticism 1981–1991* (1992; New Delhi: Vision, 1996).

——. *Midnight's Children* (London: Jonathan Cape, 1981).

Safran, William. "Diasporas in Modern Societies: Myths of Homeland and Return," *Diaspora: A Journal of Transnational Studies* 1.1 (1991): 83–99.

Sharrad, Paul. "Mena Abdullah's Untranslatable Diasporic Identity," in *The Literature of the Indian Diaspora: Essays in Criticism*, ed. A.L. McLeod (New Delhi: Sterling, 2000): 252–61.

Sissons, Ric, & Brian Stoddard. *Cricket and Empire: The 1932–33 Bodyline Tour of Australia* (Sydney: George Allen & Unwin, 1984).

Tinker, Hugh. *The Banyan Tree: Overseas Emigrants from India, Pakistan and Bangladesh* (London: Oxford UP, 1997).

van der Veer, Peter, ed. *Nation and Migration: The Politics of Space in the South Asian Diaspora* (Philadelphia: U of Pennsylvania P, 1994).

Waddell, Charles E., & Glenn Vernon. "Ethnic Identity and National Identification: The Social Construction of Commitment of Indian Immigrants to Australia," *Studies in Third World Societies* 39 (March 1987): 13–23.

Walker, David. *Anxious Nation: Australia and the Rise of Asia 1850–1939* (St Lucia: U of Queensland P, 1999).

❦

MONIKA FLUDERNIK

Imagined Communities as Imaginary Homelands
The South Asian Diaspora in Fiction

Introduction

N OVELS AND SHORT STORIES by prominent South
Asian writers have tended to concentrate on a number of
key topics and themes. These include, for one, a variety of
exoticist treatments of the Indian subcontinent, usually focusing on the
passions of Indian men and women, the alluring and threatening setting of the Indian subcontinent (in which figure an emphasis on
poverty vs riches, a fantasy-like enactment of the improbable and mysterious, and the chaos, dangers and political corruption of the Indian
metropolis), as well as the intricacies of the Indian social hierarchy,
especially the caste system. Typical representatives of this exoticist
genre are the works of Salman Rushdie, Gita Mehta, Vikram Chandra,
Arundhati Roy, or the recent novel by Amitav Ghosh, *The Glass
Palace*. Moreover, these texts frequently resuscitate the complexities
of the Indian storytelling tradition – latently an influence in the many
tales within the tale. (This can likewise be treated as an orientalist
feature, since the exuberance of storytelling observable in such novels
invokes oriental models of the *Pañcatantra* and the *1001 Nights*.)
Secondly, a good many texts concentrate on the story of emigration to

the West, focusing on issues of assimilation, professional success, and the difficulties of social acceptance. Where such themes tend to be primarily employed in the traditional context of immigration literature, they frequently coincide with the topoi familiar from Jewish-American literature. The similarities are particularly pronounced because, like Jewish immigrants to the USA, (South) Asian Americans were first discriminated against, encountering racist hatred and social alienation, and later – owing to their educational and professional qualifications – managed to acquire respectability, social acceptance and professional elite status within a generation of arrival. (South) Asian Americans – despite being visible minorities within the USA and Canada – became 'white' in terms of their fast assimilation process and thereby repeated the much slower success of Irish and Jewish immigrants earlier in the twentieth century, while getting ahead of the non-immigrant minorities of Native Americans and African Americans[1] as well as the recent arrivals of Hispanic, African and East Asian groups.[2] American novels of the Indian immigration story therefore frequently echo the patterns of older, familiar immigration novels. This can be observed in Bharati Mukherjee's *Jasmine* (1989) or in the short stories of Divakaruni, Singh Baldwin and Parameswaran.

British South Asian literature, by contrast, often presents a much more negative picture of the host country (a clear reflection of racial hostility and unrest in Britain, and of the subsumption of Indians among "blacks"). Indian fiction set in Britain, moreover, emphasizes the multicultural framework, in the sense of South Asians finding themselves to be merely one group among other immigrant groups. British South Asian fiction is particularly concerned with in-group and out-group phenomena (setting oneself apart from West Indians as well

---

[1] Non-immigrant in terms of voluntary immigration.

[2] On the current distribution and regional/religious makeup of North American vs British South Asians, see Karen Leonard, "State, Culture, and Religion: Political Action and Representation among South Asians in North America," *Diaspora: A Journal of Transnational Studies* 9.1 (2002): 21–38.

as from the British mainstream, preserving one's cultural roots). In this second, more negative version of the immigration story, which I would like to call the novel of exile, the security and emotional refuge provided by the immigrant community are emphasized and set in opposition to the hostile environment. (See, especially, Anita Desai's *Bye-bye Blackbird*, 1971, and Kamala Markandaya's *The Nowhere Man*, 1972.)[3] The embattled status of the immigrant community leads to an idealization of the home country – a feature also typical of the traditional novel of exile or immigration – and this idealization is contrasted with the multicultural processes of negotiation entertained with the surrounding alien immigrant groups.

From these scenarios spring those setups that have become famous from the films of Hanif Kureishi, in which the various immigrant groups develop a positive counterculture, a salad bowl (preserving their indigenous cultural ingredients) in which the one missing or marginal item is the native Briton, and in which the salad sauce – in contrast to the American salad-bowl idea – adds new spice and alien flavours to the mixture, eliminating any 'RP' residues of standard British life-style. These novels therefore, properly speaking, belong to the genre of the multicultural novel rather than to the novel of immigration.

The topic with which this volume is concerned, the diaspora, can now be seen to emerge among and between three types of texts: a) the traditional immigration and assimilation story; b) the novel of (cultural) exile; and c) the multicultural novel – and needs to be treated as a both constitutive and submerged element of these subgenres.

Thus, in the traditional immigration and assimilation story, immigrants flock together for safety reasons, have idealized memories of their home country and maintain contact with India. In the novel of

---

[3] Susheila Nasta, in her recent *Home Truths: Fictions of the South Asian Diaspora in Britain* (London: Palgrave, 2002), devotes three chapters to immigration problems and discusses Samuel Selvon's *The Lonely Londoners* (1956) as well as Naipaul's *The Mimic Men* (1967) in this context.

(cultural) exile this is also the case, and the urgency of rememorization and idealization becomes exacerbated through the failure of assimilation (even if assimilation with a difference). In the multicultural novel, the native community is conceived as theoretically more open and flexible. There is usually a generational barrier, with the older generation still caught in the immigration and assimilation plot, and the younger generation heading towards interrelation with other minority groups or towards fundamentalist positions. In these novels, the diaspora is not a strong element.

The next question to pose is whether there are not a number of diaspora novels that concentrate on the situation of diasporic South Asians. What would then qualify as a diaspora novel?

The protagonists of a diaspora novel, preferably, need to be at least second-generation immigrants. They have established themselves in a new home abroad. This first criterion of long residency is an optional criterion in my definition.

Secondly, and more importantly, these protagonists must be part of a flourishing community in the host country that retains contacts with the mother country and (ideally) with South Asians across the globe.

Third, the group preserves the image of an idealized homeland.

Fourth, the group is in the process of creating a self-image abroad, an imagined community of diasporic Indianness in the context of American, Canadian or British multiculturalism.

Hence the title of this essay, conjoining the imagined community (Benedict Anderson) of the South Asian diasporic identity with the imaginary homeland (Rushdie) that is receding into the mists of fiction and fantasy.

Traditionally, it took longer for immigrants to constitute a diasporic community, and in fiction the individual plot of immigration and its hazards and eventual successes stood at the centre of the representation. However, recent migration patterns and modern technology suggest that diasporas can now emerge faster, and contacts with the homeland and other South Asians are facilitated by the internet and the ubiquitous video culture as well as by cheaper flights to and from the subcontinent.

I therefore see novels and short stories by South Asian expatriates as falling into four relevant groups:

1 the novels of immigration and cultural exile that concentrate on an individual's journey of assimilation;
2 multicultural novels;
3 diaspora novels in which the collective identity of Indian migrants, expatriates and notabene second or third generation immigrants is at stake; and
4 cosmopolitan novels in which South Asian expatriates are portrayed as individuals (outside a diasporic community) and in which the process of assimilation either has been successfully completed or is not focused on the binaries of India vs. America/Britain. In these novels the main South Asian protagonist is frequently married to a Westerner or person from another (non-South Asian) nationality and ethnicity. Sunetra Gupta's texts belong to this last category.

It needs to be noted right away that almost none of these subgenres can be located in pure form. Thus Mukherjee's *Jasmine*, which is a novel of immigration and individual achievement, nevertheless contains an early section describing the New York Indian diaspora which the eponymous heroine has to leave behind. Kureishi's multicultural works, likewise, document a diasporic setting that is being transcended by the multicultural activities of the younger generation. Even the cosmopolitan novel, despite being focused on individuals, often contrasts the culturally 'free-floating' protagonist(s) with more settled members of the expatriate community.

The following table summarizes the major features of the four types:

common setting:	I	II	III	IV
First-World metropolis	immigration novel	multicultural novel	diaspora novel	cosmopolitan novel
individual focus	x			x
group focus		x	x	
nostalgia for homeland	x		x	
expatriate set primarily against host	x	x		(x)
expatriate vs. other minorities		x	x	(x)

In the remainder of this essay I want to discuss two novels for each of these four categories, but will structure my remarks to contrast representations of the 'old' and the 'new' diasporas.

The most unexpected result of my research has been the realization that pure diaspora novels are extremely rare, and that most of them tend to focus on protagonists trying to break out of the ethnic and cultural fold of their expatriate community. This may relate to the marketability of South Asian literature. The most numerous texts belong to the exoticist subgenre and are not discussed in this essay, since they have a South Asian setting. Next to this, the immigration scenario is the most popular genre, followed by the multicultural and cosmopolitan novels. The diaspora novel, whose claim to the reader's interest relies on insider status, naturally speaks to the expatriate community itself; to the extent that it propagates a separatist ideology, it is therefore liable to antagonize a large number of readers. Adding a protagonist who is starting to break away supplies a figure to the text who can become a focus of empathy for the mainstream reader, particularly to the extent that the South Asian community is experienced as a restrictive social space by Western readers, especially women.[4] From this perspective, the predominance of female protagonists is worth noting. In fact, M.G. Vassanji's *No New Land*, in my reading experience, seems to be almost the only male diaspora text of recent times.

What I find particularly interesting is my second immediate finding: namely, the (as yet) comparative rarity of the diaspora genre in contrast to the celebration of diasporic existence in literary criticism. Whereas the multicultural novel and the cosmopolitan novel seem to fictionalize some of the enthusiasm of Bhabhian hybridity and the free-floating identities à la Mishra's "diasporic imaginary" (1996), the properly diasporic novel, like the immigrant novel, is often concerned with the negative aspects of life in the expatriate community and shows little enthusiasm for diasporic existence *per se*. In my opinion, therefore, the most flourishing fashion in critical theory has so far no equivalent literary status. However, since a large number of South Asian authors are also literary critics, this situation may soon change.

℘

---

[4] Compare Pnina Werbner's remarks in a recent article: "With less dramatic results, other works in the new wave of British South Asian novels and films nevertheless also (like *The Satanic Verses*) aim to debunk sacred South Asian values. Their overt message is one of tolerance and hybridity, set against a background of racist Britain; such a message enables these works to reach out successfully to mainstream audiences and to a small elite of British South Asian intellectuals. But I would argue that the motivating allegories and central plots of the new South Asian diasporic aesthetics lie elsewhere: their subject is the sexual politics of the family represented by the struggles of a younger, British-born generation against arranged marriages imposed by authoritarian, coercive, gerontocratic elders. The new novels and films promote images of transgressive sexuality – gay, inter-racial or interethnic love marriages and illicit cohabitation – to make their point. They satirize an older generation's profligate consumption, false ethics, superstitious religiosity, blind prejudices, and obsession with honor and status." See Pnina Werbner, "Introduction: The Materiality of Diaspora – Between Aesthetic and 'Real' Politics," *Diaspora: A Journal of Transnational Studies* 9.1 (2002): 11.

The 'Old Diaspora' in South Asian Literature

The novels that I wish to discuss in this first subsection focus on expatriate communities of a long-standing and traditional type such as the Caribbean South Asian diaspora and the East African diaspora. Most prominent among these, of course, is the work of V.S. Naipaul, particularly his masterpiece *A House for Mr. Biswas* (1961). In this section I would, however, like to discuss two other texts, Harold Sonny Ladoo's *No Pain Like This Body* (1972) and M.G. Vassanji's *Uhuru Street* (1992), with a glance at Naipaul's *A Bend in the River* (1979) and Vassanji's *The Gunny Sack* (1989).

The most prominent feature of this old type of diaspora[5] concerns the long-standing expatriate existence of these groups. Both communities have been in the country for several generations and have given up any idea of migrating back to India. Both communities arose from indentured labour colonies and therefore had a history of erstwhile loneliness, poverty and near-slavery work conditions. These beginnings have developed into more prosperous circumstances, with the most typical occupation being that of a vendor or merchant.

In addition, in the Caribbean, farming needs to be added to the job list. Ladoo's book is particularly interesting, since it focuses on those segments of the South Asian population that have failed to attain social mobility and, despite being owners of the land, have lapsed into hopeless destitution and demoralization. Moreover, the function of the community as a safety net and support system features prominently in the novel.

In contrast to the old diaspora, many novels about the new diaspora are set in academic circles, among professionals and media people,

---

[5] The distinction between an old and a new diaspora goes back to Vijay Mishra: see his "The Diasporic Imaginary: Theorizing the Indian Diaspora," *Textual Practice* 10 (1996): 421–47.

and many characters are recent immigrants. The new diaspora also differs from the earlier indentured labour communities by being a self-enclosed oasis in the midst of African or Afro-Caribbean society, with the white man off limits (Naipaul's *A Bend in the River* being an exception to this). By contrast, the new diaspora is located in the metropolis, where it is bound to rub shoulders with mainstream white culture as well as coming into conflict with other immigrant or minority groups.

The African old diaspora thus closely resembles the diaspora of Sephardic Jewry, whereas the more recent diaspora corresponds to Ashkenazi immigration to the West. I will return to some further remarks that link theoretical descriptions of the diaspora with the texts under discussion.

In Vassanji's *Uhuru Street* and Ladoo's *No Pain Like This Body*, the South Asian community is represented as both a nurturing and a strangling home. Thus, the primary support for the protagonists is always the family, and only after the immediate family is there the larger home of the ethnic community. In immigration novels such as David Dabydeen's *The Counting House* (1996), the relationship between husband and wife is the focus; later, more properly 'diasporic' novels tend to concentrate on parents and children. The community in both types of diasporic texts is a community of friends, schoolmates, clients and neighbours, and it is also a stronghold in times of crisis when the official representatives of the community are called upon to exercise their authority.

In *Uhuru Street*, which starts with a series of children's stories and nostalgic reminiscences of the good old days in Dar es Salaam, this critical point comes when the first-person narrator's younger brother Aloo wins a scholarship to the California Institute of Technology, and the mother (a widow) goes to seek help from Mr Velji, the former administrator of the school. It is thanks to the advice of Mr Velji that the mother is persuaded to allow her son to leave, even though she

knows he will not return or even marry a white woman.[6] Since the
ticket to the USA is also clearly a problem, the financial help of the
community will additionally be required (73–74).

Whereas, in "Leaving," the Asian community had clearly exerted a
benevolent influence over the family, in "Ebrahim and the Businessmen" the community is presented as split between the rich businessmen and those that they have traditionally excluded from their circles.
Ebrahim Kanji's father had been an outspoken student who demanded
an investigation into the presumed mismanagement of community
funds. As a consequence, he was persecuted by the community's
leaders, was unable to secure a well-paid job, and was kept down
socially as well. Now his son Ebrahim is an official in the new African
government which is pushing through the nationalization of private
property. The leader of the community, Jaffer Teja, now needs help,
and after some deliberation, Ebrahim decides to commit forgery for
the community: this is the way in which he is going to turn himself
into a rich businessman and take revenge for his father's humiliation.

The obsequious behaviour of the businessmen is contrasted with
their earlier contempt of the protagonist when they did not see him as
one of their own. Now he is being called by his first name and adopted
as "our boy":

> Ebrahim now knocked on the door of the Tejas, one of Dar's lead-
> ing business families. After being peeped at through the spy hole he
> was received by their daughter.
>   'Why, Ebrahim! Come in. So nice to see you.'
>   'I've come to see the businessmen.'
>   'Big shot, eh?'

---

[6] M.G. Vassanji, *Uhuru Street: Short Stories* (Toronto: McClelland &
Stewart, 1992): "'Well,' said Mr. Velji, 'it would be good for his education.'
He raised his hand to clear his throat. Then he said, a little slowly: 'But if you
send him, you will lose your son'" (76). And: "'Promise me that if I let you
go, you will not marry a white woman.' 'Oh mother, you know I won't,' said
Aloo" (78). Further page references are in the main text.

Ebrahim remembered the days when he walked barefoot, when this girl would pass him in derision.

[...]

'Ah, Minister! Come in, come in, please!' Jaffer Teja greeted him with typical exaggeration and escorted him in, seating him prominently on a sofa. Teja was a middle-aged man with a pockmarked face and, like many of the businessmen present, wore a Kaunda suit.

'Our boy Ebrahim,' he announced exultantly, 'is with the Vice President's Office. This is a proud moment for all of us.' He looked up as if to offer thanks to God.

'What can I do for you, gentlemen?', Ebrahim asked, sipping the tea that had been offered him and helping himself to a savoury from the serving table that had been placed in front of him. They are grovelling at my feet, he thought with satisfaction. If only Father had lived to see this day.

'Ebrahim ... Ebrahim....' Jaffer Teja, who was obviously the spokesman of the group, began, shaking his head. He was sitting in a chair close to Ebrahim and facing him. 'You know what has befallen us, our people ... all their life's savings ... the savings of their fathers....'

What Teja was referring to was the recent take-over of properties that were let out for rent in a socialisation move by the government. Only the houses that were occupied by the owners were exempt from the take-over.

'You know how they made their money ... They came as paupers, sold peanuts, popcorn, seeds ... and little by little, through hard work, morning and night, they earned and saved. They did not put their money even in the banks! They were too scared to do so. All they dreamed of was a piece of land, to build something on it, something they could call their own, the prize of their hard labour.' (97–99)

The daughter of the house treats Ebrahim like an old friend, even ending up sitting on the armrest of his chair (99), and Teja tries to inveigle him into their plan by the false fiction that Ebrahim's help will benefit the Indian community who are under siege from the government. Thus he first signals that the formerly despised Kanji son is now "our boy Ebrahim," and then he goes on to paint Ebrahim's responsibilities as lying with "his" community. The harangue about "our people" and their life's savings – underlined by the sentimental story of how they

all started out as petty merchants and acquired their property through
"hard labour" – is aimed at giving Ebrahim a bad conscience and at
creating empathy for the community. Ebrahim must be made to identify with them.

Since the same men had earlier used their quite significant social
and financial capital to ruin his father's life, Ebrahim is of course
unlikely to sympathize with these people's concerns; he uses the
opportunity to get his back own, and he delights in the new position of
power that their need has afforded him. The community is still strong,
even if Ebrahim can insidiously make its mechanisms work for his
own personal profit and for his revenge.

"Breaking Loose" shows the relationship between the Indian community and its African surroundings. Whereas the Africans are frequently shown in inferior and even menial positions in the other
stories (see, especially, "Ali," which deals with domestic service), in
"Breaking Loose" an interracial love affair between Yasmin and the
African Daniel Akoto is described. Yasmin is meeting one of the African teachers, and this causes much gossip. When he comes to the shop
of her parents, her mother explodes:

> The sight of Akoto in her shop that day had driven her mother into a
> fit. By the time he had left the shop hugging the gramophone she was
> raging with fury. 'There are no friendships with men – not with men
> we don't know ...' she said to Yasmin.
> 'The world is not ready for it,' her father said quietly. (87)

By being forced to triangulate her position in relation to Indian culture,
Africa and the West, Yasmin rediscovers India as an imaginary homeland beyond the immediate traditions of Dar es Salaam's Indian community:

> India was not just the past, or the community, or even the jealous
> Indian communities of Dar. India was a continent, a civilisation, a
> political entity in the world. Only recently it had emerged from a long
> struggle for independence. (88)

What Yasmin discovers is true of Uhuru Street as a whole – a pre-occupation with Tanzania as home (usually in contrast with England or America, to which many characters are in the process of migrating), with India as a vague origin responsible for present-day "ancient customs, unchanged for generations, remotely related to the world around her" (88). In fact, the old Indian diaspora in Africa and the Caribbean used to be little troubled with the homeland, and even less troubled with a hostile environment until the rising African nationalism after colonial devolution.

Harold Sonny Ladoo's novel *No Pain Like This Body*, like (parts of) Dabydeen's *The Counting House* written in the local vernacular, provides a grim picture of the destitution and demoralization of latter-day Indian farmers in the Caribbean. The story of a drunken and lazy father ("Pa"), his abuse of "Ma" and the children, the death of one child, the funeral, and the final catastrophe when Ma goes mad – all this characterizes the deficiencies of the Indian community as against the little help Ma's father is able to provide. The family's poverty is of the most dire colouring: the children have nearly no clothes, the hut consists of a few barrels and sacks for furniture, and there is never any proper food, much less money for medication or funeral fees to the fake brahmin[7] who supervises the funeral rites. Nevertheless, the community does help to transport the children to and from the hospital, and at the wake communal gossiping, shaming of the husband and female bonding are in evidence.

The wake also demonstrates the survival of oral traditions. The priest tells stories (90–92), as do the female gossips. Besides the Hindu rites of the funeral, many superstitions and cosmological explanations are alluded to in the text which – though written in the authorial mode – uses the language and mind-frame of one of the com-

---

[7] Harold Sonny Ladoo, *No Pain Like This Body* (Caribbean Writers Series; London: Heinemann, 1972): 98. Further page references are in the main text.

munity: "The sun jumped inside the sea to sleep and the night crawled as a fat worm over the face of Tola" (71).

> The sky twisted lake a black snake and the clouds rolled and rolled and rolled as a big spider; the wind shook Tola in rage and the rain pounded the earth; the lightning came out of the mouth of the darkness like a golden tongue and licked the trees in the forest and the drum ripped through the darkness like a knife. They moved deeper and deeper into the forest, and they felt the rain falling upon their heads from heaven. (134)

The irresponsibility of Pa contrasts with the care given to Ma and the children by her immediate relatives Nanny and Nanna. The community, though sympathetic to Ma's plight, does not help her against Pa, who upholds his male privileges and gains some sympathies from the women as an attractive man. To this extent, Ladoo's (unlike Naipaul's) depiction of the traditional diaspora is less idealized than Vassanji's.

The old diaspora, one can conclude, was a legitimate object of nostalgia, since little conflict with the ethnic surroundings took place. However, dissent within the Asian community, the difficult situation of marriages, and inter-generational strife clearly play a large role in the fictional representations of these communities. To some extent, the novels convey an atmosphere of self-centredness and isolation that is typical of a culture that takes itself to be the measure of all things. To this extent, the old Indian diaspora fails to evince that yearning for the homeland, that exposure to the strangers surrounding the community, which is so prominent in descriptions of diasporic existence.

The New Diaspora:
From Immigration to Multicultural Celebration
and on to Cultural Self-Sufficiency

Traditional immigration novels frequently thematize the South Asian diaspora as a safety net and support system in alien lands. Thus, in

Mukherjee's *Jasmine*, it is the expatriate community that welcomes, feeds and houses the bereft widow and illegal immigrant. This community is then shown to be restrictive as well as nurturing to the female protagonist, and she leaves it in quest of a very individual immigration and *Bildungsroman*-oriented quest. Most immigration novels do not describe such a break-away from the expatriate community but focus instead on the compromises, adaptations, hybrid refunctionalizations and partial revolts undergone by South Asian immigrants and their children as they try to maximize the advantages of the communal safety net and the freedoms afforded by life in the West. Particularly for women, this process of wrenching free from traditional expectations and the opportunities of making their own way in the professional or executive sphere constitute a huge challenge, which is frequently depicted in the texts.

A very comic example can be found in Yasmine Gooneratne's *A Change of Skies* (1991), in which it is the wife who becomes the more successful immigrant, gaining the college unheard-of sums in their fund-raising effort by exploiting their copy of the *Kamasutra* for a sensational exhibition at the college fair. In this redeployment of Indian sacred art for sexual voyeurism and fund-raising purposes, the renamed Jean Mundy manages to get the best of both worlds.[8]

In what follows I would like to concentrate on a few short stories and on Meera Syal's novel *Life Isn't All Ha-Ha Hee-Hee* (1999).

In Shauna Singh Baldwin's collection *English Lessons*, several stories illustrate these problems of community life abroad. In the story "Toronto 1984," Piya is breaking away from Indian life by refusing to wear salwar kameez and acquiring a car of her own to go to work. Meanwhile her parents are planning to send her to India to get her

---

[8] For a good discussion of Gooneratne's novel, see Lothar Bredella, "Interpreting Cultures: Yasmine Gooneratne's novel *A Change of Skies*," in *Critical Interfaces: Contributions on Philosophy, Literature and Culture in Honour of Herbert Grabes,* ed. Gordon Collier, Klaus Schwank & Franz Wieselhuber (Trier: Wissenschaftlicher Verlag Trier, 2001): 371–82.

married off. However, when Indira Gandhi is assassinated by a Sikh, Piya's trip is cancelled for safety reasons. Piya, meanwhile, has come round to a more positive evaluation of her ethnic origins since she refused to stand for the British Queen and was called a "damn Paki"[9] by her employer.

Piya's context is that of a diaspora community. Not only is her intended marriage settled through relatives at home; all the other services that the family uses are Sikh as well:

> What's the matter? Not the flight? What happened? Who got shot? She got shot? Mrs. Indira Gandhi? When? Early morning in Delhi – two hours ago. Who did it? Was it a Hindu – like the one who killed Mahatma Gandhi? What – a Sikh did it? Son, stop it. You must not show happiness – what will people say? [...] Cancel the flight, son. Yes. A Brahmin has been killed and every Hindu will be looking for blood. [...] Call the airport taxi – the owner's family is also Sikh. They will understand.[10]

This is very reminiscent of Mukherjee's depiction of Professorji's integration into a Hindu community in New York:

> There were thirty-two Indian families in our building of fifty apartments, so specialized as to language, religion, caste, and profession that we did not need to fraternize with anyone but other educated Punjabi-speaking Hindu Jats. There were six families more or less like Professorji's (plus Punjabi-speaking Sikh families who seemed friendly in the elevator and politically tame, though we didn't mingle), and three of the families also had aged parents living in.[11]

> Nirmala worked all day in a sari store on our block. Selling upscale fabrics in Flushing indulged her taste for glamour and sophistication. The shop also sold 220-volt appliances, jewelry, and luggage. An adjacent shop under the same Gujarati ownership sold sweets and

[9] Shauna Singh Baldwin, *English Lessons and Other Stories*, ed. Laurel Boone (Fredericton, New Brunswick: Goose Lane, 1996): 63.

[10] Singh Baldwin, *English Lessons*, 66–67.

[11] Bharati Mukherjee, *Jasmine* (New York: Fawcett Crest, 1989): 129–30.

spices, and rented Hindi movies on cassettes. She was living in a little corner of heaven.[12]

Unlike Professorji and Nirmala, Piya manages to transcend her South Asian roots, but she does not fully assimilate to Canadian life. By taking coffee rather than tea, by insisting on a vacation for family reasons, and by re-adopting South Asian habits at home, she signals a new balance: on the job, she refuses to assimilate completely, and returns to the cultural fold in private:

> My boss sat down first at our table. 'What's your problem?' he said.
>   'I cannot stand for the British Queen.'
>   [...]
>   I pushed my chair back, rose to my feet and walked out of the banquet hall to the coat rack. There, with shaking hands, I lifted my coat onto my shoulders. I left the door open so that the freezing Dundas Street air could choke them if there was justice ...
>   I drove my new car home. On the radio a blind dark man was singing. 'I just called to say I love you ...' Bibiji met me at the door with sweet hot milk and elaichi and I wore a salwar kameez to dinner.
>   But today it never happened and the boss was jovial at the coffee machine. 'How's our little Paki?' he said. I pretended not to hear and poured myself a styrofoam cup of bitter coffee instead of my usual cup of tea.[13]

Chitra Banerjee Divakaruni's *Arranged Marriage* (1995) offers a full range of immigration to diaspora stories. "Silver Pavements, Golden Roofs" tells of racial violence; "The Disappearance" of a wife leaving her violent husband – using the opportunity to escape afforded by American life; "Affair" of two Indian women breaking away from their arranged marriages. In all of these stories, the job world is white but their family life and circle of acquaintances are Indian. Robbie Clipper Sethi's short story "The Bride Wore Red" (1996) also starts out from a diasporic-immigrant environment but expands into inter-racial marriage. The central place of the Indian community in these

---

[12] Mukherjee, *Jasmine*, 127.
[13] Singh Baldwin, *English Lessons*, 63–64.

stories documents the continuing importance of a diaspora setting. Nevertheless, even in these stories, it is family connections more than the expatriate community that provide the characters with the necessary support system. This becomes most obvious in "Missing Persons," where Leslie is taken up by her Indian family-in-law when her husband Surinder abandons her.

In another story, "Grace," the American wife who is a painter, is incommoded by month-long visits from her husband's parents from India. After she has separated from him, she starts to understand how community works. Her final painting is of two Indian women belonging together:

> The lines of her portrait blurred in front of her. She tried a wash. By night-fall she had managed to blend the foreheads of the women into the cityscape behind them. They no longer stood out as distinctive figures, individuals, together; they were disappearing fast into the big, gray city. Still, the painting needed something. Grace opened a tube of primary red, put a dab of paint on the tip of her finger and touched a dot above each figure's eyes.[14]

A particularly humorous story is "The White-Haired Girl," a first-person text in which Mataji comes to visit her son Hermeet and is welcomed by his girlfriend Goodie, the blonde (ie, white-haired) woman. Goodie, after a lot of grumbling about the marriage, eventually reconciles Mataji to the mixed marriage by producing a son in prime time ahead of her (Mataji's) sister's son.[15]

The Bride Wore Red, therefore, thematizes attempts at diasporic homogeneity which are being undermined by interracial marriages and assimilation to the American way of life. In the texts I have discussed so far the positive and negative aspects of the expatriate South Asian community for individual protagonists have balanced each other. The diaspora accounts for a good measure of safety and nurturing, but it

---

[14] Robbie Clipper Sethi, *The Bride Wore Red: Tales of a Cross-Cultural Family* (Bridgehampton NY: Bridge Works, 1996): 98.

[15] Sethi, *The Bride Wore Red*, 66.

also stands in the way of complete assimilation. In the business world and in interracial marriages the expectations and norms of South Asian culture and those of the North American mainstream are in conflict, and a resolution of the conflict needs to be negotiated individually by each protagonist.

A much more typical rendering of the new diaspora can be observed in Hanif Kureishi's *The Buddha of Suburbia* (1990), in which the old diaspora of Indian shopkeepers and their families, complete with an arranged marriage for the daughter, is superseded in the younger generation by a generally more extensive youth culture of a multi-ethnic cast in which narrowly Indian, Muslim and Hindu values start to evaporate whereas, at the same time, fundamentalists are beginning to create enclaves of ethnic purity which they are determined to police by violence and intimidation. Kureishi's second film, *Sammy & Rosie Get Laid* (1988), more clearly illustrates a multicultural diaspora which includes a prominent Indian subsection but is otherwise peopled by a great number of other ethnic and sexual minorities. The film *East is East* (1999) also has sequences of going to Bradford, in this way providing a glimpse of a different, more traditional kind of diaspora.[16]

The best example of a diaspora novel is perhaps Meera Syal's *Life isn't all Ha-ha Hee-Hee* (1999). Syal's second novel takes the more traditional Indian diasporic community which she described in *Anita and Me* (1996) further into a flourishing professional diaspora. Where-as, in *Anita and Me*, the Indian family was living in a house next to English people and visits by their Indian relatives caused some uproar in the neighbourhood, in Syal's second novel the dramatis personae all are Indians and some of them also live in typically ethnic communities. Like immigration novels, *Anita and Me* thematized the conflict with English mainstream culture; by contrast, *Life Isn't All Ha-Ha Hee-Hee* is diasporic, to the extent of ignoring Englishness and concentrating on Indian–Indian relationships and problems. Although the

---

[16] See Susheila Nasta, *Home Truths*, 211.

plot is fairly familiar – the breaking-up of two marriages, adultery, (Indian) women finding their own feet – the focus of the text on one ethnic community tells its own story: for these characters, England no longer counts except as a convenience; their set of acquaintances are all South Asian, their interests focus on a warm close-knit community of friends. This shift in emphasis relates not only to the absent theme of interracial conflict but also to the change in perspective from parental to marital problems. While *Anita and Me* had still treated little Meena's problems of being a good child, and many other novels and short stories focus on the intergenerational conflicts, Syal's second novel leaves all the problems of arranged marriages and visiting parents behind to concentrate on men and women in the modern world. Nevertheless, these protagonists are part of a closely knit community of friends. They are not left alone with the disasters that befall them – the women support each other very caringly, and the Indian community runs several support-systems, like the office in which Sunita works. Tania, despite being a top professional, also realizes that her partner needs to be from the same ethnic group for things to work out. Women's emancipation is the major theme of the novel, but unlike a number of other texts that see the liberation of Indian wives from patriarchal households as an unalloyedly positive move, the book makes it quite clear that such liberation has its drawbacks, as instanced in successful but lonely Tania. Nevertheless, the plot provides for a moderately happy ending, with Tania forgiven by Sunita and Chila.

A particularly interesting aspect of the novel comes through the film that Tania is producing and which serves as a catalyst for Sunita and Chila in their personal development. Thanks to the film, Chila realizes her status as a plaything in Deepak's doll's house, and the audience gets a sense of the life in an ethnic community. The film has the function of doing some PR work for the South Asian community, but it backfires as a multiculturalist project. The film upsets too many people; they feel it undermines their self-confidence in their own culture. Tania's project, to make money out of ethnicity *and* to do something for the community at the same time, is a problematic one; but in the end it helps to refocus the women's sense of community.

As a consequence of this setting, what develops is a panoramic picture of a happy diasporic community that is self-supporting and vibrant. Although Syal's novel is perhaps the closest one can get to a literary depiction of the South Asian diaspora, its credentials do not tally completely with critical criteria applicable to the diaspora: there is practically no communication with the home country and no nostalgia for it, nor can one observe exemplary hostility to the community in the host country, and there is absolutely no desire to return to India.

I would like to round off my discussion by a brief analysis of Meena Alexander's *Manhattan Music* (1997). This novel retains some features of the typical Indian diaspora, especially in the case of Sandhya's roots with her family in India. In other respects, the setup corresponds more closely to the cosmopolitan setting of Gupta's novels, with Sandhya married to a New York Jew, and her friends a cultural mix (Draupadi comes from an Indian, Fiji and Caribbean background; Rashid has Egyptian and African roots). The novel – typically for the cosmopolitan novel – involves miscegenation and cultural hybridity, but on the whole fails to celebrate this mixture. Instead, the unrootedness of the characters, especially Sandhya's disorientation, occupies the foreground, although Draupadi's creativity as an artist may also be related to her mixed origins. The novel, untypically for a cosmopolitan setting, and even more untypically for a diaspora novel, really concerns immigration problems, or problems of transplantation to a new culture. It is particularly interesting for its contrasting of the successful Jewish diaspora, to which Sandhya's husband belongs, and the problematic status of diaspora for the South Asian female protagonist. As Susheila Nasta has shown so forcefully for the triple displacement of Parsis and Sikhs in the South Asian diaspora, Sandhya has become divorced from her Malayalam linguistic roots and thrown into Hindi and English; her departure from India has propelled her to America, but that, too, is a threatening cultural mix, in which she is supposed to

adapt to a new life-style, new clothes, new habits, and to become a
Jewish wife as well. Predictably, Sandhya ends up feeling imprisoned
by her husband's ethnicity and American expectations. Unlike Draupadi and Rashid, who have grown up in a multicultural setting, she is
unable to negotiate the differences and hybridities of her surroundings.

As in the case of Kureishi's *The Black Album* (1995), Alexander's
novel additionally thematizes Muslim fundamentalism in the figures
of Rashid's room-mate and Sandhya's psychologically unbalanced
sister. Unlike Kureishi, however, Meena Alexander presents a
fundamentalism that has evolved into downright terrorism, in uncanny anticipation of 9/11.[17] The fundamentalist card is no longer an
ethnic or even religious one; its violence becomes part of a threatening New York, equally worrisome to Sandhya as her experience of
being attacked by racists (133–34), and the same shattering impact is
made by her passion for Rashid (203).[18] Unlike Sandhya, her cousin
Sakhi has become an assimilated American, and she is perhaps the
most 'diasporic' person in the novel. With her garden in New Brunswick, Sakhi has "seize[d] time" the correct way (209), not by halting
it, as Sandhya tried to do. As Sakhi says, "we are all migrants [...]
from the past" (211). Later in this chapter, the women decide to do a
Diwali celebration even though they "didn't have a direct link with
India. After all, they were all part of the diaspora" (213). And in this
gentle easing into muted ethnicity Sakhi manages to provide Sandhya with a livable immigrant identity which does not require a
multicultural background. In Draupadi's celebration of the diaspora
and Jay's "diaspora ditties" (158), Draupadi and Jay both "try and
seize a border where newness flashed by" (159), but these solutions
are not for Sandhya. She has to be content with the "Manhattan
Music" (211) of Central Park in whose lake Sandhya finds herself at

---

[17] Meena Alexander, *Manhattan Music* (San Francisco CA: Mercury
House, 1997): 116–17, 190. Further pages references are in the main text.

[18] The passage figures Draupadi's artwork on Hiroshima and hints at
Sandhya's impending suicide attempt.

last when, at the end of the novel, "slipping sandals onto feet still damp with the lake water, Sandhya Rosenblum walked quickly into the waiting city" (228).

Conclusion

On the basis of the preceding analyses, it seems to me that most literary representatives of the South Asian diaspora, except for the old diaspora in Naipaul's work, do not really accord with critical descriptions of the diasporic imaginary as outlined by (literary) critics like Cohen, Clifford and Mishra. On the other hand, analysing the above texts for the usability of the concept has been a stimulating exercise which has definitely helped to refine my understanding of the recent literary traditions in South Asian literature. As we have seen, there are a number of texts that move in the direction of representing a new type of Indian diaspora, yet these texts foreground cultural homogeneity among diversity without the nostalgic imaginary homelands so prominent in traditional conceptions of the diaspora. Expatriate South Asians, in these texts, are clearly converting their imagined communities into real ones, transferring their imaginary homelands abroad. If diasporic imaginary there is, its emotional roots are now clearly in the transplanted culture without immediate reference to India. Those most affected by their South Asian homeland are the new immigrants who need to go through the same processes of adjustment as their elders, only with a better chance of preserving their culture and, at the same time, of being accepted professionally. As with the Jewish diaspora in the opinion of Beate Neumeier (see above), the South Asian expatriate community has a greater chance of flourishing in the USA than in Great Britain, where social unrest is endemic and a large community of the old diaspora with its social problems subsists. Enthusiastic depictions of expatriate life are good only for the professional classes. Diasporic consciousness in the new diaspora has become less ethnic and more cosmopolitan, less traditional and more constructed. It is family and friends, rather, than the 'diasporic community', that now provide emotional support to expatriates. As with the old diaspora, one encounters privatism and a shyness to confront the mainstream other in these novels. From that perspective, the new diaspora, after all, is perhaps not that different from the old.

WORKS CITED

Alexander, Meena. *Manhattan Music* (San Francisco CA: Mercury House, 1997).

Anderson, Benedict. *Imagined Communities: Reflections on the Origin and Spread of Nationalism* (London: Verso, 1983).

Bredella, Lothar. "Interpreting Cultures: Yasmine Gooneratne's novel *A Change of Skies*," in *Critical Interfaces: Contributions on Philosophy, Literature and Culture in Honour of Herbert Grabes*, ed. Gordon Collier, Klaus Schwank & Franz Wieselhuber (Trier: Wissenschaftlicher Verlag Trier, 2001): 371–82.

Dabydeen, David. *The Counting House* (London: Jonathan Cape, 1996).

Desai, Anita. *Bye-bye Blackbird* (1971; Delhi: Orient, 1991).

Divakaruni, Chitra Banerjee. *Arranged Marriage: Stories* (Garden City NY: Doubleday Anchor, 1996).

Frears, Stephen, dir. *Sammy and Rosie Get Laid* (London: FilmFour International, 1987).

Ghosh, Amitav. *The Glass Palace* (London: HarperCollins, 2000).

Gooneratne, Yasmine. *A Change of Skies* (New Delhi: Penguin India, 1992).

Kureishi, Hanif. *The Black Album* (London: Faber & Faber, 1995).

——. *The Buddha of Suburbia* (London: Faber & Faber, 1990).

——. *Sammy & Rosie Get Laid* (London: Faber & Faber, 1988).

Ladoo, Harold Sonny. *No Pain Like This Body* (London: Heinemann, 1972).

Leonard, Karen. "State, Culture, and Religion: Political Action and Representation among South Asians in North America," *Diaspora: A Journal of Transnational Studies* 9.1 (special double issue: "Diasporas"; 2002): 21–38.

Markandaya, Kamala. *The Nowhere Man* (1972; Bombay: Sangam, 1975).

Mishra, Vijay. "The Diasporic Imaginary: Theorizing the Indian Diaspora," *Textual Practice* 10 (1996): 421–47.

Mukherjee, Bharati. *Jasmine* (New York: Fawcett Crest, 1989).

Naipaul, V.S. *A Bend in the River* (London: André Deutsch, 1979).

———. *A House for Mr. Biswas* (1961; London: André Deutsch, 1984).

———. *The Mimic Men* (1967; Harmondsworth: Penguin, 1984).

Nasta, Susheila. *Home Truths: Fictions of the South Asian Diaspora in Britain* (London: Palgrave, 2002).

O'Donnell, Daniel, dir. *East is East* (London: Miramax, 1999).

Parameswaran, Uma. *The Sweet Smell of Mother's Milk-Wet Bodice* (Fredericton, New Brunswick: Broken Jaw Press, 2001).

———. "Dispelling the Spells of Memory: Another Approach to Reading Our Yesterdays," in the present volume, xxxvii–lxiv.

Rushdie, Salman. *Imaginary Homelands: Essays and Criticism, 1981–1991* (London: Granta, 1991).

Selvon, Samuel. *The Lonely Londoners* (1956; London: Longman, 1994).

Sethi, Robbie Clipper. *The Bride Wore Red: Tales of a Cross-Cultural Family* (Bridgehampton NY: Bridge Works, 1996).

Singh Baldwin, Shauna. *English Lessons and Other Stories*, ed. Laurel Boone (Fredericton, New Brunswick: Goose Lane, 1996).

Syal, Meera. *Anita and Me* (London: Flamingo, 1996).

———. *Life Isn't All Ha-Ha Hee-Hee* (London: Doubleday, 1999).

Vassanji, M.G. *The Gunny Sack* (London: Heinemann, 1989).

———. *No New Land* (Toronto: McClelland & Stewart, 1994).

———. *Uhuru Street: Short Stories* (Toronto: McClelland & Stewart, 1992).

Werbner, Pnina. "Introduction: The Materiality of Diaspora – Between Aesthetic and 'Real' Politics," *Diaspora: A Journal of Transnational Studies* 9.1 (special double issue: "Diasporas"; 2002): 5–20.

୫

Ulfried Reichardt

Diaspora Studies and the Culture of the African Diaspora

The Poetry of Derek Walcott, Kamau Brathwaite and Linton Kwesi Johnson

We are all Caribbeans now in our urban archipelagos [...] perhaps there's no return for anyone to a native land—only field notes for its reinvention.[1]

roots [...] are a conservative myth, designed to keep us in our places.[2]

T HE CONTEXT in which the recent centrality of the diaspora concept emerged is the overwhelming globalization process observable in politics, economics and culture. Cultural studies have been responding to this development by increasingly investigating transnational and transcultural phenomena. Within the framework of these developments, a focus on diasporic cultures and 'identities' helps us to better understand a contemporary world-system and its ramifications which so far have mostly been described with

---

[1] James Clifford, quoted in Caren Kaplan, *Questions of Travel: Postmodern Discourses of Displacement* (Durham NC & London: Duke UP, 1996): 127.

[2] Salman Rushdie, *Shame* (London: Jonathan Cape, 1984): 125.

reference to economics and communications technology.[3] National
boundaries are of only limited relevance with regard to changes in
economics, migration, and cultural flow today:

> Transnational connections break the binary relation of *minority* com-
> munities with *majority* societies – a dependency that structures pro-
> jects of both assimilation and resistance.[4]

In terms of theory, diaspora studies partake in a shift from static
notions of tradition and cultural rootedness, that is spatial concepts, to
temporal and temporally dynamic ones (which are linked to individual
and group migrations). With regard to identity, there is a conceptual
change from substance to performance, from being to doing, from
essence to context-dependent actions. The governing thesis of my
essay, therefore, is that the study of diaspora cultures enacts a necessary shift from essentialist conceptions of identity to a focus on dynamic exchanges between people and cultures; moreover, that it
acknowledges the hybridity, contingency and mixing of contemporary
identities, cultures and societies.

I shall first discuss the shift from the notion of multiculturalism to
the concept of diaspora within the context of cultural studies; then I
shall consider more closely the specificities, contexts and functions of
the African or black diaspora. Having delineated the particular situation in the Caribbean, which can be seen as the prototype of a region
populated by diasporic peoples, I shall discuss the differing, in some

---

[3] Of course, "world systems" already existed before the modern Euro-
American one gained dominance, and moreover, the signs of globalization we
discern today are to be understood as accelerated and intensified forms of
exchange and contact which have existed since the sixteenth century. Kenneth
Surin stresses that it is now "accepted that world-systems have existed for at
least a millennium and that their accompanying paranational formations have
existed for just as long." Kenneth Surin, "Afterthoughts on 'Diaspora'," *South
Atlantic Quarterly* 98.1–2 (1999): 309.

[4] James Clifford, "Diaspora," in *Migration, Diasporas and Transnationalism*, ed. Steven Vertovec & Robin Cohen (Cheltenham & Northampton MA:
Edward Elgar, 1999): 224.

respects even opposed, positions and aesthetic strategies of Derek Walcott's and Edward Kamau Brathwaite's poetry, and finally look at the work of Linton Kwesi Johnson, a West Indian living in Britain.

From Multiculturalism to Diaspora

The term 'diaspora' was only brought into the contemporary cultural debate after the notion of multiculturalism had been fully established and had begun to be contested from within the field of cultural studies. Multiculturalism refers to the recognition of the coexistence of different cultures within one nation. The term was first used with regard to the relationship between the anglophone and francophone populations in Canada; both cultures were declared to be (nominally) equal and to have the same rights. Contemporary debates about multiculturalism concerned the conflicts resulting from the presence of incompatible and in certain cases even incommensurable cultural assumptions and values within the same national framework, as much as the acceptance of cultural difference as potentially permanent. The main thrust of the politics of multiculturalism, therefore, was to achieve tolerance of cultural difference rather than assimilation and acculturation. The theoretical backdrop to this concept, however, was that ethnic 'identities' were regarded as stable, fixed and unchangeable, precisely because the concept of a multicultural society was employed to counter the pressure towards assimilation to the Euro-American culture. Identity as something given rather than as a process of development was the key in what was called "identity politics."

The main impetus of this "politics of recognition"[5] was to end ascriptions of inferiority to, and denigration of, people of colour and

---

[5] "The background premise of these demands is that recognition forges identity, particularly in the Fanonist application: dominant groups tend to entrench their hegemony by inculcating an image of inferiority in the subjugated. The struggle for freedom and equality must therefore pass through a revision of these images. Multicultural curricula are meant to help in this process of

people from other cultures. In order to achieve this aim, proponents of multiculturalism presented cultural (ethnic, racial) identities as 'authentic' and homogeneous, even in the face of a long and constitutive history of racial mixing and mutual cross-influencing in the Americas. In order to revise the asymmetry of the process of hybridization – up to then always conceived of as moving towards the dominant white majority culture and its values – the process of cross-fertilization itself was ignored strategically. This move can be understood in the context of what Gayatri Spivak has called "strategic essentialism." You have to claim a distinct standpoint and identity if you wish to emancipate yourself from a hegemonic cultural regime.[6]

Nevertheless, whenever boundaries are dissolved, new distinctions are inevitably introduced. The claim to an ethnic identity without regard to differences in age, gender, location and so on could not be kept up for long. Moreover, one soon had to acknowledge that, on the one hand, such vertical orderings stayed linked to the former hierarchy which they merely invert, and, on the other, that such ascriptions of "authenticity" and of a unified identity proved to be static and constrictive precisely to those who would like to liberate themselves from such constraints. You do not want to move from one restrictive notion of culture and identity to another. Furthermore, majority groups themselves obviously do not possess a pure culture either; rather, theirs has also evolved in exchange and negotiation with minority cultures. Finally, since multiculturalism was usually understood to apply to relationships within national boundaries, experiences shared by members of ethnic groups *living in different countries* were neglected.

---

revision." Charles Taylor, "The Politics of Recognition," in *Multiculturalism: A Critical Reader*, ed. David Theo Goldberg (Oxford: Blackwell, 1994): 97.

[6] Even if such a recourse to authenticity seems somewhat strained now, we should remember that the bourgeoisie used rather similar strategies in their effort to break the dominance of feudal society. Authenticity has been the most successful battle-cry since the eighteenth century (as Lionel Trilling and others have shown).

Consequently, new ways of thinking about the conditions of coexistence, simultaneity and exchange between cultures had to be sought.
The diaspora concept therefore came to be employed to designate
shifting alliances and new positionings within changing contexts.

The Term 'Diaspora'

Delineating the history of diasporas, Robin Cohen distinguishes between victim diasporas,[7] an experience mainly shared by Jews, Africans and Armenians, and other, more positive forms of diasporic
settlements which "can be seen as galvanizing a new creative energy
outside the natal homeland."[8] While he remarks that the current usage
of the term favours the meaning of a "victim diaspora,"[9] he points out
that in the modern era, many forms of trade or business diasporas
exist. Therefore, diaspora as enforced dispersal was never the only
facet of the term's meaning. Any consideration of the concept and the
predicament of diasporic existence has to take into account this double

---

[7] "Bonds of language, religion, culture and a sense of a common fate im-
pregnate such a transnational relationship and give to it an affective, intimate
quality that formal citizenship or even long settlement frequently lack." Robin
Cohen, "Rethinking 'Babylon': Iconoclastic Conceptions of the Diasporic Experience," in Vertovec & Cohen, ed. *Migration, Diasporas and Transnationalism*, 257.

[8] Cohen, "Rethinking 'Babylon'," 252. Cohen argues that "though the
word 'Babylon' often connotes captivity and oppression, a re-reading of the
Babylonian period of exile can thus be shown to demonstrate the development
of a new creative energy in a challenging, pluralistic context outside the natal
homeland. This ancient form of what might nowadays be called 'multiculturalism' can be regarded as a precursor of the 'hybridity' phenomenon (i.e,
a productive cultural exchange)"; Cohen, "Rethinking Babylon," 255.

[9] Cohen writes that "the idea that the 'diaspora' implied forcible dispersion
was found in Deuteronomy (28:25). [...] The destruction of Jerusalem and the
razing of the First Temple in 586 BC created the central folk memory of a
diasporic experience – enslavement, exile and displacement"; Cohen, "Rethinking Babylon," 252.

inflection of the term: on the one hand, the experience of dislocation, displacement and exterritoriality, and, on the other, the creative, productive and syncretic energies inherent in a situation of multiple identification and movement. Cohen concludes: "It may be that diasporas, seen as forms of social organization, have pre-dated the nation-state, lived within it and now may, in significant respects, transcend and succeed it."[10]

The term 'diaspora', as it is used today in cultural and social studies, first of all allows us to establish new links and connections. Rather than continuing to practise, for instance, African-American studies in isolation, we have now shifted to African diasporic studies, which analyse cultures of African-descended people in the USA, the Caribbean, Latin America, and Europe.[11] More generally, the term acknowledges the transnational character of many cultures and ethnic, religious and racial affiliations. James Clifford points out "that contemporary diasporic practices cannot be reduced to epiphenomena of the nation-state or of global capitalism."[12] Rather, he speaks, quoting Roger Rouse, of "transnational migrant circuits" and calls for "comparative, intercultural studies".[13] Emphasizing the difference between older and more recent uses of the term, he adds that

> decentered, lateral connections may be as important as those formed around a teleology of origin/return. And a shared, ongoing history of

[10] Cohen, "Rethinking 'Babylon," 263.

[11] Paul Gilroy criticizes the construction of canons "on an exclusively *national* basis – African-American, Anglophone Caribbean, and so on"; Gilroy, *The Black Atlantic: Modernity and Double Consciousness* (Cambridge MA: Harvard UP, 1993): 33.

[12] Clifford, "Diasporas," 215.

[13] Clifford, "Diasporas," 216. Discussing different definitions of the term, Clifford sums up the main features of diaspora as "a history of dispersal, myths/memories of the homeland, alienation in the host country, desire for an eventual return, ongoing support of the homeland, and a collective identity importantly defined by this relationship" (218).

displacement, suffering, adaptation, or resistance may be as important
as the projection of a specific origin.[14]

These elements underline the fact that the current meanings and uses
of the term show important differences when compared with the
original Jewish diaspora: the point of origin (the homeland) loses
importance in comparison with the trajectory of migration and the
shifting contexts within which people actually live. Furthermore, the
concept of diaspora has to be distinguished from "(1) the norms of the
nation-states and (2) indigenous, and especially autochthonous claims
by 'tribal' peoples,"[15] and – I would argue – also from (3) immigration,
from (4) travel (merely temporary residence in a foreign country) as
well as from (5) exile. In my definition of these terms, the difference
between diaspora and exile, notions which are often used interchange-
ably, lies in the fact that exile describes the predicament of individuals
whereas diaspora refers to the collective experience of groups or
peoples.

As I have argued, the term 'diaspora' is also employed strategically
to destabilize and disrupt the notions of ethnic identity and authenticity which had become dominant since the 1960s and were used to
insist on cultural (or ethnic, racial etc) difference within a discourse
which focused primarily on differences *between* groups. Particularly
since the early 1990s, the emphasis shifted from the differences
between to those *within* groups and communities.[16] Seen in this context, diasporic identities are understood as performatively constructed
rather than as stable, fixed and rooted entities. This shift therefore
signals a dynamization and de-essentialization of the identity-concept.
Focusing on the position of enunciation of post-colonial subjects,
Stuart Hall remarks that "instead of thinking of identity as an already
accomplished fact [...] we should think [...] of identity as a 'produc-

[14] Clifford, "Diasporas," 219.

[15] Clifford, "Diasporas," 220.

[16] One important political event which contributed to the questioning of
loyalties along the lines of cultural "identity" was the Rushdie Affair.

tion', which is never complete, always in process."[17] Accordingly, "diaspora experience [...] is defined, not by essence or purity, but by the recognition of a necessary heterogeneity and diversity."[18] Diaspora in this sense is used as a way of indicating that for people coming from different cultures there exist multiple areas of identification – the country of origin, the country of residence, perhaps another minority culture in the country of residence, and, moreover, that these identifications also vary according to age or gender and can change over time. This last point leads to a further crucial feature of the concept of diaspora. It involves a constitutive temporal dimension which stands in marked contrast to the spatial orientation implied by definitions of ethnic or cultural identity and belonging based on the metaphor of 'roots'. Diaspora people are *en route*: they come from somewhere, the old home which is linked with the past, they live in their new country in the present, and they might even be on their way to another place which will provide a not yet determined future. The concept of diaspora thus combines both *roots* and *routes*, as Paul Gilroy puts it in a felicitous pun,[19] and it also focuses on the discussion of the (potential) transience of the sojourn of an ethnic group in a specific country: "diaspora communities are 'not-here' to stay."[20] The focus on diasporic situations thus involves an important conceptual shift from a concern with the past to one with the future:

> Praxis indicates a project and thus refers to the future, to the production of something that does not yet exist; identity, on the other hand, suggesting a totality that is always already present, refers everything back to a past – not a past to be overcome, though, but rather one that respects a fullness and an ideal. As a result, the present is completely captured and immobilized by the past [...] Conceptualizing today's diasporas as constellations of cultural and political actions, as projects

---

[17] Stuart Hall, "Cultural Identity and Diaspora," in *Contemporary Postcolonial Theory*, ed. Padmini Mongia (London: Arnold, 1996): 110.

[18] Hall, "Cultural Identity and Diaspora," 119–20.

[19] Gilroy, *The Black Atlantic*, 190.

[20] Clifford, "Diasporas," 224.

rather than congealed totalities, thus confers an epistemological dimension upon these praxes.[21]

In other words, it is the shift from identity to identification, from the local region to transnational movement, or from space to time, which is most important.

Such a conception of diaspora, however, has not gone uncontested. Thus Cohen argues that Hall's notion of diaspora "is post-modern in the sense that he wants to use the notion of diaspora to describe contemporary identities, while none the less lifting the notion from [...] its moorings in the catastrophic, victimizing and territorializing tradition."[22] Even while Cohen is critical of the emphasis given to what he calls "victim diasporas," he also has doubts about a tendency to project the image of the rootless and free-floating "postmodern nomad" onto groups which, even if they left their homes voluntarily and the trip turned out to be advantageous for them, still have to struggle with the conflicts resulting from dislocation and adaptation to a new and different cultural and social environment. Caren Kaplan even suggests that the celebratory use of the notion of diaspora might be self-reflexive, as it frequently occurs when diasporic intellectuals of the postmodern nomad type refer to themselves.[23] Thus, the term 'diaspora' also functions within specific social and discursive contexts. A similar argument has been made by Zygmunt Bauman with regard to the negative social consequences of globalization; he speaks of "the unbreakable unity between 'globalizing' and 'localizing' pressures" and

---

[21] Valentin Y. Mudimbe & Sabine Engel, "Introduction," *South Atlantic Quarterly* 98.1–2 (1999): 5–6.

[22] Cohen, "Rethinking Babylon," 261.

[23] Kaplan, *Questions of Travel*, 124. She also claims that "reviewers and critics construct 'authentic public voices of the Third World' by celebrating cosmopolitan authors who can appear exotic even when they have similar 'tastes, raising, repertoire of anecdotes, current habitation' as those very same reviewers and critics" (124).

emphasizes *"the concentration of freedom* to move and to act" which is available only to few people when seen on a global scale.[24]

While diaspora studies thus certainly constitute an important and necessary corrective to investigations that are linked to identity politics, one should nevertheless be careful not to misrepresent the situation of contemporary migrants and diasporic people (who have lived in another country for longer periods) by projecting onto them postmodernist concepts of fragmented and constantly shifting identities that are characteristic of persons who can be seen as partaking in the latest social developments of modernization.

The African Diaspora

The deportation of Africans as slaves to the Americas since the sixteenth century was the biggest enforced emigration and the largest migration in known history. Conservative accounts now estimate that about ten million Africans were brought to the Americas.[25] The triangular trade between Europe, the west coast of Africa, and the Americas (the Caribbean, Brazil and North America) and the plantation economy centering on the production of sugar were highly profitable, at least until the middle of the eighteenth century. As a consequence, until the nineteenth century, the American continent should be regarded first of all as an extension of Africa, as Albert Wirz puts it.[26] For every European who came to the Americas before 1820 four or even five Africans were brought into the continent. European settlers were in the majority only in a few areas, for instance New England.

---

[24] Zygmunt Bauman, *Globalization: The Human Consequences* (Cambridge: Polity, 1998): 70.

[25] Albert Wirz, *Sklaverei und kapitalistisches Weltsystem* (Frankfurt am Main: Suhrkamp, 1984): 36.

[26] Wirz, *Sklaverei und kapitalistisches Weltsystem*, 36.

Only with new waves of immigration in the nineteenth century did America become a predominantly white continent.[27]

As Africans continued to live on the African continent, it was argued that after emancipation New World Africans could, at least potentially, return there. Yet, diasporic Africans did not share any common language, ethnicity, culture or (tightly circumscribed) religion among themselves, nor did they share these with the many African tribes and populations, which were themselves to a high degree ethnically and politically differentiated. As the slaves came from many different regions and cultures, tribal units or nations, they never constituted a homogeneous group in terms of culture, language, religion and values. Whereas they had been as differentiated in Africa as Europeans were among each other in Europe, on arrival in the New World they were "rendered" (uniformly) "black." Common to the African diaspora, however, is a shared history of slavery, oppression and racism, as well as forced adaptation and assimilation. Africans in the Americas also share expressive forms which stem from African culture but were developed outside of Africa, like specific types of music and rhythm, syncretistic religions, retrospective historical narratives, and specific forms of cultural expression. The usefulness of the notion of the African diaspora lies in the fact that it allows us to investigate the similarities and continuities between the cultures and social situations of African-descended people in North America, the Caribbean, Latin America and Europe.

Even while the African diaspora is thus different from the Jewish prototype, which shares a religious set of texts, memories of expulsion and the aim to return to Israel, the idea of an exodus stemming from Jewish diasporic history constituted an important point of orientation for Africans during and after the period of slavery. Zionism and pan-Africanism, which since the nineteenth century strove for the unity of

---

[27] Wirz, *Sklaverei und kapitalistisches Weltsystem*, 37.

all African peoples, share common traits.[28] While, during the period of colonialism, Haiti, Liberia, Sierra Leone and Ethiopia, because they were independent states, constituted important points of orientation and models for self-organization for Africans in America, such a cultural or political unity never existed in Africa as a whole, and African Americans were often disillusioned when they went back there. Consequently, while the cultural concept of *négritude* gained a certain influence, a political network of alliances never properly materialized.

The question of the degree to which African diasporic cultures retain African elements remains contested. Richard Roberts deconstructs the authenticity of "Africa" itself by claiming that its "image" is, at least to some extent, a construction of colonialism and ethnography.[29] Furthermore, the view which postulated a strong West African cultural continuity in the New World has since been invalidated. Roberts sums up the research of Sidney Mintz and Richard Price, who

> [...] conclude that 'African-American social and cultural forms were forged in the fires of enslavement.' [...] their interpretation is based on a model of great cultural innovation, in which Africans in the diaspora developed unique cultural forms under their particular historical circumstances. African New World cultures were unique developments that drew on vast reservoirs of cultural knowledge from a wide range of origins, but were fashioned in new ways under the

---

[28] Gilroy, *The Black Atlantic*, 211: "The precise genealogy of the diaspora concept in black cultural history remains obscure, but George Shepperson, who comes closest to providing it, has pointed to the fundamental impact of Blyden's Pan-African formulations on legitimising the importation of the term and to the significance of the *Présence Africaine* project in making it credible. The link between these phases of modern black Atlantic political culture is supplied by Négritude."

[29] Richard Roberts, "The Construction of Cultures in Diaspora: African and African New World Experiences," *South Atlantic Quarterly* 98.1–2 (Winter 1999): 177-90. He writes: "Chanock took an extreme position when he argued that the invention of tradition in the early colonial period effectively distorted the precolonial past because the traditions invented created a cognitive grid of practices of daily life which were projected into the remote past and thus distorted the messiness of actual experience" (178).

conditions of slavery and racism. There was never one African culture of diaspora, but rather many African New World cultural experiences.[30]

This insight, Roberts claims, "challenges the political program of race-based organisation among Africans in the diaspora."[31] In an article published in 1971, Orlando Patterson had already attacked the emphasis given at the time to African history by black activism in the USA. Refuting attempts to understand the experience of Africans in America by reconstructing African history, even if there obviously were certain continuities, he insisted on a comparative methodology.[32] This is precisely what transcultural and transnational diaspora studies attempt to do. In the same vein, Stuart Hall maintains that the "common history of transportation, slavery, colonisation [...] does not constitute a common *origin*, since it was, metaphorically as well as literally, a translation."[33]

Rather than investigating the African diaspora mainly by reference to the African continent, it is therefore more productive to shift the focus on the proposition that the contact and intermixing between Africans, and between Africans and Europeans since the sixteenth century constitute a fundamental dimension of modernity. To capture the historical horizon of this economy of cultural, economic and political exchanges, Gilroy introduces the notion of "the Black Atlantic,"

---

[30] Roberts, "The Construction of Cultures in Diaspora," 187.

[31] Roberts, "The Construction of Cultures in Diaspora," 188. He elaborates: "For Africans in the diaspora, the concept of the motherland remains part of an imagined community, but one with only a weak capacity to sustain collective political action. V.Y. Mudimbe is absolutely right, then, to suggest that diasporas conceive of themselves, insofar as they do, within the cognitive grid of a Western paradigm of identity reconceived from a marginal position. The motherland calls precisely because the real world so often requires constant and painful accommodations from a marginal position" (188).

[32] Orlando Patterson, "Rethinking Black History," *Harvard Educational Review* 41.3 (1971): 315.

[33] Stuart Hall, "Cultural Identity and Diaspora," 114.

which, he suggests, one should conceive "as one single, complex unit of analysis in [...] discussions of the modern world and [...] use it to produce an explicitly transnational and intercultural perspective."[34] Consequently, he criticizes afrocentrists because they neglect to consider the interdependence of black and white cultures and people. Rather than relying on a retrospectively constructed African tradition as a unifying feature, he emphasizes the dynamic cultural and political forms which evolved in the exchange and contact that characterize the African diaspora.

The component that most importantly creates a coherence and common, if certainly diversified, diaspora culture, is linked to the expressive forms which were developed by African-descended people in the New World. These forms are a hybrid mix of African, European, and other cultural elements forged into an expressive culture elaborated by black people outside of Africa. For an understanding of the diaspora it is important to note that these cultural ingredients are not locally fixed. One significant example is the history of how hip hop music evolved. It was Jamaicans that brought their sound systems to the South Bronx in New York in the 1970s.[35] Later, hip hop was taken up by black West Indians in Britain and has now become a musical form also used in Europe and Africa. Moreover, it constitutes a (black) model of performance which has influenced much of contemporary popular culture. Quoting James Brown's report about his experience with music in Africa – he met African musicians who played an African version of his own African American music – Gilroy argues that

> the circulation and mutation of music across the black Atlantic explodes the dualistic structure which puts Africa, authenticity, purity, and origin in crude opposition to the Americas, hybridity, creoliza-

---

[34] Gilroy, *The Black Atlantic*, 15.

[35] Gilroy, *The Black Atlantic*, 33: "In conjunction with specific technological innovations, this routed and re-rooted Caribbean culture set in train a process that was to transform black America's sense of itself and a large portion of the popular music industry as well."

tion, and rootlessness. There has been (at least) a two-way traffic between African cultural forms and the political cultures of diaspora blacks over a long period.[36]

As the relatively recent example of the emergence of hip hop music shows, the Caribbean has played a major role within the exchanges and movements which characterize the African diaspora. A large percentage of Africans who were enslaved and shipped to the New World were brought to the Caribbean, including many who were then to become slaves in North America. In the early twentieth century, several important writers of the Harlem Renaissance were West Indians. Today, many black British writers and intellectuals originally came from the islands, and several contemporary Caribbean writers live in the USA. The Caribbean is thus an important site of historical and cultural exchange within the world of the Black Atlantic, and its cultures and literatures constitute privileged instances for investigating the cultural dynamic of the African diaspora.

The Situation in the Caribbean

As almost no members of the original Indian population of the Caribbean islands, the Arawaks and the Caribs, survived, all inhabitants of the Caribbean since the sixteenth century have come from elsewhere. The majority are descendants of African origin brought to the islands as slaves. Therefore, the culture which developed in the archipelago retains African traces to a larger extent than does North American black culture. Yet there are also European, Indian, Chinese, Jewish and other people present. Drawing on Aimé Césaire and Léopold Senghor, Stuart Hall usefully distinguishes between the "*Présence Africaine, Présence Européenne,* and *Présence Américaine*" with

---

[36] Gilroy, *The Black Atlantic*, 199.

regard to the situation of Afro-Caribbeans.[37] None of these presences, however, exists in 'pure' form:

> The Third, 'New World' presence [...] is the juncture-point where [...] strangers from every other part of the globe collided [...] It is the space where the creolisations and assimilations and syncretism were negotiated. [...] The 'New World' presence — America, *Terra Incognita* — is therefore itself the beginning of diaspora, of diversity, of hybridity and difference, what makes Afro-Caribbean people already people of a diaspora.[38]

Politically, moreover, the Caribbean is extremely fragmented today. The federation established in 1958 among ten territories of the British West Indies had already dissolved by 1962. Jamaica as well as Trinidad and Tobago became independent in 1962, Barbados and British Guiana in 1966, and Grenada and the Bahamas in 1974. Thus, since the 1960s, many Caribbean islands have been involved in nation-building. Postcolonialism in the Caribbean involves the search for, and construction of, national identities that are expected to create unity and coherence, a tendency which runs counter to the acceptance of multiple affiliations and divided loyalties characteristic of diasporic identities.[39] At the same time, many people, in particular writers, left the islands and went to Britain or the USA. Thus, most black writers living in Britain belong to "re-migrant" groups and are what Cohen calls "a diaspora of a diaspora."[40] Indeed, it is interesting to note that the concept of the African diaspora has been mainly developed by black Britons from the Caribbean, whereas until recently it has rarely been used within the USA.[41]

---

[37] Hall, "Cultural Identity and Diaspora," 116.

[38] Hall, "Cultural Identity and Diaspora," 119–20.

[39] As Hall points out, the Caribbbean situation "positions Martiniquans and Jamaicans as *both* the same *and* different"; Hall, "Cultural Identity and Diaspora," 114.

[40] Cohen, "Rethinking Babylon," 261.

[41] Two of the main theoreticians of the concept, Stuart Hall and Paul Gilroy, are black West Indians living in Britain.

Thus we can say, first, that many Caribbean artists and writers tend to be more concerned with the construction of a Caribbean culture and 'identity' than with an African diasporic affiliation, although such an African identity nevertheless constitutes an important ingredient in the emergent hybrid Caribbean cultures. Secondly, the concept of diaspora has been primarily used and developed by black West Indians living in Britain. It is important to keep this framework in mind when we approach the work of the two most famous West Indian poets, Derek Walcott and Edward Kamau Brathwaite. I will also discuss the texts of Linton Kwesi Johnson, who was born in Jamaica and has lived in Britain since the age of eleven, and who is said to have invented "dub poetry."

Walcott and Brathwaite, two poets who are frequently discussed in juxtaposition, take two opposed positions with regard to the situation of the African diaspora in the Caribbean. While Brathwaite claims an African heritage in order to liberate himself from colonial culture, Walcott accepts the hybrid cultural situation in the Caribbean and claims a multifaceted and multidimensional heritage. Both poets are concerned with the creation and definition of a specifically Caribbean literature and culture. Nevertheless, Walcott puts the emphasis on the genuine newness of a culture that covers a broad spectrum of traditions, whereas Brathwaite stresses the dominant African element. In a somewhat oversimplified manner, one can say that Walcott thinks of the diaspora as a culturally productive experience, as a paradigm of (multi-) cultural creativity, whereas Brathwaite focuses more on the dimensions of what Cohen calls a "victim diaspora." Johnson in turn creatively develops Walcott's multiculturalism and Brathwaite's Africanist diaspora to account for a specifically Caribbean diasporic consciousness among the British Caribbean community.

Derek Walcott

> I who am poisoned with the blood of both,
> Where shall I turn, divided to the vein?
> I who have cursed
> The drunken officer of British rule, how choose
> Between this Africa and the English tongue I love?
> ("A Far Cry from Africa")

To investigate Walcott's view of the diaspora, I shall look at his poem "Names." This poem, which is dedicated to Edward Brathwaite, crystallizes the history of African-descended West Indians in the history of their language.[42] It represents the diaspora as a linguistic process, as the development and creation of a new language by way of a re-interpretation of the enforced colonial language. Thus, the poem describes a trajectory. First, the enslaved Africans were stripped of their original languages, producing almost a *tabula rasa*, which, however, is seen as a source of creativity ("My race began as the sea began, / with no nouns, and with no horizon"). As the memories of Africa were lost on the Middle Passage, Caribbean history began with the 'now' of the arrival on the islands: "I began with no memory, / I began with no future, / but I looked for that moment / when the mind was halved by a horizon." "That moment" emphasizes the being-there rather than the having-come-from, the present rather than the past. On their voyage across the unbounded sea, which was their first encounter with de-racination, with the loss of their familiar world, Africans, uprooted and torn from the only cosmos they knew, were adrift in a world without words and without precedent in the range of their former experience. When they arrived on the islands, they looked for that moment when the world was defined again, "halved by a horizon." A horizon introduces a contour, marking the unmarked continuum by introducing, in

---

[42] Derek Walcott, "Names" (1976), *Collected Poems 1948–1984* (New York: Farrar, Straus & Giroux, 1986): 305–308.

Gregory Bateson's words, a (first) difference which makes a (further) difference, rendering it knowable. Yet the poet has never found that moment, as the first people who were brought to the islands ("the goldsmith from Benares, / the stone-cutter from Canton") are forgotten. Rather than a horizon appearing in the West, the horizon vanishes in the memory of the East. For Walcott, what West Indians are is what they became and how they created themselves in the archipelago of the Americas. In a gesture of erasure, the first strophe stages the predicament of diaspora as a stripping-away and loss of a familiar world, and the ensuing loneliness which is a solitude of words.

The poem presents this process as a drama of reduction. The Africans are left with "that cry, / that terrible vowel, / that I!" Yet this "I" is not an expression of subjectivity; rather, the arrivants are reduced to their mere being, unable to communicate – the "I" is a presemiotic sound signifying nothing. In this radical reduction to corporeality, however, the new beginning is already latent. "No nouns" implies that they did not possess anything, not even a past or memories, which are a form of property and thus (in the thinking of Pierre Bourdieu) cultural capital. To emphasize the transience and fragility of the slaves' predicament, the poem uses the image of their "tracing" their names in the sand with a stick; yet these are erased again by the sea (which is their history).[43] Slaves were cut off from their "roots," yet they were *en route*. Walcott is not interested in the reconstruction of African con-

---

[43] Cf Walcott's poem "The Sea is History" (1979; *Collected Poems 1948–1984*, 364–67). According to Aleid Fokkema, in Walcott's poetry the sea is "a symbol of identity without belonging. Between the trap of 'roots,' identity connected to belonging (hence the politics of inclusion and exclusion), and the free-floating, lying, endless deferral of identity that deprives of meaning, Derek Walcott offers us a version of identity that is protean, unattached, but, ideally, whole, not alienated from itself, its past, its community"; Fokkema, "On the (False) Idea of Exile: Derek Walcott and Grace Nichols," in *(Un)Writing Empire*, ed Theo D'haen (Cross/Cultures 30; Amsterdam & Atlanta GA: Rodopi, 1998): 110–11.

tinuities; he accepts the historical "cut" and focuses on what has emerged since Africans began to live in the Western hemisphere.

The European colonizers who took possession of the Caribbean archipelago used their own language to name the landscape and settlements. For Walcott, there is a discrepancy between the words, nouns as names in particular, which evolved in a specific historical, geographical and sociocultural context in Europe and the translation of these names into the Caribbean world. Stressing the gap between the elegance of European culture and "the uncombed forest, / [...] uncultivated grass," the colonizers could only use "belittling diminutives" like "little Versailles" to familiarize the strange and set it in a relation of inferiority to Europe. Their power is first of all one of naming:

> Being men, they could not live
> except they first presumed
> the right of every thing to be a noun.
> The African acquiesced,
> repeated, and changed them

The right to name, to take possession, is taken for granted by the colonizers. Walcott combines the topos of Adamic language, the dream of every poet to name things, with the impulse of every colonizer to take possession of what he has conquered by naming it, but also to familiarize the unfamiliar.[44] Subjugated Africans in the New World did not revolt against European naming practices but rather repeated the European names, yet "signifying" on them.[45] They repeated the European words and phrases, but with a signal difference, with a different voice, inflection, and altered meaning. This process of incipient creolization

---

[44] Homi Bhabha, "Freedom's Basis in the Indeterminate," *October* 61 (1992): 55: "Claims to identity must never be nominative or normative. They are never nouns when they are productive; like the vowel, they must be capable of turning up in and as an other's difference and of turning the 'right' to signify into an act of cultural translation."

[45] See Henry Louis Gates, Jr., *The Signifying Monkey: A Theory of African-American Literary Criticism* (Oxford: Oxford UP, 1988).

is described as a subversive and creative form of appropriation and acculturation out of which something new emerged.

Coming from Santa Lucia/Sainte Lucie, Walcott takes the multi-lingual situation of the island as exemplary. No forgotten African language is supplanted by English; rather, the creole of the first colonial power, French creole, is confronted with the English of the later masters. Thus, the already creolized word '*baie-la*' is superseded by the English 'bay'. In the Caribbean, according to Walcott, there is no original (African, for instance), no firstness exists; rather, what one finds are intrinsic processes of mixing. While the Africans, by way of the well-known stereotype, are called children, the poem also stages an opposition between the younger Africans and the once young but now older Europeans, making the Africans into the innovators, the bearers of the new:

> and children, look at these stars
> over Valencia's forest!
>
> Not Orion,
> not Betelgeuse,
> tell me, what do they look like?
> Answer, you damned little Arabs!
> Sir, fireflies caught in molasses.

The Africans re-name things; they invent new metaphors that are catachreses in the original sense. They find metaphors for something they do not yet know the name for. Being addressed as "little Arabs," they are misrecognized as familiar 'Others'. The same linguistic process occurs when they invent names for the stars taken from their own familiar world. The word "firefly," however, is itself already a catachresis; it is secondary to the terms 'fly' and 'fire'. Molasses, by contrast, as a native American term, is specific to the landscape; it is made from the geographically typical sugar cane. These lines thus constitute a poetic *mise-en-scène* of creolization, of hybridization without an origin; this is 'signifying' in the sense of mimicry and at the same time involves linguistic change. Even while creolization occurs within a social situation of domination and radical asymmetry, the linguistic development of Caribbean speech is not 'primitive' but representative of the way in which languages generally evolve.

For Walcott, the creative act of the new beginning in the New World is symptomatic of Caribbean culture. He claims that

> what would deliver [the New World Negro] from servitude was the forging of a language that went beyond mimicry, a dialect which had the force of revelation as it invented names for things, one which finally settled on its own mode of inflection, and which began to create an oral culture of chants, jokes, folksongs, and fables; this, not merely the debt of history, was his proper claim to the New World. For him metaphor was not symbol but conversation, and because every poet begins with such ignorance, in the anguish that every noun will be freshly, resonantly named, because a new melodic inflection meant a new mode, there was no better beginning.[46]

Walcott accepts the mixed character of Caribbean culture, which for him implies a double heritage. This "split within," which cannot and must not be mediated, is precisely what Homi Bhabha has theorized as the seminal feature of cultural hybridity and which can be regarded, moreover, as a defining characteristic of diaspora identity in the contemporary sense.[47] Walcott does not conceive of identity as spatially fixed by descent ('roots') but as evolving temporally by the trajectory of one's life ('routes'). As a consequence, he most emphatically opposes afrocentric gestures concerning language: "Our bodies think in one language and move in another [...] the language of exegesis is English."[48]

---

[46] Derek Walcott, "What the Twilight Says" (1970), in *What the Twilight Says: Essays* (London: Faber & Faber, 1998): 15. He adds that "our quarrels about genealogy, our visionary plays about the noble savage remain provincial, psychic justifications, strenous attempts to create identity" (18).

[47] See Ulfried Reichardt, "Hybridity, Time, and Recursivity," in *Crossover: Cultural Hybridity in Ethnicity, Gender, Ethics*, ed. Therese Steffen (Tübingen: Stauffenburg, 2000): 13–21.

[48] Walcott, "What the Twilight Says," 27.

However, the acceptance of the African and the European legacies does not involve a sense of alienation for Walcott. Against V.S. Naipaul's famous verdict that "nothing has ever been created in the West Indies and nothing will ever be created" he sets his own vision: "Nothing will always be created in the West Indies [...] because what will come out of there is like nothing one has ever seen before."[49] The diasporic situation is precisely the Caribbean's "legacy," its chance, and its contribution to world culture. Consequently, he argues that Naipaul attacks not just the Caribbean cultural situation but, rather, "the American endeavour" in general, the project of a "New World" culture that has been hybrid from the beginning. Accordingly, his figure for the Caribbean is not Prospero/Caliban, but Robinson Crusoe.[50] Claiming that the "truly tough aesthetic of the New World [...] refuses to recognise it as a creative force,"[51] he adopts Walt Whit-

---

[49] Derek Walcott, "The Caribbean: Culture or Mimicry?" (1974), in Hamner, ed. *Critical Perspectives on Derek Walcott*, ed. Robert D. Hamner (Washington DC: Three Continents, 1993): 54. Fred D'Aguiar comments: "Walcott argues that by internalising the ruler's culture and re-invigorating it to suit the new surroundings, colonised people defied the very foundations of enslavement, effectively achieving their own self-emancipation. [...] Mimicry therefore becomes 'an act of imagination' rather than the mindless 'aping' of a hollow people that V.S. Naipaul sees"; D'Aguiar, "Ambiguity without a Crisis? Twin Traditions, the Individual and Community in Derek Walcott's Essays," in *The Art of Derek Walcott*, ed. Stewart Brown (Bridgend: Seren, 1991): 164.

[50] See Walcott, "The Figure of Crusoe" (1965), in Hamner, ed. *Critical Perspectives*, 33–40. Cf, further, Patricia Ismond, "Walcott versus Brathwaite" (1971), in *Critical Perspectives*, 235: "The significance of his 'acceptance' of the Western World [...] availed him as a strategy for consciousness that, having been absorbed and modified in his environment over the centuries, becomes as much his property as that of the former masters. So that he feels free to mould it, bend it to his purposes, now to expose its shortcomings, now draw upon its strengths – as completely as the original possessors."

[51] Derek Walcott, "The Muse of History" (1974), excerpted in *The Postcolonial Studies Reader*, ed. Bill Ashcroft, Gareth Griffiths & Helen Tiffin (London & New York: Routledge, 1995): 371.

man's enthusiastic vision of the New World as being exclusively characterized in terms of the future rather than being defined by the past:

> I accept this archipelago of the Americas. I say to the ancestor who
> sold me, and to the ancestor who bought me, I have no father. [...] I
> give the strange and bitter and yet ennobling thanks for the monu-
> mental groaning and soldering of the two great worlds.[52]

While he acknowledges the "American" experience and history, he
regards Caribbean (including afrodiasporic) cultures as genuinely new
and charged with creative potential.[53]

There is yet another dimension to the poem I have been examining.
In contrast to the process it describes, its language is not specifically
(Afro-)Caribbean; diction, metre, rhythm, and structure are standard
English. The form of the poem itself is not hybrid. Rather than showing traces of creolization, it delineates and presents the process in its
meaning only. One could argue, therefore, that Walcott's aesthetic remains within the limits of European culture and that he expands its
range, but does not oppose the Western tradition. The way in which
the Caribbean experience is mediated shows that the poem is written
for an audience which 'reads' poetry, knows the conventions of reading the lyric, and thus shares a certain (European) education. The
specifically aesthetic and formal features of African diasporic cultures,
expressive forms which emerged from oral sources and centre on performative and rhythmic qualities, are missing from Walcott's poetry.
His work thus translates the Caribbean experience into a modernist
form.

---

[52] Walcott, "The Muse of History," 373–74.

[53] As he said in his Nobel Prize speech, "Antillean art is this restoration of
our shattered histories, our shards of vocabulary, our archipelago becoming a
synonym for pieces broken off from the original continent. And this is the
exact process of the making of poetry"; Derek Walcott, *The Antilles: Fragments of Epic Memory; The Nobel Lecture* (New York: Farrar, Straus &
Giroux, 1992): np.

Edward Kamau Brathwaite

Edward Kamau Brathwaite's poetry differs significantly from Walcott's, formally as well as politically. Their main differences concern their views of the diasporic situation of African-descended people in the Caribbean: how important is Africa as a focus, how significant is African-based cultural difference in comparison to the mixture and cultural as well as racial and ethnic hybrids which have evolved in the Caribbean basin since the sixteenth century? Their attitudes with regard to these questions, however, do not merely constitute value-judgements; rather, they imply aesthetic strategies concerning the function and cultural politics of their poetry. By stressing the linguistic difference between anglophone Caribbean cultures and British culture, Brathwaite also produces a declaration of mental and cultural independence from Britain.

Brathwaite delineates his poetic project plastically by opposing the pentameter to the calypso. Whereas the pentameter stays linked to the European cultural and geographic context in which it developed, the calypso is the metrical, musical and rhythmical form which is specific to the particular history, population and geography of the Caribbean. It is the folk expression of the African-descended people on the islands. Pointing out that "in terms of [...] our perceptual models, we are more conscious (in terms of sensibility) of the falling snow [...] than of the force of the hurricanes,"[54] he stresses that only the vernacular spoken in the Caribbean, which he defines as "nation language,"[55] offers him a

---

[54] Edward Kamau Brathwaite, *History of the Voice: The Development of Nation Language in Anglophone Caribbean Poetry* (London & Port of Spain: New Beacon, 1984): 8.

[55] "Nation language is the language which is influenced very strongly by the African model, the African aspect of our New World/Caribbean heritage. English it may be in terms of some of its lexical features. But in its contours, its rhythm and timbre, its sound explosions, it is not English, even though the words, as you hear them, might be English"; Brathwaite, *History of the Voice*, 13.

medium "to get a rhythm which approximates [...] the *environmental experience.*"[56] As "nation language" is based on an oral tradition, "the noise that it makes is part of the meaning. [...] I want to get the sound of it, rather than the sight of it."[57] Therefore, even when he uses standard English, Brathwaite's poems are meant to be heard rather than to be read. As has often been pointed out, his poems are most impressive when he performs them publicly.[58]

In his most famous work, the trilogy *The Arrivants*, Brathwaite enacts a trajectory from the slave experience in the Caribbean colonies (focusing on the figure of [Uncle] Tom) to Africa and back again to the islands. It is a journey back in history, an exploration of African roots, and of the contemporary situation of the African diaspora in the Caribbean. Like Walcott, Brathwaite starts out with the experience of loss and negativity, which he nevertheless laments:

> for we who have achieved nothing
> work
> who have not built
> dream
> who have forgotten all
> dance
> and dare to remember
>
> the paths we shall never remember
> again:
> [...]
>   and now nothing
>
> nothing
> nothing.[59]

---

[56] Brathwaite, *History of the Voice*, 9.

[57] Brathwaite, *History of the Voice*, 17.

[58] Interestingly enough, he names T.S. Eliot as the poet who influenced him the most: "What T.S. Eliot did for Caribbean poetry and Caribbean literature was to introduce the notion of the speaking voice, the conversational tone"; Brathwaite, *History of the Voice*, 30.

[59] Edward Kamau Brathwaite, "Tom" (*Rights of Passage*, 1967), *The Arrivants: A New World Trilogy* (Oxford: Oxford UP, 1973): 13.

Yet even when he returns from Africa – in the second part of the trilogy, he dives deep into African history, mythology, and rituals – he still finds emptiness in the archipelago:

> But my island is a pebble.
> [...]
> Seeds will not
> take root on its cool sur-
> face.[60]

If there is "salvation," it lies in the sound and rhythm of words:

> stretch the drum
> tight hips will sway
>
> stretch the back
> tight whips will flay
>
> *bambulula bambulai*
> *bambulula bambulai*
>
> kink the gong gong
> loop and play
>
> ashes come.[61]

The trilogy, however, ends on a tentatively hopeful note:

> hearts
> no longer bound
>
> to black and bitter
> ashes in the ground
>
> now waking
> making
>
> making
> with their
>
> rhythms some-
> thing torn
>
> and new.[62]

---

[60] Brathwaite, "Pebbles" (*Masks*, 1968), *The Arrivants*, 196.

[61] Brathwaite, "Jouvert" (*Islands*, 1969), *The Arrivants*, 267.

An example of Brathwaite's vernacular poetry is "Horse weebles:"

> Sellin biscuit an salfish in de plantation shop at pie
> corner, was another good way of keepin she body an soul-seam
>   together
>
> she got she plot of cane, she cow, she fifteen pigeons in a coop,
> razzle-neck fool-hens, a rhode islan' cocklin,
> yam, pumpkin, okro, sweet
> potato, green pea bush.[63]

The scene takes place in a village shop and represents the ordinary life
of common people; most vegetables the lady sells were originally
brought from Africa, like yams, okra and sweet potatoes. The lines are
structured by the rhythm of the non-standard "nation language" spoken
in the anglophone Caribbean. The linguistic 'difference' of the vernacular which results from the fact that we restitute the standard equi-
valents, allows the poet to create a rhythm and sound which stands in
marked contrast to European metres: "she got she plot of cane, she
cow, she fifteen pigeons in a coop." The non-standard use of the pro-
noun "she" as a possessive produces an internal rhyme through intense
repetition. There is also an improvisatory dimension, based on the oral
tradition, and syncopation, which can be traced back to African forms
of rhythm. Further along, the poem directly employs spoken voices:
"*evenin missis / evvy, miss / maisie, miss / maud, olive / how you?
How / you, eveie, chile?*" The performative qualities of this exchange
supersede its semantic thinness; it is life as it is enacted in spoken language that interests Brathwaite. Thus, the poem emphasizes the con-

---

[62] Brathwaite, "Jouvert," *The Arrivants*, 269–70. Cf the comment of Laurence Breiner: "The broad movement of *The Arrivants* is historical and
dialectical, going back from the Caribbean to Africa, not in hopes of reentering
a dream but in order to bring a meaningful Africa to bear on the experience of
the Americas"; Breiner, "Edward Kamau Brathwaite," in *Dictionary of Literary Biography*, vol. 125, ed. Bernth Lindfors & Reinhard Sander (Detroit &
London: Gale Research, 1993): 23.

[63] Edward Kamau Brathwaite, "Horse weebles," in *Mother Poem* (Oxford:
Oxford UP, 1977): 38.

trast to the colonial 'high' English tradition both in its form and in its content.

When Brathwaite explicitly thematizes the historical and cultural situation in the Caribbean, he uses oppositions like those between the North and the South, between the powerful and the powerless, and presents the history of African people in the New World from the perspective of the victims. Yet he does not offer an alternative vision. The two main areas he dramatizes are the everyday life of black West Indians and the history of colonialism, slavery and racism which, in his view, is still very much inscribed in the actual present on the islands. To delineate this historical horizon, Brathwaite, particularly in his later work, such as *X/Self*, uses many names—names which do not only signify violence and domination, but also the counter-power of the non-Europeans. To use one of Nietzsche's terms, these names are fragments of "monumental history": "Now dying at aachen / I prophesy the downfall of the empire"; "Rome burns / and our slavery begins"; "sarawak / arawak / samarkand"; "asuto mokheti namibia aziania shaka the zulu kenyatta the shatt."[64] One could say that these noun-sequences enumerate the ruins of European, African, and American history. They represent the remnants of the process by which the populations of the three continents became intertwined in the era of colonialism. The poems pile these names up and juxtapose them, presenting "a heap of broken images."[65] Brathwaite thus emphasizes the destructiveness of the history of the encounter between Africans and Europeans. Such is Brathwaite's view of the situation which led to the African diaspora and which still characterizes its present social and cultural situation.

Accordingly, Brathwaite's favoured temporal perspective is the past. His view of the diaspora experience is characterized by suffering,

---

[64] Edward Kamau Brathwaite, *X/Self* (Oxford: Oxford UP, 1987): 29, 31, 35, 73.

[65] T.S. Eliot, "The Waste Land," in *The Waste Land and Other Poems* (New York & London: Harcourt Brace Jovanovich, 1962): 30.

destruction, loss and negation. In contrast to Walcott, he does not see a
new beginning,[66] but continues to stage the burden of a traumatic past
which is not yet worked through:

> Where then is the nigger's
> home?
>
> In Paris Brixton Kingston
> Rome?
>
> Here? Or in Heaven?
>
> [...]
>
> Will exile never
> end?[67]

While his poems find at least some solace in the cultures of Africa,
they can also be understood as elegies to an identity which has been
lost long ago. In this sense, Brathwaite's view of the African diaspora
is reminiscent of the way in which the Jewish diaspora kept alive the
idea of Israel in their ritualized and melancholy incantation of
memories of the lost homeland. Brathwaite's work is an elegy to a lost
origin, even while he acknowledges that Africa is not his homeland.

∅

Let us now compare Brathwaite and Walcott. An important difference
between the two poets concerns their use of the poetic voice. Whereas
Walcott usually speaks as an "I," Brathwaite's poems frequently present different voices, yet rarely use a lyrical "I." The emphatic shift to

---

[66] Brathwaite, quoted in Breiner, "Edward Kamau Brathwaite," 20, argues
"that the idea of creolization [...] has to be modified into a more complex
vision in which appears the notion *of negative or regressive creolization*: a
self-conscious refusal to be influenced by the Other." On the other hand, as
Breiner maintains, Brathwaite also seeks to account for the ways in which
blackness [...] can, as a result of creolization, become a *cultural* element for all
West Indians."

[67] Brathwaite, "Postlude/Home" (*Rights of Passage*), *The Arrivants*, 77.

subjectivity which occurred in English poetry in the mid-eighteenth century is missing in Brathwaite's work. Instead, he speaks representatively for the people, the folk. Rather than as an isolated individual, the West Indian writer, he states, should be seen as an "agent of society."[68] Even when he depicts individuals, he retains a collective view of black West Indians. His intention is to express and, more importantly, to create a coherent cultural identity, and he does this through the creation of a form which is distinct from European traditions and based on African models. For the same reason, he reiterates the history of slavery and racism as the shared narrative of the African diaspora. Walcott, by contrast, speaks as an individual, a particular product of a cultural mix rather than as a type or representative of a group. Thus he deploys the aesthetic and poetic forms that have emerged within Western culture since print was invented and modern individualism developed.

When we attempt to generalize these observations with regard to the question of the meaning and use of the concept of diaspora, we are confronted with a chiastic structure and a somewhat paradoxical conclusion. Brathwaite's work retains many features of the traditional notion of the diaspora, like the orientation toward the past, an original homeland (Africa) and culture, using the sound of the vernacular and the African rhythms for what I want to call a "regeneration through sounds." Walcott, by contrast, employs a (post)modern concept of diaspora which is comparable to the one put forward by Hall, Gilroy and Clifford and which resembles Bhabha's notion of "hybridity." Yet with regard to individuality, Walcott still uses a modern poetic "I," even while he stresses his experience as being culturally "divided by the vein." I suggest, therefore, that we are looking at a self-reflexive deployment of modernity, not at its transcendence. In Brathwaite, however, the modern European concept of individuality is retained only in vestiges. By employing older (communal) models of person-

---

[68] Quoted in Breiner, "Edward Kamau Brathwaite," 20.

hood, by insisting on the bard's function as griot and on the communal voice in his poetry, he goes beyond modernity precisely by returning to premodern conceptions of self-being.

Such a position could be seen as a form of regression if contemporary media theorists (like Marshall McLuhan and Joshua Meyrowitz) had not argued that the effect of the contemporary shift in the forms of communication and the development of the electronic media and new technologies had, precisely, led to a change in the relation between the public and private aspects of contemporary existence. McLuhan provocatively speaks of a new tribalism. Brathwaite's sound-, voice-, rhythm-, and performance-oriented poetry, then, in a sense seems more 'contemporary' than Walcott's writing, which is still very much written for solitary reading. As has often been shown, our modern form of individuality emerged in Europe in the context of the inception of print culture. If this observation is correct, then a form of poetry like the one found in Brathwaite's work, but also in voice- and performance-oriented poetry and art generally, shows affinities with forms of expression that are linked to changes in communication structure as a result of the new media. Postliteral and preliteral cultural forms show many similarities.

Brathwaite's poetry, therefore, even while he focuses on the past, uses the link to African and African-derived forms to devise a thoroughly contemporary poetic form. In our 'postmodern' world, the calypso, which is geared towards what in chaos theory is called "turbulent flow," might be better equipped to capture our sense of radical contingency – better, that is, than the iambic pentameter, which stays linked to a linear, ordered world-view characteristic of Euro-American modernity. At the same time, what in Brathwaite is gained in rhythm, performativity and audience-as-community orientation is lost in self-reflexivity and complexity, since these strategies require the possibility of reiteration, which is only possible in reading and writing. Walcott's poetry, as we have seen, does not only express, but also reflects on, the diasporic situation, and, most importantly, it celebrates the multifaceted mixture of cultures in the Caribbean as genuine and creative newness evolving into the future.

Linton Kwesi Johnson

Linton Kwesi Johnson's work adds several further shades to the spectrum of African diasporic poetry. He left Jamaica at the age of eleven and has since lived in Great Britain (London). Accordingly, he is a member of the black "diaspora of a diaspora" in England and his experience reflects a doubly diasporic situation. While he uses Jamaican patois and reggae rhythms in most of his poems, thematically he focuses on the situation of black West Indian immigrants in Britain. The situation of black people in Britain is very different from that in the Caribbean and the USA, as they have been a large community in Britain only since World War II and are thus recent immigrants.

The most important factor for Johnson concerns the fact that for him his place of origin and descent is the Caribbean, Jamaica in particular. He does not mention Africa, and his links with African cultural elements are mediated by Caribbean culture. Moreover, he is very critical of afrocentric ways of thinking.[69] If there is a connection to African culture, it consists in the hybridized and reinterpreted forms developed by Rastafarianism, which for him are "part of my historical heritage and a part of my cultural roots."[70] What is significant for him are Rasta music and, in particular, the ways in which the Rastafarians use language.[71] While Rastafarianism itself is a relatively recent

---

[69] Billy Bob Hargus, "Linton Kwesi Johnson: Interview January 1997," in http://www.furious.com/perfect/lkj.html: "You can't tell the children that all of us were kings and queens because if there were kings and queens then they must have ruled over somebody else."

[70] Hargus, "Linton Kwesi Johnson."

[71] "Rasta is important for me on that level – as a cultural force that broadened our consciousness and opened our consciousness to our African heritage and our African ancestry"; Hargus, "Linton Kwesi Johnson."

phenomenon (it began in the 1930s) and has to be understood within the cultural and social context of the Jamaican situation at the time, its image of Africa is largely imaginary.[72] As a black British citizen, Johnson stands in a relation of double distance to Africa. Jamaica is his original homeland, and it is the culture of the islands, the Afro-Caribbean hybrid culture represented by Walcott and Brathwaite among others, which constitutes his first tradition. Moreover, he also points out that he discovered black literature in his youth when he began to be politically active, "particularly the work of W.E.B. Du Bois, the Afro-American scholar whose *Souls of Black Folk* inspired me to write poetry."[73] Johnson's situation thus exemplifies the multiply centred and interlinked identities of members of the African diaspora in Britain. The place of origin is the already diasporic Caribbean black culture, while England as the land of immigration is also seen as 'home' to a certain degree. In *Dread Beat and Blood*, he has said, the message is: "We are here to stay in England":

> I like England. I like the temper of life, the tempo. They have strong democratic traditions, there's a strong libertarian tradition there. There's a greater level of tolerance I find there than I'd find anywhere else.[74]

Moreover, while he retains strong cultural links with Jamaica, in particular through the use of the Jamaican patois and reggae rhythms, he does not idealize the political life and society of the Caribbean, as can be seen in an elegy he wrote after his father's death:

> an wen mi reach mi sunny isle
> it woz di same ole style
> di money well dry

---

[72] For the notion of imaginary Africas, see Kwame Anthony Appiah, *In My Father's House: Africa and the Philosophy of Culture* (New York: Oxford UP, 1992), where he speaks of the "Invention of Africa" (3–27).

[73] Hargus, "Linton Kwesi Johnson."

[74] Eric Beaumont, "Linton Kwesi Johnson: Black Power, People's Black," in http:/ctomag.com/ may16cto/lkj.html.

di bullits dem a fly
plenty innocent a die
many rivahs run dry
ganja plane flyin high
di poor man im a try
yu tink a lickle try im try
holdin awn bye an bye
wen a dallah cant buy
a lickle dinnah fi a fly[75]

This critical perspective on Jamaica is significant; the poem underlines the fact that Johnson does not look back at Jamaica nostalgically. His are split or, rather, plural affiliations, hence his roots cannot be reduced to an 'essential' black Caribbean identity. Henry Louis Gates, Jr., in a different context, writes of the quest "for affinities, not roots."[76] Johnson has such an affinity with the Caribbean.

In terms of the style of his poetry, Johnson cites Edward Brathwaite as his main influence and an important point of departure:

He incorporated the rhythms of Caribbean speech, jazz rhythms, blues rhythms, calypso rhythms and so on. In a sense, what I've been doing with reggae, what I call reggae poetry is to consolidate that revolution that was started by Brathwaite in terms of the language and in terms of the aesthetics.[77]

If we take Johnson as a representative of the next generation of poets of Caribbean descent, we realize that the groundwork of searching for a Caribbean idiom in poetry, a rhythm, diction and tone which are specific to, and expressive of, the Caribbean region and culture, especially of the black Caribbean experience, has already been done, and that the poetry of Brathwaite and others now constitutes the basis for the work of later artists. Johnson can draw on a tradition of black

[75] Linton Kwesi Johnson, "Reggae fi Dada" (1984), in *The Penguin Book of Caribbean Verse in English*, ed. Paula Burnett (Harmondsworth: Penguin, 1986): 77.

[76] Quoted in Kobena Mercer, *Welcome to the Jungle: New Positions in Black Cultural Studies* (London & New York: Routledge, 1994): 29.

[77] Hargus, "Linton Kwesi Johnson."

Caribbean poetry, adapt it to new cultural and media contexts, and
continue to develop its aesthetic.

Johnson's poetry is at once directly political and aesthetically innovative. He is said to have invented "dub poetry" (he prefers the term
"reggae poetry") in Brixton in 1973.[78] Dub poetry is important because
it introduced a new poetic form to the British scene and contributed to
a revival of poetry. Today, dub, reggae and rap poetry as well as slam
poetry are key expressive forms which have helped to bring poetry
back into literary life as performance. Dub poetry can best be described as 'performed speech', and the crucial element is verbal
rhythm. It is performed either with music, mostly reggae, or *a cap-
pella*. As the following poem shows, Johnson's poetry combines political critique with an elaborate and innovative, highly rhythmical,
musical and performative poetic form:

> Muzik of blood
> Black geared
> pain rooted
> heart geared;
>
> [...]
>
> it is the beat of the heart,
> this pulsing of blood
> that is a bubblin bass,
> a bad bad beat
> pushin gainst the wall
> whey bar black blood.[79]

The verbal rhythm in this poem is analogous to the rhythm of reggae
music;[80] it is clearly non-European, performance-oriented, and based
on the speech patterns of the Jamaican patois. Yet at the same time,

---

[78] Tom Terrell, "Linton Kwesi Johnson," in http://imusic.artistdirect.
com/showcase/contemporary/lintomjohnson.html.

[79] Linton Kwesi Johnson, "Bass Culture," in Johnson, *Dread Beat and
Blood*, intro. Andrew Salkey (London: Bogle-L'Ouverture, 1975): 57.

[80] There is also a record version of the poem where it is accompanied by
reggae music; musical and poetic rhythms interact.

the poem also dramatizes the predicament of black existence in the diaspora. The poems' main concern is with the struggle against the racism black people still experience in Britain.

Johnson's poetry and music thus opens up a further perspective on the African diaspora. Being a successful poet, performer and recording artist, he contributes to black music and black popular culture, which constitute significant and influential elements within today's global culture. Black expressive forms, music in particular, are no longer marginal phenomena but important, widely recognized forms of contemporary culture. However, this does not imply that the social situation of black people in Britain (or the USA) is not still jeopardized by residual racism and social inequality. This is the crucial paradox of the strong visibility/audibility and presence of African diasporic cultures today. Accordingly, in Johnson's texts it is not the search for a cultural identity and an African past that interests the poet, but the critique of social inequality and the present struggle for a better, more democratic and just future for the black British community. Cultural identity is no longer the main concern, as African-diasporic expressive forms are well-accepted aspects of contemporary culture, yet social equality is still a project to be achieved. Within this endeavour, political coalitions are more important than the search for one's roots.

Caribbean language and music give Johnson the aesthetic and cultural means to express his social aims. Nevertheless, he bases his critique of racism and inequality on Western democratic values ('tolerance').[81] His links with the African diaspora include shared expressive forms on the one hand and the ongoing experience of racial discrimination on the other, yet at the same time he deals very specifically with the situation in Britain. Seen from this perspective, we could use the term 'glocalization' in the sense that black culture con-

---

[81] Johnson speaks of his hope of making "some progress in advancing the humanist project"; http://www.reggaesource.com/artists/linton_kwesi_john son/interview 1999.html.

nects the members of the African diaspora, yet that it is at the same
time adapted to and reinterpreted in specific local contexts.

To conclude. The contemporary, modified concept of diaspora
enacts a shift from statically conceived notions of culture and cultural
identity to dynamic and performatively constructed ones. It thus helps
us describe the cultural contacts and multicentred mixtures and fusions
which characterize our contemporary transnational, transcultural, and
globalized world. Whereas the concept of multiculturalism tended to
focus on constellations within national boundaries, diaspora studies
foreground the constant movements, exchanges and hybrid cultural
and social processes which are defined as inherently creative. With
regard to the African diaspora, this focus on the diaspora helps to
counter afrocentric constructions of black identity, which tend to
neglect the complexity of the history of slavery and the full range of
cultures that evolved in the Americas, focusing instead on the inter-
connectedness of New-World cultural forms among communities of
African descent.

WORKS CITED

Appiah, Kwame Anthony. *In My Father's House: Africa and the Philosophy of Culture* (New York: Oxford UP, 1992).

Bauman, Zygmunt. *Globalization: The Human Consequences* (Cambridge: Polity, 1998).

Beaumont, Eric. "Linton Kwesi Johnson: Black Power, People's Power: A Conversation with Linton Kwesi Johnson," http://ctomag.com/may16cto/lkj.html.

Bhabha, Homi. "Freedom's Basis in the Indeterminate," *October* 61 (1992): 46–57.

Brathwaite, Edward. *The Arrivants: A New World Trilogy* (Oxford: Oxford UP, 1973).

——. *History of the Voice: The Development of Nation Language in Anglophone Caribbean Poetry* (London & Port of Spain: New Beacon, 1984).

——. *Mother Poem* (Oxford: Oxford UP, 1977).

——. *X/Self* (Oxford & New York: Oxford UP, 1987).

Breiner, Laurence A. "Edward Kamau Brathwaite," in *Dictionary of Literary Biography: Twentieth-Century Caribbean and Black African Writers*, ed. Bernth Lindfors & Reinhard Sander (Detroit MI & London: Gale Research, 1993): 8–28.

Burnett, Paula, ed. *The Penguin Book of Caribbean Verse in English* (Harmondsworth: Penguin, 1986).

Clifford, James. "Diasporas," in Vertovec & Cohen, ed. *Migration, Diasporas and Transnationalism*, 215–45. Originally published in *Cultural Anthropology* 9.3 (1994): 302–38.

Cohen, Robin. "Rethinking 'Babylon': Iconoclastic Conceptions of the Diasporic Experience," in Vertovec & Cohen, ed. *Migration, Diasporas and Transnationalism*, 253–65. Originally published in *new community* 21 (1995): 5–18.

D'Aguiar, Fred. "Ambiguity without a Crisis? Twin Traditions, the Individual and Community in Derek Walcott's Essays," in *The Art of Derek Walcott*, ed. Stewart Brown (Bridgend: Seren, 1991): 157–68.

Eliot, T.S. *The Waste Land and Other Poems* (New York and London: Harcourt Brace Jovanovitch, 1962).

Fokkema, Aleid. "On the (False) Idea of Exile: Derek Walcott and Grace Nichols," in *(Un)Writing Empire*, ed. Theo D'haen (Cross/Cultures 30; Amsterdam & Atlanta GA: Rodopi, 1998): 99–113.

Gates, Henry Louis, Jr. *The Signifying Monkey: A Theory of African-American Literary Criticism* (New York & Oxford: Oxford UP, 1988).

Gilroy, Paul. *The Black Atlantic: Modernity and Double Consciousness* (Cambridge MA: Harvard UP, 1993).

Hall, Stuart. "Cultural Identity and Diaspora," in *Contemporary Postcolonial Theory: A Reader*, ed. Padmini Mongia (London: Armold, 1996): 110–21. Originally published in *Identity: Community, Culture, Difference*, ed. Jonathan Rutherford (London: Lawrence & Wishart, 1990): 222–37.

Hamner, Robert D., ed. *Critical Perspectives on Derek Walcott* (Washington DC: Three Continents, 1993).

Hargus, Billy Bob. "Linton Kwesi Johnson: Interview," in http://www. furious. com/perfect/lkj.html.

Hecker, Judy. "Reggae Source Interview. Dub Statesman: An Interview with Linton Kwesi Johnson" in http://www.reggaesource.com/artists/linton_kwesi_johnson/interview1999.html

Ismond, Patricia. "Walcott versus Brathwaite" (1971), in Hamner, ed. *Critical Perspectives*, 220–36.

Johnson, Linton Kwesi. *Dread Beat and Blood*, intro. Andrew Salkey (London: Bogle-L'Ouverture, 1975).

Kaplan, Caren. *Questions of Travel: Postmodern Discourses of Displacement* (Durham NC & London: Duke UP, 1996).

McLuhan, Marshall. *The Medium is the Message* (New York: Random House, 1967).

Mercer, Kobena. *Welcome to the Jungle: New Positions in Black Cultural Studies* (London & New York: Routledge, 1994).

Meyrowitz, Joshua. *No Sense of Place: The Impact of Electronic Media on Social Behavior* (New York & Oxford: Oxford UP, 1986).

Mudimbe, V.Y., & Sabine Engel. "Introduction," *South Atlantic Quarterly* 98.1–2 ("Diaspora and Immigration"; 1999): 1–8.

Patterson, Orlando. "Rethinking Black History," *Harvard Educational Review* 41.3 (1971): 297–315.

Reichardt, Ulfried. "Hybridity, Time, and Recursivity," in *Crossover: Cultural Hybridity in Ethnicity, Gender, Ethics*, ed. Therese Steffen (Tübingen: Stauffenburg, 2000): 13–21.

Roberts, Richard. "The Construction of Cultures in Diaspora: African and African New World Experiences," *South Atlantic Quarterly* 98.1–2 ("Diaspora and Immigration"; 1999): 177–90.

Rushdie, Salman. *Shame* (London: Jonathan Cape, 1983).

Surin, Kenneth. "Afterthoughts on 'Diaspora'," *South Atlantic Quarterly* 98.1–2 (1999): 275–325.

Taylor, Charles. "The Politics of Recognition," in *Multiculturalism: A Critical Reader*, ed. David Theo Goldberg (Oxford: Blackwell, 1994): 75–106. Originally published in *Multiculturalism and the "Politics of Recognition"* (Princeton NJ: Princeton UP, 1992): 25--73.

Terrell, Tom. "Linton Kwesi Johnson," in http://imusic.artistdirect.com/showcase/contemporary/lintonjohnson.html.

Trilling, Lionel. *Sincerity and Authenticity: The Charles Eliot Norton Lectures 1969–1970* (Cambridge MA: Harvard UP, 1972).

Vertovec, Steven, & Robin Cohen, ed. *Migration, Diasporas and Transnationalism* (Cheltenham & Northampton MA: Edward Elgar, 1999).

Walcott, Derek. *The Antilles: Fragments of an Epic Memory: The Nobel Lecture* (New York: Farrar, Straus & Giroux, 1992).

——. *Collected Poems 1948–1984* (New York: Farrar, Straus & Giroux, 1986)

——. "The Caribbean: Culture or Mimicry?" (1974), in Hamner, ed. *Critical Perspectives*, 51–57.

———. "The Figure of Crusoe" (1965), in Hamner, ed. *Critical Perspectives*, 33–40.

———. "The Muse of History" (1974), excerpted in *The Postcolonial Studies Reader*, ed. Bill Ashcroft, Gareth Griffiths & Helen Tiffin (London: Routledge, 1995): 370–74.

———. "What The Twilight Says" (1970), in *What The Twilight Says: Essays* (London: Faber & Faber, 1998): 3–35.

Wirz, Albert. *Sklaverei und kapitalistisches Weltsystem* (Frankfurt am Main: Suhrkamp, 1984).

∅

SANDRA HESTERMANN

The German-Turkish Diaspora and Multicultural German Identity
Hyphenated and Alternative Discourses of Identity in the Works of Zafer Şenocak and Feridun Zaimoğlu

Introduction

NOTHING HAS SHAPED AND CHANGED our global land-scape more radically and drastically during the last century than modern mass migrations. Currently, the number of immigrants worldwide has passed the 100-million mark. Germany, with its high economic status, its political power and stability, a rela-tively generous welfare system and, until recently, liberal and flexible asylum laws, "has become a new diaspora for an eclectic body of dis-placed people."[1] With around 7.3 million guest workers, refugees, artists, writers, intellectuals and professionals, more than two million of whom are of Turkish origin, Germany is the most important country of immigration in Western Europe. The presence of by now three generations of Turkish immigrants has marked all aspects of German

---

[1] Azade Seyhan, "Paranational Community/Hyphenated Identity: The Turks of Germany," http://jsis.artsci.washington.edu/...rams/europe/wendep/ SeyhanPaper.htm. Online 09/10/00, 1.

life. Germans have grown accustomed to shopping at a nearby Turkish
grocery, they enjoy their lunch at one of the popular fast-food 'döner'
restaurants or spend their evenings dancing to Turkish-Oriental pop
and rap music. It is therefore not surprising that the Turkish element
has also become a noticeable and increasingly natural factor in all
areas of German culture, high and low, in the cinema, literature, the
visual arts, theatre and cabaret. The purpose of this essay is to indicate
the extent to which the literary expression of the Turkish community,
particularly of the second and third generations, has given rise to a
diasporic Turkish-German consciousness that proposes new alternative identities – neither German nor Turkish – which are re-negotiated,
reproduced and re-created in this 'other' or 'third space,' as Bhabha
has termed the "interstitial passage"[2] where cultures meet and merge.

In the first section of this essay, I will introduce the history and
nature of the German Turkish diaspora and briefly compare its most
salient features with another community, that of the South Asian diaspora in Great Britain. The comparability of these two communities
and the adoption of Vijay Mishra's distinction between 'old, exclusive' and 'new border' diasporas allows us to see the Turkish-German
diaspora within the larger context of global diaspora histories. The
second section of the essay is dedicated to presenting an overview of
the genealogy of Turkish-German literature, after which I will direct
my attention to the contemporary generation of Turkish-German 'axial
writers'. A close analysis of works by Zafer Şenocak and Feridun
Zaimoğlu shall demonstrate that this literature has left the ethnic
ghetto behind and is not even exclusively confined any longer to the
geographical, national or even linguistic boundaries of Germany. In
my analysis of Zafer Şenocak's hybrid novel *Gefährliche Verwandtschaft* ('Dangerous Family Relations')[3] and Feridun Zaimoğlu's
collections of testimonial declarations and interviews *Kanaksprak: 24*

---

[2] Homi Bhabha, *The Location of Culture* (London: Routledge, 1994): 4.
[3] Zafer Şenocak, *Gefährliche Verwandtschaft* (Munich: Babel, 1998).

Misstöne vom Rande der Gesellschaft and *Koppstoff: Kanaka Sprak vom Rande der Gesellschaft*,[4] I will illustrate how these writings of the new diaspora of the border produce, re-negotiate and modify the prevailing concept of German identity. Through the deployment of a subversive use of language and the creation of essentially hybrid genres of literature, Şenocak and Zaimoğlu contribute to creating multicultural, hyphenated and new diasporic forms of German identities which are no longer either German or Turkish, but fluid bi-, tri-cultural concepts or radically new ones, as the portraits of the 'Kanakster' will show.

A Short History of the German/European Diaspora: 'Exclusive' or 'Border' Diaspora?

The Turkish diaspora community is scattered all over Europe and currently stands at around three million, constituting the largest non-European immigrant group in the European Union; two thirds of them live in Germany, forming – ironically speaking – Turkey's sixty-eighth province.[5] The vast majority have settled in the industrial north and in the German capital city of Berlin.[6] The history of Turkish migration to

---

[4] Feridun Zaimoğlu, *Kanaksprak: 24 Misstöne vom Rande der Gesellschaft* (Hamburg: Rotbuch, 1995); *Koppstoff: Kanakasprak vom Rande der Gesellschaft* (Hamburg: Rotbuch, 1998).

[5] Turkey has sixty-seven provinces, and the Turks who live in Germany are often referred to as constituting the sixty-eighth province. Ruth Mandel, "Shifting Centres and Emergent Identities: Turkey and Germany in the Lives of Turkish Gastarbeiter," in *Muslim Travellers: Pilgrimage, Migration, and the Religious Imagination*, ed. Dale F. Eickelmann & James Piscatori (Berkeley: U of California P, 1990): 153.

[6] The figures given by Ural Manço for 1996 are the following: Germany: 2,014,300 (66.4%), France 261,000 (8.6%), Netherlands 260,100 (8.6%), Austria 142,200 (4.7%), Belgium 119,000 (3.9%), Switzerland 79,400 (2.6%), United Kingdom 58,200 (1.9%), Sweden 35,700 (1.2%), Denmark 35,700 (1.2%), Italy 15,000 (0.5%), Norway 10,000 (0.3%), Total (Western Europe) 3,034,500 (100%). Again, one-fourth (23.1%) of the immigrants have settled in North Rhineland-Westphalia; however, the highest density of the Turkish

Europe is a relatively recent one, going back to the late 1950s and
early 1960s when Turkey faced serious economic problems. Extensive
unemployment among the population of Southern and Eastern Anatolia led to mass migration into Turkey's cities in the north and on the
coast (Ankara, Istanbul, Izmir). As a result, thousands of peasants who
were facing social misery and poverty in the urban ghettos decided to
look for work abroad. The first Turkish guest workers came to Germany as early as 1957, but organized mass labour emigration under the
auspices of the Turkish Republic only started on 31 October 1961 after
Turkey signed its first recruitment agreement with Germany.[7] Both
parties considered this 'selling and buying' of labour as a temporary
arrangement, and could hardly have foreseen the consequences.[8] The
first migrants were almost all men, but from the late 1960s onwards
these male guest workers were joined by their families. Thus, in spite
of the implementation of a recruitment ban on foreign labourers from
non-European countries in 1973, the Turkish population in Germany
continued to increase at a considerable rate.[9] From the mid-1970s to
the beginning of the 1980s, the Turkish migrants availed themselves of

population is to be found in the German capital city of Berlin, which hosts
close to five percent of the total number of Turkish immigrants in Europe. See
Ural Manço, "Turks in Europe: From a garbled image to the complexity of
migrant social reality," www.allserv.rug.ac.be/~hdeley/ umanco5.htm. Online
21/11/00: 4.

[7] Further recruitment agreements with France, Belgium, the Netherlands
and Switzerland were to follow in subsequent years.

[8] See Faruk Şen & Andreas Goldberg, *Türken in Deutschland: Leben
zwischen zwei Kulturen* (Munich: C.H. Beck, 1994): 9–26. See also Çiğdem
Akkaya, Yasemin Özbek & Faruk Şen, *Länderbericht Türkei* (Darmstadt:
Wissenschaftliche Buchgesellschaft, 1998): 305–308.

[9] The demographic statistics state an increase of 57% in 1969, 46% in
1979, 39% in 1972, 28% in 1971 and again 18.3% in 1975. Except for 1980,
when the percentage reached 15% because of family reunification, the average
increase of the Turkish population in Germany after the late-1970s has been at
around four percent. Source: *Jahrbücher des Statistischen Bundesamtes*
(Wiesbaden), quoted in Şen & Goldberg, *Türken in Deutschland*, 15.

the law allowing for family reunion, and married Turkish partners, so that today there exists an almost equal number of female and male Turkish migrants. Between 1983 and 1984, Germany implemented the *Gesetz zur Förderung der Rückkehrbereitschaft von Ausländern*, a programme of financial incentives which paid those Turkish migrants willing to return to Turkey a lump sum as well as the money they had paid into the pension scheme. Only a small minority accepted this offer; the vast majority remained in Germany as permanent residents.[10]

Mostly of rural South-Anatolian and East-Anatolian origin, the Turkish migrants transferred whole village communities to Germany. This family-based and geographically oriented societal structure is called '*hemşeri*-ties' (ie, families of the same village tending to cluster in the same quarter of the city or town when they come to Germany). These are marked by preservation of the native language. Lack of educational qualifications explains the employment of large numbers of Turkish migrants as semi-skilled or unskilled workers in the manufacturing industry. Additionally, the elimination of blue-collar jobs in favour of white-collar jobs has contributed to cementing the status gap between Germans and the immigrant Turkish population.[11] In this respect, the 'Turkish phenomenon' resembles that of other migrant minorities. Their situation can be compared with that of North African immigrants from Morocco, Tunisia and Algeria who settled in French-speaking areas of Europe, or with the South Asian population in Great Britain. However, both of these latter groups have their origins in the colonial-imperial past of France and England dating from the eigh-

---

[10] *Statistisches Jahrbuch für die Bundesrepublik Deutschland 1994*, quoted in Eva Kolinsky, "Non-German Minorities in German Society, " in *Turkish Culture in German Society Today*, ed. David Horrocks & Eva Kolinsky (Providence RI & Oxford: Berghahn, 1996): 83.

[11] Kolinsky, "Non-German Minorities," 93–94. See also Friedrich Heckmann, "Nation und Integration von Migranten in Deutschland," in *Was ist ein Deutscher? Was ist ein Türke? Alman olmak nedir? Türk olmak nedir?*, Deutsch-Türkisches Symposium 1997, ed. Türkeiprogramm der Körber-Stiftung (Hamburg: Edition Körber-Stiftung, 1998): 181–95.

teenth to the early twentieth century. 'Modern migrant communities' were not constituted by forced dispersal from their original homelands (which had been the case in the prototypical Jewish diaspora). Yet in many ways the Turkish, South Asian and North African migrant communities display characteristics that correspond to the criteria listed by Robin Cohen as common features of the current (and increasingly fashionable) notion of diaspora.[12]

Tom Cheesman illustrates the special affinity between the South Asian diaspora and the Turkish diaspora in Europe[13] as follows: both diasporas are

a) constituted largely by mass labour migration in the 1950s to 1970s followed by family reunions and large-scale sojourning or migration on the part of students, entrepreneurs and professionals, and refugees,
b) marked by religious differences from the 'host' societies,
c) implicated in the long-term histories of European expansion, orientalism and westernization,
d) marked by major internal ethnic, religious and ethno-national differences or 'communal' tensions, as well as other political and social differences,
e) in recent post-migrant generations, marked by striking upward social mobility and by increasingly complex patterns of return, repeat and transversal migration.[14]

---

[12] Robin Cohen, *Global Diasporas: An Introduction* (Seattle: U of Washington P, 1997): 26. See above, Introduction.

[13] Cheesman, "Axial Writing: Transnational literary/media cultures and cultural policy," www.transcomm.ox.ac.uk/wwwroot/cheesman.htm. Online 09/10/2000: 6. The South Asian diaspora is estimated at nine million, five million of whom have emigrated to Great Britain. Cf Vijay Mishra, "The Diasporic Imaginary," *Textual Practice* 10.3 (1996): 443.n 2.

[14] This social mobility cannot, of course, be applied to all members of the post-migrant generation; there is often a sharp discrepancy between those who achieve full integration in professional and social regard and others who remain excluded from any active participation in German social, political and professional life. Mançu states that only six percent of the 18- to 25-year-olds of Turkish descent in Germany are in higher education, compared to an

Ural Mançɔ, a sociologist, shares Cheesman's views regarding a comparison of the features of the Turkish diaspora with those of other ethnic minorities in the English-speaking world:

> Turkish immigrants seem to have developed a community logic that shares several features with the minority integration model that reigns in the English-speaking world, regardless of the host country's immigration policies and prevailing philosophy of integration. With regard to Turkish immigrants, talking about community life is tantamount to talking about dense community ties confined to the island-space of a working-class neighbourhood. Europe's Turkish immigrants appear to cultivate their difference. They are in the process of weaving a unique cross-border diaspora identity in terms of its magnitude and demographic weight.[15]

---

average of thirty percent of German students. See Mançɔ, "Turks in Europe," 14. These figures are confirmed by Elçin Kürsat–Ahlers, who states that a mere 6% of Turks passed their A-Level exams (*Abitur*): ie, qualified for entry into higher education. See Kürsat–Ahlers, "The Turkish Minority in German Society," in Horrocks & Kolinsky, *Turkish Culture in German Society Today*, 117–30. — The 1980s witnessed a wave of re-migration among many Turks from the first generation, but not all of them ended up staying in Turkey. Some came back to rejoin their family – children and grandchildren who would not accompany their parents – but continue to travel between Turkey and Germany, spending half of the year with their relatives in Turkey and the rest of the year in Germany.

[15] Mançɔ, "Turks in Europe," 6. The genesis of the Chinese-Canadian diaspora reveals striking parallels with the Turkish-German diaspora. Although the official status of the Chinese as immigrants had already been confirmed by the Chinese Immigration Act of 1923, the hostile attitude toward Chinese migrants only started to change after World War II, after the dissolution of imperial power and the advent of independence in the colonies. All this triggered the process of slow integration of Chinese migrants into Canadian mainstream society and culture, but it was to take another generation for these Chinese-Canadians to find their own voice in literature. The emergence of the first generation of writers came in the early 1960s. The development of Chinese-Canadian writing thus runs parallel to the growing need for acceptance in Canadian society. Today's literature reveals the main interest of Chinese-Canadians as trying to establish the relation of their community to the mainstream white community, which creates an essentially hyphenated iden-

Both the Turkish and the modern South Asian diaspora in Great Britain are the result of a lack of economic perspectives in the original home countries, constituting what Vijay Mishra has described as a new "diaspora of the border."[16] Yet, although Cheesman's and Manço's comparison with other modern diaspora communities such as the South Asian or North African ones in Great Britain and France is justified by these obvious parallels, it is nevertheless essential to point out some peculiarities of the Turkish diaspora in Germany, especially with regard to the particular role of Islam in Turkish culture.

In contrast to the large majority of Hindus among the South Asian diaspora, whose religion has traditionally met with sympathy or even enthusiasm in Western culture and whose 'negative' cultural characteristics (the caste system) does not form part of the diasporic culture, the image of Islam has traditionally been defined in radical opposition to Western culture and society, giving rise to a whole array of negative stereotypes. These stereotypes have portrayed the 'Muslim Other' as an enemy, as an alien, aggressive and hostile conqueror, and as a menace to Western civilization. This pejorative image of Islam continues to determine the German attitude towards Turkish co-citizens, especially in connection with the rise of fundamentalist Islamic movements such as the mullah regime in the Republic of Iran or the former terror regime of the Taliban in Afghanistan. Naturally, this view of Islam is extremely biased and hardly takes into account the heterogeneity of Islam, which comprises at least as many different schools and sects as does Christianity. Besides, Islam has already become part of our everyday life, constituting the largest religious community after

---

tity. The sense of being Chinese-Canadian lies at the heart of Canada's metamorphosis into today's multicultural society. Canada extended the Bilingualism Act from 1963 (English/ French) to the Multiculturalism Act, S.C. 1988, c.31. See Ronald B. Hatch, "Chinatown Ghosts in the White Empire," in *Intercultural Studies: Fictions of Empire*, ed. Vera & Ansgar Nünning (*anglistik und englischunterricht* 58; Heidelberg: Carl Winter, 1993): 193–209.

[16] Mishra, "The Diasporic Imaginary," 422.

the Christian churches. Whereas Christian religions are structured hierarchically, Islam does not have an official representative body: ie, it does not have hierarchical organizations comparable to those of the Christian churches. Whereas official Islam is part of the Sunna confession in Turkey, where it is controlled by the National Board of Education and the Presidium for Religious Affairs, there also exist a number of other Islamic groups. Some of the most influential ones – in Turkey as well as in Germany – are the 'Süleymanci-Movement' (*Verband der islamischen Kulturzentren e.V.*), the 'Nurculuk-Movement' (*Islamische Jama'at un-Nur*), and the 'Islamic community Milli Görüş' (National Perspective).[17]

One must acknowledge, however, that the aversive German attitude to these religious groups is understandable insofar as almost all of these neo-Islamic groups are characterized by fundamentalist tendencies. They in turn display a negative attitude towards Europe, which is not directed against the scientific–technical basis of modern civilization itself but is highly critical of its "dangerous"' consequences. This ambivalent view of Western society finds expression in what could be called an 'occidentalist discourse' in which the 'Western Other' is described in terms of immorality and corruption.[18] Stereotypically, the 'German Other' is criticized for his/her allegedly religious indifference and for having succumbed to such vices as pornography, promiscuity and drug abuse. These fundamentalist Islamic groups are usually much more popular in the diasporic communities than in Turkey, which can be explained by their strong involvement in the cultural and social affairs of their people. They provide the diasporic community

---

[17] Compare the description of Islamic organizations in Germany in Ursula Spuler–Stegmann, *Muslime in Deutschland: Nebeneinander oder Miteinander?* (Freiburg, Basel & Vienna: Herder, 1998): 109–28.

[18] For a discussion of 'occidentalism', see Sandra Hestermann, "'Meeting the Other – Encountering Oneself': Paradigmen der Selbst- und Fremderfahrung in ausgewählten anglo-indischen und indisch-englischen Kurzgeschichten" (unpublished doctoral dissertation, University of Freiburg, 2002).

with a stable point of reference to which they may turn for guidance, orientation and help. They also help to foster a sense of pride and identity in an environment which, by a majority of Turkish migrants, is seen as hostile and prejudiced against them.

It is therefore understandable that so many Turkish migrants should turn to religion, professing an assiduous devotion they would not have adopted in their home country. This particular religious discourse, which serves as a crucial source for the formulation of a positive cultural identity, is taken up by two of Feridun Zaimoğlu's protagonists, and constitutes one central feature of an exclusive tendency within the new Turkish border diaspora.[19]

As Mishra points out, the type of the "old, exclusive diaspora" describes the old Indian diaspora of the sugar plantations, a result of the British imperial policy of hiring indentured labourers in the nineteenth century. The term "new diaspora," however, is applied to the mass labour emigration of Indians to the Western metropoles of Canada, the USA and Great Britain. The old diaspora tended to re-create an imitation of its home country, a kind of India *en miniature*, which constructed Indianness via artefacts, rituals, books, food, etc. Due to the preservation of family and community structures and the native language, the identity of the migrant was defined in terms of cultural segregation. The new diaspora, however, is typically characterized by the border-crossing of its members, particularly with reference to the second and third generation who arrived during their childhood or were born in the host countries.

As regards the first generation of Turkish migrants (and Indian migrants), however, it seems as if in addition to the characteristics of the new diaspora, the features of the old exclusive diaspora still remained valid. Certainly, the first Turkish migrants did not come as

---

[19] Compare the testimonials by Yücel, 22; Islamist, "Im Namen des Allerbarmers" (In the Name of the Merciful), in Zaimoğlu, *Kanaksprak*, 137–34; and Hatice, 22, student of the law, "Alles in dieser Welt ist vergänglich" (Everything in this world shall pass), Zaimoğlu, *Koppstoff*, 67–71.

indentured labourers, but they were treated as second-class citizens who did not enjoy the legal status of immigrants as did the Indians or Pakistani in Great Britain. They were *Gastarbeiter*, guest workers, who were hired for a temporary period of time to fill vacant jobs in the manufacturing industry. The work was hard, dirty and badly paid. In contrast to the Indian immigrants to the UK, these Turkish labourers had never really coexisted with a European culture or language before immigrating to Germany. From the beginning they regarded their stay in Germany as a temporary one (just like the former South Asian indentured labourers), which induced them to preserve their traditional cultural values. Their lack of knowledge of the German language and culture led to a ghettoization in which the structure of a closely knit community provided stability and orientation. The gradual change of the first generation of Turkish labourers from the status of temporary guest worker to permanent resident exacerbated the sense of unbelonging, since the carefully fostered Turkish identity was now threatened by mainstream German culture and society. In response to the prejudices and social discrimination which they had to face,[20] these first Turkish migrants created an idea of Turkey which – owing to its geographical and temporal distance from the home country – increasingly acquired the contours of an "imagined community."[21]

More recently, the easy availability of the modern mass media and the affordability of cheap travel to and from the home country have resulted in a collapse of geographical distance from Turkey. However, visits to the home country soon led to disillusionment with Turkey among the first generation, who were treated as outsiders. As a result, these migrants started to adopt different values shared with other diaspora community members who had the same migrant cultural back-

[20] On the German view of foreigners, see Dietrich Thränhardt, "Patterns of Organization among Different Ethnic Minorities," *New German Critique* 46 (1989): 12–14.

[21] Benedict Anderson, *Imagined Communities: Reflections on the Origin and Spread of Nationalism* (London: Verso, 1983).

ground. Although still abiding by the fantasy of an eventual return
(which is delayed until an undetermined date), they replaced this ob-
jective with a discourse of return or multiple returns which take place
in the form of annual vacations. This attitude, however, does not apply
to many Turkish migrants of the second and third generation. Unlike
their parents or grandparents, they do not have any original memories
of their home country. For them, Turkish reality gets transformed into
a myth in which flourish very vague notions derived from the stories
told by their families. These young Turks of the second and third generation have grown up in a 'vacuum culture' and construct their identity
as a consciously 'hyphenated' one. For them, Turkey is a foreign
country whose population calls them *alamancılar* (*Deutschländer* or
"Germaners") – a Turkish term designating their mimicked German-
ness, which is but an imperfect, flawed version of the original.[22]

[As a consequence, the Turks of the second and third generation do
not share the nostalgia of their fathers' and/or grandparents' generation, but have to create an identity of their own which is no longer
exclusive but cross-cultural or even multicultural. The positive description of these seemingly privileged members of the "diaspora of
the border" in terms of a hybrid, intercultural identity figures as an
important subject in contemporary Turkish-German literature that
challenges the prevalent German homogenizing notions of nation and
German culture.] The authors of this body of literature belong to a
group of second- and third-generation 'German' Turks who are characterized by upward social mobility and transnational status. They are
cosmopolitans, or at least bi-cultural citizens – border-crossers who
move freely and comfortably between the German and Turkish cultures and between Berlin and Istanbul. Thanks to higher education and
a sovereign command of the German language, it is not difficult for
these border-crossers to relate positively to their 'hyphenated' identity.

---

[22] Compare Homi Bhabha's concept of "colonial mimicry"; Bhabha, "Of
Mimicry and Man: The Ambivalence of Colonial Discourse," in Bhabha, *The
Location of Culture*, 85–92.

Yet the border, which has a positive connotation for these cosmo-politan Turks, does not necessarily have the same meaning for every-one who belongs to the category of the "diaspora of the border." In fact, a large majority of second- and third-generation Turks do not maintain any social contacts, or at best, only occasional contacts with Germans in their free time.[23] Border-crossing for these Turks does not feature a dialectical cultural exchange that takes place in the contact zone. For them, the border acquires the meaning of a line of separa-tion. This dilemma of living in two separate worlds is additionally aggravated by the fact that many of the young Turks who experience exclusion, stigmatization and threat from mainstream German society also feel imprisoned by their families. Although members of this generation hardly know their parents' country of origin and are unable to sympathize with their traditional, conservative point of view, they have nevertheless established strong emotional ties with their Turkish origins, often built around their religious identity as Muslims. This identification with Islam and the social and cultural environment of Turkish housing areas, resembling so-called ethnic enclaves, offer positive points of reference which stand in sharp contrast to the hostile world outside. Although cultural border-crossings may prove extreme-ly enriching for highly educated and fully integrated Turkish residents, for others they constitute an increasing sense of ambivalence and insecurity. The consequence is not a fruitful exchange of cultures, but, more often, a persistence of cultural segregation.

Moreover, the Turkish minority in Germany, due to its insecure legal status, faces a far more difficult situation than does the South Asian diaspora in Great Britain, the USA, Canada and Australia. In these countries, ethnic diversity is being promoted and endorsed by a politics of multiculturalism, affirmative action and anti-discrimination laws. Kürsat–Ahlers rightly points out that a society does not

---

[23] According to research conducted in Berlin, 34% of young Turks had no contact and 30% only occasional contact, while 30% reported frequent contact with Germans. See Kürsat–Ahlers, "The Turkish Minority," 117.

automatically qualify as multicultural simply because it contains large numbers of ethnic minorities. In Germany, the concept of multiculturalism was only introduced into political debates in the late 1980s, and even then it did not have any real effect on Germany's official self-image as a homogeneous society.

The authors of *Länderbericht Türkei* discuss this issue in relation to Germany's principle of *ius sanguinis*, which is responsible for the shaky legal status of those migrants of the second and third generations. Despite having been born in Germany or having grown up in this country, these Turks are not automatically considered citizens of this country (as is the case in countries like France, which applies *ius soli*). Although they have never lived in any country but Germany, they remain foreigners, *Ausländer*. They are holders of a residence permit which is unlimited in theory but may be cancelled at any time. In extreme circumstances they might have to face expulsion. Until recently, any demand to legalize the status of Turkish migrants of the second and third generation was rejected by the federal government, which argued that such a regulation could only be valid in a country of immigration, a label that did not apply to Germany. In 1998, though, the new coalition government between the SPD and the Environmental Party agreed to at least partly modify naturalization regulations. In order to facilitate the naturalization and integration of Turkish migrants, children of foreign parents may be accorded full citizenship if at least one parent was born in Germany or immigrated to Germany before his or her fourteenth birthday. Yet this citizenship is still not accorded automatically. Candidates have to opt for either Turkish or German citizenship, as dual citizenship is not accepted by German law.[24] Only in 2001 did the pressing need for skilled workers in Germany's booming high-tech economy induce the major political parties of Germany to finally agree to adopt an official definition of Germany as a country of immigration. However, the immigration law (*Zuwan-*

---

[24] See Akkaya, Özbek & Şen, *Länderbericht Türkei*, 312.

derungsgesetz) passed on 22 March 2002 is in many aspects restricted to immigrants qualifying as highly skilled professionals, who may be naturalized after a period of ten years of uninterrupted residency in Germany.[25]

The adoption of the term 'multicultural' has so far only been a "question of semantic change," as it has not yet led to any considerable sociocultural change or political redefinition of the concept of nation.[26] Thus, as Haselbach argues, "it makes sense to distinguish between multiculturality (ie, the makeup of society in its ethnic and cultural mix) and multiculturalism (that is, actual political policies arising from multiculturality)."[27] Yet the prevalent discourse on foreigners and 'Others' in German culture and society as well as the increase in ethnic tension and conflict (open attacks on foreigners motivated by racism and xenophobia) clearly show that the idea of multiculturalism has not yet taken root in German political and cultural consciousness. Politically, the Turks of Germany are denied most of the rights that full citizenship would guarantee. At the same time, multiculturalism is both a reality and a tourist bonus. The demography of cities like Cologne or Berlin with the multicultural composition of such quarters as Kreuzberg in Berlin and "Little Istanbul" in Cologne's "Neuköln" reflects the indisputable character of multiethnic Germany. Local governments do not hesitate to appropriate the cultural diversity created by the Turkish community as tourist attractions and celebrate a multicultural ambience which is belied by the insecure legal situation of today's Turkish migrants.

The new German-Turkish literature takes up these contradictions by positively re-casting the fact of belonging 'neither here nor there' in

---

[25] See
http://www.bundesregierung.de/top/dokumente/Artikel/ix_70428.htm.

[26] See Kürsat–Ahlers, "The Turkish Minority," 114.

[27] Dieter Haselbach, "Multicultural Reality and the Problem of German Identity," in *Multiculturalism in a World of Leaking Boundaries*, ed. Dieter Haselbach (Münster: LIT, 1998): 211.

the mould of multicultural and hyphenated identities. These alternative
identities, which emerge as integral parts of the Turkish diaspora community, are not represented as inferior to the national concepts of
German or Turkish identity. Nor is cultural assimilation regarded as a
necessary prerequisite for successful integration. The new diaspora
literature thus offers positive models of identification, making way for
a cultural and linguistic diversity which ultimately contributes to the
formation of Germany as a multicultural society.

The Turkish-German Literature of Diaspora: *Gastarbeiterliteratur* of the 1960s to Turkish-German Literature of the 1990s[28]

Works by today's Turkish-German writers have become of interest to
foreign scholars working on German literature, who place them within
the broad context of global diaspora writings.[29] This context has to a
large extent been ignored by German scholars in Germany, among
whom the recent flood of literary production has sparked very little
interest. Instead, scholars in departments of German literature still
apply the term 'migrant minority literature', thus allocating to these
writers a marginal role in the production of German literature. By analogy with the lack of acceptance and recognition of Turks as full mem-

---

[28] There are numerous publications which discuss the authors of the "Gastarbeiterliteratur" or "Migrantenliteratur" of the 1960s to 1980s. For further
reference, see Hartmut Heinze, *Migrantenliteratur in der Bundesrepublik*
(Berlin: Express, 1986); *Kalte Heimat*, ed. Karen König & Hanne Straub
(Reinbek bei Hamburg: Rowohlt, 1984); Anna Picardi–Montesardo, *Die Gastarbeiter in der Literatur der Bundesrepublik Deutschland* (Berlin: Express,
1985); Ulrike Reeg, *Schreiben in der Fremde* (Essen: Klartext, 1988); and
Eine nicht nur deutsche Literatur, ed. Irmgard Ackermann & Harald Weinrich
(Munich: Piper, 1986).

[29] See, for example, the course on "Multiculturalism in Germany" offered
by the German Faculty of the University of Michigan: www.rc.lsa.umich.
edu/programs/german/amulti.htm, Online 23/10/00.

bers of German society, this absence of interest in their literature
renders the Turkish minority literarily invisible and subject to a
totalizing German discourse which defines and objectifies 'the Other'
along categories (white/non-white, German/foreigner) which leave no
room for fruitful dialogue. 'The Other' is silenced in favour of a
monocultural and monodiscursive paradigm.[30] As Azade Seyhan
states,

> in the institutional treatment of Germanistik both in this country
> [USA] and in Europe there is very little acknowledgement of the
> multicultural intervention in established literary scholarship by the
> growing numbers of ethnic minorities – Turks, Yugoslavs, Greeks,
> Spaniards, Italians, Portuguese. The politicisation of the minority
> question in West Germany, the emergence of relatively established
> minority organizations, the aggressive, self-styled participation of
> minority artists and writers in the cultural sphere, and the political
> tensions that accompanies the emerging visibility of the ethnic sign
> have left only a marginal and aleatory trace in the German
> curriculum.[31]

Consequently, the Italian Germanist Immacolata Amodeo blames German studies for their silence on the literary quality of the work of
immigrant writers,[32] and Russel Berman claims that it is "not much of
an exaggeration to claim that German literary studies still gives
priority to the 'white boys of Weimar' or subsequent authors who fit
the mould."[33] Apparently, what has been completely overlooked by
these German critics is the drastic paradigm shift – on the thematic as

---

[30] Compare Azade Seyhan, "Introduction" to *New German Critique* 46
(special issue on "Minorities in German Culture"; 1989): 4–5.

[31] Seyhan, "Introduction," 5.

[32] "Schweigen über die Ästhetik der Literatur ausländischer Autoren in der
Bundesrepublik"; Immacolata Amodeo, *"Die Heimat heisst Babylon": Zur
Literatur ausländischer Autoren in der Bundesrepublik* (Opladen: West-
deutscher Verlag, 1996): 199, quoted in Marilya Veteto–Conrad, "'Innere Un-
ruhe'? Zehra Çirak and Minority Literature Today," *Rocky Mountains Review*
(Fall 1999): 59.

[33] Russel Berman, quoted in Seyhan, "Introduction," 5.

well as literary level – in the fictional works of Turkish-German writers between the 1970s and 1980s and the generation of the 1990s. Veteto–Conrad highlights a development in German-language literature which is marked by a move away from the early genre of *Betroffenheitsliteratur*[34] ('literature of the affected'), which was often interpreted as symptomatic of Turkish inability to integrate and adjust to German culture.

This paradigm shift is discussed in detail by Veteto–Conrad in her study *Finding a Voice* (1996) in which she deals with the works of German-language Turkish writers up to 1990. She sets out with a presentation of *Gastarbeiterliteratur* or *Betroffenheitsliteratur*, which focused on the destiny and plight of the marginalized Turkish migrants in a German society that was neither prepared nor willing to integrate these foreigners into their social lives.[35] Most of this literature was

---

[34] This term was coined by Franco Biondi and Rafik Schami in their essay "Literatur der Betroffenen," in *Zu Hause in der Fremde: Ein bundesdeutsches Ausländer-Lesebuch*, ed. Christina Schaffernicht (1981; Reinbeck: Rowohlt, 1984): 136–50. In 1980, Biondi and Schami were the central figures in setting up the so-called PoLi-Kunstverein ('Polynationaler Literatur- und Kunstverein') and the publishing collective Südwind, who organized a series of anthologies of literary texts in German by immigrant writers. See Robert Burns, "Images of Alterity: Second Generation Turks in the Federal Republic," *Modern Language Review* 94.3 (1999): 744.n1.

[35] Cf Wolfgang Riemann's bibliography *Über das Leben in Bitterland* [On Life in Bitterland], which lists works of German-Turkish literature and Turkish literature in Germany from the turn of the nineteenth/twentieth century to the late 1980s. The author eschews the terms *Gastarbeiter-Literatur* ('guest workers' literature'), *Migrantenliteratur* ('migrant literature') or *Ausländerliteratur* ('foreigners' literature') and employs the more neutral term *Deutschland-Literatur* ('Germany Literature'), in order to indicate the fact that recent German-Turkish authors have shifted their thematic preoccupation from the figure of the *Gastarbeiter* to broader subjects. He cites the following works: Aras Ören, *Eine verspätete Abrechnung oder der Aufstieg der Gündogus* (1988), and Güney Dal, *Der enthaarte Affe* (1988). Wolfgang Riemann, *Über das Leben in Bitterland: Bibliographie zur türkischen Deutschland Literatur und zur türkischen Literatur in Deutschland* (Wiesbaden: Otto Harrassowitz, 1990): vii–xx.

originally written in Turkish and then very often translated into German by dilettante translators, so that its significance related mostly to its biographical content and sociopolitical implication rather than its literary value.[36] The authors of this first generation clearly addressed their works to 'the Other': ie, the non-*Gastarbeiter*. It served to inform mainstream Germans about the economic misery, the crisis of identity and the cultural confusion experienced by the Turkish migrant worker. They especially foregrounded the 'clash of civilizations' which they experienced, for these early guest workers did not have anything in common with their new host country. They encountered a new language, completely different from their mother tongue,[37] a new religion, a new life-style that was modern and urban whereas the migrants' home environment had been extremely traditional and even part of a backward rural society characterized by a low literacy rate. But, most important of all, they encountered a German culture that was not prepared to accept all these people in the first place.

This inhospitability on the part of their host country, expressed in the term *"Bitterland,"* became a central concern of the writers of the first generation, among whom Aras Ören stands out as the most representative and prolific. His concern with the social problems of the Turkish working class in Germany aligns his texts with what could be

---

[36] Veteto–Conrad criticizes this attitude by quoting an article by Klaus Frain, "Genervt von Herkunftsfragen," on Çirak, Ören and Şenocak, in Berlin's *zitty* magazine (December 1996): 28–31. However, at the same time, Veteto–Conrad acknowledges that many non-German authors who published their works in the 1980s, did not in fact have sufficiently "mature literary ability," so that reception tended to be sociocultural rather than based on literary criteria. See Veteto–Conrad, "Zehra Çirak and Minority Literature Today," 59.

[37] The Turkish language is a non-Indo-European language. It is characterized by certain peculiar morphophonemic, morphotactic, and syntactic features: vowel harmony, agglutination of all suffixing morphemes, free order of constituents, and head-final phrase structure – all of these untypical of Indo-European languages.

called proletarian literature.[38] Another early Turkish writer is Saliha
Scheinhardt, an Anatolian woman who came to Germany with her
German fiancé at the age of seventeen, and who has, in her chiefly
semi-biographical work, focused on the aspect of cultural segregation
experienced by young women and girls. Her concentration on the fate
of Turkish women, however, carries the risk of perpetuating many of
the current clichés, which are neither realistic nor helpful to the cause
of the emancipation of Turkish women.[39] Veteto–Conrad also discusses the works of Turks of the second generation who have not only
chosen German as their medium of literary expression but increasingly
reject the labels of *Gastarbeiter* and migrant literature, claiming that
these categorizations of Turkish-German authors ultimately support a
ghettoization of Turks in terms of 'otherness': ie, as different from
mainstream authors.[40] As Veteto–Conrad points out, today's Turkish
community is essentially heterogeneous, which makes it difficult to
systematize their literature.⎡ It seems as if Turks do not have much in
common apart from their cultural background. However, the issue of
cultural identity in all its facets remains a decisive factor in the lives
and literature of these 'new' Turkish writers, who have started to

---

[38] See Marilya Veteto–Conrad, *Finding a Voice: Identity and the Works of
German-Language Turkish Writers in the Federal Republic of Germany to
1990* (New York: Peter Lang, 1996): 13–20.

[39] Veteto–Conrad strongly attacks Scheinhardt for the pathos in her semi-
autobiographical stories, which "despite their established allure for German
audiences, does the women whose lives she has documented [...] no favors,"
in Veteto–Conrad, *Finding a Voice*, 66.

[40] Compare Veteto–Conrad, *Finding a Voice*, 23–25. This 'ghettoization'
was also unwittingly furthered by the publication of three anthologies of work
by Turkish authors, whose exclusivity and titles suggest a focus on the Turkish
migrant's peripheral and marginal existence. See the following, all edited by
Irmgard Ackermann and issued by the Deutscher Taschenbuchverlag in
Munich: *Als Fremder in Deutschland* (1983); *In Zwei Sprachen leben* (1983);
Türken deutscher Sprache: Berichte, Erzählungen, Gedichte von Ausländern
(1984).

adopt the diasporic German-Turkish identities of people "who root themselves in ideas rather than in places."[41]

Today's most prominent authors who have either made a conscious choice to use German as their literary language, or for whom German is actually their first language, such as the women writers Aysel Özakin, Alev Tekinay, Emine Sevgi Özdamar and Zehra Çirak, or the male authors Kemal Kurt, Feridun Zaimoğlu and Zafer Şenocak, to name but a few, are no longer part of the original 'old, exclusive diaspora' of the first generation of Turkish migrants. They constitute the new Turkish "diaspora of the border." Unlike the first generation of Turkish writers, today's German writers of Turkish origins claim for their writing the status of any other literature in the German language. Their texts do not only deal with the problems of migrant experience of the first Turkish guest workers, although the fear and insecurity engendered by social exclusion clearly affects all generations.[42] The sense of the cultural dislocation of her parents' generation becomes, for example, the subject of Renan Demirkan's *Schwarzer Tee mit drei Stück Zucker* ('Tea with three lumps of sugar', 1991). Yet the majority of today's writers are less concerned with the question of 'roots' and 'origins'. Rather, they are making an active contribution towards redefining German culture and society as multicultural. Against the foil of perceiving German identity as an essentially heterogeneous, multinational and multi-ethnic concept,[43] these writers do not understand themselves or their protagonists as being alienated from German society. As Veteto–Conrad puts it, "the issue is not whether they belong in Germany, but how to adjust to the fact of belonging." [44]

All of the writers listed above, but especially Özdamar, Zaimoğlu and Şenocak, belong to a cosmopolitan group of 'axial writers' who, according to the definition suggested by Cheesman, are authors whose

---

[41] Seyhan, "Paranational Community/Hyphenated Identity," 1.

[42] See Burns,"Images of Alterity," 744.

[43] See Veteto–Conrad, *Finding a Voice*, 49.

[44] Veteto–Conrad, *Finding a Voice*, 49.

> biographical [background] includes different countries of childhood
> and adult residence; family histories of migration; and a travelling
> professional life, in which time is regularly divided between two or
> more localities which are connected by axes of historical and
> contemporary diaspora movements.[45]

In Great Britain, axial writers like Salman Rushdie and Hanif Kureishi
were crucial in triggering the boom of South Asian writing in English.
These writers, together with axial intellectual critics such as Stuart
Hall, Paul Gilroy, Homi Bhabha and Clifford Geertz as well as the
American philosopher Charles Taylor,[46] have made important contributions to the ongoing debate on multicultural and cosmopolitan
issues. The extent of their influence on shaping contemporary British
society and culture as that of a multicultural one becomes visible in the
shift they brought about in the critical and policy discourses in Britain's leading cultural institutions. These no longer employ the mar-
ginalizing term "ethnic minority," but that of "cultural diversity."[47]
Moreover, this development is reflected in a project launched by the
British Council entitled "Re-Inventing Britain," which contains a
manifesto by Homi Bhabha. According to Bhabha, the new cosmopolitanism has already rendered the problem of identity passé and
poses other more urgent questions, such as citizenship in a context of a

---

[45] Cheesman, "Axial Writings: Transnational literary/media cultures and
cultural policy," http://www.transcomm.ox.ac.uk/wwwroot/cheesman.htm.
Online 09/10/00: 3.

[46] See Lothar Bredella, "Human Rights and Understanding Foreign Cultures Between Relativism and Universalism," in Haselbach, *Multiculturalism*,
251–77.

[47] The change in German-Turkish literature is nicely captured in the expression "from 'Pappkoffer' [suitcase made of cardboard] to Pluralism," part
of the title of an essay on the development of migrant writing in the Germany.
See Sabine Fischer & Moray McGowan, "From Pappkoffer to Pluralism: On
the Development of Migrant Writing in the German Federal Republic," in
Turkish Culture in German Society Today, ed. David Horrocks & Eva
Kolinsky (Providence RI & Oxford: Berghahn, 1996): 1–22.

transnational migration or the relation between 'consensus' and 'community' within secular intellectual culture.[48]

A similar shift is taking place in Germany. Since the beginning of the 1990s, German writers of predominantly Turkish origin have for the first time won national and international prizes. Emine Sevgi Özdamar received the prestigious Ingeborg Bachmann Prize in 1991 for her novel *Das Leben ist eine Karawanserei, hat zwei Türen, aus einer kam ich rein, aus der anderen ging ich raus* (1992) ('Life is a Caravanserai') and Zehra Çirak won the Hölderlin Prize for poetry in 1994. The broad range of German-Turkish writers is reflected in the numerous literary and artistic genres: Akif Pirinçci has specialized in crime novels; Zehra Çirak and Dilek Zaptçioğlu represent the lyric female voice; Emine Sevgi Özdamar is not only a novelist and playwright but also an actress. Osman Engin is a cabaret artist and a satirical novelist. Other young authors – Selim Özdağan, author of Western-style road novels, Renan Demirkan, and Kemal Kurt, with his celebration of global and cosmopolitan culture in his novel *Ja, sagt Molly* ('Yes, says Molly', 1998) – have become role models for the younger generation of Turks. As well as this, Aras Ören and Güney Dal, although they write in Turkish, have had a substantial impact on German literature. Last but not least, there is Zafer Şenocak, poet, essayist and novelist, and Feridun Zaimoğlu, *l'enfant terrible* of contemporary German literature. The diversity of the themes and genres deployed by these authors testifies to their successful escape from the cultural ghetto to which they had previously been confined. Especially the works of Şenocak, Zaimoğlu and Özdamar, which have been translated into other European languages and were reviewed in journals like *Newsweek* and the *Economist*, have shaped the literary landscape of Germany.[49] However, whereas the German cultural em-

---

[48] Cheesman, "Axial Writings," 5.

[49] See Tom Cheesman & Deniz Göktürk, "German Titles, Turkish Names: The Cosmopolitan Will," www.new-books-in-german.com/feature3.htm. Online 09/10/00: 1.

bassies and the Goethe-Institut have recognized the growing interest in these writers abroad, appropriating them as cultural ambassadors of the 'multicultural metropoles' of Germany, the political recognition of these writers and their fellow compatriots remains a highly problematic and sad affair.

Multicultural Identity in Zafer Şenocak's *Gefährliche Verwandtschaft*: "I'm the son of culprits and victims"

Gefährliche Verwandtschaft ('Dangerous Relations',' 1998) is a hybrid novel that combines a major plot with other narrative subplots, all of which are additionally commented upon by the insertion of texts presented in the form of flyers, testimonials and interviews with Turkish-German migrants, excerpts from diaries, bits and pieces of statistics, economic newspaper reports, and historical reports (eg, biographical details about Kemal Mustafa Atatürk, the demolition of the Berlin Wall and German reunification), as well as passages from private letters, essays, aphorisms, etc.[50]

The frame-narrative focuses on the present life of the first-person narrator Sasha, a writer of Turkish-German-Jewish origins and a fictional alter ego of the author. The novel starts with Sasha's visit to a notary in Munich. At the occasion of the reading of his parents' will, he receives a heavy silver box, formerly in possession of his parents, which contains twenty diaries of his grandfather, all written in Arabic and Cyrillic script and dating from 1916 to 1936. These diaries trigger the narrator's decision to write a novel about his Turkish grandfather, although he is not able to decipher the diaries. He speaks no Turkish, and even if he did, he would not be able to decipher the Arabic script. He thus experiences a double alienation from his grandfather, which is due not only to his ignorance of the Turkish language but also to the

---

[50] Cf the German montage novel of the 1960s and 1970s.

fact that the birth of the modern Turkish Republic involved a drastic rupture with its Ottoman (Arabic-Persian) tradition. At the same time, while the narrator sets himself the task of writing a novel, the novel develops into a rewriting of German and European history seen from the perspective of a Turkish-German-Jewish cosmopolitan. This task not only presents a challenge to the established historical truth, but also forces the author–narrator to face the history of his own origins.

The fictional re-invention of his grandfather's life, focusing on the years around the birth of the Turkish Republic, becomes a reflection of the narrator's own quest for identity. This quest is revealed as an attempt to fix himself and others in particular frames of reference, creating closeness and distance between people that will ultimately determine their identity. The narrator's confrontation with his own past is seen as a painful but unavoidable process. The loss of his family and the degree of alienation from his father, reiterating the alienation between his grandfather and his son, the narrator's father, is overcome by a concept of identity that makes up for the experience of loss and provides him in turn with the stability, comfort and intimacy that the family had supplied in his childhood.

Thus, the narrator's identity is located at the interstices of cultures. Neither German nor Turkish, his identity is not defined on the basis of a determinable geographical territory, but resembles the cross-woven pattern of the peregrinations of a migrant who continues to oscillate between Istanbul, Berlin, Munich and the USA. In the meantime, the narrator's girlfriend Marie is busy reconstructing the historical past of the same period. She is working on a documentary that centres on the biography of Talat Pasha, an important figure in the history of the Turkish Republic. Unlike her boyfriend, who has always preferred the "private side of history," Marie is obsessed with finding the "truth" about the historical protagonist. While she does research in libraries and archives and travels to historical places in order to interview witnesses or at least relatives of witnesses, the narrator, who is at first reluctant to have the diaries translated, decides to use these private letters and notes as well as conversations with friends as his sources of inspiration.

This main story is continually interrupted by numerous flashbacks to previous events in the writer's life (childhood, early adulthood, his exile as writer in residence in the USA, anecdotes and stories from his family's past) which provide insights into the lives of his Turkish grandfather (his father's father, whose story parallels that of Talat Pasha and his "*Opa*" or grandfather: ie, his mother's Jewish father). The novel thus tells not just one story, but several, which are inter-linked and resemble a set of Chinese boxes, with one story embedded in the next one. In addition, the narrator provides numerous meta-fictional comments in which he discusses the process of writing the novel.

The re-construction or, better, re-invention of his own history is exemplified by the sentence "I am a grandson of victims and culprits!" The "victim" side refers to his mother's father, his "*Opa*," which is a German affectionate form of address, equivalent to the English "Grandad." As a member of the Jewish-German bourgeois merchant class, he lived in Munich before Hitler and his antisemitic politics forced him to emigrate to Istanbul in 1934. In Istanbul he belonged to the fast-increasing exile community of German refugees, who played an important part in the modernization of the young Turkish Republic. Religion, though traditionally regarded as part of the cultural heritage and identity, was far less important than the pride the narrator's *Opa* took in their humanist tradition, represented by the great works of German literature. It is this humanist heritage that the first-person narrator feels indebted to and not the Arabic-Persian-Turkish tradition from which he was cut off because of his residence in Germany. Whereas his mother's father managed to rescue the family through early emigration, all of the other family members on his mother's side became victims of the Holocaust. The narrator's mother grew up in Istanbul, got married to a Turk (the narrator's father), and both returned to Germany in 1954 to join the rest of the family.

The "culprit" side refers to his father's father, his grandfather, who
was one of the leaders responsible for the Armenian deportation. To
him, the narrator has but a very distant relationship, which is expressed in the much more formal form of address, namely *"Grossvater"*
('Grandfather'). Owing to his grandfather's early death in 1936 and
the lack of information, the narrator's knowledge about his grandfather
remained very incomplete. Only the receipt of his grandfather's diaries
eventually awakens his interest in reconstructing his grandfather's life.
In the course of the novel, the narrator gradually puts together the
fabric of his 'novel-to-be written'. While doing so, the author–narrator
compares this process of writing to his grandfather's diary. Whereas a
diary reveals what the writer wants to keep secret from prying eyes,
the novel provides the opportunity for the writer, his protagonists and
the reader to invent themselves. This is exactly what is happening in
the present novel: the author–narrator re-creates and re-invents himself
in the act of writing, as he manages to acquaint the reader with his
family history, which, in turn, consists of re-invented fictional biographies. Through the particular way in which the author–narrator
links the different strands of narratives, interweaving private and historical biographies, he achieves a Rushdie-esque "chutnification of
history."[51] As a result, the narrator not only proposes to write his
grandfather's and his family's story but at the same time attempts to
re-write Turkish and German history. As the narrative proceeds, the
Jewish-German diaspora becomes aligned with the Turkish-German
diaspora of the present time. Hereupon, the narrator's friend, Heinrich,
an expert in the Jewish-German history of the nineteenth century,
makes the following striking remark: "Die Deutschen haben nichts aus

---

[51] Compare the narrator-figure Saleem Sinai, born on the stroke of midnight at the instant of India's independence, who tells his own private version
of the history of the young Indian nation. While doing so, he equates the
making of pickles with the preservation of time and history, "the feasibility of
the chutnification of history; the grand hope of the pickling of time!" Salman
Rushdie, *Midnight's Children* (1981; London: Picador, 1982): 459.

der Geschichte gelernt […] jetzt haben sie sich die Türken ins Land geholt. Dabei sind sie noch nicht einmal mit den Juden zurecht-gekommen."[52]

Yet the narrator is not only concerned with Germany's and Turkey's contemporary or recent history, but is also interested in the history of the Ottoman Empire – a heterogeneous empire which had guaranteed the coexistence of different peoples and religions for 800 years – and the fundamental role it played in Western European history. The foregrounding of this 'other' side of the coin of Turkish history is set against the 'official' European history, according to which the Turks had been represented with negative terms such as *Türkenangst* (Turkish scare) and *Türkenjoch* (Turkish oppression). This biased representation of the Turkish 'Other' wholly excludes the long history of tolerance, peace and cultural achievement characteriz-ing the Ottoman regime. The narrator therefore suggests an alternative view of history by focusing on the similarities, not the differences, in Turkey's and Germany's history. Consequently, he deems the break of modern Turkey with its Ottoman tradition to have been as drastic and severe as the partition of Germany, or argues that the founding of the Turkish Republic, which resulted in the deportation and the genocide of Turkey's Armenian population, may be compared to Nazi Germany and its genocide against the Jews.[53]

By equating seemingly disjunct and distant histories, the intention of the author–narrator is revealed as an attempt to reconstruct and re-narrativize European history. This history eschews separation between 'East' and 'West'; instead, it highlights the extent to which the Jewish diaspora, on the one hand, and the Turkish diaspora, on the other, have interbraided German and Turkish history. Ultimately, this crossing and

---

[52] Zafer Şenocak, *Gefährliche Verwandtschaft* (Munich: Babel, 1998): 82: "The Germans have not learned anything from history […] now they have brought the Turks to their country, yet they couldn't even get along with the Jews." Translations in the following are my own.

[53] Senocak, *Gefährliche Verwandtschaft*, 75.

mixing of histories constructs German history and cultural identity as being fundamentally multicultural. According to the narrator, this would not only allow for a German-Turkish dialogue to take place, but would make it possible to imagine a tri-cultural exchange between Germans, Jews and Turks, or Christians, Jews and Muslims.[54] The narrator proceeds to argue that the dissolution of the German-Jewish or, rather, German-Turkish dichotomy would actually liberate both sides from their respective victim and culprit trauma.

The break with historical, racist and religious stereotypes is taken up again on a metanarrative level. At the heart of the novel, we are presented with four 'seemingly' non-fictional statements by Turkish migrants of the second and third generation. All of them propose a definition of German society, of which they consider themselves to be an integral and vital part. In his *"Rede an die Deutschen"* ('Speech to the Germans'), the first speaker, a broker called Ali, claims to be the rightful successor to the present German generation. Turning the tables on the Germans, he assumes that the former guest workers have by now surpassed their former masters, whom they are about to replace: "Wir sind die Deutschen von morgen. Nieten seid ihr, fett und ängstlich, macht Platz, wir kommen."[55] Kamile, a fashion designer, describes herself as bi-cultural, which has allowed her to grow up as an emancipated German woman, whereas her Turkish self has re-mained the child of her parents. The author, Zafer himself, confronts the reader with an account of his childhood. His autobiographical essay describes his experience of 'otherness' on his first arrival in Germany. However, as the author acknowledges, once the foreignness of the other culture and language wore off, he was never troubled by questions of whether or not Germany was his home: "Wenn man ein

---

[54] Senocak, *Gefährliche Verwandtschaft*, 89–90.

[55] Senocak, *Gefährliche Verwandtschaft*, 96: "We are the Germans of tomorrow. You're a bunch of losers, fat and scared; get out of the way, here we come."

geborgenes Zuhause hat, wird die Frage, wo dieses Haus steht, uner-
heblich. Unser Haus stand in Deutschland."[56]

On the fictional level, the first-person narrator breaks with another
set of stereotypical expectations on the part of the reader. His narrator
is not a merely autobiographical portrait of the author (compare the
narrator's self-description, 69). His mother-tongue is not Turkish, but
German. The author–narrator claims he does not even speak Turkish,
as he is one of those second-generation Turkish migrants who – thanks
to the intellectual, cultural and germanophile background of their
parents – grew up with German as their first language. He is not even a
'pure' Turk, which deconstructs another stereotype, but the son of a
cross-cultural, cross-racial and cross-religious couple, with his mother
being a secularized Jew (more German than the Germans themselves)
and his father coming from one of the prestigious Turkish bourgeois
families of Istanbul. Thus, Turkey is not his 'mother country' – the
Turkish always use the female 'anadolu' – but his 'father country',
which corresponds to the German 'Vaterland'. Born in Munich, but
conceived in Istanbul and of Turkish-German-Jewish origin, the
narrator–author now moves between Istanbul, Berlin, Munich and the
USA. This mobility has turned him into a true transnational or 'axial'
writer. In his search for his origins, which may give his life stability,
he is no longer confined to one geographical location, but constantly
oscillates between cultures.

Zafer Şenocak, as this analysis illustrates, is the representative of a
new multicultural discourse of Turkish-German hybrid writers in
which the boundaries of fiction and reality are blurred. The concept of
an alternative German identity is mirrored in the form of the novel.[57]

---

[56] Senocak, *Gefährliche Verwandtschaft*, 105: "If you've got a safe home,
it doesn't matter where this house is located. Our house was in Germany."

[57] Another example of this hybridizing process can be found in Alev
Tekinay's *Nur der Hauch vom Paradies* ('Just a Whiff of Paradise'), where
his first-person narrator Engin writes an autobiographical prose work. The narrator not only develops a positive attitude towards his origins: ie, Turkish

Feridun Zaimoğlu: *Kanaksprak*:
Ethnic identity and 'süppkültür' of the 'Kanakster'

Feridun Zaimoğlu regards himself as a literary advocate of the 'Kanakster',[58] a term derived from the German pejorative slang expression 'Kanake' for Turks. Zaimoğlu himself describes his work as that of a chronicler who records the struggles of Turkish migrants of the second and third generation. With his books *Kanaksprak: 24 Misstöne vom Rande der Gesellschaft* ('Kanak-Speak: 24 Discords from the Margins of Society', 1995), *Abschaum – Die wahre Geschichte des Ertan Ongun* ('Scum: The True Story of Ertan Ongun', 1997)[59] and *Koppstoff: Kanaka Sprak vom Rande der Gesellschaft* ('Headcloth: Kanakasprak from the Margins of Society,' 1998), he has established himself as the mouthpiece of those Turkish migrants who have not managed full integration into Germany, where they are despised and stigmatized as

---

language and culture, but is additionally converted to a specific multicultural philosophy which is finely expressed in the following metaphorical image: "Unsere Wurzeln sind in der Türkei und unsere Blüten gehen in Deutschland auf, einem Baum, der Schmerzen hat, weil er sich ständig fast 3.000 Kilometer biegen muß, von den Wurzeln zu den Blüten" ('Our roots are in Turkey but we are blossoming in Germany, [we are] a tree in agony, which has to keep stretching over a distance of 3,000 kilometres, from its roots to its blossoms'); Alev Tekinay, *Nur der Hauch vom Paradies* (Frankfurt am Main: Brandes & Apsel, 1993): 94, quoted in Burns, "Images of Alterity," 755.

[58] Feridun Zaimoğlu is one of the founders of a politico-cultural movement of Turkish migrants of the second and third generation, called Kanak-Attak. The members of Kanak-Attak fight against all forms of racism and discrimination in Germany. See "Manifesto," www.kanak-attak.de/main. htm. Online 11/09/2001.

[59] *Abschaum* tells the story of the criminal Ertan Ongun and his tragic downfall, leaving him entangled in drugs, deaths, prison and tears. In the meantime, Ertan Ongun has become a kind of model anti-hero for the young Turkish migrant community, who even address their fan-post to Zaimoğlu's protagonist.

"Kanaken."[60] Yet in Turkey they are labelled *alamancılar* (*'Deutsch-länder'*), who, because of their inadequate knowledge of Turkish and their cultural alienation from their parents' and grandparents' home-land (which most of them have only visited during their annual summer vacation), are discriminated against as people 'who do not belong'. As a result, these 'Kanakster' do not identify either with their parents' and grandparents' generation or with their 'original home country' Turkey. Zaimoğlu's *Kanaksprak* contains a series of testi-monials which give voice to the beliefs, fears, opinions, desires and, above all, aggressions and frustrations of present-day Turkish migrant society. True to his self-image as chronicler, Zaimoğlu goes out into the streets, bars, discos and other public spaces, where he meets the interview partners whose stories he records. The type of language used in these testimonials is Zaimoğlu's ingenious literary re-creation of "kanaksprak"[61] – a pseudo-oral[62] adaptation of the Turkish migrant

---

[60] See "'Was deutsch ist, bestimmen wir': Dokumentation der Talkshow III nach neun (N3) mit Feridun Zaimoğlu, Heide Simonis, Wolf Biermann, Norbert Blum und Harald Juhnke," *iz₃w* (Februar–März 2000): 39.

[61] Zaimoğlu defines 'kanaksprak' in his introduction to his work, explain-ing the traps of orientalist folklore he had to avoid in order to render the talk of his interview partners as authentically as possible. 'Kanaksprak' is described as a kind of creole with secret codes and signals, related to the "Free-Style Sermon in rap-music." The 'Kanakster' speaks his own mother tongue badly, and is hardly fluent in German either. His vocabulary thus consists of a mish-mash of words and expressions which exist in neither of the two languages. His talk is accompanied by a rich language of gestures and symbolic signs, giving evidence of his physical presence. See Zaimoğlu, *Kanaksprak*, 12–14.

[62] Pseudo-orality in literary communication designates the use of typically oral and written linguistic strategies to convey a sense of orality. Although it may be highly suggestive of spokenness by featuring typical linguistic patterns of speech, it contrasts sharply with the spontaneous and unplanned nature of oral discourse. The literary representation of oral discourse will always remain an 'imperfect', artificial version of real-life speech. For further reading, see Paul Goetsch, "Fingierte Mündlichkeit in der Erzählkunst entwickelter Schrift-kulturen," *Poetica* 17.3–4 (1985): 202–18, and *Mündliches Erzählen im*

ethnolectal form of Turkish-German speech, called 'Kanakensprache' or *Türkendeutsch*, a mixture of standard Turkish, colloquial Anatolian dialect and colloquial and slang German.[63] Zaimoğlu claims that his poetic imitation of the 'kanaksprak' pursues the aim of creating an authentic linguistic image which may, in contrast to the so-called *Immigrantenliteratur*, give the 'Kanake' his own language and voice in literature.

In *Kanaksprak*, the author concentrates on the male subculture of the criminal milieu in the Kanakster ghettos located in Kiel, which is also supported by the lack of variety in the depiction of the protagonists' speech characteristics. His interview partners are neither the friendly assimilated Turkish neighbour of the "Ali-type,"[64] nor the intellectual, highly educated academic. The voices represented come from the members of a third generation of Turks who live on the margins of both societies. As part of a Kanakster subculture, they are rappers, break-dancers, unemployed loafers, travelling merchants at flea-markets, prostitutes, homo- and transsexuals, patients in psychiatric asylums, etc. Only two testimonials by a poet and a sociologist – presumably semi-fictional alter egos of the author – stand out, as they are phrased almost in standard German.

Disillusioned with German society, these *alamancılar* Turks of the third generation ("*Alemannen*" in Zaimoğlu's poetic adaptation) have started to adopt the negative heterostereotypes of German society in order to distinguish their identity from the type of the "good Ali"

Alltag, fingiertes mündliches Erzählen in der Literatur, ed. Willi Erzgräber & Paul Goetsch (Tübingen: Gunter Narr, 1987).

[63] For further information on linguistic features of frequent patterns of non-native German, often called '*Türkendeutsch*', see Jannis Androutsopoulos, "From the Streets to the Screens and Back Again: On the mediated diffusion of ethnolectal patterns in contemporary German," paper presented to the ICLaVE I Conference, Barcelona, 29 June 2000, draft version, date of online publication: 3 August 2000, http://www.rzuser,uni-heidelberg.de/~iandrout/papers/iclavedraft.html. Online 21/11/2000: 1-15.

[64] Zaimoğlu, *Kanaksprak*, 31.

whose assimilation has turned him into a slave. Accused of behaving like "bonitos" or "apes," as they are content to mimic the life-style of the Germans, the assimilated Turks are despised for having succumbed to the 'slave's' desire to become like their 'masters.' Ali is rather blunt about the behaviour of these assimilated Turks, "weil er sich dem Einheimischen zwischen die ollen arschbacken in den Kanal dienert, und en kakaoüberzug als ne art identität pflegt."[65] Susan, a female Kanakster in Zaimoğlu's second 'kanaksprak-novel' *Koppstoff*, reveals the 'passing' of both groups as a ridiculous attempt to hide their 'true colour': ie, their ethnic origins: "N gebleichter Brother ausm Kongo und n Türkengirl mit Frisierstabblondlöckchen."[66]

However, their identity as 'Kanakster' also distances these Turkish migrants from their parents' generation, who are described as fossilized and backward-looking. Three recurrent central subjects around which the formation of the Kanakster identity is constructed are music, comparison and identification with American blacks, and sexuality.

In the testimonials of rappers like Abdurrahman, Ali or Bayram, a break-dancer, the function of music is frequently compared with the role of black music in the USA, where it helped the black community to create a black consciousness in which the pejorative label of 'blackness' is revalorized into a label of ethnic pride. Turkish rap music achieves the same goal via a positive re-definition of the insulting and stigmatizing label of "*Kanake.*" When employed by the Turkish migrant in his lyrics, the term is re-instrumentalized and re-charged with a positive meaning and serves as an identification-tag that provides the Kanakster with an independent and proud personality. Turkish rap musicians, just like their black fellow musicians, are convinced of having a mission. By appropriating the music for their own needs, they propose an alternative to white pop music, which is based

[65] Zaimoğlu, *Kanaksprak*, 32: "because he kisses the German's ass in the gutter and cultivates brown-nosing as some sort of identity."

[66] Zaimoğlu, *Koppstoff*, 36: "A bleached brother from the Congo and a Turkish girl with blonde styling brush curls."

on the ideas and values of German mainstream society that shuts them out. The 'Kanakster' music helps them to voice their own ethos and value-system,[67] which lends stability to their identity as 'Germany's blacks'. Music becomes a way of redemption, of finding one's own voice, the right pose (as a dancer) and the right code of conduct. All these factors constitute the 'Kanakster's' "good attitude," which serves to establish a positive self awareness: "Wir schwimmen nicht mit dem strom. Wir machen nen eigenen strikten strom, wo jeder 'n Fluss ist und aufföhrt 'n gottverschissenes rinnsaal zu sein."[68]

The comparison between blacks and Turks is also reinforced by statements such as the following: "Wir sind hier allesamt nigger, ne ganze menge anderssein und anres leben."[69] Thus, the 'Kanakster' identifies himself with the image of the Turkish underdog, who is put into ghettos like black people in the USA. On account of the ghetto situation, the Turkish migrant is denied the privilege of participating in a multicultural society. The ghetto is seen as equivalent to the poorest quarters of the east side of town, whereas the rich town lies in the west, on the other side of the city. The bridge linking both parts can, however, only be crossed in one direction.

The importance of sexuality is illustrated in no fewer than five testimonials – by Büyük (a self-proclaimed sex-machine), by Dschemal-

---

[67] Cultural diversity has not only become part of German literature, but other areas, especially pop music, have proved to have a particularly important share in rendering a culture 'multicultural'. Cf the Berlin bands '3. Generation' and 'Kanacks with Brains', young Berliners of Turkish origin trying to cope with living in two cultures by means of music. Whereas the former band claims to make music for everyone ("we are all humans"), the latter claims to stand for the rights of the marginalized by fighting openly against the discrimination they suffer in everyday life because of their 'foreign' appearance.
[68] Zaimoğlu, *Kanaksprak*, 41-42: "We don't swim with the tide. We make a beautiful current all of our own, where everybody's his own river and stops being a bloody rivulet."
[69] Zaimoğlu, *Kanaksprak*, 25: "We're all niggers here, [which means being] a whole lot different and a different life."

eddin (a male prostitute), by Azize (a transsexual), by Lem, a pimp and by Ercan, a gigolo. Their testimonials celebrate sexuality as an expression of virile masculinity. Such a concept of manhood is vital for asserting a particular 'Kanakster' sexual identity. Its male chauvinism ridicules German men's apparent failure to satisfy the sexual needs of their women. By exposing the women's extravagances and perversions, the prostitute–customer relationship is unmasked as the continuation of a master–slave relationship which reflects the German Nazi past and the crimes committed against the Jewish population. In Ercan's testimonial "Sex ist Händeschütteln" ('Sex is shaking hands'), he narrates a strange encounter with a rich lady who insists on calling him "my handsome Jew" despite his protests that he is just a simple *Kümmel*.[70] All these protagonists make use of the exotic orientalizing stereotype of the virile and expert lover to prove not only their championship in the area of love, but also their moral superiority: "Mercy is the true vitamin – der alemanne denkt er hat zu viel von was, aber er hat zu wenig von was."[71]

Typically, all the protagonists reject a specific hyphenated label that classifies them as having two cultures within their reach. Being a 'Kanakster' means something completely new. It is a form of identity that is not consciously concerned with reconciling two different cultural origins (although their hybrid form of language suggests the contrary), but is regarded as a new and effective strategy of survival:

> Diese scheiße mit den zwei kulturen steht mir bis hier, was soll das, was bringt mir 'ne kultur schnak mit 2 fellen, auf denen mein arsch keinen platz hat, nen fell streck ich mir über'n leib, damit mir nicht bange wird, aber unter'n arsch brauch ich verdammich bloß festen boden, wo ich kauer an der erde.[72]

---

[70] Zaimoğlu, *Kanaksprak*, 70–71. (Ger. *Kümmel* 'caraway seed' = Turk.)

[71] Zaimoğlu, *Kanaksprak*, 81: "The Kraut thinks he's got too much of something, but he's got too little of everything."

[72] Zaimoğlu, *Kanaksprak*, 96: "I am fed up with this crap about 'two cultures'. How is this talk about culture with its two skins supposed to help me,

Kadir, the sociologist, expresses the same dilemma in a less metaphorical way by painting a portrait of his father's generation, the old
Turkish diaspora, whom he accuses of being unwilling to abide by
their state of temporariness. His description vividly recalls another
picture of old men speaking about home – those sitting on the veranda
of Hanuman House in V.S. Naipaul's *A House for Mr Biswas*:[73]

> Sie sehen aus wie janitscharen in billigen polyesterhemden. Sie sind
> fürchterlich schlecht gekleidet und haben winters gesprungene
> unterlippen. Sie ernähren sich von teig und fett und haben eine ganz
> bestimmte art, brotrinde in ungesunde saucen zu tunken. Sie ver-
> zeihen ihren söhnen nicht, daß diese über plastikkloschüsseln
> gebeugt oder unter stromzählern masturbieren. Sie lieben ihre söhne
> als erzeuger von dicken enkeln. Auf hochzeiten tragen die frauen
> schlimme gewänder mit rüschen und langen schleppen wie
> entenbürzel, und die feierlichen dicken männer betrinken sich und
> haben kümmel am borstigen bart, der mit wichse gerichtet von
> kleinen glanzsprenkeln glitzert. Den hochprozentigen anisschnaps
> nennen sie löwenmilch und können augenblicklich vor kummer in
> tränen ausbrechen. Ihre nostalgie ist dumpf, ihr haß wirkt sieben
> katzenlebenlang. Ihr deutsch ist lächerlich, ihr türkisch grob dialekt,
> ihr vaterland immer noch die türkei, aus der sie mit zwiebelsäcken
> beladen zurückkehren, als wären in dem ungläubigen Land alle
> reserven aufgebraucht [...][74]

---

when my ass doesn't have enough room. I need a skin to cover my body, so I
won't be afraid, but underneath me, dammit, I just need firm ground if I'm
crouching on the earth."

[73] See V.S. Naipaul, *A House for Mr Biswas* (1961; London: André
Deutsch, 1984): 193–94.

[74] Zaimoğlu, "Haß wirkt sieben Katzenleben lang," in *Kanaksprak*, 101-
102: "They look like janissaries in cheap polyester shirts. They're appallingly
dressed and they've got chapped lower lips in winter. They live on dough and
fat and have a certain way of dipping bread crusts in unhealthy sauces. They
can't forgive their sons for masturbating bent over plastic toilet-seats or beneath electricity meters. They love their sons as begetters of fat grandsons. At
weddings the women wear awful clothes with frills and long trains like ducks'
tails, and the solemn fat men get drunk and have caraway seeds on their bristly
beards, glistening with pomade. They call their strong aniseed brandy lion's

Mehmet finally draws a neat conclusion by writing a manifesto of the Kanakster identity that clearly separates 'us' ('*sie*') from 'them' ('*man*'):

> Sie sind menschenmüll, eine verschwendung in den straßen der metropolen, sie haben das spiel verloren, weil die karten gezinkt sind, die man ihnen in die hand drückt. Deshalb sind sie kanakster, deshalb bin ich ein kanake, deshalb bist du ein kanake. Wir sind bastarde [...] kreaturen ohne sinn und rechten verstand.[75]

The 'kanake' emerges as a synthetic product made to function as part of the mechanism in a factory. A 'kanake' is someone who mirrors and reflects the vices, dirt and abysses of (German) society. He is an object of projection, who serves as the living conscience of the nation: by adopting the negative heterostereotypes and transforming them into images of active resistance, the 'kanake' is enabled to achieve a positive re-definition that shifts him from the margin to the centre of attention.

Through the literary rendering of the 'kanaksprak', Zaimoğlu thus creates a 'Joycean text' through which he manages to re-order the semantic codes within the German language and give it new life. He thus politicizes the German language towards a new semiotics, re-creating 'tarcaneze', a pidgin yet highly artistic literary form of German, turning it into a literary jargon, a linguistic vehicle that becomes

---

milk and can burst into tears at the drop of a hat. Their nostalgia is dull, their hatred lasts the nine lives of a cat. Their German is ridiculous, their Turkish a coarse dialect, their home is still Turkey, from where they return laden with sacks of onions, as if all the provisions of this godless country had been used up."

[75] Zaimoğlu, *Kanaksprak*, 109–10: "They are human garbage, a waste in the streets of the big cities. They have lost the game, because the cards that were thrust into their hands were marked. That's why they're kanakster, that's why I'm a kanake, that's why you're a kanake. We're poor bastards [...] creatures without sense and proper reason."

the carrier of the identity-politics of the 'Kanakster'.[76] The originally negative hetero-image of the 'Kanake' is adapted by the 'Kanakster' and recharged in the process with positive identification values and the use of a specifically creolized Turkish-German slang. As a result, the protagonists emerge as part of an ethnic 'Kanakster süppkültür' whose members are determined to reject any kind of alien definitions and labels. In spite of the great variety of speakers portrayed, the 'kanaken-spraken' in both collections (*Kanaksprak* and *Koppstoff*) retain a sufficient number of common features to convey the impression of a unifying yet heterogeneous diasporic 'Kanakster' consciousness.

Thus, the testimonials of these *almancılar*, *Deutschländer*, become a powerful manifesto of identity, which, however, is not synonymous with any stable or fixed image of the 'Kanakster'. By including women and men from all areas of society, the Turkish diaspora group represented in the two collections becomes another microcosmic reflection of German society at large. Neither German nor Turkish, they set out to construct an alternative self-image that emancipates itself from both German and Turkish stereotypes, prejudices and clichés.[77] The 'Kanakster' is a confident voice from the diasporic Turkish-German community, which has made itself at home in Germany. Whether the Germans acknowledge or deny it, the Turks of Germany have come to stay:

---

[76] Androutsopoulos points to the recent trend of adapting Turk-German for artistic purposes (spoken genres include comedy acts, radio shows, song lyrics, broadcast commercials, and films; written genres include literature, comic strips etc). While Feridun Zaimoğlu was certainly the first to re-create Turkish migrant speech in his books *Kanaksprak* (1995) and *Abschaum* (1997), which was adapted for the screen in 2000 under the title "Kanakattack," the "starting-point of the trend," claims Anadroutsopoulos, was the film entitled *Knocking on Heaven's Doors* (1996) directed by Thomas Jahn. See Anadroutsopoulos, "From the Streets to the Screens," 5–6.

[77] See Jamal Tuschik, "Heimat ist altmodisch: Deutschländerinnen bestimmen ihren Standort: Feridun Zaimoğlu dokumentiert Widerständlichkeit," junge welt (7 October 1998), http://www.jungewelt.ipn.de/beilagen /bl3/015.htm. Online 16/11/2000.

Ja, die Bastarde kommen, aber nicht mit Döner, export-ladenkitsch, Multikultigetrampel, tränenreicher "In der Fremde"-Literatur und schlechtem Rap, goldbehangen im Sultanschick und anatolische Lieder lallend, wie's der Deutsche gern hätt, wenn überhaupt, sondern mit Qualität, erlernter deutscher Disziplin, angeborenem Feuer unterm Arsch, mitgebrachtem Kulturkoffer, nicht loszuwerdender Sentimentalität und erworbener widerstandsfähigkeit, denn was nicht tötet, härtet angeblich ab, und es hat uns nicht umgebracht. Hat jemand Angst bekommen? Aber nicht doch. Wer auf unserer Seite steht, braucht keine Angst zu haben.[78]

The two authors have illustrated how the German multicultural environment has produced new forms of diasporic existence in which German and Turkish identities have become hybridized in an emergent diasporic kanakster identity.

Biographical Data

Zafer Şenocak

Born in Ankara in 1961, Şenocak has lived in Germany since 1970. Since 1979, he has been publishing poetry in both German and Turkish, and fiction, drama and essays in German. A leading voice in contemporary German debates on national identity and multiculturalism, he has also spent several semesters teaching on US campuses in recent years. He has also written several essays tackling cultural and political issues of Germany and Turkey, Europe and Islam, 'East' and 'West'.

---

[78] Zaimoğlu, *Koppstoff*, 61: "Yes, the bastards are coming, but not with döner-kebab and laden with cheap export trash, loud and multicultural with tearful 'In-a-foreign-country' literature and bad rap, draped in gold and sultan's costumes and babbling Anatolian songs, as the Germans would like to have them; if they come, then it's with quality – acquired German discipline, innate zeal, cultural baggage, a sentimentality that cannot be shed, and with acquired resistance. What doesn't kill you only makes you stronger, or so they say, and it hasn't killed us. Is anyone afraid? Oh no, whoever's on our side need not be afraid."

Feridun Zaimoğlu

Born in 1964 in Bolu, Anatolia, has lived in Kiel, Germany (except for short periods) for thirty-two years. He studied medicine and art and became Germany's *enfant terrible* and promoter of 'Kanak-Attack' with the publication of his first two books, called *Kanaksprak* (1995) and *Abschaum – Die wahre Geschichte des Ertan Ongun* (1997). His first epistolary novel *Liebesmale, Scharlachrot* (2000) established his reputation as a creator of original poetic prose writing.

WORKS CITED

Ackermann, Irmgard, ed. *Als Fremder in Deutschland* (Munich: Deutscher Taschenbuchverlag, 1982).
——, ed. *In Zwei Sprachen leben. Berichte. Erzählungen, Gedichte von Ausländern* (Munich: Deutscher Taschenbuchverlag, 1983).
——, ed. *Türken deutscher Sprache. Berichte, Erzählungen, Gedichte* (Munich: Deutscher Taschenbuchverlag, 1984).
——, & Harald Weinrich, ed. *Eine nicht nur deutsche Literatur: Zur Standortbestimmung der Ausländerliteratur* (Munich: Piper, 1986).
Adam, Heribert. "German and Canadian Nationalism and Multiculturalism: A Comparison of Xenophobia, Racism and Integration," in Haselbach, ed. *Multiculturalism in a World of Leaking Boundaries*, 193–210.
Akkaya, Çiğdem, Yasemin Özbek & Faruk Şen. *Länderbericht Türkei* (Darmstadt: Wissenschaftliche Buchgesellschaft, 1998).
Anderson, Benedict. *Imagined Communities: Reflections on the Origin and Spread of Nationalism* (London: Verso, 1983).
Androutsopoulos, Jannis. "From the Streets to the Screens and Back Again: On the Mediated Diffusion of Ethnolectal Patterns in Contemporary German," Paper presented to the ICLaVE I Conference, Barcelona, 29 June 2000, http://www.rzuser.uni-heidelberg.de/~iandrout/papers/iclavedraft.html.Online 21/11/2000: 1–15.
Bhabha, Homi. *The Location of Culture* (London & New York: Routledge, 1994).
——. "Of Mimicry and Man: The Ambivalence of Colonial Discourse," in Bhabha, *The Location of Culture*, 85–92.
Biondi, Franco, & Rafik Schami. "Literatur der Betroffenen" in *Zu Hause in der Fremde: Ein Bundesdeutsches Ausländer-Lesebuch*, ed. Christina

Schaffernicht (Fischerhude: Atelier im Bauernhaus; Reinbeck: Rowohlt, 1984): 136–50.

Bojadzijev, Manuela, & Vassilis Tsianos (Kanak Attack). "Mit den besten Absichten: Spuren des migrantischen Widerstandes," in *IZ₃W* 244 (April 2000): 35–38.

Bredella, Lothar. "Human Rights and Understanding Foreign Cultures between Relativism and Universalism," in Haselbach, ed. *Multiculturalism in a World of Leaking Boundaries*, 251–77.

Brinker–Gabler, Gisela, & Sidonie Smith, ed. *Writing New Identities. Gender, Nation, and Immigration in Contemporary Europe* (Minneapolis & London: U of Minnesota P, 1997).

Burns, Robert. "Images of Alterity: Second Generation Turks in the Federal Republic," *Modern Language Review* 94.3 (1999): 744–57.

Cheesman, Tom. "Axial Writing: Transnational Literary/Media Cultures and Cultural Policy," www.transcomm.ox.ac.uk/wwwroot/cheesman.htm. Online 09/10/2000, 1–8.

——, & Deniz Göktürk. "German Titles, Turkish Names: The Cosmopolitan Will," www.new-books-in-german.com/feature3.htm. Online 09/10/2000, 1–2.

Cohen, Robin. *Global Diasporas: An Introduction* (Seattle: U of Washington P, 1997).

Dal, Güney. *Der enthaarte Affe,* tr. Karl Koss (*Kilları yolunmuş mayum,* Munich: Piper, 1988).

Demirkan, Renan. *Schwarzer Tee mit drei Stück Zucker* (Cologne: Kiepenheuer & Witsch, 1991).

Eickelmann, Dale F., & James Piscatori, ed. *Muslim Travellers: Pilgrimage, Migration and the Religious Imagination* (Berkeley: U of California P, 1990).

Erzgräber, Willi, & Paul Goetsch, ed. *Mündliches Erzählen im Alltag, fingiertes mündliches Erzählen in der Literatur* (Tübingen: Gunter Narr, 1987).

Fischer, Sabine, & Moray McGowan. "From Pappkoffer to Pluralism: On the Development of Migrant Writing in the German Federal Republic," in Horrocks & Kolinsky, ed. *Turkish Culture in German Society Today,* 1–22.

Goetsch, Paul. "Fingierte Mündlichkeit in der Erzählkunst entwickelter Schriftsteller," *Poetica* 17.3–4 (1985): 202–18.

Haselbach, Dieter. "Multicultural Reality and the Problem of German Identity," in Haselbach, ed. *Multiculturalism in a World of Leaking Boundaries,* 211–28.

——, ed. *Multiculturalism in a World of Leaking Boundaries* (Münster: LIT, 1998).

Hatch, Ronald B. "Chinatown Ghosts in the White Empire," in Ansgar & Vera Nünning, ed. *Intercultural Studies*, 193–209.

Heckmann, Friedrich. "Nation und Integration von Migranten in Deutschland," in *Was ist ein Deutscher? Was ist ein Türke? Alman olmak nedir? Türk olmak nedir?* Deutsch-Türkisches Symposium 1997, ed. Türkeiprogramm der Körber-Stiftung (Hamburg: Edition Körber-Stiftung, 1998): 181–95.

Heinze, Hartmut. *Migrantenliteratur in der Bundesrepublik* (Berlin: Express, 1986).

Hestermann, Sandra. "'Meeting the Other – Encountering Oneself': Paradigmen der Selbst- und Fremderfahrung in ausgewählten anglo-indischen und indisch-englischen Kurzgeschichten" (unpublished doctoral dissertation, University of Freiburg, 2002).

Horrocks, David, & Eva Kolinsky. *Turkish Culture in German Society Today* (Providence RI & Oxford: Berghahn, 1996).

König, Karen, & Hanne Straub, ed. *Kalte Heimat* (Reinbek bei Hamburg: Rowohlt, 1984).

Kolinsky, Eva. "Non-German Minorities in German Society," in Horrocks & Kolinsky, ed. *Turkish Culture in German Society Today*, 71–111.

Kürsat–Ahlers, Elçin. "The Turkish Minority in German Society," in Horrocks & Kolinsky, ed. *Turkish Culture in German Society Today*, 113–35.

Kurt, Kemal. *Ja, sagt Molly* (Berlin: Hitit, 1998).

Manço, Ural. "Turks in Europe: From a Garbled Image to the Complexity of Migrant Social Reality," http://allserv.rug.ac.be/~hdeley/umanco2.htm. Online 21/11/2000: 1–17.

Mandel, Ruth. "Shifting Centres and Emergent Identities: Turkey and Germany in the Lives of Turkish Gastarbeiter," in Eickelmann & Piscatori, ed. *Muslim Travellers*, 153–71.

Mishra, Vijay. "The Diasporic Imaginary," *Textual Practice* 10.3 (1996): 421–47.

Naipaul, V.S. *A House for Mr Biswas* (1961; London: André Deutsch, 1984).

Nünning, Ansgar, & Vera Nünning, ed. *Intercultural Studies: Fictions of Empire* (*anglistik & englischunterricht* 58; Heidelberg: Carl Winter, 1993).

Ören, Aras. *Eine verspätetet Abrechnung oder der Aufstieg der Gündogus*, tr. Zafer Şenocak & Eva Hund (Frankfurt am Main: Dagyeli, 1988).

Özdamar, Emine Sevgi. *Das Leben ist eine Karawanserei, hat zwei Türen, aus einer kam ich rein, aus der anderen ging ich raus* (Cologne: Kiepenheuer & Witsch, 1992).

Picardi–Montesardo, Anna. *Die Gastarbeiter in der Literatur der Bundesrepublik Deutschland* (Berlin: Express, 1985).

Reeg, Ulrike. *Schreiben in der Fremde* (Essen: Klartext, 1988).

Riemann, Wolfgang. *Über das Leben in Bitterland. Bibliographie zur türkischen Deutschland Literatur und zur türkischen Literatur in Deutschland* (Wiesbaden: Otto Harrassowitz, 1990).

Rushdie, Salman. *Midnight's Children* (1981; London: Picador, 1982).

Şen, Faruk, & Andreas Goldberg. *Türken in Deutschland: Leben zwischen zwei Kulturen* (Munich: C.H. Beck, 1994).

Şenocak, Zafer. *Gefährliche Verwandtschaft* (Munich: Babel, 1998).

——. "There's a Crack in the Handle," tr. Tom Cheesman, in www.swn.ac.uk/conferences/transcomm/senocak.htm. Online 09/10/2000.

Seyhan, Azade. "Introduction" to *New German Critique* 46 (special issue "Minorities in German Culture"; 1989): 4–5.

——. "Paranational Community/Hyphenated Identity: The Turks of Germany," http://jsis.artsci.washington.edu/...rams/europe/wendep/Seyhan Paper.htm. Online 09/ 10/2000, 1–5.

——. "Scheherazade's Daughters. The Thousand and One Tale of Turkish-German Women Writers," in Brinker–Gabler & Smith, ed. *Writing New Identities*, 230–48.

Spuler–Stegmann, Ursula. *Muslime in Deutschland: Nebeneinander oder Miteinander?* (Freiburg, Basel & Vienna: Herder, 1998).

Tekinay, Alev. *Nur der Hauch vom Paradies* (Frankfurt am Main: Brandes & Apsel, 1993).

Thränhardt, Dietrich. "Patterns of Organization among Different Ethnic Minorities," *New German Critique* 46 (1989): 10–26.

Tuschik, Jamal. "Heimat ist altmodisch: Deutschländerinnen bestimmen ihren Standort: Feridun Zaimoğlu dokumentiert Widerständlichkeit," *junge welt* (7 October 1998) in www.jungewelt.ipn.de/beilagen/bl3/015.htm. Online 16/11/2000.

Veteto–Conrad, Marilya. *Finding a Voice: Identity and the Works of German-Language Turkish Writers in the Federal Republic of Germany to 1990* (New York: Peter Lang, 1996).

——. "'Innere Unruhe'? Zehra Çirak and Minority Literature Today," *Rocky Mountain Review* (Fall 1999): 59–74.

"Was deutsch ist bestimmen wir! Dokumentation der Talkshow III nach neun (N3) mit Feridun Zaimoglu, Heide Simonis, Wolf Biermann, Norbert Blüm und Harald Juhnke," *iz₃w* 243 (2000): 38–41.

Zaimoğlu, Feridun. *Abschaum: Die Geschichte des Ertan Ongun* (Hamburg: Rotbuch, 1997).

——. *Kanaksprak: 24 Mißtöne vom Rande der Gesellschaft* (Hamburg: Rotbuch, 1995).

——. *Koppstoff: Kanakasprak vom Rande der Gesellschaft* (Hamburg: Rotbuch, 1998).

——. *Liebesmale, Scharlachrot* (Hamburg: Rotbuch, 2000).

℗

Contributors

VERA ALEXANDER studied English, German and Italian philology and education at the Universities of Cologne, Freiburg and Norwich and has an MA from the Centre for Colonial and Postcolonial Studies, University of Kent at Canterbury. She is co-editor with Monika Fludernik of *Romantik* (2000) and has written articles on several post-colonial writers from the Indian subcontinent. She is currently completing her doctoral research at the University of Saarbrücken on the role of migration and education in selected Indo-English novels.

BRYAN CHEYETTE is Professor of Twentieth Century Literature at the University of Southampton. He is the author of *Constructions of "the Jew" in English Literature and Society: Racial Representations 1875–1945* (1993) and *Muriel Spark* (2000) and is currently working on a study entitled "Diasporas of the Mind: British-Jewish Writing and the Nightmare of History." He is also the editor of *Between 'Race' and Culture: Representations of "the Jew" in English and American Literature* (1996), *Contemporary Jewish Writing in Britain and Ireland: An Anthology* (1998) and *Modernity, Culture and "the Jew"* (1998, with Laura Marcus).

MONIKA FLUDERNIK is Professor of English Literature at the University of Freiburg, Germany. She is the author of *The Fictions of Language and the Languages of Fiction* (1993), *Towards a 'Natural' Narratology* (1996), and *Echoes and Mirrorings: Gabriel Josipovici's Creative Oeuvre* (2000). As well as editing special journal issues on second-person fiction, language and literature, and (with Donald and Margaret Freeman) new cognitive developments in metaphor, she has edited four essay-collections: *Hybridity and Postcolonialism: Twentieth-Century Indian Literature* (1998), *Das 18. Jahrhundert* (with Ruth Nestvold, 1998), *Romantik* (with Vera Alexander, 2000), and *Fin de siècle* (with Ariane Huml, 2001). Work in progress includes a project on the development of narrative structure in English literature between 1250 and 1750 as well as a study of prison settings and prison metaphors in English literature.

SANDRA HESTERMANN has recently completed a doctorate on "Meeting the Other – Encountering Oneself: Paradigms of Self and Other in Selected Modern Anglo-Indian and Indian-English Short Stories" in the English Department of Freiburg University, Germany. Since 1997 she has been a member of an interdisciplinary research project on identities and alterities in postcolonial literatures in English. An article entitled "'Voices out of the closet': Lesbian Sexuality and Feminist Identity in Indian-English Prose" is forthcoming.

FEROZA JUSSAWALLA is Associate Professor of English at the University of Texas at El Paso. She specializes in postcolonial literatures and theory and in children's literature. She is the author of *Family Quarrels: Towards a Criticism of Indian Writing in English* and co-author of *Interviews with Writers of the Post-Colonial World*. She edited *Conversations with V.S. Naipaul*, which includes previously published interviews with the author.

BEATE NEUMEIER is Professor of English Literature at the University of Cologne. Her research interests are postmodern and postcolonial theory and gender studies. She is the editor of *Jüdische Literatur und Kultur in Grossbritannien und den USA nach 1945* (1998). She is the author of *Gender and Madness in English Renaissance Drama* (forthcoming) and *Spiel und Politik: Aspekte der Komik bei Tom Stoppard* (1986) and editor of *Engendering Realism and Postmodernism: Contemporary Women Writers in Britain* (2001).

UMA PARAMESWARAN was born in India. She has lived in Winnipeg, Canada, since 1966. Her first critical volume, *A Study of Representative Indo-English Novelists* was published in 1976. Her most recent critical volume is on Kamala Markandaya (2000). She is also the author of several volumes of poetry, drama and fiction, including *What was Always Hers*, which won the 2000 Jubilee Award for the best collection of short fiction published by a Canadian author in 1999. She is married to a mathematician, and they have one daughter.

MAKARAND PARANJAPE is Professor of English at the Jawaharlal Nehru University, New Delhi. A widely published scholar, critic, poet and columnist, he is the author and editor of several books. His most recent publications include his third collection of poems, *Used Book* (2001), and a collection of critical essays entitled *In Diaspora: Theories, Histories, Texts* (2001).

ULFRIED REICHARDT teaches at Mannheim, Germany. His books include *Postmodernity Seen from Inside: The Poetry of John Ashbery, A.R. Ammons, Denise Levertov, and Adrienne Rich* (1991, in German) and *Alterity and History: Functions of the Representation of Slavery in the American Novel* (2001, in German). He is the editor of special issues of the journal *Amerikastudien/American Studies*: *Engendering Manhood* (1998, co-edited with Sabine Sielke); and *Time and the African American Experience* (2000).

MINOLI SALGADO teaches English at the School of African and Asian Studies, University of Sussex, England, where she is the Convener for the MA programme in Colonial and Postcolonial Cultures. She has a special interest in literature from the South Asian diaspora and has published widely in the field. Her most recent publications include her contributions to *British Culture of the Postwar* (2000) and *A Reader's Guide to the Contemporary Short Story in English* (2001).

ROY SOMMER teaches English literature and cultural studies at the Universities of Cologne and Giessen. His doctoral dissertation, *Fictions of Migration*, a study of contemporary black British literature, was published in 2001. Other publications include essays on intercultural pedagogy, narrative theory and the functions of literature. He is currently working on articles on transgeneric narratology, time and narrative (with Ansgar Nünning), Salman Rushdie (with Bruno Zerweck) and David Dabydeen.

URSULA ZELLER taught at the University of Zurich before joining the Zurich James Joyce Foundation as curator. She is co-editor of *A Collideorscape of Joyce: Festschrift for Fritz Senn* (1998) and author of *James Joyce – "thought through my eyes"* (2000), and has provided the new German translation of "Penelope" (2001), the final chapter of *Ulysses*. She has published various essays on Joyce and contemporary literature, with a special interest in Jewish aspects. She is currently studying for an additional degree in Jewish studies at the University of Lucerne.

∅

Index

Printed in the United Kingdom
by Lightning Source UK Ltd.
126702UK00001B/70-87/A